1988

PRINCIPLES AND STYLES OF ACTING

Alfred Lunt and Lynn Fontanne in *O Mistress Mine* by Terence Rattigan.

PRINCIPLES AND STYLES OF ACTING

EVERETT M. SCHRECK

(RICHARD MORRILL)

Formerly of Ohio State University

With contributions by
WILLIAM R. McGRAW
Ohio University
and
FABER B. DeCHAINE
University of Oregon

ADDISON-WESLEY PUBLISHING COMPANY
Reading, Massachusetts • Menlo Park, California • London • Don Mills, Ontario

To my wife, Dorothy, who, with her practical
advice, unceasing encouragement, and patient
helpfulness, has become in a very real sense
part author of this book

Preface

This book is designed for individuals who wish to study seriously the art of acting. The reasons and objectives for study may be quite diverse. Some people will undoubtedly be drawn to the study of acting in order to broaden their understanding and appreciation of this popular art. Others may wish to achieve a greater self-confidence, poise, and freedom of expression before an audience. Many, undoubtedly; will wish to acquire a knowledge of acting so that they may teach it, while others may themselves hope to become professionals. The principles and exercises presented here should prove helpful in fulfilling the needs of each student, whatever his specialized objectives may be.

The two parts of the book are interrelated and could readily be used for one extensive course in acting. Part One, Principles of Acting, is planned to meet the needs of the beginning actor, while Part Two, Styles of Acting, may serve as an advanced course. The emphasis on style in Part Two is a unique feature of the book. The importance given to types and styles of acting is justified when one considers that, in each instance, the actor performs in a particular type and style of drama. In reality, style is the common denominator and the sine qua non of all acting. To play each character, the actor must give careful consideration to the type of play and to the appropriate style of performance. This obligation, which places great demands upon the actor, cannot be avoided. The actor must have a knowledge of style as it relates to historical periods and as it is reflected in the play script. He must also acquire special skills in mastering the subtle techniques whereby a particular style may be expressed.

The authors hold the opinion that acting is a unique art, embodying specific principles and techniques. These must be learned and put into practice by the aspiring actor if he hopes to achieve excellence in his art. Even the individual most gifted by nature must train and discipline his voice and body in order to meet the rigorous demands of acting.

This book does not endorse any one system of acting to the exclusion of another. Rather, it takes a pragmatic approach, utilizing those principles and techniques which will help the actor meet the exacting requirements of his art more successfully. Creating a character for the stage is a twofold process involving *impression* and *expression*. With respect to the former, the principles codified by Stanislavsky in *An Actor Prepares,* and currently called "The Method" in the United States, are most helpful. The second part of the process, expression, requires varied and refined techniques. It is the lack of technical training which handicaps many American actors and often denies them the opportunity to play in non-realistic dramas. Each of the currently popular systems of acting, the natural (Stanislavsky) and the technical, complements and strengthens the other. It is the authors' firm conviction that all highly accomplished actors utilize both systems, in differing degrees, as the specific play and character may demand. Only through a variation in the admixture of the two systems is the actor able to perform successfully in the diverse types and styles of drama.

Acting is a *performing* art. Mastery is acquired by doing. Consequently, scenes from many types and styles of dramas are provided here as practice material. Although general principles are included as guides for the playing of the major types and styles of plays, the authors have avoided stating arbitrarily just how the scenes should be played. It is felt that considerable freedom should be given in this matter to both instructor and student.

A substantial amount of material has been included which may seem to some to be within the province of the play director. In no sense do the authors intend that the actor should encroach upon the prerogatives of the director. Each of the authors has had years of experience as a teacher of directing as well as of acting, and each is as sensitive to the director's sphere as he is to the proper domain of the actor. It is well-known among teachers of acting and directing, however, that the two arts unavoidably overlap. One cannot teach acting without including certain principles of play directing. The reverse is equally true. It is the opinion of the authors that the actor will be benefitted in many ways if, in addition to his proficiency as an actor, he has some knowledge of the principles of directing. Moreover, the inclusion of material in the area of directing in this book, primarily devoted to acting, extends its scope and renders it useful as a text in a course such as Stage Arts, in which both acting and directing are taught.

Santa Monica, California   E.M.S.
April, 1970

Foreword

In writing a foreword to a book such as this, I am constrained to think of it as a preface to a preface, for all that is contained in this book is a preface to that moment when an actor steps before an audience for the first or the last time—yes, the last time—for an actor must continually refresh himself and find new things within his art previously unrevealed. With his study of the principles of his craft, the actor sometimes behaves as a computer does, rearranging that which is fed into it when something new occurs in the equation. Acting is a mystic thing; it is not altogether a mixture of knowledge and careful study, nor is it improvisation or inspiration or discipline; it is a combination of these elements held in suspension by that inexplicable factor, "the gift." One cannot be taught to act; one can only be exposed to the essence of it as one is exposed to the rays of the sun—some people tan beautifully, some burn terribly, and some are unaffected.

The matter of the actor's knowledge is expanded here even into the realms of the dramatist and the director. It does the actor no harm to be made acquainted with all elements of the theater for he is only one part. His role is not creator but interpreter. Oh, it has been said from time to time that an actor "created" a certain role, but this is impossible. Rubenstein does not create Chopin when he plays the piano; he interprets Chopin. The actor can add to, or enhance, a role by certain qualities, or, by the same token, he can destroy the characterization intended by the author; but it is not his business to create.

When actors do try to create, curious things can happen. Once, during one of the rehearsals for a story on the television series called "Mama," a young actor was cast for a sort of Jack London part: a successful man from the Klondike on his way back east with the gold he had dug. The actor was tall and handsome and rugged in appearance —good typecasting, one might say. But he had worked out for himself a characterization which had no relation to the period or background of the situation, or to the story itself. In vain the director explained to him his place in the sequence of the plot; during every rehearsal he stuck to his own interpretation and every night he went home to his drama coach. Finally, when he doggedly refused to change his misconception of the role, the director said to him: "You have an idea that the theater is a democratic institution in which every person has a right to his own opinion, but you are mistaken; the theater is a dictatorship and *I'm* the dictator. Now, are you going to play this role as it was intended, or not? If not, you're fired." The young egotist stalked out.

Of course, the theater is democratic in the sense that each person is important and of equal value—the small part is necessary to the big part and the young folk necessary to the old folk—but somebody has to be the boss, and it is not the actor.

This book gives the actor rules, but we all know rules can be broken. As the old adage says, "The exception proves the rule." But rules do not make an actor. If a person is bent on a career in the theater, all of the information within these covers is of value, but one must never forget about the *gift*. The painter, the composer, the writer, *and* the actor must have an indefinable gift within him.

How does the actor know if he has a gift? He prepares himself and then faces the people in the audience. *They* tell him.

In the meantime, the actor will find this book rewarding and fascinating.

Peggy Wood

Contents

Part One
Principles of Acting

Chapter one

Introduction to Acting

In acting take Nature as your model — but never fall into the error of attempting to present Nature in the stead of art.

David Belasco

THE NATURE OF ACTING

Of all the arts, acting is perhaps the most difficult to define, analyze, or evaluate. It has been termed the highest of the arts by some and disparaged as mere craftsmanship by others. It is not uncommon for an actor to receive high praise for his characterization by one critic and yet, for the same performance, be adversely criticized by another. Undoubtedly, there are many reasons for the varying reactions to an actor's performance; the most basic ones are certain truths such as the following:

1. *The way the audience responds to the actor and his performance is often conditioned by the degree of audience identification with the character.* For instance, people are inclined to respond favorably to an actor when he is playing a character with whom they can empathize.

2. *It is often difficult for the audience to differentiate the personality of the actor from the character he is portraying.* Whether an actor is giving an excellent performance of the character or is merely playing himself is, at times, impossible to determine. If an actor invariably fails to submerge his personality in the character, his acting may be evaluated as inferior. Typical of such an evaluation was a critic's comment in *Theatre Arts Monthly* some years ago in regard to George Arliss' performance in the role of Cardinal Richelieu. The critic stated that Arliss gave an excellent performance of George Arliss in the robes of the Cardinal. Without questioning the validity of this criticism, we must, however, grant that all acting is inextricably enmeshed with the personality of the actor.

Katherine Cornell, an actress of recognized distinction, has stated that her characterizations are, in each case, portrayed through her own personality. Indeed, one might compile a considerable list of actors and actresses who leave the imprint of their personalities on the characters they play. The moot point is, has the personality of the actor been subordinated to that of the character, or has the actor's personality been so dominant as to be detrimental to his performance? The degree to which an actor must strive for complete identification with the character varies with the type and style of the play. A detailed discussion of this point is given in Part Two.

3. *Live acting (in contrast to filmed performances) is ephemeral and transitory.* It cannot be held, or fixed for later study and analysis. It is a thing of the moment and may never be quite the same in succeeding performances. In this respect, the arts of acting, dancing, and singing are alike. They are in contrast to the painter's art, which is fixed on canvas, the sculptor's art, which may be fixed in stone or clay, the composer's art, recorded in notations on the score, and the writer's art, preserved in words on the printed page.

4. *Acting must come into being at a specified time and place.* The actor, unlike the composer, the painter, the sculptor, and the writer, cannot choose the time and place most propitious for his creative efforts. Since the audience will not wait long for him to engender a mood and assume a character, the actor must develop a technique of acquiring the appropriate mood even though his emotions may be quite remote from those of the character.

Definition of acting

There are many definitions of acting. For this reason, it seems pertinent to consider what acting means to certain individuals who, through the passage of time, have achieved great renown and success in this field. A distinguished representative of this group, Henry Irving, appropriately stated: "Now, what is the art of acting? . . . It is the art of embodying the poet's creations, of giving them flesh and blood, of making the figures which appeal to your mind's eye in the printed drama live before you on the stage."[*]

Probably the name of Laurette Taylor is still well known to some contemporary theater-goers. If not recalled for her long list of successes from 1912 to her retirement in 1928, she will be remembered for her return to the stage seventeen years later in a remarkable portrayal of Amanda Wingfield in Tennessee Williams' *The Glass Menagerie.* During one of her earlier successes, as Mrs. Midget in Sutton Vane's *Outward Bound,* Miss Taylor gave a newspaper reporter this provocative definition of her art: "Acting is the physical representation of a mental picture and the projection of an emotional concept."[†]

Another thought-provoking definition is that of one of America's most illustrious actors, John Barrymore: "Acting is the art of saying a thing on the stage as if you believed every word you utter to be as true as the eternal verities of life . . ."[‡]

In simplest terms, acting is the purposeful, controlled imitation of the manners and emotions of other human beings. It is the progressive development and concise projection of the life of the character.

Qualities of art

There are certain universal principles of art which are applicable to acting. These are unity, selectivity, emphasis and proportion, intensification, and a masterly control of the medium.

Unity. This might be called the sine qua non of all art. Unless the artist applies the principle of unity to some degree in his work, meaningless confusion may be the result. Unity implies a oneness or singleness of concept and an absence of

---

[*] Henry Irving, "The Art of Acting" (1885), *The Drama.* London: William Heinemann, 1893, p. 40.

[†] Toby Cole and Helen Krich Chenoy (eds.), *Actors on Acting.* New York: Crown, 1959, p. 517.

[‡] Helen Ten Broeck, "From Comedy to Tragedy; an interview with John Barrymore," *Theatre Magazine,* New York, July 1916, p 23.

irrelevant elements. To observe this principle an actor must have a clear and concise concept of the character and its goals. In the process of developing this character, the actor employs economy in his vocal manipulation and physical action.

Selectivity. Every artist must select from the mass of available materials only those which are useful to his purpose. Without selectivity there is no art — only raw nature. Although the playwright has carefully selected the dialogue of the play, the actor must select the appropriate actions and vocal elements to create an acceptable interpretation of the author's meaning. Sir John Gielgud said: "Yes, you've got to be heard and you've got to be seen. But you must select what you want to make the people hear and see and draw attention to it at the right moment and not at the wrong one."* Selectivity is expressed in another way by Katherine Cornell, who has said that one of the chief problems of the actor is to decide what *not* to do on the stage.

Emphasis and proportion. The human mind seems to demand a focal point, an anchorage, or a place to rest. In a painting the observer seeks the most important object; in a novel or play he searches for the central idea or core of meaning. By means of emphasis the important elements are made to stand out vividly, while those of lesser importance are suppressed. By means of proportion each segment of a work of art is given its appropriate degree of importance.

An actor uses emphasis and proportion in a variety of ways. In portraying a character, he emphasizes those particular traits which add clarity and meaning to the character's action, and subordinates the less important facets of the

character's nature. The dominant characteristic may be one of several human tendencies such as envy, jealousy, or cupidity, and the chief motivation may be ambition, power, or greed. The actor determines the particular objective of the character and in the process of pursuing this goal, he communicates the character's individual traits to the audience. This principle is discussed at greater length in Chapter 8.

Intensification. By means of unity, selectivity, order, and emphasis, art is given another quality: intensification. In art the ingredients of life are rearranged, sharpened, quickened, heightened, and magnified. The colors on the painter's canvas are more brilliant than those in nature. The purple shadows under the eaves of houses are more intense than real shadows, for instance. In a similar manner, the actions in a play move more swiftly and the characters are more heroic, impassioned, romantic than those in real life. On the stage, we accept Cyrano de Bergerac although, in life, we may never have met his counterpart. It is this intensification of life on the stage that makes the theater a place of excitement and enchantment. To achieve this intensification, the actor must approach his characterization with understanding, sincerity, and depth of feeling, utilizing certain essential physical and vocal techniques to raise the character above the commonplace.

Mastery of the medium. It is a universal axiom that a true artist is a master of his medium. The artist, Heifetz, plays the violin with such mastery that it seems to be a simple achievement. In like manner, the performance of a difficult role by an accomplished actor appears effortless. Too often an artist's ease of execution is mistaken for an inborn talent rather than skill, but even if an artist possesses special aptitudes, the seeming ease in performance is the result of more than innate talent. It derives also from a technical mastery

---

* John Gielgud, "And Keep Your Mouth Shut," *The New York Times*, 2 May 1965, p. 1.

of the artist's medium. "Art is always a matter of skill, and skill is always the result of sincere study and labor."*

The duality of acting

We have considered certain similarities between acting and the other arts. Let us now observe a marked dissimilarity. In all the arts, except dancing, singing, and acting, the artist is separated from the instrument or medium of his expression. The painter works with pigments, canvas, and brush; the sculptor works with clay, stone, and chisels; and the musician produces tones and rhythms with instruments. These tools, materials, and instruments, within certain limits prescribed by their respective natures, are responsive to the artist's will, but are apart from him. In contrast, the actor is his own instrument. He is the player and the person played upon.

Thus we see both subjective and objective phases in acting. Subjectively, the actor must feel, to a degree at least, the emotions of the character he is playing. He should seem to "live the part," to give the impression that he is ruled by the character's passions. He should seem to be swept along by the action of the play. Yet, at the same time, the actor must keep a certain degree of objectivity and detachment. He must maintain his own individuality and self-control, and be conscious of the fact that he is in a theater, playing to an audience. He should be aware of how his posture, movements, gestures, and vocal patterns are adjusted to the character he is portraying and to the theater in which he is performing. Through this objectivity, the actor can be in control of his character and of the situation.

The subjective and objective phases of acting should blend and supplement each other. Over-

---

* Charles H. Woolbert and Severina E. Nelson, *The Art of Interpretative Speech*. New York: F. S. Crofts, 1947, p. 43.

emphasis of either phase is likely to be detrimental. Too much subjectivity in acting may result in loss of control, overemotionalization, ineffectiveness, or a lack of artistry and communication. Too much objectivity may bring about insincerity, superficiality, or exhibitionism and thus destroy the truth and credibility of the character. Consequently, one of the chief problems of the actor is to maintain, at all times, a happy balance between these two phases of acting. It is this dual nature which makes acting one of the most difficult of all the arts to master. A further discussion of the duality in relation to style is presented in Part Two.

BASIC REQUIREMENTS FOR ACTING

The preceding discussion suggests two basic requirements for acting: talent and technique. However, the art of acting is certainly more complex than these terms imply. Basic requisites for the actor are discussed briefly here since, in succeeding sections, an opportunity is provided to explore the actor's resources and to discuss in depth the particular skills which he must acquire.

Talent

It is generally believed that artistic talent is, in large part, inborn. There is no question but that certain individuals possess an exceptional ability to paint, to play a musical instrument, to dance, or to act. What comprises this special ability in a particular art is difficult to define. However, there are certain attributes which all talented actors seem to possess and which, in varying degrees, may be cultivated and refined.

Imagination. Imagination is the ability to draw upon past experiences and re-create new images from them. The actor must be able to leave the world of actuality and enter into an imaginary world.

Sensibility. Talented actors, in common with other artists, possess a highly developed sense perception. They are more responsive to the sights, colors, and sounds of their environment and generally react with high emotional intensity.

Sense of rhythm and tempo. Since there are no specific time indicators in the play script comparable to those in the musical score, the actor must innately sense the appropriate rhythm and timing. This he does from a penetrating study of the script: its lines, actions, situations, locale, and characters.

Imitative ability. Although actors are often admonished not to imitate, acting is, in large part, really pure imitation. The degree of the actor's mimetic skill is often the measure of his artistry in characterization. In order to imitate, an actor must have a keen sense of hearing, to detect variations of tone and pitch, combined with a highly responsive and coordinated neuromuscular system.

Personal magnetism. Most actors possess an outgoing, dynamic, expressive personality. The stage character often requires that the actor establish a pleasing, harmonious rapport with his audience. Although all actors may not be classed as egocentric extroverts, they nonetheless must be able and willing to communicate, without inhibitions, the inmost thoughts and emotions of the stage character.

Emotional feeling. Actors are highly emotional individuals. The very nature of their profession demands not only that they feel intensely but also that they be able to express their emotions in a wide and varied range. A note of caution, however, should be entered here. Although an actress may shed real tears on the stage, her emotions are not actual but make-believe. There is always the danger that emotional expressions such as laughter, crying, or hysteria may get out of control, to the detriment of the play and the embarrassment of the audience. An actor does

well to heed John Gielgud's admonition: "It's a great pleasure to shed real tears on the stage, but if you overdo it, the audience doesn't cry at all, as I found to my cost."* The expression of emotion on the stage is discussed further in Chapter 3.

Technique

Technique is the second essential requirement of the actor's art and complements his talent. The truly sincere student of acting can further develop his talent through the perfection of certain basic skills and an attempt to acquire unwavering personal discipline. As Tyrone Guthrie so aptly stated in describing the career of Katherine Cornell, "... let no one suppose that Miss Cornell's career has been achieved simply by the light of nature, without art, without technique, without the grinding attention to duty which is needed to maintain a star in orbit."†

Webster's dictionary defines the word *technique* as "the method or the details of procedure essential to expertness of execution in any art..." In the process of gaining expertness there are no shortcuts, no easily learned methods, no books of rules which will guide the actor in establishing a complete rapport with his art.

Self-discipline. Self-discipline is necessary to achieve the intellectual and emotional control that the actor must maintain in his work. Though often implied rather than stated, the concept of self-discipline permeates all discussions of acting. Such discipline demands a total concentration of the actor upon the task at hand in order to gain mastery of body and voice as mediums of expression.

---

* Gielgud, "And Keep Your Mouth Shut," p. 3.

† Tyrone Guthrie, "The Star's the Thing," *The New York Times Magazine*, 23 October 1960, p. 111.

THE CREATIVE PROCESS

Every work of art involves two distinct processes: impression and expression. An impression in the artist's mind causes him to seek expression in some form. A work of art may originate from an idea, an incident, a mood, or a view of an impressive scene. Gutzon Borglum's idea for "America's Shrine of Democracy" resulted in his carving the faces of four great Americans on the side of Mt. Rushmore in the Black Hills. Chopin's mood, created by sitting alone in his castle during a storm, brought forth his *Fifteenth Prelude*. Michelangelo's vision of the Last Judgment resulted in the magnificent fresco on the wall of the Sistine Chapel. Thus, there is a concept or impression at the core of every creative effort.

The artist may see quite clearly the form of the product before he begins to shape his materials; or his artistic creation may progress by gradual stages. Handel composed the *Messiah* in the amazingly short period of twenty-four days. In contrast, Anton Chekhov's masterpiece, *The Cherry Orchard*, underwent major revisions in concept and mood for a period of almost three years. But each must have had a vivid impression in his mind to point the way and suggest the means to his ultimate goal. In like manner, the actor must gain a vivid and clear impression of any character he will portray, for it is obvious that he cannot proceed until this phase of the creative process is clearly defined.

It is not enough for the artist to be imbued with an impression however. Regardless of the clarity of the original concept, most artists must rework, polish, and refine their materials before the final satisfactory creation is achieved. The actor is no exception. If he wishes to be honored with the name of artist, he must not only have a clear concept of his desired goal but must also be willing to work tirelessly for perfection. He must have at his command the particular skills necessary to fully communicate his impression, to bring it into being in some form. Chopin and Michelangelo were masters of the necessary techniques and could communicate their concepts into auditory and visual terms, polishing and refining their products into final form. So, too, the actor works to perfect his art form and to give it clarity.

Each art form has its own unique characteristics, dictated by the nature of the material used — paint, clay, stone, words, musical tones, or bodily movement. Each artist must master his medium and know the technical means for its complete expression. As Alexander Dean has pointed out, "The purpose of technique in all the arts is the same, namely, to make the concept or subject matter clearer, more effective, more compelling, more moving. . . ."*

It is thought by some that the actor is an exception among artists in the need for technique. The assumption is that if an actor understands the play and the character and feels the appropriate emotion, the communication will take care of itself. This is far from true. It is quite possible for an actor to experience true emotions, have a very vivid concept of the character, and yet (through faulty technique or a lack of skill) fail to communicate his thoughts and feelings to the audience. In a lecture at Ohio State University, Mary Morris, an accomplished professional actress, stated that in her early years on the stage she was often seething with inner emotions which failed to reach the audience. She gradually learned from her colleagues the technical skill of imparting her character's emotions to the audience.

It is not uncommon for an amateur actor to say to his director, "I know what you want me to do, but I don't know how to do it." Although this statement is an admission of a lack of technical skill, it must not be assumed that this lack is characteristic only of the amateur. Many pro-

---

* Alexander Dean, *Fundamentals of Play Directing.* New York: Farrar & Rinehart, 1941, p. 9.

fessional actors are deficient in certain techniques needed to meet the unusually taxing requirements of nonrealistic dramas. This opinion is strongly held by Tyrone Guthrie, one of the most competent directors of the modern theater. For his production of *Mary Stuart* at the Phoenix Theatre in New York, he imported actors from the Shakespeare Festival Company of Stratford, Ontario, giving the following statement as his reason: "I was convinced that a play like *Mary Stuart*, demanding an operatic breadth of speech and movement, could hardly be cast with American actors."* He goes on to say that for many years American actors have had no training in the necessary technical equipment. Lack of theatrical technique is, in Guthrie's opinion, due to a number of factors: the intimate "natural" style of acting which is demanded for the movies and television, the general preoccupation of the American theater with realistic dramas, and its almost total neglect of classic dramatic literature. He commented further that "little journalistic plays generate a little and limited acting style; such a style, in turn, is inappropriate and inadequate for the performance of great works."†

SYSTEMS OF ACTING

In the theater tradition of the western world, two principal systems of acting have developed. The French, or technical system, is the name given to one. The Stanislavski system, commonly called "the Method" in the United States, is the other. Each of these systems has its loyal disciples and practitioners. The French system has a long and illustrious history which reached its peak in the

great acting tradition of the eighteenth century in England. The principles and techniques of this approach to acting were systematized by François Delsarte in the latter part of the nineteenth century. Delsarte's system was an analysis of the techniques used by the voice and body in the communication of emotions. The portrayal of each emotion was catalogued in terms of postures, gestures, head positions, and expressions of the eyes, eyebrows, and mouth. In a period when characters were grandiose and statuesque, when the dialogue was rhetorical and highly poetic, when the plots were artificial and exaggerated, this technical approach to acting was generally accepted. Such "theatrical" acting, with its lack of conformity to actual life, did not appear incongruous to the audiences of the eighteenth and nineteenth centuries. But the technical system did produce astounding results. For example, the French actress Sarah Bernhardt — "the Divine Sarah" — was noted not only for her technical skill but also for her superb powers to enthrall and move her audiences deeply.

The gradual trend throughout the history of the theater has been toward greater verisimilitude. It is interesting to note that while methods of staging underwent radical changes, the style of acting generally held to an established tradition. Following the lead of Emile Zola, who expostulated that "either the theatre will become naturalistic or it will not be at all," many playwrights began to write about life as it actually was. Naturalistic plays were labeled "slice-of-life" dramas since they portrayed characters not in the conventional, theatrical manner but in terms of unglamorized life.

This new style of writing demanded a radically different style of acting. The most influential pioneer in the new, realistic style of acting and staging was unquestionably Duke Georg of Saxe-Meiningen, whose acting troupe achieved wide acclaim and distinction. André Antoine had seen the Duke's troupe and was

* Tyrone Guthrie, *A Life in the Theatre*. New York: McGraw-Hill, 1959, p. 244.
† *Ibid.*, p. 245.

greatly impressed. Adopting many of the Duke's methods, Antoine in 1887 founded the Théâtre-Libre in Paris, where for seven years his revolutionary ideas in acting and staging astounded and impressed the audiences and visiting critics. Following in Antoine's footsteps, in 1889 Otto Brahm opened the Freie Bühne in Berlin and put into practice the principles which he had earlier expounded in an essay entitled "Old and New Acting."

Out of this concern for truth to life in the theater, the Stanislavski system of acting developed. Turning from the technical and external manifestations of the character, Stanislavski focused his attention on the *inner* processes of man. He sought to engender the emotion within the actor which, if it were right for the character and the situation, would then produce the desired effect on the audience. Various techniques of impression were developed by Stanislavski, for example, the "if" situation: "What would I, as a character, do *if* I were in this situation?" Stanislavski admonished his actors to draw on "emotional memory" as an aid to finding the true feeling of an emotion. Through "units and objectives," a complex character-action is broken down, simplified, and its step-by-step development toward an ultimate goal is unfolded. The world renown of the Moscow Art Theatre, under Stanislavski's direction, is ample testimony to the effectiveness of this system, particularly in naturalistic and realistic styles of production. Certain disciples and practitioners of the Stanislavski system have, in recent years, departed somewhat from Stanislavski's theories. They have tended to base their system of acting, the Method, on the first publication of his principles, *An Actor Prepares*. They have neglected his later publications, notably *Building A Character*, which includes the importance of technique in acting.

Each of the systems, the technical and the Method, has its inherent strengths and weaknesses, and neither, to the exclusion of the other, is wholly adequate for all the requirements of the actor's art. The technical system is particularly advantageous for certain period dramas where a high degree of stylistic acting is required. Conversely, the Method is highly effective for realistic and naturalistic dramas. Many actors and some directors (notably Tyrone Guthrie) consider the Method inadequate for many styles of acting, particularly for those of historical periods. In practice, both of these systems are used in varying degrees by accomplished and intelligent actors. As Norris Houghton pertinently states:

"The Stanislavski system is really only a conscious codification of ideas about acting which have always been the property of most good actors of all countries whether they knew it or not. Its basis is the work of the actor with *himself* in order to master 'technical means for the creation of the creative mood, so that inspiration may appear oftener than is its wont'. "*

These two systems, the technical and the Method, are interdependent and complementary. The actor would be wise not to follow one system to the exclusion of the other, but rather to adapt the best principles of each to his purpose, according to the unique requirements of the particular role.†

---

* Norris Houghton, *Moscow Rehearsals*. New York: Harcourt, Brace, 1936, p. 57. Quoted by permission of Norris Houghton.

† This particular point has often been reinforced in panel discussions on the art of acting and in conversations which the authors have had with contemporary actors.

Development of the Actor's Resources

Good actors, like good plays, are made of flesh and blood, not bundles of tricks.

Raymond Massey

In the Introduction certain basic requirements of acting were discussed, the importance of self-discipline was emphasized, and the necessity of adequate technical training was stressed.

In the following discussion, opportunity will be provided for the actor to make a study of himself and to acquire a knowledge of his own possibilities and limitations. A conscientious application of the principles set forth here should result in characterizations of greater breadth and depth.

MENTAL DISCIPLINE

Developing a positive attitude

One of the first and most obvious problems of the young actor is that of developing self-confidence. A sound approach to this problem is striving to acquire a *positive* attitude. This means that the actor must believe in himself and feel that he has something of worth to offer. Stated in another way, a positive approach means that the actor should concentrate on his endowments rather than on his imperfections. Various mental fears, such as, "I'll look silly, forget, or make a mistake," must be suppressed and controlled. Negative attitudes greatly hinder an actor's natural abilities and obstruct his chances for success. The actor must realize that all creative work requires courage and that the actual difficulties are often not as insurmountable as first imagined.

Aids in developing self-confidence

There are a number of ways in which the actor may replace a negative attitude with a positive one. The following suggestions are given to aid him in developing self-confidence.

1. *The actor should not be alarmed by nervousness and anxiety.* He should bear in mind that, on occasion, all performers have stage fright. Even the most seasoned actors are not without "first night jitters."

Instead of becoming panicky, the actor must control his fears and prevent his inner anxiety from harming his performance. Contrary to the usual conception, a certain degree of tension is beneficial. It quickens the reflexes, increases bodily energy and vitality, heightens the sensory reactions, and stimulates the actor to a more energetic and spirited performance. Not infrequently, an actor gives his best performance on an opening night. Too much relaxation and self-confidence often results in a phlegmatic performance. On the other hand, uncontrolled stage fright can be detrimental. It may so tense the muscles that free and easy movements are inhibited and may cause such a corresponding tension of the vocal bands that a natural and flexible delivery is prevented.

2. *The actor should be thoroughly prepared.* Fears and tensions often arise from a feeling of insecurity and inadequacy. Insufficient line and "business," or action, memorization may easily lead to stage fright. Knowing thoroughly what one has to do, and the "when" and "how" to do it, is a great boon to composure. A thorough preparation greatly contributes to an actor's feeling of self-assurance.

3. *The actor should concentrate on the character, not on himself.* In playing a character, the actor is often required to express ideas and emotions normally hidden and repressed in real life. For an inexperienced actor, this is one of the primary causes of inhibition. If he bears in mind that it is the character who performs the action and that he is only the instrument, he may, without embarrassment, express thoughts and feelings that would be disconcerting in real life. It follows then that the actor should, in so far as possible, suppress his individuality and keep uppermost in his mind the thought, "This is what the character would do." When the action is well planned, purposeful, controlled, and believable, the audience is quite willing to accept the actor as the character.

4. *The actor should take stock of his assets and find increased confidence in them.* If an actor is a person with average talents, he has reason to believe that, with hard work, he may achieve a certain degree of success. It is imperative that he believe in himself as a competent performer. The very fact that he has been cast by the director indicates he has some degree of capability in acting. In addition, he may take comfort in the thought that, in all likelihood, he has more ability to act than the majority of those sitting out front. Otherwise, he would be a spectator with someone else playing his role. Every performer should believe that he is equal to the task at hand.

5. *The actor should not overemphasize the importance of either the success or failure of his performance.* A play is not life. If something goes wrong, if the actor gets a bad review, he is not ruined forever. The chances are, the "catastrophe" will soon be forgotten by everyone else and life will go on much as it did before.

6. *The actor should bear in mind that his audience is allied with him, that it is "pulling for" the cast, and that it wishes the performance to be supremely successful.* The audience is there to be entertained and it is usually willing to do its full share in fostering a successful production.

If the actor keeps these six points in mind, his stage fright should be forestalled.

PHYSICAL PREPARATION

Developing a flexible body

It is obvious that the aspiring actor should possess a physical instrument free from impediments. An artistic performance requires the most perfect instrument. The concert violinist performs on a Stradivarius; the pianist plays on a concert grand; and the painter chooses the best oils and brushes available. In like manner, the actor needs the most flexible and responsive body possible for his performance.

Fortunately, most of us are endowed with bodies free from defects. However, a healthy body is of no avail until its potentialities are brought under control and mastered. This involves the development of bodily coordination and the eradication of bad posture, ungainly movements, and distracting mannerisms. Depending on the actor's particular endowments or deficiencies, the development of a flexible body may require exercises over a long period of time. Particularly helpful are exercises in pantomime, fencing, and dancing.

Relaxation. As applied to acting, the concept of relaxation is frequently used but often misunderstood. Relaxation is a relative term. In actual practice, it must be a muscular condition somewhere between the extremes of inertia and rigidity. Creative activity is impossible if either of these extreme conditions exists. Acting demands a vigorous muscular tone, but the tension must be controlled and must never be allowed to reach a condition in which freedom of physical action or vocalization is hindered.

Extreme muscular tension is usually the result of anxiety and fear. When this negative attitude, which is usually unwarranted, is replaced by positive thinking, a more normal and controlled physical state results. Muscular tension is relieved by physical activity. The athlete is often very tense before the contest but once he is in the game a normal muscular tone soon results. Before the performance, it is often advisable for the actor to go through some simple calisthenics to loosen and relax overtense muscles.

Poise and bodily control. Closely related to controlled muscular tension is poise. Some teachers of acting think poise is a better term than relaxation. Poise includes both a mental and a physical adjustment to a particular situation. It embodies mental composure and physical control. Stage poise is not easily achieved and often requires years of training and experience, but it is a prime essential for any artistic performance. Poise not only enables the actor to be at his best, physically and vocally, but it also allows the audience to be at ease, thus heightening its enjoyment of the performance.

Exercises which aid in physical preparation

1. From an erect position, release muscular tension so that the body slumps and almost collapses on the floor. Repeat, until the body no longer feels tense.
2. To relieve tight neck muscles, rotate the head in a clockwise and then counterclockwise motion.
3. Let the arms hang freely and shake them.
4. Advance two or three steps to greet a supposed friend, then recoil as from an enemy.
5. Practice simple dance steps of your own invention. Strive for ease, grace, and poise.

TRAINING THROUGH IMPROVISATION

An improvisation is an unrehearsed, unpolished exercise. It differs in this respect from a performance. In such an exercise, the actor should concern himself primarily with *who* he is, *where* he is, and *what* are the environmental conditions.

Values of improvisation

Undoubtedly, there is no better way to begin the training of an actor than through improvisation since it permits him to experiment, explore, invent, even make mistakes, and thereby discover himself. Here the actor is given a freedom of action and interpretation not usually possible in a specific character part in a play. In performance situations the actor is subject to the concepts of the author, the dictates of the director, and the interplay with other characters. In improvisation the actor must, in a sense, be playwright and director. His creative powers are taxed, his imagination stimulated, and his resources fully challenged and tested. When an inexperienced actor is given a role in a play, his lack of training is often glaringly evident. As a result, the communication of the author's thoughts is often faulty or inadequate and the characterization is frequently misconceived. In improvisation, an actor speaks only the dialogue which his own thoughts and feelings dictate, and he executes only the actions which the situation and the character require. Consequently, a beginning actor often achieves greater credibility in his improvisation than in an assigned role.

Improvisation also has definite values in the acted play. Certain roles, particularly in comedy and farce, require some improvisation. This inventive "business" (sometimes called by-play) is not included in the script. Yet its inclusion by the imaginative actor often adds greatly to the comedy of a scene and to a more complete realization of the character. The inclusion of such improvisation in the performance, however, is not devoid of some danger. If left to the discretion of an uninhibited actor, improvisation is likely to get out of hand, creating confusion and consternation for the other actors in the scene and resulting in possible damage to an entire performance.

Excellent as improvisation may be for the training of the actor, it should be relegated to the classroom and to the rehearsal periods of the play. By the time the play reaches the performance date, everything should be set. During the run of the play, all spontaneous "improvements" should be avoided. This does not mean that an important change in lines or action may not be incorporated into a performance after the opening night. But such changes should be left to the decision of the director. Each member of the production who is affected by the change should be informed. The new lines or action should be rehearsed, set, and recorded in the prompt book. Nothing new should be added without consultation with the director

since nothing in a performance should be left to chance. Shakespeare's admonition to the players seems pertinent here: "... let those that play your clowns speak no more than is set down for them."

Principles of improvisation

Planning. The question may well be asked, how much preliminary planning should an actor make for an improvisation? Obviously, detailed planning would hamper the actor, stifle his imagination, and defeat the very purpose for which the improvisation was devised. On the other hand, no planning might easily lead to a chaotic and confused demonstration. It is helpful for the actor to have a clear concept of his improvisation — its definite point of departure, its development, and its destination. In other words (to borrow from Aristotle), a good improvisation should have "a beginning, middle, and end." A comparison might be made to the scenarios used by the actors of *commedia dell'arte*.* In the original Italian form a skeleton of the scene was provided which, within its general framework, permitted the actor freedom to invent and improvise as his imagination and fancy dictated.

Mood. The general mood of an improvisation should be predetermined. One must decide if the effect is to be comic or serious. In spite of the fact that the line which separates the comic from the tragic may be extremely thin, the actor must know which mood he wishes to develop, since appropriate action for comedy would be totally wrong for a serious scene. A further discussion of mood is presented in succeeding chapters.

Style. Since style is a subtle and complex matter, a discussion of this aspect of acting is usually reserved for the advanced actor. Nevertheless,

---

* Pierre Louis Duchartre, *The Italian Comedy.* New York: John Day, 1929, pp. 50–56.

acting does not take place in a void. The beginning actor must place his improvisation in some specific relationship with the real world. He should determine whether he is portraying life as it actually is or some departure from real life, such as a romanticized or stylized treatment. In the beginning stages of his study, it is highly advisable for the actor to limit himself to real life as he knows it, and to reserve until later any attempts to represent the various stylistic departures from reality. A detailed discussion of style in acting is presented in Part Two.

Character type. Situation and character are interrelated and dependent, one on the other. The situation determines the action of the character, and the type of character determines what he will do in a particular situation. For example, all individuals register definite reactions on seeing a murder victim, but the kind of reaction is conditioned by background and training. Consider the reaction of an average young man as compared to that of a police commissioner. Since all emotional reactions are variable, the actor must have a clear concept of the type of character he is portraying and of how its background and training will condition its reactions to a given set of circumstances.

Studies in improvisation

Observation. The primary study for the actor is human nature, the fountain source of his inspiration and expression. He must constantly observe people, determining their habits, mannerisms, and ways of reacting to diverse situations. For example, he must observe how individuals express joy, exultation, grief, and despair, or how they bid their friends good-bye. From these observations the actor will discover that, in a given situation, behavior patterns vary, that they depend on such factors as the mental and social conditioning of the characters involved. After careful observation of these factors, the actor will reach the conclusion

that people are idiosyncratic and that *general* assumptions regarding human behavior are unreliable and invalid. Yet despite individual differences, the actor must find those elements of commonality in each situation or emotion which will convey conviction and credibility. He must discover what is true for a particular individual and circumstance, within the compass of the particular emotion he wishes to express.

The following exercises are designed to aid the actor in developing his powers of observation.

1. Describe in detail a familiar scene or recent event.
2. Observe and reenact how a waitress sets a table.
3. Pack a suitcase or a trunk in the manner of a boy going to camp, a girl leaving for a weekend visit, a woman going abroad, or a man departing on a business trip.
4. Observe various eating habits in a restaurant. Select one individual and reenact his manners. Try not to copy merely the external characteristics. Seek the inner motivation for the eating manner. Perhaps the man may be extremely hungry; the woman may be very dainty and fastidious.
5. Visit a depot, air terminal, or dock, and observe the manners of travelers saying good-bye. The action will be characterized by the individual and by circumstances such as who is leaving, for how long a time, and for what purpose. With these circumstances in mind, reenact a parting scene.

Sensitivity. As mentioned in the Introduction, acting requires a highly sensitive mechanism in order that the actor may receive and transmit psychological impulses. This requires more than a flexible, coordinated body. Even though athletes possess highly developed physiques, it is doubtful that their training (valuable as it is) qualifies them to function as artistic performers.

The actor must be responsive to the whole gamut of sensations and emotions. He must, on occasion, react to horrible sights, ominous sounds, the taste of bitter medicine, and the handling of unpleasant objects. In the process of developing sensitivity, a recalling of past sensations of like or similar nature will be helpful. For example, the actor may recall how he felt and reacted to such experiences as extreme pain, nausea, fainting, gnawing hunger, oppressive heat, extreme cold, or exhaustion.

In the following exercises, strive for the re-creation of a true inner feeling. Do not rely on external clichés to portray each particular sensation.

1. Recall an experience in which you were obliged to handle or touch unpleasant objects, such as the "cat's eye" or "brains" at a Halloween Party, or some grimy, dirty object. Re-create the experience in detail.

2. Arrange a bouquet of thorny roses.

3. Recall an experience of intense, stifling heat. Reenact the experience.

4. You are a member of a captive audience with no graceful way of escape. The room is becoming colder and colder. How would you react to this situation?

5. You have been out in the bitter cold for hours. Now you have come into a shack whose potbellied stove seems quite warm in contrast. Strive to make your actions and sensations realistic.

6. From your experience in a chemistry laboratory, recall an unpleasant odor, such as that of hydrogen sulphide. If such an experience is not included in your background, re-create a similar reaction to the odor of a skunk.

7. Recall your experience in having to take a distasteful medicine. Re-create the experience.

8. Recall a very frightening experience. Draw on your emotional memory in reenacting the scene.

9. Recall a situation in which you were very nervous. It may have been one similar to the following: making a public appearance, meeting an important person, or interviewing a dignitary. Recall your sensations and reenact the scene.

10. Recall other examples of similar experiences which will develop your ability to receive and communicate sensations.

Imagination. Imagination is the faculty which carries the actor beyond the immediate and real into the realm of the make-believe. Frequently, the actor is required to go beyond his exact knowledge of life experiences in portraying a character, and must place a great deal of dependence on his imagination. Drawing on past experiences, sensations, and emotions, he combines them to create a new image. For example, how does Macbeth feel and act after the murder of Duncan? It is obvious that the actor has had no comparable experience, yet he must make his actions and vocal expressions believable. In such an extreme emotional situation the actor may, by using his imagination and drawing on similar experiences of horror, remorse, and regret, piece together a believable portrayal of Macbeth's emotions. But, as a note of caution, the actor should be wary of unrestrained flights of fancy. Imagination is grounded in reality and although it may soar, it must never lose contact with actual life.

In the following exercises, let past experiences stimulate your imagination in creating the image of the character or the details of the scene.

1. Select a character in a fanciful or unreal situation such as the following:

a. Rip Van Winkle, waking up after sleeping for twenty years.

b. Death appearing to Everyman.

c. The witch in *Snow White*.

d. Goldilocks when discovered by the Three Bears.

Let your imagination dwell on each character and the situation until you have a clear image.

2. Imagine yourself a pilot. You have bailed out of your plane and come down in a wild, unknown region. Ponder the situation and your reactions.

3. You are a young wife and have been left alone at night in your country home for the first time. Imagine your reactions to a knock at the door.

4. Accidentally, you have been locked in a park late at night, alone. There seems to be no way of getting out. Imagine your reactions to this situation.

5. Select a character from *The Diary of Anne Frank*. Imagine its reactions to the various sounds which may precede discovery.

6. You return home and discover that three gangsters have taken possession of your house and are holding the other members of the family as prisoners.

7. Use your imagination in the selection of incidents, or characters, and draw on your past experiences to aid in the re-creation of the character, situation, or mood.

Concentration. This term, so applicable to the actor, means freeing the mind of all irrelevant matters and becoming absorbed in thoughts or actions of immediate concern. Although in many real life situations concentrated attention may be involuntary, on the stage (with its many distractions) the actor must often exercise *forced* attention. He must not allow the unexpected sounds in the audience, a passing fire truck, or any of the many accidental happenings during the run of a show to disrupt his train of thought. Although the development of the thought or action of the scene may relate to the past or the future, concentration is a matter of the present. The "blow-up" or mental blank, which is not uncommon with actors, is usually caused by lack of concentration. For a

moment, the actor has allowed his mind to wander to some irrelevant matter such as what he has to say or do in another scene, or the quick change he has to make. Thoughts which have no bearing on the immediate action should be erased from the mind.

Life on the stage is highly concentrated. Time and action move with great rapidity. One has only to forget a line or wait for a delayed entrance to realize that a pause of a few seconds on the stage seems interminable. The actor must not only concentrate on his own lines and actions but he must also give close attention to what the other characters are saying and doing. Above all, he must be constantly aware of how the audience is reacting to what is happening on the stage. Concentration of the degree required for acting may be acquired by a heightened interest in the character, its motivation and objectives. This highly important facet of acting develops within the framework of mental discipline.

Consider the following exercises which are designed to increase the actor's powers of concentration.

1. You are a police inspector at the scene of a crime. Concentrate on the situation. Reconstruct a possible theory as to how the crime might have been committed. List all the possible relevant matters and circumstances.

2. Try reading aloud from a book while listening to conversation. This exercise will demonstrate that one cannot give concentrated attention to two or more activities at the same time.

3. Choose a dramatic character such as Sadie Thompson, Hedda Gabler, Cyrano de Bergerac, or the Nurse in *Romeo and Juliet*, and concentrate on the interesting facets of the character and on what motivated his or her actions. Use one of these characters as an improvisation in which the emphasis is on concentration.

4. Explain an idea, a process, or a complicated game to a companion.
5. Observe and listen attentively to a scene or exercise by another member of the group and then reenact as much of the action and dialogue as you can recall.

Additional Exercises for Improvisation

1. You are waiting for an important letter or message. The nature of the message and what it contains are left to the imagination of the actor. Create the scene in detail.
2. A student returns to his dormitory room for a valuable object. He searches but cannot find it. Various thoughts and suspicions rush through his mind. Decide on the nature and value of the object, and develop the scene.
3. A young wife goes to the air terminal to meet her husband who is returning from service overseas. He is not with the passengers on the scheduled plane. Through your imagination, develop the situation to a logical and believable conclusion.
4. Imagine yourself a kleptomaniac in a department store. Determine the direction which the scene may take and its conclusion.
5. You are celebrating your birthday. Determine all the pertinent circumstances of the party. React to the various guests and the gifts received.
6. You are a harassed mother on a day when everything seems to go wrong. Decide on the mood and the specific details of the scene.
7. You are called into the company manager's office. You are expecting a raise. Decide on the development of the scene and the final action.

Stage
Terminology
and Technique

*The ideal creation is one in which there is perfect
proportion of concept and technique.*

Alexander Dean

Over a period of centuries, the theater of the
western world has developed its own terminology,
techniques, and conventions. Since these are well
known to every professional actor, it is essential for
each aspirant to learn the "tools of the trade" as
soon as possible. A knowledge of stage terminology
and technique (1) aids the beginning actor in
taking stage directions, (2) enhances his playing
ability with other actors in the scene, (3) increases
the effectiveness of his playing, and (4) helps to
provide skillful execution of plot action and stage
business.

THE ACTOR AND THE STAGE

Since it is assumed that every professional actor
knows the terminology and technique of his art,
the following principles are provided chiefly for
the benefit of the novice. A knowledge of them is
essential as background.

Stage areas

As a matter of convenience for both actor and
director, sections of the stage may be designated
as distinct playing areas. The number of areas
may be determined by the size of the stage or the
total amount of stage space needed for a particular
production, or may merely be the number of
areas traditionally referred to by certain directors.
The contrast in Figures 1 and 2 illustrates the
variance in use of specific areas as designated by
individual directors. Some find that the more
detailed the division of areas, the more difficult it
becomes for a novice actor to adjust to his new
environment.

Conventionally, a division into six areas seems
to have gained most common usage. These
conventional areas are called *up right* (UR), *up
center* (UC), *up left* (UL), *down right* (DR), *down
center* (DC), and *down left* (DL).

In spite of differences of opinion as to the
definite number of areas on a stage, common

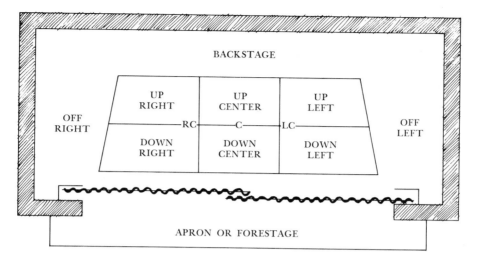

Figure 1. Stage areas.

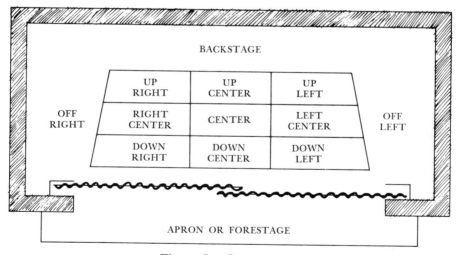

Figure 2. Stage areas.

agreement has been reached on a few facets of the labeling process. For example, it should be noted that the portion of the stage nearest the audience is always termed *downstage* and that farthest from the audience is termed *upstage*. No doubt this distinction and the resultant terminology origi-

nated with the Teatro Olimpico, completed in 1584 by Vincenzo Scamozzi. The stage floor of this early Renaissance theater was actually higher at the back than at that spot closest to the audience. Scamozzi felt that the use of a "raked" stage heightened the perspective illusion. Other architects followed Scamozzi's practice. The sloping stage became so conventional that it may still be found in theaters built as late as the nineteenth century. These terms remain appropriate in our modern theaters where, due to the laws of perspective, the level stage floor seems to be higher at the back than at the front when viewed from the modern sloping auditorium.

Stage directions are always given from the viewpoint of the actor, not the audience. Stage right or stage left indicates that part of the stage to the actor's right or left as he faces the theater auditorium.

The relative importance of stage areas

It will help the actor in his playing of various types of scenes if he realizes the relative importance and conventional uses of each stage area. The center portion of the acting area, comparable to the center of a painting, is the area of greatest interest. It is not surprising that stars of the eighteenth and nineteenth centuries often monopolized this area of the stage. Generally, important scenes (particularly scenes of dramatic conflict) are played in the central portion of the stage rather than at either side. In like manner, the downstage areas are generally stronger than the corresponding upstage areas. Consequently, the six conventional stage areas indicated earlier are classified from strongest to weakest as follows: down center, up center, down right, down left, up right, and up left. Because of its inherent weakness, the up left area is used much less than the other stage areas. When of necessity it is used for important scenes, an additional strength value, by means of steps, levels, or balcony, is often provided. Obviously, the importance of stage areas is less significant on the arena or the thrust stage.

In addition to placing the important scenes of a play in the strong areas, the important or dominant character in a scene is generally given a stronger area than the characters of less importance. An exception to this rule is not using the strong area down center for the dominant character in a scene requiring ensemble playing. Although occupying the strongest area, the character would be in a disadvantageous playing position in that he would be forced to turn upstage and away from the audience in playing to the other characters in the scene. Thus, knowing the strength values of the stage areas will help the actor to determine his own stage positions and he will require fewer stage directions.

It is helpful when the actor remembers that, in addition to the strength factors, stage areas have individual connotative, denotative, and mood values. Alexander Dean used the term "tonal qualities" to express the various mood values of different areas.* For example, *down center* is hard, intense, and strong. Here one may logically play scenes of strong conflict, fights, quarrels, etc. On the other hand, scenes of extreme violences, murder, and torturing are generally moved upstage where the effect is softened and made more acceptable to an audience. *Up center* is more aloof, regal, and formal. Here it is appropriate to play scenes of state and royal occasions, or romanticized love, or scenes which do not contain an inherent intimate quality. *Down right* has a warm and intimate feeling which makes it ideal for scenes of confession. *Down left*, according to Dean, is colder, less intimate, and more formal. Here one may play scenes of intrigue, conspiracy, or sophisticated love. *Up right* has less warmth and is more remote than down right, where one might appropriately play scenes of romance. *Up left* has a cold, distant quality. Quite commonly, dream and supernatural scenes are played in this area. It is here that the spirit, Elvira, usually makes her appearance in Noel Coward's play *Blithe*

---

* Alexander Dean, *Fundamentals of Play Directing*. New York: Farrar & Rinehart, 1941, p. 212.

Spirit. The appearance of the mysterious and magical character, Applegate, in the musical *Damn Yankees* (by Abbott and Wallop) may be staged up left. Playing a scene in the area which contributes the appropriate tonal quality heightens the dramatic effectiveness of the play and produces a mood value which otherwise might be minimized or lost. Again, these concepts apply particularly to the proscenium stage.

Body positions

There are five conventional body positions for the actor in relation to his audience. These positions are as follows.

1. *Full-front*. The actor faces directly toward the audience.

2. *Quarter position*. He faces left or right about forty-five degrees from the full-front position.

3. *Profile*. He faces directly stage right or stage left.

4. *Three-quarter*. He is in a position halfway between profile and full-back either to stage right or left.

5. *Full-back*. He faces the back wall of the stage with his back to the audience.

As in the case of the stage areas, the different body positions also have varying strength values. The strongest is full-front. For example, if five actors are on stage, each representing one of the five body positions, the actor in the full-front position will receive the greatest emphasis, providing all the other factors which have a bearing on emphasis are equal. The remaining body positions from strength to weakness are quarter, profile, full-back, and three-quarter. It will be noted that, as the actor turns away from the audience, his position decreases in emphasis. The exception to this is the full-back position which is stronger than a three-quarter. The emphasis which an actor receives in the full-back position

may be explained by (1) the unusual quality of the position and (2) the emphatic breadth of the body as compared with the three-quarter position. It is obvious that an actor must harmonize the strength of his playing position with the significance of his lines and with the dominance of the character in the scene. In other words, an actor does not take a weak body position when he should dominate the scene or has important lines to deliver. Conversely, he does not take the full-front position while delivering relatively unimportant lines, unless there is a good reason for doing so.

The body positions of the actor should harmonize with the dialogue, the quality of the scene, and the style of the play. Consequently, no one body position is held for any length of time. As the character's lines vary from important to unimportant, his body positions change. In serious drama or tragedy the same body position, with slight variations, may be held for a number of speeches.

Each different type and style of drama demands variation and adaptation of the actor's body positions. In modern realistic or naturalistic dramas, which seek to create an illusion of reality, all the body positions may be put into use. However, the full-front is used less frequently than others. Even so, when the actor uses the full-front position he usually does not look directly at the audience or indicate an awareness of its presence. In the nonrealistic styles and in productions of historical dramas, the actor not only plays in the full-front and one-quarter positions but also frequently addresses himself directly to the audience. A more detailed discussion of the uses of body positions for various styles of acting is presented in Part Two.

Directions for change of body positions

In addition to the five body positions listed previously, the following terms are used when a change in the actor's position is desired by the director.

Open up. This means to turn the body more toward the audience. For example, to open up, the actor might turn from a profile to a quarter position or to full-front.

Close in or *turn in.* The actor turns away from the audience and toward the center of the stage, as for example, turning from quarter position to profile.

Turn out. The actor turns away from the center of the stage to the right or to the left. If the actor were playing left of stage center in the full-front position and were given the direction to turn out, he would turn left to approximately the quarter position.

Frequently, the director must give directions to his cast which have no direct bearing on the interpretation of the scene, but rather serve to "dress the stage" or improve the aesthetic qualities of the stage composition. In this category, the following terms are typical.

Forward. The actor moves one or more steps in the direction which he is facing, keeping the same body position.

Backward. The actor moves backward one or more steps and keeps the same body position.

Downstage. This direction, with varying distances, means for the actor to move the required distance directly toward the front of the stage and assume the same body position he had before moving.

Upstage. The actor moves directly upstage, a specified distance, and takes the same body position.

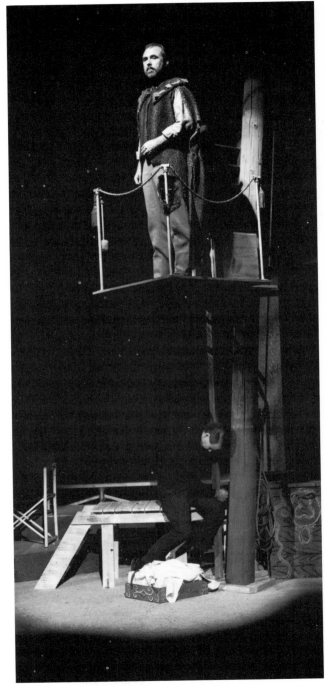

Plate 1. *J.B.* by Archibald MacLeish. Emphasis by means of level. Ohio State University. Director: Charles Ritter. Photograph: Department of Photography, Ohio State University.

Devices for achieving character emphasis

Although character emphasis and focus are chiefly the concern of the director, the actor should know the techniques of gaining emphasis or audience attention when the nature of the scene demands that one character stand out in relation to the others. In addition to the strong body positions and strong stage areas, the six methods which follow are used to gain emphasis.

Levels. In theatrical terminology, levels refer to distances above the stage floor. The use of level is one of the most effective ways of achieving emphasis for a single character. When all other factors are more or less equal, the character in the highest position, or level, receives the most emphasis. For example, in the scene from *J.B.*, Mr. Zuss' position on the platform gives him far greater emphasis than that given to Nickles below. (See Plate 1.)

There is one exception to the rule of greater emphasis to the character on the higher level. When one character is sitting, kneeling, or lying on the floor, and all the others are standing, the character in the lowest position receives emphasis because of contrast or unusual position. For example, note the crouching figure of Orestes in Plate 2.

Because of the strength value of level, a character usually stands for important speeches. If very strong emphasis is needed he may play on a raised platform, on steps, or on a balcony.

Space. A character standing or sitting alone receives more emphasis than a member of a group or mob. This device of gaining emphasis through spatial relationship is sometimes abused by a performer who desires more for himself than is justified for the character. He refuses to allow other actors to play near him. But space as a means of emphasis is often justified and necessary. The nature and quality of the scene and the importance of the character, not the actor, should be the guiding considerations. In the scene from *Dark of the Moon*, Barbara Allen is appropriately isolated from others who appear in the scene. She is, therefore, given greater emphasis. (See Plate 3.)

Plate 3. *Dark of the Moon* by Howard Richardson and William Berney. Emphasis by space, body position, and visual focus. West Virginia University. Director: Charles D. Neel.

Plane. The stage is divided by a number of imaginary lines running parallel to the footlights. The distance between these lines is about the width of the human body. The strongest plane is nearest the footlights; each plane decreases in strength value from downstage to upstage. Although the plane nearest the audience is very strong, it can seldom be used, particularly in stage center in a modern realistic production. In the down center stage plane, the actor is at a disadvantage since he must turn to the three-quarter or full-back position in order to play to other characters in the scene. However, the downstage plane may be used effectively in productions of certain historical plays, as indicated in the scene from *Medea* by Euripides. (See Plate 4.)

Line. In a drawing or painting, the eye tends to follow lines. If these lines converge at a point, the eye is led to that spot. Similarly, on the stage, if an actor is placed at the apex of a triangle, he will receive emphasis due to the actual lines in the composition. This triangle may vary in form with

Plate 4. *Medea* by Euripides (adapted by Robinson Jeffers). Emphasis by plane, strong area, and visual focus. Bowling Green State University. Director: Lael J. Woodbury.

Plate 5. *The Importance of Being Earnest* by Oscar Wilde. Emphasis by the position of the characters at points of a triangle and full-front body positions. University of Iowa. Director: David Schaal.

its apex upstage, on either side, or even down-stage. The photographs of *The Importance of Being Earnest* and *Uncle Vanya* (Plates 5 and 6) illustrate how emphasis by the use of line can be found in different types of composition. In the first the character in the center of the composition is at the apex of the triangle, but the apex has shifted to the right of center in the second scene. In *Uncle Vanya*, the emphasis on the upstage character is also due to position, level, and contrast.

Visual Focus. It is well known that a person is drawn to look where others are looking. If we see a group of people looking at the sky, we are impelled to look up also. In the theater the audience is inclined to focus its attention on the character toward whom the other characters in the scene are looking. In the scene from *Mary Stuart* (Plate 7), strong emphasis is placed on Mary in the downstage point of the triangle. This type of

emphasis is termed visual focus. The emphatic character in a scene should receive visual focus from one or more characters. The greater the number of characters focusing on the principal character, the stronger will be the emphasis. Since the audience should usually look at the character who is speaking, the visual focus may shift from character to character with the dialogue.

Contrast. We notice the object that is different or unusual. Involuntarily, our attention is directed to the soldier who is out of step or the dancer in the chorus who is out of position. On the stage, the character who is in contrast to the other characters will receive emphasis. The contrast may be one of body position, level, or bodily attitude. In the scene from *Samson Agonistes* (Plate 8), the character of Samson is given emphasis chiefly by his unusual position in contrast to that of Dalila.

Plate 6. *Uncle Vanya* by Anton Chekhov. Emphasis by position at the apex of a triangle and by elevation. University of Michigan. Director: Richard Burgwin. Photograph: F. W. Ouradnik.

Plate 7. *Mary Stuart* by Friedrich Schiller. Emphasis by position at the downstage point of the triangle and by visual focus. Ohio State University. Director: Everett M. Schreck. Photograph: Department of Photography, Ohio State University.

Thus we see that the actor has a number of devices whereby he may bring emphasis to his character. It should be remembered that it is the character, not the actor, that must be emphasized, and then only when it is justified and meets the approval of the play director.

The actor's position in relation to other actors in the scene

The scene with two actors. The positions of actors in a scene are governed by their relative importance as characters. When two characters are of equal importance, the scene is *shared*. Emphasis on each character is practically equal. The shared scene is usually played in the quarter position as shown

Plate 8. *Samson Agonistes* by John Milton. Emphasis by contrast and the unusual position of the character. Dartmouth College. Director: Henry B. Williams. Photograph: David Pierce Studio.

Plate 9. *Once Upon a Mattress* by Jay Thompson, Marshall Barer, and Dean Fuller. Shared scene in the quarter position. Ohio University. Director: Rex McGraw. Photograph: Bruce A. McElfresh.

in the photograph of *Once Upon a Mattress* (Plate 9). This relationship is well adapted for scenes of comedy with equally divided dialogue. It allows each character to open up, yet play to the other.

The shared scene may be played in a variety of body positions, providing that the emphasis on each character is approximately equal. In the scene from *The Importance of Being Earnest* (Plate 10), Cecily is playing in an almost full-front position while Gwendolen is slightly above in the quarter position. In the letter-reading scene from *The Merry Wives of Windsor* (Plate 11), both Mistress Ford and Mistress Page are playing in the quarter position but are turned away from each other. This character relationship may be used in a scene in which each character is attempting to conceal something from the other or in which each

character is displeased with the other. The intellectual and emotional relationship may be changed by varying the distance between the two characters. The profile positions are usually taken when the scene is a heated argument or quarrel. For example, note the characters in the scene from *The Sea Gull* (Plate 12).

When one character is more important, he may take a position in a plane above a second character, thus giving himself greater emphasis. This is called a *given* scene, since the downstage character has literally given the scene to his companion. Such a relationship is used when the upstage character is the more dominant one in the scene, has more important lines to speak, or has longer speeches. In the scene from *Major Barbara* (Plate 13), the character of Bill Walker is domi-

Plate 10. *The Importance of Being Earnest* by Oscar Wilde. Shared scene using full-front and quarter positions. Ohio State University. Director: Everett M. Schreck. Photograph: Department of Photography, Ohio State University.

Plate 11. *The Merry Wives of Windsor* by William Shakespeare. Shared scene with characters turned away from each other. Denison University Theater. Director: William Brasmer.

nant; consequently, the scene is given to him by the character, Price, who has his back to the audience.

Whether a scene is shared or given, the relative position of the actors depends upon (1) the importance of each character, (2) the nature of the scene, (3) the intellectual and emotional relationship of the characters, and (4) the style of the play and the production. In realistic pro-

ductions the characters play more directly to each other, while in the nonrealistic and historical ones characters play less directly, open up more, and frequently use the full-front position, as indicated in the scene from *The Lark* (Plate 14). The character relationships are, of course, not static but are being altered almost constantly throughout the play with the changes in the dramatic situation.

Plate 12. *The Sea Gull* by Anton Chekhov. Shared scene in profile. Brandeis University. Director: Morris Carnovsky.

Plate 13. *Major Barbara* by George Bernard Shaw. A given scene. University of Miami. Director: Jack Clay. Photograph: David Greenfield.

Plate 14. *The Lark* by Jean Anouilh (adapted by Lillian Hellman). Scene played in full-front position. Ohio State University. Director: Everett M. Schreck.

Plate 15. *The Imaginary Invalid* by Molière. Triangle scene. University of Delaware. Director: C. Robert Kase. Photograph: Action! Photo Lab.

Plate 17. *A Doll's House* by Henrik Ibsen. Uneven grouping of three characters. Vassar College. Director: Mary Virginia Heinlein. Photograph: Howard Green.

Plate 16. *The Tempest* by William Shakespeare. Three-character scene with almost equal spacing. Yale University School of Drama. Director: Frank McMullan. Photograph: Arnold Baker.

The upstage position is generally considered the most advantageous one for the actor. In this position, he may play directly to the other characters in the scene and, when in the more open body position, receive more emphasis. Other characters are forced to turn upstage while playing to the upstage actor and, consequently, lose emphasis. Experienced actors sometimes take unjustifiable advantage of this device to gain emphasis for themselves. If allowed to do so by the director, an actor will maneuver into the upstage area when this position is not justified by the relative importance of his character. In a production of *The Merry Wives of Windsor* some years ago, starring Otis Skinner, Minnie Maddern Fiske, and Henrietta Crosman, it was amusing to observe each of these masters in the art of gaining personal emphasis jockeying for the upstage position.

Plate 18. *The Importance of Being Earnest* by Oscar Wilde. Artificial and formal qualities are conveyed by equal spacing. Yale University School of Drama.

Director: Frank McMullan. Photograph: Commercial Photo Service.

Scene after scene moved gradually from the downstage to the upstage areas.

The scene with three characters. In most stage situations where three actors appear together in a scene, their stage positions form the points of a triangle. Obviously, stage triangles may differ greatly in size and form, as may be seen by carefully examining Plates 15, 16, 17, and 18. The spatial relationship of characters is considerably diverse, as is the placement of the triangle's apex. It will be noted in comparing the photographs of *The Imaginary Invalid* and *The Tempest* that the uneven spacing of characters in the former provides a more interesting grouping than the more evenly spaced scene in the latter. The grouping of the three characters in the scene from *A Doll's House*, while differing very little in spatial relation-

ship from the *Tempest* scene, depicts an entirely different mood since the tension is shown as somewhat more relieved.

In general, actors should avoid the equal division of space between them since equal spacing is formal, lacks subtlety, and may even suggest artificiality. The equal spacing in the photograph of a scene from *The Importance of Being Earnest* (Plate 18), in contrast to spacing in the other scenes (Plates 15, 16, and 17), shows how the artificial quality of a play may be conveyed by the manner of its staging.

Although the emphatic character is usually in the upstage position of the triangle, it is possible to give emphasis to another character in the group. This may be achieved through one of the following devices: (1) level, (2) body position, (3) space, or (4) visual focus, as is indicated in the scenes from *J.B.*, *Orestes*, *Dark of the Moon*, *Mary Stuart*, and *Samson Agonistes*, in Plates 1, 2, 3, 7, and 8.

When the scene contains four or more characters, the arrangement of the individual actors becomes more the concern of the director, but here also, the actors should be aware of their stage positions and strive to avoid straight lines, even spacing, or "faulty covering."

ACTING TECHNIQUES

Standard individual techniques

What should appear to be the most natural actions for performers to execute are, too frequently, those in which they look most awkward and amateurish. When required to execute the appropriate techniques of standing, sitting, kneeling, falling, turning, or gesturing, the beginner often fails to recognize how these actions on the stage differ from the same basic actions he has been using all his life. It is in the development of such standard individual techniques that the actor begins to put into practice the concept that action on the stage must be heightened, intensified, and refined.

Standing. Since the manner of standing is often indicative of character, no hard and fast rules can be formulated regarding the actor's stance. However, in the playing of so-called straight parts, the posture is erect but not stiff. The head is up, the shoulders pulled back, and the chest lifted. The weight of the body is kept forward on the balls of the feet, which form a medium sized base. The entire body should be comfortable and relaxed. This position gives the actor an appearance of poise, and permits him to move readily in any direction. Any posture which calls undue attention to itself and is inappropriate to the character should be avoided.

Sitting. As in the case of standing, the manner of sitting should be expressive of the character.

Ladies and gentlemen of breeding usually sit erect and do not slouch. When permitted by the particular characterization, professional actors customarily sit on the front portion of the chair in an erect posture. This position gives the character a more energetic, alert appearance and the ease of rising is facilitated.

The act of sitting down in a chair should be as unobtrusive as possible. Unless it has some significance to plot or character, it should not call attention to itself. A not uncommon fault of the amateur is to start to sit, then stop and look to see if the chair is still there. The trained actor moves to the chair, finds its position with the back of his leg, and sits with the least amount of mechanical difficulty or distraction.

Kneeling. With the emphasis on realism in the contemporary American theater, kneeling has all but disappeared as a common stage practice. Some plays, however, particularly the ones of historical periods, require kneeling for certain characters. In such cases, the actor usually kneels on his downstage knee. This gives his body a position more open to the audience. The act of kneeling and rising should be easy and graceful with as little attention as possible directed to the physical effort involved. The writer remembers witnessing a performance by the late Walter Hampden as King Henry V and the scene in which Henry kneels to pray for the success of his soldiers in battle. The attention of the audience was focused on the king's face and there was little awareness of the process of kneeling or rising.

Falling. Sometimes an actor must fall in an open area where there is no opportunity to grasp objects for support. With some variations, the technique is as follows. The body becomes limp, there is some swaying or staggering, then the fall begins with a succession of momentary stops in order to break the force of the fall. The actor drops to one knee, then to the other, next to the thigh, hip and finally the upper part of the body. The fall may be made forward, backward, to the side, or in a spiral motion. In the case of more spectacular falls, such as from platforms or down steps, it would be advisable for the actor to consult a professional dancer or someone especially skilled in this technique. With practice, an actor should be able to execute a convincing stage fall without injury to himself.

Turning. One of the most frequent movements of the actor is the turn. This action away from or toward another character, which will be discussed later, is a visual means of expressing the logical and emotional content of the dialogue. Turns are usually made toward the audience so that the face of the actor is visible throughout. This rule may be broken when a turn toward the audience would seem mechanical or awkward. For example, if an actor were stage left in a three-quarter position facing up left and wished to face another actor at right center, it would be awkward to make a three-quarter movement toward the audience instead of the shorter turn away from the audience.

Gesturing. Since acting is a representation of life and not a photographic copy, the actor normally gestures more than his counterpart in real life. He must be ambidextrous, since stage business requires him to use either hand with almost equal ease. Customarily, an actor gestures with the upstage hand. For example, if he is stage right and facing stage left he gestures with the left hand. The purpose of this rule is to prevent awkwardness and to keep the actor's face in view of the audience. In like manner, the actor should give and receive props with the hand that is nearer the actor to whom it is to be given or from whom it is received.

Crossing. Contrary to the rule of courtesy in real life, crosses on stage are usually made *in front* of or *downstage* of another character. Since the moving character generally has the focus of attention, this cross keeps the emphatic character in uninter-

rupted view of the audience. There are, of course, exceptions to the rule. A character may cross behind other seated characters since, in this case, the audience's view of the moving character would not be blocked. The rule of crossing in front does not apply to minor characters, servants, or any person not having primary attention in the scene.

Approaching. As a rule, the simplest and most direct approach is used in going to an exit, an object, or another actor. Frequently, this approach is a straight line; however, in making approaches from upstage to down, or downstage to up, the curved approach is often necessary. This is particularly true if the actor wishes to arrive at a point and play a scene in a certain body position. If, for example, an actor in the down left area must approach a window in the left wall and be in an open position while he looks offstage through the window, he must use a curved approach. A direct approach, in this case, would put the actor in an unfavorable body position on arriving at the window.

The curved approach has a number of other uses: (1) it adds a flow of rhythmic movement, softness, and beauty, so essential to fantasy and romantic comedy; (2) it may be used to indicate indecision in the character; or (3) it may be used to heighten the suspense of the scene through delayed indirect action.

Entering and exiting. Most stage doors swing offstage. The exception to this is the outside door in a realistic set which should swing onstage. Doors in the side walls of the set are normally hinged on the upstage side. In making an entrance from stage left, the actor opens the door with his right hand, starts through the doorway while giving the door a closing swing. As he steps into the stage area, he turns and closes the door with his left hand. This method of entering keeps the actor open to the audience and makes the manipulation of the door easy and simple. When the actor is making an exit at stage left, he opens the door with

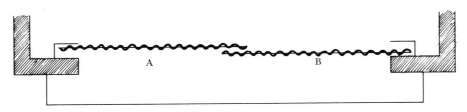

Figure 3.   Floor plan drawing of stage curtain.

his left hand, steps through the doorway, swings the door partly shut with his left hand and completes the closing with his right hand. In entering or exiting on stage right, the process is reversed.

More specific techniques are, in the main, dependent upon the type of character involved. When a butler, for instance, enters at a side door to announce a guest, he steps to the upstage side of the door, announces the name of the arriving character and exits as soon as the character has entered.

When two or more characters are entering, the character who speaks first usually enters first. This allows him to pick up the stage cue, speak to another character on stage, or turn and address the one with the later entrance. Other particular situations may vary this technique.

When two or more characters are making an exit at approximately the same time, the character with the last speech exits last. Usually, the character crosses to the exit on a previous speech so that he may make his final speech at the door and exit quickly.

When an actor or stage manager is required to pass through the stage curtain onto the apron or forestage without exposing the stage setting, the curtains are not parted but the overlap is held in place, as indicated in Figure 3. Section A is held with the right hand and section B with the left hand as the actor passes through between the two sections. In passing back through the curtains, the actor presses against section A. This allows light from the stage area to reveal the opening in the curtains and prevents the embarrassment of

hunting for the opening. The actor then takes the edge of section B with the right hand and holds it in position while he passes through the curtains.

Some common technical problems

Laughing. As a general rule, actors should avoid laughing at amusing lines or situations on the stage, since this tends to suppress the laughter in the audience. However, laughter is occasionally demanded of the character and this sometimes presents a problem. Laughter is one of the most spontaneous indications of a human emotion; but when laughter is required in a scene, the actor often lacks a natural motivation for its expression. As a result, his laughter frequently seems forced and unreal. There are several solutions to this problem. The actor may think of an amusing incident or story which might evoke a more natural and convincing laugh, or he may acquire a technique for producing a laugh. In any case, stage laughter must be simulated and not real.

Genuine laughter is an uncontrolled psychological and physiological reaction. No doubt every one has experienced amusing situations in which the laughter mounted to almost hysterical magnitude. A play cast in rehearsal often becomes convulsed with laughter over a comic incident. When this happens, the rehearsal usually stops until the cast members have completely relieved themselves of their mirth. Since genuine laughter cannot be controlled or terminated at will, it has no place in a stage performance. However, knowing the physical basis of laughter will help the actor to achieve a believable, simulated laugh.

In laughing, air is first expelled from the lungs so that only a little more than the residual air is left. The sound of laughter is actually executed by the rapid expulsions of air between the slightly tensed vocal folds. The physical force for the laughing action is produced by the somewhat convulsive contractions of the intercostal and abdominal muscles. If this action is prolonged, it causes the often referred to "aching sides."

The sound or tone of the laughter may be one of several vowels. For example, the "ha, ha" is usually on the sound of *a* as in "father." Girls usually giggle on one of the *e* vowel sounds. There are various kinds and types of laughter from the belly laugh or guffaw to the almost quiet chuckle.

Crying. The manner of expressing emotions on the stage is being constantly debated. William Archer made an extensive inquiry into this problem and published the results of the study in the January, February, and March, 1888, issues of *Longmans Magazine.* Archer found that many actors admitted that, when the occasion demanded it, they shed tears in performance. Since certain actors are capable of *forcing* tears, the genuineness of such crying is open to doubt. The difference of opinion seems to rest on the degree of emotional feeling and on the manner of its expression.

The following opinion by David Belasco is in accord with those who contend that emotions on the stage are make-believe rather than actual.

"To assert that any actor must or even can really feel, when acting, all that he represents — assuming, of course, that he is representing any vital or even vivid emotional experience — is merely to maintain what is manifestly nonsensical. In acting there never can be, in the very nature of things, any real feeling."*

---

* Toby Cole and Helen Krich Chenoy, *Actors on Acting.* New York: Crown, 1949, p. 503.

Although it is helpful to the actor to feel, to a degree, the emotions associated with crying, he should not give way to *real* crying. He would lose control of his emotional expression if he permitted himself to shed real tears. Also, a demonstration of real emotion rather than simulated is likely to be aesthetically disturbing to the audience. It is doubtful anyone would admit that the uncontrolled, extreme bereavement occurring in real life would be acceptable on the stage. Art is make-believe, pretense, the seeming rather than the actual. When the real replaces the illusion of the real, the product ceases to be art. Thus, the actor should give a convincing *illusion* of crying, often gaining the effect best by restraint rather than by exaggeration. An attempt to contain and subdue the expression of an emotion is often more moving and effective than an unrestrained outpouring of vocal and physical demonstrations.

The effect of crying may be made quite convincing by uneven and convulsive inhalations and exhalations, with or without vocalized sounds. This breath action is accompanied by spasmodic movements of the chest, shoulders, and abdominal muscles. When possible, it is advisable to turn the face away or partly cover it from the audience. The mouth should be left uncovered so that both the sounds of crying and the character's lines will be audible. The actor should not attempt to say lines and cry at the same time. The sobs may be interspersed between words or lines.

Killing. Various methods of taking a life are represented on the stage; the most common are shooting, stabbing, strangling, and poisoning. Some of these methods will be considered here, first in relation to the killer and then to the victim.

Shooting. In the action of shooting, actors should follow these rules:

1. Shoot across stage or upstage. Never point a gun directly at the audience, if it can be avoided.

2. Shoot slightly to one side of the victim. When the gun is aimed across stage, as is usual, the audience cannot detect that it is not pointed directly at the victim. This technique prevents the possibility of injury from the gun wad.

3. Stand several feet from the victim to avoid the danger of powder burns.

4. The victim should be tense and register an emotion appropriate to his awareness of the killer.

5. At the moment of the shot, the victim should stagger slightly and place his hand over the "wound." The victim does not usually fall immediately when shot unless the bullet strikes the spinal cord, or unless he is shot by a large calibre weapon, such as the ·45. An effective device for the victim is to grasp for support objects such as chairs, tables, draperies, etc. The attempt to support the body by reaching for nearby objects adds a realistic and convincing note to the scene and also helps the actor to break the force of the fall.

6. If possible, the victim should fall in an upstage area or behind furniture. A "dead" body on the floor in full view of the audience is a distraction which may destroy the effectiveness of the remainder of the scene.

7. If the victim must fall in view of the audience, his position should be parallel to the footlights or his head should be towards the audience.

Stabbing. When the killing is done with a dagger, either the killer or the victim must cover the actual killing. If the killer is upstage of the victim, the stab may be made in the victim's back in the following manner. The killer's arm moves quickly until almost touching the victim. Then the motion is slowed and the dagger is turned so that the fist strikes the body with lessened force. The weapon should be "withdrawn" after the blow with an indication of difficulty to give the

illusion that it has actually been driven home. The dagger should be dropped quickly to the floor or hidden, if possible, so that the audience does not see the absence of blood. An exception is the stabbing scene in *Julius Caesar* in which the blood becomes a significant bond between the assassins.

When stabbing with a sword or a rapier, the positions of the killer and victim should be upstage and parallel with the footlights. The thrust of the weapon is between the arm and body of the victim on his upstage side. An indication of force is used both in the thrust and in the withdrawal of the weapon. The sword should be disposed of quickly by dropping it to the floor or returning it to the scabbard. The action of the stage duel with either the rapier or the sword must be carefully rehearsed. Nothing can be left to chance or improvisation. Each movement must be planned, rehearsed, and memorized in order to prevent the possibility of injury.

Poisoning. If the "death" of the character results from the taking of poison, the actor should consult a physician to learn the varying effects of the particular kind of poison on a victim. Knowing these facts, the actor will be able to give a more convincing illusion of death by poisoning.

Strangling. This method of killing is usually done in one of the upstage areas in order to soften the emotional impact on the audience. The victim may be forced to his knees, bent backward over a table, sofa, chair, or thrust to a prone position on a bed or the floor. If in a prone position, the victim's knees may be drawn up toward the torso to give a stronger indication of real strangulation. Usually, the head of the victim is toward the audience. There must be the illusion of physical exertion by both victim and killer. Gradually the physical exertion of the victim subsides until he finally falls limp.

Removing the body. The carrying of a supposedly dead body is difficult to do with any degree of ease or grace as there is always the danger of producing a comic effect. The following rules for carrying a body off the stage will tend to eliminate the unwanted laughter.

1. Have a sufficient number of characters carry the body so that there is no apparent physical effort. Four or six usually are adequate.
2. Carry the body to the nearest exit.
3. If possible, have other characters cover part of the action.
4. Carry the body off head first with the head slightly higher than the feet.
5. Carry the body in a horizontal position and, in particular, avoid letting its middle portion drag on the floor.

When carefully done, the carrying of a body after a death scene may produce a very dramatic effect. A notable example was the carrying of Sir Laurence Olivier as Hamlet in the final scene of the well-known motion picture.

The stage fight. As in the case of the duel with sword or rapier, the stage fight must be carefully planned. Each party must know what the other is going to do. Very little physical exertion is actually used for the struggle and blows are carefully faked. The crew fight in the original stage production of *Mr. Roberts* (by Heggen and Logan) was convincing; yet probably no actor received bodily injury, although the action was repeated several times a week. Undoubtedly, no actor ever changed a single movement or reaction.

The love scene. The mood of a love scene may be broken abruptly by inappropriate laughter caused by the actor's lack of poise and skill. If he is mindful of a few basic principles, the actor may eliminate an embarrassing audience reaction. The emotional build of the love scene should progress gradually and smoothly. The distance between the couple should gradually decrease as the scene progresses. A uniform tempo in movement and business should be maintained. If the couple is sitting on a sofa, for example, the action may be

somewhat as follows. The man may move one arm to the back of the sofa, then place his hand on the woman's shoulder or take one of her hands in his. She may lean her head back on his shoulder, while both provide other pieces of business of an endearing sort used in leading up to the final embrace and kiss. If the woman tilts her head upstage and the young man inclines his downstage, the actual kiss may be "covered" from the audience.

If the couple is in a standing position, the following procedure may be used. The young man may first take the girl's hand. As she moves nearer, he may drop her hands and place his hands on her waist. The girl may use such reactions as adjusting the man's tie. As they move into the final embrace, the man's right arm goes around the girl's waist while his left hand rests on her shoulder. In the final embrace, ease and poise will be greatly facilitated if the young couple will assume the foot positions used in ballroom dancing. In this love scene the kiss may be covered, if desired, in a manner similar to that described for the sitting love scene.

It is not our intention to imply that all love scenes should follow the procedure described. To do so would make the scene very mechanical. The bits of business mentioned are merely suggestions; many others of a similar nature may be used. The important points to remember in playing a love scene are (1) the emotional build should be slow and steady; (2) as the scene progresses, more visual indications of endearment should be included; and (3) the tempo and rhythm of the scene should be maintained with no sharp or sudden breaks.

Eating and drinking. These mundane essentials should not be permitted to interrupt the flow of dialogue or dramatic action; consequently, most eating and drinking on the stage is either faked or the quantity consumed greatly minimized. There are several reasons for this: (1) "property" food is usually not very appetizing; (2) it is difficult to talk when the mouth is full of food; and (3) with food or liquid in the mouth, there is always the danger of choking. The following suggestions should help to solve the technical problems of eating and drinking on the stage.

1. When possible use dishes and glasses which are not transparent. This prevents the audience from seeing just how much food or liquid they contain.
2. Use food that is easy to chew and swallow, such as scrambled eggs, cottage cheese, or ground beef.
3. Place only small helpings of food on the plate.
4. Take time in cutting the meat. Toy with the food.
5. Take only small morsels of food into the mouth.
6. Chew in a way that fakes a larger intake of food.
7. Fill glasses only partially.
8. Take little or no liquid from the glass, but give the illusion of drinking.
9. Time your eating and drinking to coincide with the dialogue of another character.

Each of these directions must, of course, be modified in accordance with the nature of the character and situation.

The double take. When properly executed, this is a very effective device in comedy and farce. As the term implies, there are two parts to the action, a wrong response followed by the right one. The double take may comprise several forms of response and reaction, either both verbal, both physical, or combined verbal-physical or physical-verbal. In each instance, the double take is brought about by mental distraction, or muddled or illogical thinking, each reaction coming at a very rapid pace. Consequently, the character is impelled to say or do the wrong thing and must then make the correction. If the tempo of the action were slow, the character would have time to make a rational and proper verbal or physical reaction and thus eliminate the need for a correction.

An example of a verbal double take might be the following dialogue.

SHE: You're so marvelous.

HE: Yes.

SHE: You're so sweet.

HE: Yes.

SHE: You're so kind.

HE: Yes.

SHE: And you're so generous.

HE: Yes.

SHE: But you're a fool.

HE: Yes. . . . No!

A typical physical double take is found in *Arsenic and Old Lace.* Mortimer is hurriedly going about the living room, picking up objects and opening bureau drawers, looking for his manuscript. He opens the lid to the window seat in which there is a dead body. His action is so fast that he has crossed to the middle of the living room before he realizes what he has seen. He makes an abrupt stop, turns, and cautiously comes back to the window seat for another peek. It should be remembered that a rapid tempo is the essential ingredient for a believable double take.

Chapter
four

Stage
Movement

Suit the action to the word, the word to the action; with this special observance, that you o'erstep not the modesty of nature.

Shakespeare

The importance of the physical aspects of acting can scarcely be overemphasized. Since the eye is a more receptive organ than the ear, what the actor does often takes precedence over what he says. The truth of this point is aptly stated in Emerson's well known quotation: "Do not say things. What you are stands over you the while, and thunders so that I cannot hear what you say to the contrary." If there is a contradiction between what the character says and what the character does, the observer will, in most cases, believe the action. The very nature of drama, namely, "a story told in action," puts a heavy responsibility on the physical phase of acting. The actor should bear in mind that his physical actions carry to all parts of the theater when often individual lines are lost. For this reason, he should be doubly sure that his physical actions are controlled, purposeful, and meaningful.

An actor's body, then, is a highly expressive instrument of his art. As mentioned earlier, most of us are endowed with a physique that is free from serious impediments. But an actor's body should be more than this. It must be trained, brought under control, and disciplined before it becomes his medium for artistic expression. It should give him poise, balance, coordination, and a complete responsiveness to internal and external stimuli.

FUNCTIONS OF STAGE MOVEMENT

Although stage movement may generally be considered the prerogative of the director, in reality it is character motivated. For this reason, the actor should understand the purpose and significance of all movement. It is only through understanding that he may bring greater truth and credibility to his physical action.

To heighten plot action

The primary purpose of movement is to aid in telling the dramatic story. Action, as the late

George Pierce Baker stated many years ago, is a basic essential of drama. The movement which is an integral part of the plot is usually indicated by the playwright in the stage directions or the dialogue, but this constitutes only a fraction of the total movement necessary for a complete interpretation of the play. Much additional movement must be *invented* by the actor or the director in order to heighten the dramatic effect or make a particular moment in the scene more meaningful. All plot action must be executed with such skill, clarity, and economy of effort that no undue attention is attracted to the mechanics of the movement.

To establish mood

Stage movement has a significant bearing on the mood of the scene. Basically, movement within a scene is determined by (1) the kind of emotion the character is experiencing, (2) the intensity of the emotion, and (3) the type of character.

Certain emotions require an outlet in extreme physical movement while others are expressed by inaction. During the stock market crash in the autumn of 1929, many financiers were pacing the floors of their offices as the ticker tape recorded the falling stock prices. There were instances of men leaping to their deaths from office windows. In other times of deep depression of spirit, however, men may be completely inactive.

The same emotion may cause varying reactions in different people. In a play, the type of character as well as the emotion determines the amount of stage movement to be used in creating the mood of a particular scene. Roughly, characters may be placed in two groups: the active, and the meditative, or introspective. Othello is representative of the former and Hamlet of the latter group. If these two characters had been reversed, Othello would undoubtedly have killed the king, Claudius, at the first opportunity, and Hamlet would have seen through the villainy of Iago.

A scene must be evaluated for its mood in order to know the amount of movement needed. An increase in the amount and tempo of movement will help to establish a light, gay tone, and a decrease will create a somber, serious effect. The actor must sense the varying gradations of mood within the play and adapt the amount and kind of movement accordingly.

To denote the type of play

Just as he must be sensitive to the effect of movement on the mood of the scene, so also must the actor be aware of the relationship between the type of play and the amount and kind of movement. Each type of play (tragedy, melodrama, comedy, farce) requires a special treatment of movement. In general, movement in tragedy stems from inner motivation. In contrast, movement for comedy or farce is, to a great extent, determined by arbitrary or technical considerations. An exaggerated use of movement, often with only slight motivation, is essential in order to achieve the light, hilarious mood of farce. The diverse types of plays demand these sensitive variations of movement, both in kind and amount, to enhance the spirit of the play.

To establish the style of the play

Movement is a dominant element in establishing the style of the play. Briefly, the determining factors here are the amount, manner of execution, and degree of motivation. For example, the movement for romantic styles is, in varying degrees, graceful and flowing; for classic style it is restrained and statuesque; and for expressionistic style it is often machinelike. The relation of movement to the style of the play is treated more fully in Part Two.

To indicate locale

Movement is an aid in the establishment of the play's locale. Each locality has its own tempo and rhythm, and it is chiefly through movement that this characteristic is established. Compare the tempo and rhythm of a small town railway station with that of Grand Central or the tempo of a small town newspaper establishment with that of a metropolitan daily just before going to press. In order to achieve a truthful representation, the tempo and rhythm of an actor's movement must be in tune with the play's locale.

To suggest the season

The season of the year may be suggested by movement. People move about more languidly on a hot summer day than on a cold day in winter. This difference is very noticeable in the way shoppers hurry along the street in midwinter as compared with their leisurely pace in midsummer. The actor should adjust his movements, both in amount and pace, to the make-believe climatic conditions of the particular scene.

To delineate the character

Undoubtedly, the character may be revealed to the audience through visual communication as much or even more than through auditory communication. For example, the character's age, health, and mental and emotional state may be clearly revealed by such visual characteristics as bent posture, uncertain or palsied hand movements, and slow, shuffling gait. A more thorough discussion of characterization is presented in Chapter 8.

To build a climax

Increasing the tempo and amount of movement is an effective way to build a scene to its climax. The increase in pace and number of characters moving has the psychological effect on the audience of building emotional tension, excitement, or exhilaration. Conversely, by slowing down the tempo and decreasing the amount of movement in a scene, a feeling of quietude and repose is established. Even though setting the pace of the scene is the prerogative of the director,

an actor may be more effective in his performance if he is aware of the relationship of tempo and rhythm to the play's dramatic quality.

To provide emphasis

A moving object attracts more attention than one at rest. In a play, movement may be used to attract attention to the most important character in the scene, or to emphasize significant plot action or an important line. For this reason, most of a character's movement is made while speaking his own lines. To do otherwise would result in misplaced emphasis. There are many instances that might be cited of illegitimate stealing of scenes by a minor character through the inappropriate use of movement to get attention. Such displays of exhibitionism at the expense of the production are, of course, to be deplored.

Movement is sometimes used to attract the attention of the audience to one area of the stage while action, which is not supposed to be seen, is executed in another part. This device may be used for the mysterious appearance or disappearance of a character.

MOVEMENT IN RELATION TO ENTRANCES

During the latter half of the seventeenth, and through the eighteenth, century, the manner of making entrances was, from a dramatic point of view, relatively unimportant. Since most of the action was played on the forestage or apron, entrances and exits were made through the proscenium doors which did not indicate a specific locality. These were nonillusionistic portals, serving, in the main, as a convenient means of getting on and off the stage. However, with the advent of realism and illusionistic staging, entrances assumed greater dramatic significance.

It seems appropriate at this point to make a distinction between the entrance of the actor and the entrance of the character. Not uncommonly in the past, *personal* entrances were made by actors and actresses to receive the applause of the audience. No doubt they considered this personal display a justifiable part of their "stock in trade." At a time when the actor's status was questionable, he understandably felt the need of personal advertising and promotion. As a consequence, the entrances were played up and each actor made the most of his opportunity. The play, in such instances, stopped until the display of adoration for the actor was concluded. This overt demonstration on the actor's first entrance has all but disappeared from the modern stage, although applause for a leading actor or star still persists. Many prominent actors of today ignore or play down the personalized entrance.

Our primary concern here is the entering *character*. There are at least five important requirements which the actor must consider in making his entrance. He must (1) establish the character, (2) establish the character's mood, (3) establish a relationship with the play and the onstage characters, (4) establish relationship with the locale of the scene, and (5) reveal the offstage action and mood, in case this is pertinent.

Establishing the character

The first appearance of a character is particularly significant. It is then that the audience receives the first impressions which may influence its reactions to the character for the remainder of the play. What the audience needs to know about the character must be quickly and easily discernible; anything that might create an unwarranted or mistaken first judgment should be avoided.

Due to the rapid progression of a play, there is little time for audience deliberation over what a character is supposed to be. He must be immediately recognizable as a distinct, dramatic personality. The audience tends to classify stage characters by age, occupation, or social groups; or as senior citizens, farmers, or the affluent, to mention a few categories. It also tends to classify the characters psychologically, for example, moody, gay, domineering, peevish, or garrulous. The list could be extended indefinitely. Suffice it to say, the audience wants to *know* the character. The very nature of the drama, a story told in action of some two hours' duration, demands that for the sake of clarity certain facets of the character must be heightened and others suppressed or eliminated.

Sometimes, the author enlightens the audience as to what to expect in a particular character through pertinent comments expressed by the other characters. This is the case in Molière's *Tartuffe*. Here we have one of the best examples in all dramatic literature of a build-up and preparation for a character's entrance. Tartuffe has been discussed at length by the other characters throughout Acts I and II, but it is not until the second scene of Act III that he makes his first appearance. It is obvious that Tartuffe's manner must corroborate the opinions of the other characters (with the exception of the duped Orgon) and reveal his hypocritical nature.

More commonly, there is no preliminary preparation or warning in the play text as to what the audience may expect of the entering character. Ruth's entrance in the second act of O'Neill's *Beyond the Horizon* is a shock to the audience. Three years of plot time have passed since they saw her as a young, radiant girl in love. The three years as a farm wife have taken their toll. She has lost her fresh, buoyant, girlish spirit; she is weary, disillusioned, and petulant. Work in a hot kitchen, an unsuccessful husband who is always late to lunch, and a sickly baby are contributing factors. All of these must be taken into consideration by the actress as she makes Ruth's second entrance.

The actor should not attempt to reveal everything about the character at the first entrance. All that is essential is the revelation of what the audience needs to know at that moment or what is dramatically significant. The actor, of course, knows at the beginning of the play, as the audience does not, the final outcome of the dramatic action. But what the character becomes in the later scenes should not be revealed until the appropriate time arrives; even though, in some instances, there may be hints of the character's later development. In Ibsen's *A Doll's House*, Nora's first entrance must convey the gay, irresponsible, doll-wife characteristics even though she has already shown her independence and resourcefulness in negotiating a loan to save her husband's life. The serious side of her character must be held in abeyance and revealed gradually as the drama unfolds.

It is axiomatic that the actor should be in character at the moment of his entrance. Actually, he should be in character prior to his entrance. A common practice among experienced actors is to "step into the character's shoes" some moments before the entrance cue and take five or six steps in character before the first entrance.

Establishing the character's mood

Sometimes the character's mood is established or at least suggested by the dialogue. Shakespeare did this for Hamlet in the second scene of the play, as the following lines indicate.

KING: But now, my cousin Hamlet, and my son, —

HAMLET: (*Aside*) A little more than kin, and less than kind.

KING: How is it that the clouds still hang on you?

HAMLET: Not so, my lord; I am too much i' the sun.

QUEEN: Good Hamlet, cast thy nighted colour off,
And let thine eye look like a friend on Denmark.
Do not for ever with thy vailed lids
Seek for thy noble father in the dust:
Thou know'st 'tis common; all that lives must die,
Passing through nature to eternity.

HAMLET: Ay, madam, it is common.

QUEEN: If it be,
Why seems it so particular with thee?

HAMLET: Seems, madam! nay, it is; I know not
'seems.'
'Tis not alone my inky cloak, good mother,
Nor customary suits of solemn black,
Nor windy suspiration of forced breath,
No, nor the fruitful river in the eye,
Nor the dejected haviour of the visage,
Together with all forms, moods, shapes of grief,
That can denote me truly: these indeed seem,
For they are actions that a man might play:
But I have that within which passeth show;
These but the trappings and the suits of woe.

Here we have not only a concise description of Hamlet's mood but also the outward manifestations by which the mood is conveyed to the audience: his dress, physical state, facial expression, watery eyes, and forced breath. Although Shakespeare has helped the actor by clearly delineating Hamlet's mood, the script has not removed the actor's problem of creating this mood *within* the character.

Generally, an actor is not so fortunate as to have an author such as Shakespeare clearly describe the character's mood. He must devise from the context of the play the appropriate mood of the character at the moment of his entrance. This is chiefly the actor's responsibility, although a sensitive director may help in the process of analysis and also in determining when the proper emotional chord has been struck.

Establishing relationship with the play and onstage characters

Each character has an important contribution to make to the scene. If this were not so, it would be a case of faulty playwriting and the character might well be eliminated. The character's function should, of course, be known by the actor and very shortly surmised by the audience. We know almost immediately what to expect with the entrance of Doolittle in the second act of *Pygmalion*. Shaw helpfully indicates the character's manner with the statement: "His present pose is that of wounded honor and stern resolution." Five speeches later he states (*menacingly*): "I want my daughter; that's what I want. See?" This explains the motive for his entrance and the following scene brings out the deal he plans to make with Higgins regarding Eliza.

The entering character should indicate his relationship to the other characters in the scene. For example, we should know immediately whether he is known or unknown to the other characters, whether his relationship is friendly or unfriendly. If the latter is the case, he may pause after his entrance and remain somewhat aloof until this relationship has altered.

Establishing relationship with the locale of the scene

In addition to knowing his motive for entering the scene, the character should indicate whether he is entering a familiar or unfamiliar place. If he is a frequent visitor and on good relations with the host, then his manner may be quite casual. He will know where things are located, will relate himself to the furnishings and, in a sense, make himself at home. If, on the other hand, the character is entering the scene for the first time, he may pause after entering and get his bearings, so to speak, and size up the situation. This difference in manner is well illustrated by two characters in *Dial "M" for Murder* (by F. Knott). Max, a friend of Margot, is at home, as shown by the way he helps himself to cigarettes and drinks. The unfamiliarity of the scene to Hubbard, a police officer, is indicated in the stage directions: "Hubbard looks around for a place to hang his hat. He sees coat rack by the door and hangs it up. He then strolls into the room and looks the place over, getting his bearings."

Revealing the offstage mood and action

In some instances, there is no particular offstage situation or action in which the character is involved. He may make what is termed a cold entrance, as Clarence Day does when he comes home from his office in *Life with Father*. His mood immediately changes on finding the Rector having tea with Mrs. Day. He exclaims, "Oh, damn!"

In contrast, Willy Loman enters in Miller's *Death of a Salesman* in a continuation of his offstage mood — his unsuccessful sales trip. Technically, the offstage mood and action may be revealed in a number of ways. (1) The character may enter with a slow pace and a drooping posture, indicating low spirits and failure as in the case of Willy Loman. (2) He may enter hurriedly and look for a place to hide if he is a fugitive. (3) He may enter, pause, and turn to the door as he contemplates the action which is taking place offstage. (4) He may enter stealthily as if planning a robbery. These are only a few illustrations of types of entrances indicating a continuation of offstage moods or actions and what they signify. In each case, the actor should have the mood within himself and understand clearly the character's objectives. He should not rely merely on external manifestations.

INDIVIDUAL MOVEMENT

Motivation

Physical action stems from inner motivation. Instead of resorting to external clichés, the actor should create the inner reality of a desired emotion or physical state. This is a normal and natural process. For example, when one feels depressed or elated, the body expresses these emotional conditions automatically without resorting to forced or conscious manipulation. In like manner, before the body makes a visible manifestation or reaction to an external stimulus, there must be an inner reaction. Sounds which incite fear or alarm must stimulate the corresponding inner emotions before the actor gives outward manifestations of his feeling. It is not uncommon for a beginning actor to anticipate the cue and give a false physical

Plate 19. *Richard III* by William Shakespeare. "Bad" posture, appropriate to the character. University of Minnesota. Director: Frank M. Whiting. Photograph: A.V.E.S. Photographic Laboratories.

reaction before receiving the proper stimulus to his emotion.

Technique

The emphasis on inner motivation for physical action does not eliminate the importance of acting technique. Every person has experienced a variety of emotions, but by no stretch of the imagination could one expect the average, untrained person to be able to express these emotions adequately on the stage. It is not even unusual for a somewhat experienced actor to feel an emotion and be unable to communicate it to a theater audience. This inability may be due to a number of causes: inhibition, muscular tension, or a lack of bodily coordination. The emotions, real or true as they may be, are locked within the actor.

It should be remembered that acting requires both a subtlety and a magnification of emotional expression which are not generally expressed in real life. The actor's imagination and technique must come to his aid. Consider the remorse of Othello after he learns, too late, the truth of Desdemona's fidelity. Or again, how does one give validity to Lady Macbeth's sleep-walking scene? Few individuals in real life have ever felt the intensity of such emotions. Certainly one cannot rely entirely on past experiences or emotional memories. One must *create* the appropriate inner feelings which, aided by the use of techniques, will convey convincing, outward manifestations of the various emotions. Technique must fill in the gaps where sufficient experiences and stimuli are lacking.

Physical poise

Good posture is simply that bodily carriage which is appropriate to the character. To some degree at least, this will vary with each portrayal. Obviously, an actor playing Richard III (see Plate 19) would not exemplify good posture in the usual sense of the term. In this case, a *bad* posture would be the good posture appropriate for the character.

Posture conveys the physical condition and emotional state of the character. With the approach of old age, bodily fatigue, or weakness, there is a tendency for the body to slump. In a similar manner, posture may reveal the occupation of the character. Years of working in the mines in a cramped position will undoubtedly leave their mark. Or a military man, disciplined to stand erect, will often carry this posture to advanced old age.

An actor cannot expect to find a posture appropriate to the character merely by being told to slump or stand erect. A method frequently used to find the most appropriate bodily carriage is determining "the center of gravity." Youthfulness of body and spirit usually suggests a high center of gravity. If the actor thinks "high," the action of the various parts of the body will help to convey youth and freedom from care. Age and emotional concern may produce a center of gravity much lower in the body. The back, arms, legs, and even the stomach of the character naturally slump if the actor has mentally lowered the center of gravity. The same principle also suggests the possibility of more subtle changes in the weight of the body as the moods and emotions of the character change within the framework of the play.

Posture reflects the inner man. Instinctively, various members of the animal kingdom express their attitudes by physical manifestations. A cat arches its back and makes itself appear as large as possible when it wishes to frighten an attacking dog; a beaten dog slinks off in retreat. The higher animal, man, also reacts instinctively. In a mood of defiance he draws himself up to his full height; when he is cowed, defeated, or beaten, his shoulders slump and his head droops. There are many other kinds of instinctive reactions, for example, recoiling from danger, dodging a blow, and exploding in vocal outbursts.

Gestures

Not infrequently a director is asked by an in-experienced actor, "What shall I do with my hands?" The simple answer seems to be, "Use them to express your thoughts and feelings and forget about them." But the basic problem for the troubled actor is far more complicated. The actor's self-consciousness in regard to his hands may arise from several causes. He may be inhibited, fearing to free himself and respond to his inner impulses. Or he may have his mind on himself and not be sufficiently immersed in his character. If he is truly absorbed in his role, his gestures will tend to be spontaneous and natural. Calvert's advice concerning this problem of the actor is applicable: "A good general rule to follow is: when in doubt, do nothing; never make a gesture until there is absolutely no doubt of its propriety in your mind, wait until you are compelled to make it."* Gestures should be motivated, or preceded by an inner impulse of thought and feeling.

Principles governing gestures. There are a number of guiding principles which, if properly applied, will help the actor in his use of gestures.

1. Gestures should be *appropriate to the character*. If the character is inhibited, indecisive, or nervous, the gestures will be small and lacking in definiteness and precision. If the character is an aggressive, self-assured extrovert, his gestures will be large and pointed. By a careful analysis of the character, the actor may determine the amount and type of gestures he should use.

2. Gestures should be *appropriate to the style of the play*. The amount and kind of gestures will vary from play to play in accordance with the style of writing. In naturalistic and realistic plays, gestures are small, detailed, and numerous. In classic and romantic plays, gestures are highly selective, significant, and large.

---

* Louis Calvert, *Problems of the Actor*. New York: Henry Holt, 1918, pp. 87–88.

3. Gestures should be *adapted to the size of the theater and performance*.   In an intimate style of production, gestures may be quite small — a slight movement of the hand or even the fingers — but in a large theater or in an epic production, gestures must be correspondingly large in order to carry over the greater distances. Undoubtedly, the gestures of the ancient Greek actors who played to several thousand spectators were very large and simplified.

4. Gestures should be *adapted to the costume*. Period costumes impose certain restrictions on gesturing and in certain instances dictate the manner and style.   In the Restoration and Molière periods, because of the lace on the sleeve cuffs, the hands are generally kept in a plane above the waist with the lace tossed back on the sleeve.   Otherwise, the lace draping over the hands produces an awkward, inelegant effect.   Hand gestures for the Restoration and Molière periods, therefore, should be in the upper plane of the body, and generally should be performed in a circular motion.   When costumed in period capes, the actor will of necessity need to rest his fist on his hip to better display the cape's lining and enhance the silhouette of the costume. No matter what the costume may be, the actor will find it wise to study the manners and costumes of the period and adapt his gestures accordingly. Valuable sources for information on period manners may be found in art galleries, illustrated histories, illuminated manuscripts, biographies, and period literature.

5. Gestures should be *adapted to the dialogue*. In adapting his gestures to the dialogue, the actor should consider such matters as accent, timing, and duration.   Generally, gestures, like stage movement, begin and end with the line.   Sometimes, however, the emphatic word in the line needs pointing or accenting by a gesture.   In other cases, a continuation or carry through is required for the duration of the line.   Long, flowing, embellished lines of dialogue, characteristic of the romantic style of writing, require large, flowing gestures.   On the other hand, short, broken, or staccato lines of dialogue require quick, pulsating gestures.

Lines which contain images or pictorial qualities should be accompanied by descriptive gestures.   Let us consider the ones which might accompany certain lines in the Prologue of Shakespeare's *Henry V*.

O for a Muse of fire, that would ascend
The brightest heaven of invention,
(*Both hands and arms might be extended forward and upward, terminating on "invention."*)

A kingdom for a stage, . . .
(*Both arms might be extended at the side to suggest vastness.*)

But pardon, gentles all, . . .
(*This line suggests the gesture of pleading; hands with palms up and arms extended.*)

Suppose within the girdle of these walls
(*An extended, encompassing gesture*)

Are now confined two mighty monarchies
Whose high upreared and abutting fronts
(*Hands moving upwards*)

The perilous narrow ocean parts asunder:
(*Hands are brought downward close together until the words "parts asunder" when the hands move apart, palms outward.*)

These examples will suffice to indicate the use of descriptive gestures.   A thorough study of the above Prologue will reveal many opportunities for gestures which will add fuller meaning and beauty to the interpretation.

Faults to be avoided in gesturing

1. Do not make a gesture which lacks an inner motivation and stimulus.   Such gestures usually appear forced, mechanical, and unnatural.

2. Avoid repetition. The repeated gesture is quickly observed by the audience. Strive for variety in the size, shape, and duration of the gesture.

3. Avoid small, repetitious gestures in the plane of a man's pockets. They are too far away from the center of interest and feeling, which is the face and heart region.

4. Eliminate nervous hand movements and shuffling of the feet. Such movements, when out of character, do not contribute to the interpretation of the lines and they distract and annoy the audience.

5. Avoid gestures across the body; this has an awkward appearance. In taking a prop from another actor, use the nearest hand. If an actor is standing at stage left and gestures for another character to leave the room through a door at the left, he should use the left hand.

6. Do not cover the face in gesturing. Use the upstage hand, right or left as the case may be.

Pantomime and stage "business"

Although pantomime has been termed a universal language, this art has few masters today. Yet when the actor is a master of this art, it is a fascinating and graphic medium for interpreting the character and telling the story. Anyone familiar with the silent movies starring Charlie Chaplin, a master of pantomime, will recall that the pantomimic action was so detailed and revealing that very few subtitles were needed.

An even more vivid and compelling example of the appeal and universal understanding of pantomime has been demonstrated by Marcel Marceau. Conveying both thoughts and emotions without the use of a single word, this artist of pantomime is able to hold the rapt attention of theater audiences for hours at a time. When pantomime is used to its fullest extent, it is possible for an audience to follow the story of a foreign play without understanding its language. In any type of play, pantomime may complement the dialogue, adding depth and clarity to the story.

There are a number of requirements and functions of good pantomime or of stage business. First, it should be appropriate to the play. Each play calls for a varied amount and kind of business. In a domestic comedy a great amount of business is justified and required. In high tragedy only highly significant business is included. Typical of the elimination of the mundane in high tragedy is the banquet scene in *Macbeth* in which there is very little or no actual eating or drinking. Conversely, a great amount of food is served and some eaten in the dinner scene of O'Neill's *Ah, Wilderness!* This explains why few properties are needed for tragedies, whereas those required for comedies and farces are usually extensive.

Second, pantomimic business should be appropriate to the character. It is often through pantomimic business that subtle and amusing facets of the character's nature may be revealed. The way Jeeter Lester in Kirkland and Caldwell's *Tobacco Road* prepares his toilet is quite different from that of a man of fashion. Frequently, an ingenious actor has the inclination to include a bit of business for the sake of a laugh. The real test of its inclusion or rejection is whether or not it is appropriate to the play and to the character.

Third, pantomimic business is an aid to the establishment of the climatic conditions. Whether it is cold or hot may be graphically revealed by pantomime. In the opening scene of *Street Scene* by Elmer Rice, the hot, sticky evening in New York is revealed by the attempts of the characters to loosen their clothing from their perspiring bodies.

Fourth, the mood of a scene may be established by pantomimic business. The greater the amount of business, the lighter the mood of the scene becomes. As the mood of the scene deepens or becomes more tragic, there is less business. At times of deep sadness or bereavement it is not uncommon for people to refrain, for a time, from even so essential a function as eating. On the stage, such mundane action would seem incongruous and unbefitting for the mood of bereavement. The incongruity of mundane business in a serious situation is expressed by John Worthing in the closing scene of Act II of *The Importance of Being Earnest* by Oscar Wilde. "How you can sit there, calmly eating muffins when we are in this horrible trouble, I can't make out."

Fifth, pantomimic business may indicate the degree of emotional involvement of the character in the scene. The truth of the situation in the scene from *The Importance of Being Earnest* is that, in reality, Algy is not emotionally wrought-up. He is enjoying Jack's predicament enormously. If Algy were emotionally agitated, he would probably forego the muffins.

Another example of the relationship between mood, pantomimic business, and the involvement of the character is found in the excerpt from Act IV of *Pygmalion* in the exercises at the close of this chapter. Having just returned from the garden party, Eliza is troubled and distressed over what is to become of her now that the experiment is over. She sits on the piano bench, brooding and silent. Higgins, who is not emotionally disturbed, nonchalantly walks about the room as he eats an apple. Later in the scene when Higgins also becomes disturbed, he hurls the remainder of his apple away. His mundane actions are ended. Thus we see that pantomimic business not only contributes to the mood of the whole scene but also indicates the degree and kind of the character's emotional involvement.

Facial expression

With the present day emphasis on close-ups in motion pictures and television, the actor's face has become increasingly important as an expressive medium. This is not to say that the actor's face has not been the focal point of his characterization throughout the entire history of acting. As was mentioned in the Introduction, during the latter part of the nineteenth century facial expressions, representing the various emotions, were specifically described and catalogued. There were definite arrangements of the mobile parts of the face to convey emotions such as joy, hate, anger, and bereavement. Undoubtedly, this method of emotional expression has been used by many actors, but such mechanical devices may easily lead to false acting and hollow characterization. Although no definite rules or guiding principles may be laid down regarding the use of the face to express motion, it seems a wise and safe procedure to let the face respond to and reflect the character's inner thoughts and emotions.

As the face is the principal area of the body for emotional expression, so the eyes are the chief focal point of that expression. The eyes are appropriately called the "windows of the soul." Properly used, the eyes may reveal more than words. (Note Shylock's eyes in Plate 20.) The effective power of the eyes for the expression of inner feeling is aptly expressed by a poet during Garrick's time in the following couplet:

"A single look more marks the internal woe
Than all the windings of the lengthened *oh*."*

It is impossible to lay down specific rules for the actor to follow in the expressive use of the eyes. The safest guide would seem to be to follow the natural impulse, heightening it by such technical devices as the particular situation might demand. Because of a curious human urge to look where someone else is looking, the eyes are a dominant factor in controlling the attention of the audience. By looking at the specific place himself, the actor is able to direct the attention of the audience to another character, to an important object, or to anticipate an entrance.

---

* Julia Marlowe, "The Eloquence of Silence," *The Green Book Magazine* 9 (March 1913): 393.

Plate 20. *The Merchant of Venice* by William Shakespeare. Expressive use of the eyes. University of Miami. Director: Jack Clay. Photograph: University of Miami Photo Center.

The time the actor's eyes focus on any one object is relatively short, as is also true of people in real life situations. If one observes two business-men in conversation in a hotel lobby, one will be aware that their eyes are constantly seeking new points of interest. Even the most devoted lovers do not look steadily into each other's eyes for more than a few moments at a time. So, too, the focal point of the actor's eyes, like the movie camera, is almost constantly shifting. This does not imply that the actor's eyes are continually rolling; the point to remember is that there is a continuous process of making and breaking the eye contact.

Reaction

Sir Isaac Newton's third law of motion states, "To every action there is always opposed an equal reaction..." To a comparable manner and degree, this is true of stage action. The action of any one character logically calls for a reaction by another character or group of characters. Since the actor is concentrating on his dialogue, it is not surprising that he sometimes overlooks this other important aspect of acting: reaction. When the director calls this omission to the actor's attention, an overreaction often follows.

A helpful approach to the problem of reaction is to determine if the reaction should be *primary*, that is, draw the interest of the audience, or only *secondary*, which may or may not engage its attention. An example of the latter is the background reaction, usually of a minor character, which gives reality to the scene. The actor should assess the situation and the importance of his character's contribution to the dramatic action. If the actor is unable to make the proper evaluation, the director should determine the degree and kind of reaction required for the best artistic effect. Although some reaction is prescribed in the play script, the major portion must be supplied by the intuition and imagination of either the actor or his director. In brief, reaction may serve a number of functions: (1) point up or clarify a line of dialogue, (2) heighten the comic or tragic effect, (3) provide truth and depth to the character, and (4) add verisimilitude to the stage picture.

TYPES OF STAGE MOVEMENT

Stage movement may be classified according to its inherent characteristics. It is imperative that the actor acquire a sensitivity for these varying qualities.

Definite

Definite movement is usually, though not always, indicated in the script. It is generally part of the plot action. It is precise, ordered, and thought controlled. The following example is an illustration of this type of movement. In a scene from the play *Interference*, a doctor attempts to eliminate the evidence of a crime in which he fears his wife may be involved. His movements, typical of his profession, are executed with careful precision and design as he puts on his gloves to avoid leaving telltale finger prints, disposes of the poisoned liquor, and removes the label from the bottle.

Indefinite

This type of movement may be suggested by the playwright, but it is more often supplied by the actor as an expression of the character's emotional and mental state. As the term indicates, this type of movement lacks precision. It is dominated by the emotions of the character rather than by his mind. Some years ago Chrystal Herne made effective use of indefinite movement in her portrayal of Mrs. Craig in the closing moments of *Craig's Wife* by George Kelly. Mrs. Craig objects to flowers in her house because they drop petals on her immaculate floor. Toward the end of the play, when she has lost her husband and practically everything dear to her, except her house, she walks aimlessly about her living room in a state of utter despair, thoughtlessly strewing petals from a bouquet of roses given to her by a neighbor.

Positive

Positive movement is emphatic, aggressive, and strong. It expresses a defiance of or resistance to opposing forces. This quality may even be expressed by standing still and refusing to move when commanded to do so. In execution, positive movement may be any one of the following: (1) moving from a weak to a stronger stage area, such as from up left to down center; (2) moving from the side of the stage toward center; (3) moving from a lower to a higher position, such as rising from a chair or straightening up; (4) moving toward another character; or (5) turning the body or the head toward another character with whom the actor is playing the scene.

Negative

Negative movement, the opposite of positive movement, implies submission, weakness, or giving in to the opposing forces. In execution, negative movement is the action opposite to each of the positive movements mentioned above. The timing of the movements and the relative degree of positive or negative movement may be suggested by either the director or the actor. Generally, movements from area to area are planned by the director, and smaller movements, such as gestures, turning the head or body, and movements within the area, are left to the inspiration of the actor. In any case, the actor should sense the motivation and stimulus for the movement, whether it is large or small, and execute its relative degree of strength or weakness.

Movement in relation to dialogue

Movement is a dominant factor in line interpretation. It may strengthen or weaken the dramatic quality or it may nullify the line's literal meaning. Only by a thorough understanding of the play and the character, combined with a keen sensitivity to line values, will the actor be able to execute the appropriate movements necessary to convey the author's intention.

TYPES OF LINES

As in the case of movement, lines of dialogue may be classified according to their inherent qualities. Each type requires a specific kind of movement for its proper interpretation.

Positive and negative lines

A positive type of line expresses such attitudes as determination, defiance, aggression, and nonconformity. For example:

"I'll tear her all to pieces."

Shakespeare, *Othello*

"I will not yield."

Shakespeare, *Macbeth*

Lines of a negative type express attitudes such as submission, self-depreciation, and lack of strength. The following examples are typical.

"O, what a rogue and peasant slave am I!"

Shakespeare, *Hamlet*

"I can't go through with it. I just can't."

Author

"There I go dreaming again — my old fool dreams."

Eugene O'Neill, *Beyond the Horizon*

The quality of the movement should correspond to the quality of the lines. The actor must assess the relative positive and negative qualities of each line and adapt his movement in order to convey the appropriate interpretation.

Generally, positive movements are combined with positive lines and negative movements with negative lines. There are, however, certain exceptions. The determining factor in each case, which the actor or the director must evaluate, is whether the character is inherently weak or strong. For example, a strong character may stand still or move toward another character while saying, "Get out of here or I'll throw you out." If a weak character utters a positive line, his inherent weakness may be conveyed by making a weak movement. For example, character *A* turns away from *B* while saying, "You can't do this to me." By this action, *A* reveals that he is unable to prevent what *B* intends to do. In a similar manner, a positive movement or attitude connotes truth or honesty while a negative movement implies falsehood. *B* accuses *A* of taking some money. *A* takes a positive attitude, faces *B* and says, "I don't know what you're talking about." Since we associate straightforwardness with honesty, we are inclined to believe that *A* is telling the truth. Suppose, instead, that *A* takes a negative position, shifts his gaze or turns away as he says, "I don't know what you're talking about." The action in this case suggests dishonesty or guilt.

When a negative or weak movement is combined with a very positive line, the effect is often one of incongruity. This device is sometimes used to obtain a laugh. The following is a typical illustration: character *A* backs away from *B* while saying to his companions, who are not restraining him, "Let me at him. I'll knock his block off."

Mixed lines

Some lines have a negative beginning and a positive ending or a positive beginning and a negative ending. Sometimes the shift of strength or attitude comes within the character's speech. These lines typify a change in attitude from negative to positive.

"All right, let's get it over with. No, wait a minute. I'm not going to do it."

The following speech is an example of a positive beginning and a negative ending.

"You're damn right I'm . . . . No, I won't fight. Thirty years ago I'd fight — five years ago. Not now . . . where's your papers?"

Talbot Jennings, *No More Frontier*

In lines of this type there is a change of intellectual or emotional attitude which must be accompanied with a corresponding change of movement.

Neutral lines

Some lines of a play are not inherently positive or negative. We call them neutral. They are often expository or fill-in lines which give a true to life quality to the scene, such as small talk or the greeting of guests. Appropriate action which is neither dramatically positive or negative should accompany such lines.

Satiric lines

In satiric writing the author is ridiculing social customs, ideas, or persons. Since the intended meaning may be just the opposite of the actual wording, the dialogue is not to be taken literally. Consequently, in playing a satire the actor must be exceptionally alert and read "between the lines" if he is to catch the author's intended meaning. The satiric expression, "Oh, she's a peach," might really mean: she's a lemon. Since lines of satire or sarcasm are generally positive in statement but negative in meaning, the essence of a line may be conveyed if the character executes a negative movement. For example, one might turn away while saying, "Oh, I'm sure you know more about it than anyone else."

Theme lines

Certain lines in a play have a decided bearing on the theme or plot. They may state the theme explicitly or express it by implication. The actor must be aware of the theme lines in the script and treat them in such a way that they will be implanted in the mind of the audience. There are several techniques which may be used to give emphasis to theme lines. The actor may (1) use a slower tempo, (2) increase the word emphasis, (3) use a higher pitch level, (4) deliver the line without accompanying movement, or (5) execute movement or business just preceding the line.

Since movement has such an important relationship to the effective interpretation of the dialogue, it behooves the actor to be thoroughly familiar with the principles involved. The following general rules will constitute a guide which may be modified to suit the particular situation.

1. Do not move on the lines of another character, particularly if they are important. The principle here concerns the desired place of emphasis. To move while another character is speaking may distract the attention of the audience from where it rightfully should be, on the character who is delivering the lines. However, if the movement is a dramatic reaction to what another character is saying, then it would be justified.

2. Do not move on important lines. By eliminating the movement, the attention of the audience is focused more strongly on the importance of the line and its significance is heightened. These examples of dialogue are typical of lines which should be spoken without movement.

"The play's the thing wherein I'll catch the conscience of the king."

Shakespeare, *Hamlet*

"Excellent wretch! Perdition catch my soul, But I do love thee! and when I love thee not, Chaos is come again."

Shakespeare, *Othello*

"What was Papa doing on the staircase?"

Lillian Hellman, *The Little Foxes*

Movement on the above lines would not only detract from their importance but would also imply the character's indifference or casualness to the thought expressed.

3. In general, do not move on a question, particularly if the question is significant. This line by Iago will receive more stress if delivered without movement.

"Did Michael Cassio, when you woo'd my lady, know of your love?"

Shakespeare, *Othello*

By the same token, movement while asking a question may indicate a lack of sincerity or real concern about the answer. For example, a hostess asks her guest, "How is your mother these days?" If she turns or moves away while asking the question, it indicates she is not really interested in the mother's state of health but is only making conversation.

4. Do not stop the dialogue of a play for unimportant business or movement, such as lighting a pipe, passing tea, or the like. Only dramatic business or plot action is capable of holding the interest of an audience without accompanying dialogue.

5. Move on a line of dialogue which requires movement, positive or negative, for its proper interpretation.

6. Move on lines which are relatively unimportant or insignificant.

7. Move on a line in which the action or business is mentioned in the line. Example: "I'm going to put the car into the garage; it looks as if it might rain."

8. Move before a line if the line is important and needs emphasis. In Victor Hugo's *Mary Tudor*, a courtier decides to arouse the people in order to force the Queen to do his bidding. To bring emphasis to the line and implant the idea in the mind of the audience, the courtier might move toward the exit, stop, and say: "Suppose we try the people."

9. Move after a line if the action or business should be emphasized. When business or action seems to coincide with the lines in the script, the actor is sometimes in doubt whether action or line should be given first. An evaluation of the relative importance of line versus action will usually resolve the doubt. In a love scene, the embrace and kiss usually follow the lines of endearment.

Timing of movement and dialogue

The timing of movement is often a troublesome problem for the actor since the relationship of action and dialogue may indicate the kind of motivation in the character. For instance, if a girl slaps a young man in the face, and then says, "I'm sorry," it indicates an impulsive, involuntary action. However, if she says, "You cad!" and then strikes him, the action is both intellectually and emotionally motivated, and also indicates an action of a more positive nature. The actor should be alert to the fact that sometimes the motivation for and execution of movement precede the actual delivery of the line, while in other instances, the reverse may be true and the action which is expressive of the line is delayed.

The timing of action in relation to the dialogue is often an indication of a character's individual traits. The impulsive person may act without thinking, while the meditative character may consider before taking action.

Usually, when a line of dialogue requires movement, the movement and the delivery of the line should coincide. The action should not only start with the beginning of the line but it should also stop at its completion. It is a common fault of untrained actors to delay the movement on an action line until the speech is half delivered. The movement should start on the first word of, "Come on, let's get started," for example. In like manner, movement should terminate with the line unless there is some logical or emotional reason for it to continue. When movement "spills over" beyond the line, it holds prolonged attention on the moving actor, thus preventing an immediate shift of audience attention to the next speaker.

The tempo and rhythm of the movement should conform to the tempo and rhythm of the line. When the movement is slowed down, it gives a serious or ponderous effect to what otherwise might be a light or casual line. It is a common tendency for actors to move too slowly for rapidly paced dialogue.

A change in the mental or emotional state of the character is usually accompanied by either a pause in the movement or by a change in its tempo or direction. A careful study of the script should indicate to the actor where the character's thoughts and emotions have changed or where logical progression has been abruptly halted for some reason. Note the sudden changes of thought and emotion in Juliet's lines in Shakespeare's *Romeo and Juliet*, Act II, Scene 5.

"The clock struck nine when I did send the nurse;
In half an hour she promised to return/
Perchance she cannot meet him: / that's not so."

The marks (/) indicate a shift in Juliet's thought and emotion. If she is pacing, as she undoubtedly will be after waiting three hours for news of Romeo, the variations of thought and feeling will necessitate a pause in the flow of movement and possibly a change in its direction. Fluctuations in the thoughts and emotions of the character, accompanied by appropriate and properly executed movement, will give additional meaning to the scene. Omitted or poorly executed, they will undoubtedly detract from the scene's effectiveness and contribute to a misinterpretation of the character.

MOVEMENT IN RELATION TO OTHER CHARACTERS

In any given situation there are three actions which a character may execute in relation to another character. (1) He may stand still. This is a negation of movement, which may indicate indifference, defiance, or extreme fear. (2) He may move nearer to the other character in the scene. This movement may be motivated by love or sympathy as in the line, "Don't cry, dear. I forgive you. Really, I do." Movement toward another character may also be a threatening action motivated by anger. For example: "You clear out of here now or I'll throw you out." (3) A character may move farther away from the other character in the scene. This action may be motivated by such feelings as dislike, irritation, hurt, anger, fear, indifference, or the desire to meditate. The following lines are typical of those which require movement away from another character.

"I know. You don't care for me any more."
"Don't sneer at me. It's cruel of you to sneer at me."
"Stop! Don't come near me."
"Perhaps I shall learn to love you, after a while. I don't know."

Each situation or line in the scene should be evaluated by the actor to determine the appropriate action for the best or most justifiable interpretation, namely, whether he should (1) remain static, (2) move nearer to the other character, or (3) move farther away.

PATTERNS OF STAGE MOVEMENT

Scenes of a play may often be characterized by a particular pattern of movement or fundamental design. The actor should be aware of how the design of the movement contributes to the interpretation of the scene, since this will determine the amount and kind of movement he will make.

The moving and the nonmoving characters

Frequently, due to the emotional and intellectual states of the characters, one may do most of the moving while the other character may remain relatively static. In the scene from *Pygmalion* presented in the exercises at the end of this section, Eliza, because of her depressed, troubled spirit, remains generally static, while Higgins, who in the earlier part of the scene is undisturbed, moves about in a casual, nonchalant manner.

Another variation of this situation occurs in a scene between Othello and Iago, Act III, Scene 3. Othello is so emotionally overwrought, thinking that Desdemona may be unfaithful, that he paces throughout the scene, while Iago, scheming and diabolical, quietly watches the havoc which he is wreaking on his victim. Iago's quiet and static manner shows his intellectual strength, assurance, and devilish plotting to overthrow the trusting Othello. Whether a character moves about or remains relatively static depends on his intellectual attitude toward the other character, the degree of emotional involvement or detachment, the kind of emotion, and its intensity. (A portion of Act III, Scene 3 from Shakespeare's *Othello* is included under Elizabethan tragedy in Part Two.) Scenes of this type, in which one character is extremely disturbed and moves almost continuously, are called pacing scenes. Such a scene becomes a technical problem in movement for both the actor and the director. The pattern of movement must be worked out so as to avoid repetition, time the pace and direction of the movement in conformity with the lines, and time the position and movement of the pacer so as not to distract from the important lines of the non-moving character. In *Fundamentals of Play Directing*, Dean suggests that the pacer follow the lines of a triangle, using various sizes and shapes, as a means of solving the technical problems of a pacing scene.* This device permits movements of diversified duration and direction to conform to the gradations in positive and negative line values.

The pursuer and the pursued

The pattern of this type of scene is obvious, but the characters and the manner in which they achieve their objectives may be as varied as the imagination of the playwright may devise. The entire plot of Shaw's *Man and Superman* is basically a pursuit. Shaw has reversed the conventional concept of the courtship, that man pursues the woman. Instead, and this is typical of Shaw's paradox, the aggressive Ann Whitefield pursues the unwilling Jack Tanner. This concept should

be kept in mind while playing the love scenes in *Man and Superman*.

The more conventional courtship scene, with the man as the pursuer, is found in Samuel Taylor's *The Happy Time*. Desmonde, a modern Don Juan, "presses his suit" for Mignonette, the maid, from the first moment that he sees her, while she retreats and tries to avoid him. If scenes of this type are to become completely meaningful and theatrically interesting, an intricate and varied movement pattern must be devised to conform to the mental and emotional attitudes of the two characters. One of the many variations of this movement pattern is the hunter and the hunted, which is well exemplified in Galsworthy's *The Fugitive*. Here the plot consists of a succession of narrow escapes as the fugitive seeks to escape the law. In scenes of this type, the hunted is rarely permitted a moment of repose or security. This quality must be expressed visually in movement.

Another variation of the pursuer and the pursued movement pattern is found in Act V of *Pygmalion*† between Higgins and Eliza. Here Eliza tries to avoid Higgins and throughout the first part of the scene is on the defensive. She is driven by successive movements from the door at stage left, where Higgins blocks her escape, across the stage to far right. Higgins, although the aggressive character in the scene, follows an advance and retreat pattern. He is drawn to Eliza, but being a confirmed bachelor he does not allow himself to succumb. This scene also contains a reversal in the movement pattern. Eliza, who has been retreating, unable to cope with Higgins' superiority, suddenly finds a weakness in his armor. From this moment, the character relationship is reversed and Eliza becomes dominant as the following lines clearly indicate.

---

* Alexander Dean, *Fundamentals of Play Directing*. New York: Farrar & Rinehart, 1941, pp. 241–42.

† From *Pygmalion* by G. B. Shaw. Copyright, 1930, by G. Bernard Shaw. Reprinted by permission of The Public Trustee and The Society of Authors.

LIZA: (*Rising determinedly*) I'll let you see whether I'm dependent on you. If you can preach, I can teach. I'll go and be a teacher.

HIGGINS: What'll you teach, in heaven's name?

LIZA: What you taught me. I'll teach phonetics.

HIGGINS: Ha! Ha! Ha!

LIZA: I'll offer myself as an assistant to Professor Nepean.

HIGGINS: (*Rising in fury*) What! That impostor! that humbug! that toadying ignoramus! Teach him my methods! my discoveries! You take one step in his direction and I'll wring your neck. (*He lays his hands on her*). Do you hear?

LIZA: (*Defiantly nonresistant*) Wring away. What do I care? I knew you'd strike me some day. (*He lets her go, stamping with rage at having forgotten himself, and recoils so hastily that he stumbles back into his seat on the ottoman*). Aha! Now I know how to deal with you. What a fool I was not to think of it before! . . . Aha! that's done you, Henry Higgins, it has. Now I don't care that (*snapping her fingers*) for your bullying and your big talk . . .

The sparring scene

In this type of scene the characters may be equally strong or weak. There is a cautious manner in which each character attempts to size up his adversary. To avoid revealing strength or weakness, each character strives to disguise his positive and negative movements. The following scene from Schiller's *Mary Stuart** is an example of this type.

LEICESTER: (*Surprised*) What ailed the Knight?

MORTIMER: My Lord, I cannot tell what angers him; — the confidence, perhaps the Queen so suddenly confers on me.

---

* Friedrich Schiller, *Mary Stuart*. Copyright, 1901, by Henry Holt. Translated by Everett M. Schreck.

LEICESTER: Are you deserving then of confidence?

MORTIMER: This would I ask of you, my Lord of Leicester.

LEICESTER: You said you wish'd to speak with me in private.

MORTIMER: Assure me first that I may safely venture.

LEICESTER: Who gives me an assurance on your side?
Let not my want of confidence offend you;
I see you, Sir, exhibit at this court
Two different aspects; one of them *must* be
A borrowed one; but which of them is real?

MORTIMER: The selfsame doubts I have concerning you.

LEICESTER: Which, then, shall pave the way to confidence?

MORTIMER: He, who, by doing it, is least in danger.

LEICESTER: Well, you are that —

MORTIMER: No, you; — the evidence
Of such a weighty, powerful peer as you
Can overwhelm my voice. My accusation
Is weak against your rank and influence.

LEICESTER: Sir, you mistake. In everything but this
I'm pow'rful here; but in this tender point,
Which I am called upon to trust you with,
I am the weakest man of all the court,
The poorest testimony can undo me.

MORTIMER: If the all-powerful Earl of Leicester
Deign to stoop so low to meet me, and to make
Such a confession to me, I may venture
To think a little better of myself,
And lead the way in magnanimity.

LEICESTER: Lead the way of confidence, I'll follow.

MORTIMER: (*Producing suddenly the letter*)
Here is a letter from the Queen of Scotland.

LEICESTER: (*Alarmed, catches hastily at the letter.*)
Speak softly, Sir! — what do I see? — Oh, it is

her picture! — (*Kisses and examines it with speechless joy — a pause.*)

MORTIMER: (*Who has watched him closely the whole time*) Now, my Lord, I can believe you.

It is evident that in a scene of this type, neither character has much freedom of stage movement until the feeling of caution, mistrust, or doubt between them has been dispelled or changed to another relationship.

The "cat" and "mouse" scene

Dramatic literature contains many examples of this type. Although there are variations, the basic pattern is the same. One character, the "cat," has the power, when the proper moment arrives, to destroy the "mouse." Dramatic interest and emotion are aroused over the techniques used to ensnare the victim and over the possibilities of his escape. Scenes of this type abound particularly in mystery plays and courtroom dramas. Here the culprit may think that he is extricating himself from complicating circumstances, when in reality the net is only more tightly drawn. In Herman Wouk's *The Caine Mutiny Court-Martial*, Commander Queeg is on the stand being questioned by the defense attorney, Lt. Greenwald. Queeg, in the beginning, thinks that he can justify his actions, but as the scene progresses, Greenwald weaves and tightens the net until Queeg is a trapped and shattered man.

The movement patterns of the "cat" and "mouse" type of scene are unique and subtle. Each character furtively watches the other. Although the movements of the cat are generally decisive and assured in contrast with the more unsure actions of the mouse, each character seeks to hide his inherent strength or his inherent weakness. The device by which the victim is eventually caught remains hidden or is only partially revealed as the scene progresses. In like manner, the mouse seeks to hide his obvious attempts to escape; relying rather on deception or a lapse of vigilance by the cat. Although the cat may move

Plate 21. *The Importance of Being Earnest* by Oscar Wilde. Scene presenting opportunities for careful timing of lines and "business" and precise action for comic effect. Wayne State University. Director: Richard D. Spear.

or turn away, seemingly ignoring the mouse, he turns at the dramatic moment to block or trap the mouse in its attempt to escape. The cat and mouse interplay is, of course, both physical and verbal.

The quarrel and make-up scene

The basic pattern of this type of scene is the alternate separation and coming together, or the widening and closing, of the space gap between the two characters. The problems which confront the actor are (1) which character is responsible for the emotional break, (2) the degree of separation, and (3) the moment of change in the intellectual and emotional relationship. The movement toward or away from a character indicates accord or discord. The physical distance between the characters may indicate their degree of emotional compatibility. This distance between characters, which conveys the desired or proper emotional relationship, must be sensed or felt by the actor or director. In some cases, the appropriate distance may be arrived at by experimentation. When *Picnic* by William Inge was on the road prior to the Broadway opening, Joshua Logan, the director, tested from performance to performance the most effective distance between the school teacher and her lover in the scene where she pleads with him to marry her. Logan found that if she were too far away, or close enough to clasp him about the knees, the audience reaction (laughter) was objectionable. He finally determined the distance where the emotional impact of the scene was acceptable and most effective.

These are only a few of the more obvious movement patterns which the actor may encounter. There are many more. In each scene the actor should ask himself: (1) Does the scene have a fundamental movement pattern? and (2) How may the movement be executed to reveal more effectively the character and the dramatic qualities of the scene?

The selected excerpt from *Pygmalion* serves specifically as an exercise in the relation of the character's mood to his physical action. Cognizance should be taken of how the character's emotional state may be revealed by action or inaction.

The first selection from *The Importance of Being Earnest* presents a number of problems: (1) a sharp contrast of characters, (2) careful timing of lines and business, and (3) precise repetition of action for comic effect. (See Plate 21.)

The second scene presents the technical problem of pointing up certain important expository facts while executing rapid farcical movements.

Practice Selections

PYGMALION

by G. B. Shaw / excerpt from Act IV*

(HIGGINS' *laboratory in Wimpole Street. Double doors are in the middle of the back wall. On the stage right wall is a fireplace, with a comfortable leather-covered easy-chair at the side of the hearth. On stage left is a grand piano with the keyboard on the upstage side. The center of the room is clear. It is midnight.* ELIZA *is seated on the piano bench, brooding and silent.*)

HIGGINS

(*Over his shoulder, at the door up center*) Put out the lights, Eliza; and tell Mrs. Pearce not to make coffee for me in the morning: I'll take tea. (*He goes out.*)
ELIZA *tries to control herself and feel indifferent as she rises and walks across to the hearth to switch off the lights. By the time she gets there she is on the point of screaming. She sits down in* HIGGINS' *chair and holds on hard to the arms. Finally she gives way and flings herself furiously on the floor raging.*

* G. B. Shaw, *Pygmalion.* Copyright, 1930, by G. B. Shaw. Reprinted by permission of The Public Trustee and The Society of Authors.

HIGGINS	(*In despairing wrath outside*) What the devil have I done with my slippers? (*He appears at the door.*)
LIZA	(*Snatching up the slippers, and hurling them at him one after the other with all her force*) There are your slippers. And there. Take your slippers; and may you never have a day's luck with them!
HIGGINS	(*Astounded*) What on earth — ! (*He comes to her.*) What's the matter? Get up. (*He pulls her up.*) Anything wrong?
LIZA	(*Breathless*) Nothing wrong — with *you*. I've won your bet for you, haven't I? That's enough for you. *I* don't matter, I suppose.
HIGGINS	*You* won my bet! You! Presumptuous insect! *I* won it. What did you throw those slippers at me for?
LIZA	Because I wanted to smash your face. I'd like to kill you, you selfish brute. Why didn't you leave me where you picked me out of — in the gutter? You thank God it's all over, and that now you can throw me back again there, do you? (*She crisps her fingers frantically.*)
HIGGINS	(*Looking at her in cool wonder*) The creature is nervous, after all.
LIZA	(*Gives a suffocated scream of fury, and instinctively darts her nails at his face.*) ! !
HIGGINS	(*Catching her wrists*) Ah! would you? Claws in, you cat. How dare you shew your temper at me? Sit down and be quiet. (*He throws her roughly into the easy-chair.*)
LIZA	(*Crushed by superior strength and weight*) What's to become of me? What's to become of me?
HIGGINS	How the devil do I know what's to become of you? What does it matter what becomes of you?
LIZA	You don't care. I know you don't care. You wouldn't care if I was dead. I'm nothing to you — not so much as them slippers.
HIGGINS	(*Thundering*) *Those* slippers.
LIZA	(*With bitter submission*) Those slippers. I didn't think it made any difference now. *A pause.* ELIZA *hopeless and crushed.* HIGGINS *a little uneasy.*
HIGGINS	(*In his loftiest manner*) Why have you begun going on like this? May I ask whether you complain of your treatment here?

LIZA	No.
HIGGINS	Has anybody behaved badly to you? Colonel Pickering? Mrs. Pearce? Any of the servants?
LIZA	No.
HIGGINS	I presume you don't pretend that *I* have treated you badly.
LIZA	No.
HIGGINS	I am glad to hear it. (*He moderates his tone.*) Perhaps you're tired after the strain of the day. Will you have a glass of champagne? (*He moves toward the door.*)
LIZA	No. (*Recollecting her manners*) Thank you.
HIGGINS	(*Good-natured again*) This has been coming on you for some days. I suppose it was natural for you to be anxious about the garden party. But that's all over now. (*He pats her kindly on the shoulder. She writhes.*) There's nothing more to worry about.
LIZA	No. Nothing more for *you* to worry about. (*She suddenly rises and gets away from him by going to the piano bench, where she sits and hides her face.*) Oh God! I wish I was dead.
HIGGINS	(*Staring after her in sincere surprise*) Why? in heaven's name, why? (*Reasonably, going to her*) Listen to me, Eliza. All this irritation is purely subjective.
LIZA	I don't understand. I'm too ignorant.
HIGGINS	It's only imagination. Low spirits and nothing else. Nobody's hurting you. Nothing's wrong. You go to bed like a good girl and sleep it off. Have a little cry and say your prayers: that will make you comfortable.
LIZA	I heard *your* prayers. "Thank God it's all over!"
HIGGINS	(*Impatiently*) Well, don't you thank God it's all over? Now you are free and can do what you like.
LIZA	(*Pulling herself together in desperation*) What am I fit for? What have you left me fit for? Where am I to go? What am I to do? What's to become of me?
HIGGINS	(*Enlightened, but not at all impressed*) Oh, that's what's worrying you, is it? (*He thrusts his hands into his pockets, and walks about in his usual manner, rattling the contents of his pockets, as if condescending to a trivial subject out of pure kindness.*) I shouldn't bother about it if I were you. I should imagine you won't have much

difficulty in settling yourself somewhere or other, though I hadn't quite realized that you were going away. (*She looks quickly at him: he does not look at her, but examines the dessert stand on the piano and decides that he will eat an apple.*) You might marry, you know. (*He bites a large piece out of the apple, and munches it noisily.*) You see, Eliza, all men are not confirmed old bachelors like me and the Colonel. Most men are the marrying sort (poor devils!); and you're not bad-looking; it's quite a pleasure to look at you sometimes — not now, of course, because you're crying and looking as ugly as the very devil; but when you're all right and quite yourself, you're what I should call attractive. That is, to the people in the marrying line, you understand. You go to bed and have a good nice rest; and then get up and look at yourself in the glass; and you won't feel so cheap.

(ELIZA *again looks at him, speechless, and does not stir. The look is quite lost on him: he eats his apple with a dreamy expression of happiness, as it is quite a good one.*)

HIGGINS   (*A genial afterthought occurring to him*) I daresay my mother could find some chap or other who would do very well.

LIZA   We were above that at the corner of Tottenham Court Road.

HIGGINS   (*Waking up*) What do you mean?

LIZA   I sold flowers. I didn't sell myself. Now you've made a lady of me I'm not fit to sell anything else. I wish you'd left me where you found me.

HIGGINS   (*Slinging the core of the apple decisively into the grate*) Tosh, Eliza. Don't you insult human relations by dragging all the cant about buying and selling into it. You needn't marry the fellow if you don't like him.

LIZA   What else am I to do?

HIGGINS   Oh, lots of things. What about your old idea of a florist's shop? Pickering could set you up in one: he's lots of money. (*Chuckling*) He'll have to pay for all those togs you have been wearing today; and that, with the hire of the jewelry, will make a big hole in two hundred pounds. Why, six months ago you would have thought it the millennium to have a flower shop of your own. Come! you'll be all right. I must clear off to bed: I'm devilish sleepy. By the way, I came down for something: I forget what it was.

LIZA   Your slippers.

HIGGINS   Oh yes, of course. You shied them at me. (*He picks them up, and is going out when she rises and speaks to him.*)

LIZA   Before you go, sir —

HIGGINS	(*Dropping the slippers in his surprise at her calling him Sir*) Eh?
LIZA	Do my clothes belong to me or to Colonel Pickering?
HIGGINS	(*Coming back into the room as if her question were the very climax of unreason*) What the devil use would they be to Pickering?
LIZA	He might want them for the next girl you pick up to experiment on.
HIGGINS	(*Shocked and hurt*) Is *that* the way you feel towards us?
LIZA	I don't want to hear anything more about that. All I want to know is whether anything belongs to me. My own clothes were burnt.
HIGGINS	But what does it matter? Why need you start bothering about that in the middle of the night?
LIZA	I want to know what I may take away with me. I don't want to be accused of stealing.
HIGGINS	(*Now deeply wounded*) Stealing! You shouldn't have said that, Eliza. That shews a want of feeling.
LIZA	I'm sorry. I'm only a common ignorant girl; and in my station I have to be careful. There can't be any feelings between the like of you and the like of me. Please will you tell me what belongs to me and what doesn't?
HIGGINS	(*Very sulky*) You may take the whole damned houseful if you like. Except the jewels. They're hired. Will that satisfy you? (*He turns on his heel and is about to go in extreme dudgeon.*)
LIZA	(*Drinking in his emotion like nectar, and nagging him to provoke a further supply*) Stop, please. (*She takes off her jewels.*) Will you take these to your room and keep them safe? I don't want to run the risk of their being missing.
HIGGINS	(*Furious*) Hand them over. (*She puts them into his hands.*) If these belonged to me instead of to the jeweler, I'd ram them down your ungrateful throat. (*He perfunctorily thrusts them into his pockets, unconsciously decorating himself with the protruding ends of the chains.*)
LIZA	(*Taking a ring off*) This ring isn't the jeweler's: it's the one you bought me in Brighton. I don't want it now. (HIGGINS *dashes the ring violently into the fireplace, and turns on her so threateningly that she crouches over the piano with her hands over her face, and exclaims*) Don't you hit me.
HIGGINS	Hit you! You infamous creature, how dare you accuse me of such a thing? It is you who have hit me. You have wounded me to the heart.

LIZA	(*Thrilling to hidden joy*) I'm glad. I've got a little of my own back, anyhow.
HIGGINS	(*With dignity, in his finest professional style*) You have caused me to lose my temper; a thing that has hardly ever happened to me before. I prefer to say nothing more tonight. I am going to bed.
LIZA	(*Pertly*) You'd better leave a note for Mrs. Pearce about the coffee; for she won't be told by me.
HIGGINS	(*Formally*) Damn Mrs. Pearce; and damn the coffee; and damn you; and damn my own folly in having lavished hard-earned knowledge and the treasure of my regard and intimacy on a heartless guttersnipe. (*He goes out with impressive decorum, and spoils it by slamming the door savagely.*) (ELIZA *smiles for the first time; expresses her feelings by a wild pantomime in which an imitation of* HIGGINS' *exit is confused with her own triumph; and finally goes down on her knees on the hearthrug to look for the ring.*)

THE IMPORTANCE OF BEING EARNEST

by Oscar Wilde / excerpt from Act II

(MISS GWENDOLEN FAIRFAX *has come down from London to see her fiancé,* ERNEST WORTHING. *She is received by* CECILY CARDEW, MR. WORTHING's *ward.*)

CECILY	(*Advancing to meet her*) Pray let me introduce myself to you. My name is Cecily Cardew.
GWENDOLEN	Cecily Cardew? (*Moving to her and shaking hands*) What a very sweet name! Something tells me that we are going to be great friends. I like you already more than I can say. My first impressions of people are never wrong.
CECILY	How nice of you to like me so much after we have known each other such a comparatively short time. Pray sit down.
GWENDOLEN	(*Still standing up*) I may call you Cecily, may I not?
CECILY	With pleasure!
GWENDOLEN	And you will always call me Gwendolen, won't you?
CECILY	If you wish.

GWENDOLEN	Then that is all quite settled, is it not?
CECILY	I hope so. (*A pause. They both sit down together.*)
GWENDOLEN	Perhaps this might be a favorable opportunity for my mentioning who I am. My father is Lord Bracknell. You have never heard of papa, I suppose?
CECILY	I don't think so.
GWENDOLEN	Outside the family circle, papa, I am glad to say, is entirely unknown. I think that is quite as it should be. The home seems to me to be the proper sphere for the man. Cecily, mamma, whose views on education are remarkably strict, has brought me up to be extremely short-sighted; it is part of her system; so do you mind my looking at you through my glasses?
CECILY	Oh! not at all, Gwendolen. I am very fond of being looked at.
GWENDOLEN	(*After examining* CECILY *carefully through a lorgnette*) You are here on a short visit, I suppose.
CECILY	Oh, no! I live here.
GWENDOLEN	(*Severely*) Really? Your mother, no doubt, or some female relative of advanced years, resides here also?
CECILY	Oh, no! I have no mother, nor, in fact, any relations.
GWENDOLEN	Indeed?
CECILY	My dear guardian, with the assistance of Miss Prism, has the arduous task of looking after me.
GWENDOLEN	Your guardian?
CECILY	Yes, I am Mr. Worthing's ward.
GWENDOLEN	Oh! It is strange he never mentioned to me that he had a ward. How secretive of him! He grows more interesting hourly. I am not sure, however, that the news inspires me with feelings of unmixed delight. (*Rising and going to her*) I am very fond of you, Cecily; I have liked you ever since I met you! But I am bound to state that now that I know that you are Mr. Worthing's ward, I cannot help expressing a wish you were—well just a little older than you seem to be—and not quite so very alluring in appearance. In fact, if I may speak candidly—
CECILY	Pray do! I think that whenever one has anything unpleasant to say, one should always be quite candid.

GWENDOLEN	Well, to speak with perfect candor, Cecily, I wish that you were fully forty-two, and more than usually plain for your age. Ernest has a strong upright nature. But even men of the noblest possible moral character are extremely susceptible to the influence of the physical charms of others.
CECILY	I beg your pardon, Gwendolen, did you say Ernest?
GWENDOLEN	Yes.
CECILY	Oh, but it is not Mr. Ernest Worthing who is my guardian. It is his brother—his elder brother.
GWENDOLEN	(*Sitting down again*) Ernest never mentioned to me that he had a brother.
CECILY	I am sorry to say they have not been on good terms for a long time.
GWENDOLEN	Ah! that accounts for it. And now that I think of it I have never heard any man mention his brother. The subject seems distasteful to most men. Cecily, you have lifted a load from my mind. Of course you are quite, quite sure that it is not Mr. Ernest Worthing who is your guardian?
CECILY	Quite sure. (*A pause*) In fact, I am going to be his.
GWENDOLEN	(*Enquiringly*) I beg your pardon?
CECILY	(*Rather shy and confidingly*) Dearest Gwendolen, there is no reason why I should make a secret of it to you. Our little county newspaper is sure to chronicle the fact next week. Mr. Ernest Worthing and I are engaged to be married.
GWENDOLEN	(*Quite politely, rising*) My darling Cecily, I think there must be some slight error. Mr. Ernest Worthing is engaged to me. The announcement will appear in the MORNING POST on Saturday at the latest.
CECILY	(*Very politely, rising*) I am afraid you must be under some misconception. Ernest proposed to me exactly ten minutes ago. (*Shows diary.*)
GWENDOLEN	(*Examining diary through her lorgnette carefully*) It is certainly very curious, for he asked me to be his wife yesterday afternoon at five-thirty. If you would care to verify the incident, pray do so. (*Producing diary of her own*) I never travel without my diary. I am so sorry, dear Cecily, if it is any disappointment to you, but I am afraid *I* have the prior claim.
CECILY	It would distress me more than I can tell you, dear Gwendolen, if it caused you any mental or physical anguish, but I feel bound to point out that since Ernest proposed to you he clearly has changed his mind.

GWENDOLEN	(*Meditatively*) If the poor fellow has been entrapped into any foolish promise I shall consider it my duty to rescue him at once, and with a firm hand.
CECILY	(*Thoughtfully and sadly*) Whatever unfortunate entanglement my dear boy may have got into, I will never reproach him with it after we are married.
GWENDOLEN	Do you allude to me, Miss Cardew, as an entanglement? You are presumptuous. On an occasion of this kind it becomes more that a moral duty to speak one's mind. It becomes a pleasure.
CECILY	Do you suggest, Miss Fairfax, that I entrapped Ernest into an engagement? How dare you? This is no time for wearing the shallow mask of manners. When I see a spade I call it a spade.
GWENDOLEN	(*Satirically*) I am glad to say that I have never seen a spade. It is obvious that our social spheres have been widely different. (*Enter* MERRIMAN, *followed by the footman. He carries a salver, table cloth, and plate stand.* CECILY *is about to retort. The presence of the servants exercises a restraining influence under which both girls chafe.*)
MERRIMAN	Shall I lay tea here as usual, Miss?
CECILY	(*Sternly, in a calm voice*) Yes, as usual. (MERRIMAN *begins to clear and lay cloth. A long pause.* CECILY *and* GWENDOLEN *glare at each other.*)
GWENDOLEN	Are there many interesting walks in the vicinity, Miss Cardew?
CECILY	Oh! yes! a great many. From the top of one of the hills quite close one can see five counties.
GWENDOLEN	Five counties! I don't think I should like that. I hate crowds.
CECILY	(*Sweetly*) I suppose that is why you live in town? (GWENDOLEN *bites her lip, and beats her foot nervously with her parasol.*)
GWENDOLEN	(*Looking round*) Quite a well-kept garden this is, Miss Cardew.
CECILY	So glad you like it, Miss Fairfax.
GWENDOLEN	I had no idea there were any flowers in the country.
CECILY	Oh, flowers are as common here, Miss Fairfax, as people are in London.
GWENDOLEN	Personally I cannot understand how anybody manages to exist in the country, if anybody who is anybody does. The country always bores me to death.

CECILY	Ah! This is what the newspapers call agricultural depression, is it not? I believe the aristocracy are suffering very much from it just at present. It is almost an epidemic amongst them, I have been told. May I offer you some tea, Miss Fairfax?
GWENDOLEN	(*With elaborate politeness*) Thank you. (*Aside*) Detestable girl! But I require tea!
CECILY	(*Sweetly*) Sugar?
GWENDOLEN	(*Superciliously*) No, thank you. Sugar is not fashionable any more. (CECILY *looks angrily at her, takes up the tongs and puts four lumps of sugar into the cup.*)
CECILY	(*Severely*) Cake or bread and butter?
GWENDOLEN	(*In a bored manner*) Bread and butter, please. Cake is rarely seen at the best houses nowadays.
CECILY	(*Cuts a very large slice of cake, and puts it on the tray.*) Hand that to Miss Fairfax. (MERRIMAN *does so, and goes out with the footman.* GWENDOLEN *drinks the tea and makes a grimace. Puts down cup at once, reaches out her hand to the bread and butter, looks at it, and finds it is cake. Rises in indignation.*)
GWENDOLEN	You have filled my tea with lumps of sugar, and though I asked most distinctly for bread and butter, you have given me cake. I am known for the gentleness of my disposition, and the extraordinary sweetness of my nature, but I warn you, Miss Cardew, you may go too far.
CECILY	(*Rising*) To save my poor, innocent, trusting boy from the machinations of any other girl there are no lengths to which I would not go.
GWENDOLEN	From the moment I saw you I distrusted you. I felt that you were false and deceitful. I am never deceived in such matters. My first impressions of people are invariably right.
CECILY	It seems to me, Miss Fairfax, that I am trespassing on your valuable time. No doubt you have many other calls of a similar character to make in the neighborhood.

THE IMPORTANCE OF BEING EARNEST

by Oscar Wilde / excerpt from Act I

CHARACTERS	ALGERNON MONCRIEFF, JOHN WORTHING, *and* LANE, *the butler.*
SITUATION	JOHN, *who is in love with* GWENDOLEN, *has dropped in to see his bachelor friend,* ALGERNON.

ALGERNON

My dear fellow, Gwendolen is my first cousin. And before I allow you to marry her, you will have to clear up the whole question of Cecily. (*Rings bell.*)

JACK

Cecily! What on earth do you mean? What do you mean, Algy, by Cecily? I don't know any of the name of Cecily. (*Enter* LANE.)

ALGERNON

Bring me that cigarette case Mr. Worthing left in the smoking-room the last time he dined here.

LANE

Yes, sir. (LANE *goes out.*)

JACK

Do you mean to say you have had my cigarette case all this time? I wish to goodness you had let me know. I have been writing frantic letters to Scotland Yard about it. I was very nearly offering a large reward.

ALGERNON

Well, I wish you would offer one. I happen to be more than usually hard up.

JACK

There is no good offering a large reward now that the thing is found. (*Enter* LANE *with the cigarette case on a salver.* ALGERNON *takes it at once.* LANE *goes out.*)

ALGERNON

I think that is rather mean of you, Ernest, I must say. (*Opens case and examines it.*) However, it makes no matter, for, now that I look at the inscription inside, I find that the thing isn't yours after all.

JACK

Of course it's mine. (*Moving to him*) You have seen me with it a hundred times, and you have no right whatsoever to read what is written inside. It is a very ungentlemanly thing to read a private cigarette case.

ALGERNON

Oh! it is absurd to have a hard-and-fast rule about what one should read and what one shouldn't. More than half of modern culture depends on what one shouldn't read.

JACK

I am quite aware of the fact, and I don't propose to discuss modern culture. It isn't the sort of thing one should talk of in private. I simply want my cigarette case back.

ALGERNON	Yes; but this isn't your cigarette case. This cigarette case is a present from some one of the name of Cecily, and you said you didn't know any one of that name.
JACK	Well, if you want to know, Cecily happens to be my aunt.
ALGERNON	Your aunt!
JACK	Yes. Charming old lady she is, too. Lives at Tunbridge Wells. Just give it back to me, Algy.
ALGERNON	(*Retreating to back of sofa*) But why does she call herself little Cecily if she is your aunt and lives at Tunbridge Wells? (*Reading*) "From little Cecily with her fondest love."
JACK	(*Moving to sofa and kneeling upon it*) My dear fellow, what on earth is there in that? Some aunts are tall, some aunts are not tall. That is a matter that surely an aunt may be allowed to decide for herself. You seem to think that every aunt should be exactly like your aunt! That is absurd! For Heaven's sake give me back my cigarette case. (*Follows* ALGERNON *round the room.*)
ALGERNON	Yes. But why does your aunt call you her uncle? "From little Cecily, with her fondest love to her dear Uncle Jack." There is no objection, I admit, to an aunt being a small aunt, but why an aunt, no matter what her size may be, should call her own nephew her uncle, I can't quite make out. Besides, your name isn't Jack at all; it is Ernest.
JACK	It isn't Ernest; it's Jack.
ALGERNON	You have always told me it was Ernest. I have introduced you to every one as Ernest. You answer to the name of Ernest. You look as if your name was Ernest. You are the most earnest looking person I ever saw in my life. It is perfectly absurd your saying that your name isn't Ernest. It's on your cards. Here is one of them. (*Taking it from case*) "Mr. Ernest Worthing, B 4, The Albany." I'll keep this as a proof your name is Ernest if ever you attempt to deny it to me, or to Gwendolen, or to anyone else. (*Puts the card in his pocket.*)
JACK	Well, my name is Ernest in town and Jack in the country, and the cigarette case was given to me in the country.
ALGERNON	Yes, but that does not account for the fact that your small Aunt Cecily, who lives at Tunbridge Wells, calls you her dear uncle. Come, old boy, you had much better have the thing out at once.

JACK   My dear Algy, you talk exactly as if you were a dentist. It is very vulgar to talk like a dentist when one isn't a dentist. It produces a false impression.

ALGERNON   Well, that is exactly what dentists always do. Now, go on! Tell me the whole thing. I may mention that I have always suspected you of being a confirmed and secret Bunburyist; and I am quite sure of it now.

JACK   Bunburyist? What on earth do you mean by a Bunburyist?

ALGERNON   I'll reveal to you the meaning of that incomparable expression as soon as you are kind enough to inform me why you are Ernest in town and Jack in the country.

JACK   Well, produce my cigarette case first.

ALGERNON   Here it is. (*Hands cigarette case.*) Now produce your explanation, and pray make it improbable.

Chapter five

The Actor's Voice*

How, how, Cordelia! Mend your speech a little,
Lest it mar your fortunes.

Shakespeare

The voice as a physical instrument and as an element of emotional projection is a fundamental concern of the actor. The object of vocal study is not only to sharpen perceptions regarding one's own voice but also to acquire techniques and controls which contribute to a well-modulated tone. It is best to maintain *intelligent self-criticism* as the descriptive and technical details are delineated. Too often the student of acting focuses on an exercise or technique as if it were a detached process. In the preparation for acting, no element can be divorced from the whole.

INSTRUMENTATION

Sound

Nearly everyone has heard the old philosophical abstraction: If a tree falls in a forest outside the range of hearing of any animal, is there sound? Physically speaking there is, because a disturbance of that magnitude in a relatively tranquil atmosphere will produce the physical phenomenon we call sound. One might ask, "Of what purpose is it to the actor to have some rudimentary knowledge of the physics of sound?" Not only will it aid him in understanding the nature of projection, but also it may greatly help him to adjust to acoustical variations in playhouses and stage sets. An illustration will demonstrate this. A famous tenor, singing the part of Radames in *Aida*, was staged for his famous first act aria at midstage, carefully placed between two enormous Egyptian columns which were backed by a comparably large temple wall. In this position he was splendidly set by lighting, costume, and scenery. He refused to accept the direction by arguing that he could be better heard down center, practically on the prompter's box. To one extent he was right,

---

* This chapter was written by Faber B. DeChaine, University of Oregon.

sound dissipates in intensity by the square law (in other words, sound is less loud in multiples of the distance from the source, not just simply one half as loud by each equal measurement), but he had oversimplified the acoustical consideration. The original position offered him a splendid "megaphone effect." He must have known little of the *reflective* characteristics of sound. His downstage position put him near proscenium baffles, massive front drapes, and the wide-mouthed orchestra pit. He should have been aware of the *dampening* effect of such surroundings. His juxtaposition to the orchestra revealed further that he knew little about the competition and balancing of sound. So, here was a fine artist who diminished his theatrical and vocal effectiveness on a false assumption about acoustics.

The nature of sound

The particles of matter which make up the gaseous substance we call air are the vehicles of sound. Since the air is highly elastic, its equilibrium after any disturbance is reinstated with incredible speed. Consequently, the actor must adapt to the competitive, dampening, and reflective characteristics of sound just as surely as he must adjust his movement and style to the size of the theater. An auditorium with some echo effect, for example, invariably demands a more deliberate phrase-pause-rate.

Sound emanates from its source in a spherical pattern. It is obvious that the resonating spaces in the actor's head provide a megaphone effect and aid in focusing the sound he makes with his voice. Keep in mind the spherical sound pattern, however, because walls, props, hands, and oral-labial manipulation can aid the actor greatly in strengthening his *projection* through his awareness of this fundamental principle.

The more intense the disturbance which makes the sound, the louder it will be. An actor can speak at varying intensities from a whisper to a yell. Most individuals can do it on command. Few, however, can increase intensity without an evident appearance of strain. This particular problem in vocal intensity is discussed later.

Intensity can be measured. For measurement, the logarithmic or exponential scale is used, expressed in decibels (db). This measurement is calibrated to differentiate between each perceptible variation in intensity; that is, each time a sound seems louder, a decibel is counted. The serious student of acting should use such tools with his intensity exercises in order to receive an accurate feedback of his capacity for loudness.

Reflection

When calling to someone outdoors on a windy day, we invariably cup our hands into the shape of a megaphone. We seem to know naturally that the atmosphere demands this acoustical compensation. Not only do we cup our hands, but also we make other more subtle acoustical accommodations. Most of us purse our lips (that is, adjust and fix our labial articulators); broaden the more natural movement of the lower jaw (that is, maximize and make more precise the dento-articulators); and tend to make each phoneme (a speech sound) distinct by careful articulation in general and by a slight elongation of *voiced* sounds. What has happened in this accommodation is that the cupped hands, the pursed lips, and the broadened jaw placement are focusing the sound through reflection. The clearness of articulation and the strengthening of voiced sounds help to remove distortion or noise. Try this natural compensating situation as an exercise. How much of the compensation can you control by varying the degree from a conversational intensity to a yell?

Dampening

The concept of dampening is obviously the opposite of reflection. The above discussion should aid the student in understanding the dampening variations in terms of his relationship to stage space. Dampening within one's own vocal mechanism, however, is a decidedly different matter. Most vocal dampening is the result of lazy articulation.

Labial. Observe your fellow students in performance. Notice how they use their lips. In some instances you will probably observe that the movement of the lips tends to be fixed, almost as if the person were in a state of local paralysis. At these times the sound is locked and dampened by the fleshy tissue and moisture of the mouth. Most persons who speak with distinct labial articulation, however, tend to use and move the lips in what seems to be an extreme manner. Labial dampening can be illustrated by this exercise. Isolate words which demand an extreme pursing of the lips, such as, cool, stool, food, more, floor, etc. Pronounce these words as you will. Then pronounce the words by severely restraining the pursing characteristics of the lips. Now, repeat the words, pursing the lips in the extreme. You should be able to hear the variation in clarity by speaking in these extremes. The actor should isolate the words in his play script which require definite labial articulation.

Dental. The same characteristics of dampening can result from the manner in which one employs dental articulation. Surely you have seen and heard people who tend to hold their lower jaws in a fixed position while they speak. Such a condition does not produce as much dampening as a fixed labial position. It can, by a combination of reflection and dampening, interfere even more with the clarity of an utterance.

The problem here relates principally to fricative phonemes which are produced as a result of friction. The fricatives are the least reinforced and are therefore, naturally, the low volume sounds. The effect is doubly true when no vocal vibration accompanies the friction. To illustrate, do the following. Isolate such words as fill, spill, lull, I'm, path, etc. Execute in a similar way the exercise mentioned above for labial articulation. Hold the lower jaw in a fixed position. Then, make it extremely manipulatable. Out of your next acting unit, isolate such words as have dominant friction sounds. Repeat the exercise using these words.

Lingual. The tongue's inactivity is the chief cause of poor articulation and oral dampening. It is not uncommon in some people for minor lingual paralysis to interfere with the clarity of articulation. More often than not, however, poor articulation is due to an incredibly fast speech rate or to simple muscular laziness. In normal speech, nearly every English phoneme requires some manipulation and placement of the tongue. All of the vowels are strongly dependent upon lingual position. You can develop a lingual experiment by varying the position of the tongue from what seems to be its normal position in uttering a vowel sound. Notice how the quality of the vowel sound tends to vary.

Nearly everyone has at one time or another been anesthetized by a dentist. This anesthetization not infrequently leaves the tongue in a state of temporary paralysis. The sluggishness of speech sometimes produced from this circumstance is not uncommon in what we mistakenly believe to be a normal pattern. You may observe in yourself a diminishing of articulatory clarity during such anesthetization. Cull from your next acting scene words which tend to contain one or two strong plosives — [b], [d], [g], [k], [p], [t], [ts], and [tz] — or fricatives, which can illustrate what will happen as a result of "lazy tongue."

There are occasionally dampening effects which are the result of an inactive velum (soft palate). Such inactivity, however, usually affects the nasal sounds and is seldom the result of sluggish or lazy articulatory manipulation. The labial, dental, and lingual articulation relates directly to a dampening effect. Retarded articulation not only fails to assist in the enunciation of the whole sound or phoneme, but also blankets out much of the necessary sound quality required for the full shaping of each speech sound. Much of this dampening effect can be diminished by a series of exercises. For particularly helpful exercises, the student is referred to "Exercises for Flexibility and Control of the Articulators" in *Training the Speaking Voice* by Virgil Anderson.*

THE VOCAL MECHANISM

The human voice is an instrument for the production of sound. The skillful and well-trained actor should know this instrument to such an extent that he can manipulate and shade any sound which that instrument can produce. Before discussing the physiology or techniques of manipulation, it is imperative for the actor to understand the nature of the vocal instrument.

The vocal instrument has the capability of making not only the usual sounds associated with speech, but also a host of other sounds which can be brought into play for artistic effect. The usual sounds associated with the utterance of phonemes common to North American English pronunciation fall into two categories: those which are accompanied by vibrations from the vocal folds and those which are produced through other physiological manipulations. It should be obvious that [s], [th], [f], [wh] are nothing more than variations of a whistle, while sounds such as [p], [t], [k] are disturbances of air caused by damming the flow of breath. Notice in both cases that the slight variation in characteristics is created by the shape of the mouth and the relative juxtaposition of the articulators. These "nonvoice" sounds

demand that the actor cultivate an extreme clarity of utterance for them.

The disturbance of the breath by vibration of the vocal folds and how that breath is subsequently shaped or stopped is the "music" of human speech. The following discussion will detail the physiology of the speech mechanism. While understanding instrumentation through physiology is important, the naming of the parts is of scant value if the student cannot bring his own instrument into play in order to enhance the clarity of his utterances.

Physiology

Figure 4, a sectional drawing of the human head, shows the relative position of the cavities of speech mechanism which relate to vocal quality and resonation. Certain muscles, which control resonation and shape the variation of those cavities, are *voluntary*, some others, *involuntary*. For example, when one utters the [m], [n] sounds, it is virtually automatic that the soft palate lowers and that primary resonation takes place in the nasal cavity. The space of this cavity cannot be manipulated. At best one can learn to manipulate the soft pallet in such a way as to add or detract from the resonation which takes place there. In the mouth and throat, however, much more variation is allowable. The musculature of the lips and the adjacent cheek muscles allow for extreme flexibility in the size of the mouth. To demonstrate this to yourself, attempt the following. Without any conscious effort to vary the musculature in the mouth or throat, utter a set of vowel sounds. While one vowel sound and one tone is being sustained, manipulate these labial muscles. Note the variation in quality of the sound. Notice, too, that certain sounds seem to be uttered with more economy than others. This simple experimentation with the labial muscles should aid you in perfecting a clearer and more economical use of breath when uttering the vowel sounds.

---

* Virgil Anderson, *Training the Speaking Voice*, 2nd ed. Oxford: Oxford University Press, 1961, pp. 253–255.

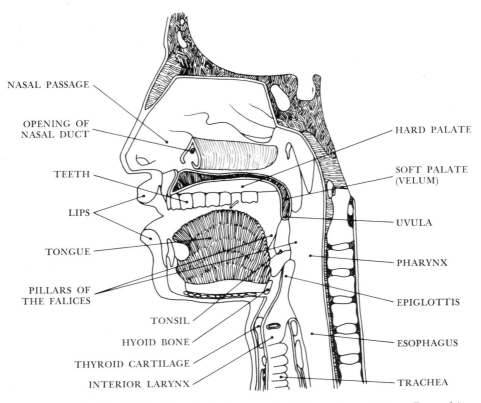

NASAL PASSAGE

OPENING OF
NASAL DUCT

TEETH

LIPS

TONGUE

PILLARS OF
THE FALICES

TONSIL

HYOID BONE

THYROID CARTILAGE

INTERIOR LARYNX

HARD PALATE

SOFT PALATE
(VELUM)

UVULA

PHARYNX

EPIGLOTTIS

ESOPHAGUS

TRACHEA

Figure 4.   Sectional drawing of the human head (courtesy of Enno Poersch).

The tongue is the largest muscle and certainly occupies the greatest space in the oral cavity. The ability to manipulate by protrusion, lateral movement, or a drawing-back action varies greatly from one person to another. Yet, it is this kind of flexibility and voluntary manipulation which contributes greatly to the actor's ability to change his tone and quality. To illustrate this, do the following. Utter simple sentences and while so doing force the tongue into depressions, protrusions, and withdrawals. Notice how evidently tonal quality varies.

The tongue and the sphincter-like muscles of the throat can be concomitantly manipulated. These manipulations usually are more difficult than those for the lips and tongue. By protruding and recessing the tongue, and by striving to make the oral cavity of maximum size, one can begin to feel the musculature of the throat constrict and relax. Such manipulation of the pharynx will be necessary if you wish to effect a variation in vocal quality successfully.

Protrusions

An understanding of the spaces within the speech mechanism and how they are manipulated must be coupled with an understanding of protrusions of bone and tissue which are natural to these cavities. The flute-like characteristic of the speech mechanism is accomplished not only by developing a "set" within the oral cavity, but also by positioning the protrusions, or blades, of the articulators in such juxtaposition that a desired sound is produced. We all know, for example, that a person without teeth sounds different after he has properly fitted dentures. This variation in quality in his case is involuntary, but the actor should be able to manipulate the dental, lingual, and labial protrusions in such a way as to effect similar variations.

One can invent for himself simple exercises to illustrate the importance of these protrusions. For example, hold your lips very tightly with only a minimum opening between them. By speaking several sentences in this highly restricted way, a given vocal quality will be realized. Then, open the mouth and utter the same set of sentences. Recognizable new vocal qualities should emerge.

Attempt this simple exercise in a similar way by manipulating the dental arches in their extreme. Nearly close the teeth and then open them wide. Attempt it again but this time bring the tongue into play: (1) use it in a rolled position; (2) use it with the tip standing up in the center of the mouth; (3) use it with the center of the tongue highly arched. These manipulations should reveal a number of variations in quality. Keep in mind the muscular stress which results because of these manipulations.

Muscles

The tongue, or glossal muscle, is the most obvious muscle within the oral and pharyngeal cavities. In natural speech this muscle, in juxtaposition with the other articulators, helps to form recognizable speech sounds. To understand the use of muscles better, consider the sounds we are apt to make which are not necessarily a part of our natural speech, such sounds as a whistle, a spitting sound, a clearing of the throat, an emission of air through the nasal cavity as in blowing the nose, a

click of the cheek as in encouraging a horse to move on, the inhalation or reverse whistle sound used to call an animal, etc. All of these extra speech sounds may not be necessary for use in building a character but they provide an opportunity to experiment with the manipulation of muscles. The production of these sounds can bring to the actor's attention muscles which are ordinarily thought to be involuntary.

BREATH CONTROL

Breathing

The manipulation of the muscles used in speech is dependent upon the production of an air stream. Consequently, the process of breathing and control of the muscles of the breathing mechanism are of considerable importance to the actor. He must master not only the manipulation of the muscles of phonation in connection with the throat, mouth, and nasal cavity, but also command the energy source which makes the sound: that is, the breath. Sheer volume is highly dependent upon energy and the amount of emission of breath used at any given time.

Notice, however, that yelling or forcing oneself to speak at an extreme intensity usually dissipates the breath very quickly and produces a state of fatigue. This is particularly true if the intensity is maintained for some time. Such a condition would be catastrophic to an actor if he were forced to speak at the level of yelling. His voice would be reduced to a whisper after a performance of high vocal intensity. If the actor is to endure as a professional, he must be able to speak at will with intensity and clarity, to control his breathing mechanism in order to produce subtle shadings of meaning as well as refined modulations of quality. These conditions are realized by voluntary, precise control and a subtle linking of the muscles involved in the speech process.

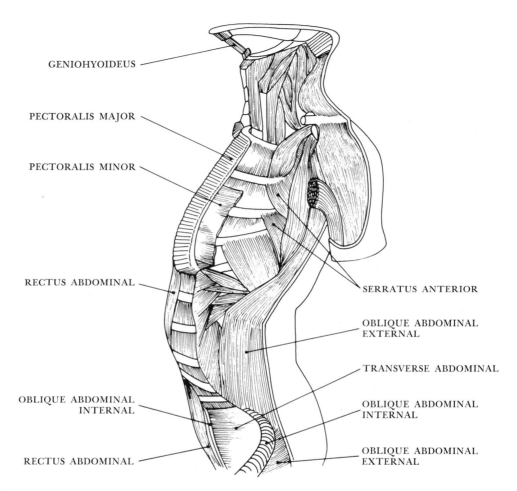

GENIOHYOIDEUS

PECTORALIS MAJOR

PECTORALIS MINOR

RECTUS ABDOMINAL

SERRATUS ANTERIOR

OBLIQUE ABDOMINAL
EXTERNAL

TRANSVERSE ABDOMINAL

OBLIQUE ABDOMINAL
INTERNAL

OBLIQUE ABDOMINAL
INTERNAL

RECTUS ABDOMINAL

OBLIQUE ABDOMINAL
EXTERNAL

Figure 5.   Frontal and sectional view of the human breathing apparatus (courtesy of Enno Poersch).

The musculature of breathing

Figure 5 shows a frontal and sectional view of the human breathing apparatus. As one inhales and exhales to a greater extent than in relaxed breathing, one can begin to identify the muscular areas or the precise muscle groups which are involved. When one breathes deeply there is a tendency to heave the chest high and pull the shoulders back. The lifting of the chest or thoracic cavity is brought about by the contraction of the inter-costal muscles which lie between the ribs. Concomitantly, the muscles in the back are tensed as they draw the shoulders up and back while they lift the rib cage.

Prove the muscle action by this exercise. Inhale by as much expansion of the chest cavity as you can. Then recite a series of lines from an acting exercise. Make a conscious effort to control the duration of exhalation as best you can. Record the time it takes. Return to a state of relaxation. Notice the subtle movement of the musculature of breathing when you are in a relatively natural state. While it is not true in all cases, most people tend to expand and contract the muscles of the abdomen more than those of the chest. Whether or not that is true in your case, cultivate a breathing procedure which forces the expansion and contraction of the abdominal muscles. You will notice when you thrust the abdomen forward that you pull down somewhat on the muscles of the chest area. There also seems to be a functioning of internal muscles.

This internal flexing is usually referred to as diaphragmatic manipulation. To be sure, the diaphragm is in use only as an adjunct to this complex muscle group. It is the *thrust* which has been referred to as diaphragmatic breathing. The serious student of acting will exercise the musculature of the abdomen and the muscles which develop this unusual internal thrust, for these groups of muscles are at the root of good breath control. One exercise most commonly used for abdominal flexing is for the actor to shadowbox and expend breath in the extreme, without making a speech sound each time he delivers a punch. Another immobile exercise is to dam the glottis, which allows a rapid buildup of breath. This naturally causes the abdominal muscles to function in the extreme. The manipulation of these muscles does not require a constant phonation which might tire the voice.

Relaxation

You will find that executing the abdominal and thoracic exercises is fatiguing for you are demanding that the muscles work in the extreme. In some cases it even causes undue tension. Since you cannot practice the phonation–resonation exercises under a state of stress, it is necessary to cultivate relaxation in breathing. Each actor should find his own threshold of tension and fatigue. When he feels that he is approaching this threshold, it is wise for him to stop the set of tensing exercises and work on a set of exercises which help produce relaxation.

To illustrate a sense of relaxation of the breathing apparatus, notice the state of muscular tension after the execution of a sustained glottal stop. To effect this condition, execute the following exercise. Take hold of a heavy object (one you cannot lift) or an object that is securely fastened to the floor. Attempt to lift the object. When you have exerted nearly all of your muscular power in the lift, attempt to speak. Notice that it is very difficult to do both. Some people cannot manage the double function at all.

It should be clear that in the lifting process the vocal muscles come into play and, in so doing, the vocal folds cut off your breathing (dam the breath). Notice further that when you attempt to lift heavy weights, you almost involuntarily synchronize your breathing and damming of breath as a preparation for excessive expenditure of energy. This exercise should sharply reveal the use of several sets of muscles for breathing. You will also experience a sense of relaxation when you release yourself from the burden of weight. This sense of relaxation can more properly be defined as fatigue, but because the expenditure of energy existed for such a short time, you recover quickly. Many people experience a rather pleasant sensation as the muscles return to their natural state of relaxation.

To understand the difference between a point of fatigue from which you can respond readily and a point of fatigue which drastically raises the threshold of tension, it will be necessary for you to engage in some strenuous physical activity for a sustained amount of time. This will put your muscles into a state of fatigue which make them virtually flaccid. You become weak and your muscles do not easily respond to voluntary manipulation.

In such a condition, breath control is difficult and in some cases the voice will quaver and play out. Nonetheless, you should execute the above two fatiguing exercises in order to experience and understand the responses of your musculature.

The following exercises will help to put you in a state of nominal relaxation without a state of fatigue. These should be executed prior to any other manipulation of the vocal mechanism.

1. Allow your head to flop out of its naturally erect position. Then rotate it while uttering the natural vowel sound "ah." It is best if you allow the whole musculature of head, neck, and shoulders to flop in this manner.
2. Let the jaw drop down. Attempt a series of yawns. Repeating this exercise will eventually produce a yawn.
3. Allow all of the musculature of the upper body to fall into a relaxed position. Allow the arms to sag and flop. Some people like to bend over at the waist and allow the upper part of the body to sway in a rhythmic manner. While in this motion, run through the vowel sounds.

If you do these exercises, you will begin to sense the kind of relaxation that resulted from the forced fatiguing exercise discussed earlier. These latter exercises, however, will leave you in a better set and tone for vocal manipulations.

Careful and repeated experience with the exercises listed will enable you to become familiar with your breathing mechanism. In addition, these exercises will increase your ability to call upon the musculature for controlled breathing and desired manipulation. What is important, of course, is that this knowledge will ultimately be brought into play for solving the essential problem of projection.

Expansive breathing is the coupling of all of the processes of breathing discussed. For effective projection, the actor begins with abdominal breathing and then couples this with thoracic breathing. Such breathing allows for a considerably greater inhalation. When you feel that you have taken in as much air as you can, you should begin a slow exhalation in reverse of the method of inhalation. That is, you should slowly reduce the expanded thoracic cavity, ultimately drawing in the abdominal muscles which are the last to be voluntarily employed.

Deliver a speech from a forthcoming acting exercise and time it. How does the time compare to the earlier time-keeping exercise? You should discover that not only can you speak for a longer duration of time, but also that the intensity of your utterance seems to have improved. When the exercise does not demonstrate such control, it is usually the result of psychological tension or an induced state of fatigue at too high a threshold.

The serious actor regulates his breathing, using the techniques described as an aid in the execution of his acting role. As he plans the phrasing for speech, the amount of inhalation and breath control needed at a given point will become apparent to him. Oddly enough, many actors do not make such an analysis, preferring to phrase by intuition.

It is this characteristic of breathing and phrasing which suggests a distinction between the singer and the actor. The singer designs his breath control and phrasing in relation to the musical composition. Actors often assume that speech allows for a greater flexibility and interpretation. Some are unconcerned with such techniques; others, who are perhaps subconsciously aware of the need for breath control, intuitively impose it. When breath control is ignored, the inexperienced actor encounters many problems in rhythm as well as in projection.

Choose a speech, or series of speeches, and develop three or four different ways of phrasing them, striving for believable interpretations. Make note of how breathing is related to these several ways you have phrased. Usually, a greater economy and a greater control of phrasing results from integrating breath control with your interpretative processes.

PHONATION

Types of sound

When one thinks of the production of sound, one usually assumes that the sound waves have been created by a vibration. This is true because the particles of matter in the atmosphere are indeed vibrating. In human speech these sound waves are set off in various ways: it is by *vibration*, *explosion*, and *friction* that phonemes are composed.

Vibration. All the vowel and diphthong sounds are the direct result of air vibration caused by the manipulation of the vocal folds within the larynx. The variation, or "color," of the sounds is caused by the shape and surface of the resonating cavities and the juxtaposition of the articulators. The sound emanating from the vocal folds is essentially the same for all vowels. The musculature of the larynx is manipulated for the control of the pitch and has little effect upon quality. The clarity of the utterance of any vowel is directly proportional to the ability of the actor to manipulate the resonating cavities and the articulators in a distinct manner. Lacking such skill, it may be necessary for him to compile a check list of words which cause him difficulty. One of the best lists for vowel sounds can be found in *Voice and Articulation Drillbook* by Grant Fairbanks.*

A common error in clarity of utterance relates to nearly everyone's tendency to produce the neutral vowel as a substitution for a distinctly shaped vowel. This is particularly true when the precise character of a vowel is in the medial group, which requires the most lingual manipulation.

Explosion and friction. There are two groups of consonants: the plosives and the fricatives. The plosives are produced by damming the air and

then allowing it to explode. The fricatives are caused by friction of the breath passing over protrusions. There are a few consonant sounds which are really a combination of the two groups. For example, notice that [p] and [b] are similar in formation except that the latter carries with it a vocal vibration. Most of the other consonant sounds are similarly paired.

Controls

It is difficult for a student of acting to identify the common errors he may be making in phonation; consequently, he must cultivate his ability to hear the sounds he makes. To assist him he can do systematic exercises using a magnetic tape recorder.

Some errors are sufficiently plentiful to deserve special consideration. They involve the elimination, substitution, addition, and fusion of separate phonemes.

There is a tendency to eliminate vowels or consonants when the word is composed of a series of seemingly incompatible sounds. It is difficult to say each required sound in such words as fifths, lists, athletics, strengths, hundredths, and warmth.

Substitution can frequently be the result of defective speech. Such substitutions as [w], [l], and [r] are not uncommon. The actor should be doubly cautious about his clarity of utterance with such sounds. Most substitutions are the result of slovenliness or dialect. The [d] and [t], for example, can sometimes have one pronunciation in Germanic languages and a different one in Romance languages. Also frequently heard is a substitution of [v] for [w], and [t] for [d]. Sounds are usually substituted unwittingly. If the vocal characteristic of a given consonant is eliminated, the result may be "liddle" for little, "ledder" for letter, "baf" for bath, "wad" for what. A common line to illustrate a good deal of elimination and substitution is "Wad ya gunna do?" for "What are you going to do?" The actor is often

---

* Grant Fairbanks, *Voice and Articulation Drillbook*, 2nd ed. New York: Harper, 1960, pp. 22–56.

surprised on receiving an accurate feedback of his speech to learn that his utterances are riddled with eliminations and substitutions not unlike those cited.

Adding sounds to words is not as common as substituting them, but it does occur with certain regional accents and in words which tend to contain silent letters. Persons living on the North Atlantic Seaboard, for example, sometimes pronounce almost a double [g] at the ends of words like long, prong, and song. Others may belabor the [r] sounds in February or library, suggesting an affectation or labored diction.

In the illustration, "Wad ya gunna do?", not only are elimination and substitution shown, but also fusion, since certain sounds carry over from one word to the other. This is quite evident when the sound used last in one word is the beginning sound in the next. This tends to happen when such words stand together as: "what time," "mug grip," "the other." There are a number of word combinations which invite fusion or elimination when the movement of the articulators would be considerable to accomplish the individual sounds. For example, in saying "all right," there is a tendency to virtually eliminate the [l] sound.

One rule applicable here is that while an actor should never cultivate a labored or affected diction, it is advisable to keep each speech sound as distinct as possible. The majority of good actors give particular attention to the consonant sounds which end words.

RESONATION

The nature of quality

The quality of the speaking voice is directly the result of controlled resonation. There are, though, secondary factors such as a partial paralysis of some of the muscles of phonation, a thickening of some tissue, or a superfluous appendage within the speech apparatus. Most of the secondary factors cannot be controlled; resonation can. It is through resonation that an actor is able to produce the unique sounds which enable him to play a variety of roles. While timing, phrasing, and accent are of comparable importance, it is the manipulation of *resonation* which primarily aids in the development of a wide range of vocal effects. Impersonations and theatrical caricatures are extremely difficult for an actor who cannot control resonation.

Spaces

We know that the quality of the musical instrument is affected by the shape and size of the resonating cavity and the composition of its walls. The voice mechanism, as the sound mechanism in musical instruments, has spaces in which overtones are produced. The musculature of phonation can be manipulated in such a way as to develop variations in tone as well as to assist in the formation of a given phoneme. The principal concern in this discussion is to deal with that space which is located above the larynx and is continuous with the openings in the head (the mouth and nostrils). The mouth, of course, is the most flexible of the resonating cavities. The formation of a phoneme is done largely through control of the devices of articulation in the mouth.

Placement

The ability to manipulate the muscles which sheathe and surround the resonation spaces differs among individuals. Those who show talent for mimicry can vary the placement of resonation easily. They have learned to convert involuntary muscles to voluntary ones. This is the task in voice placement. The various areas of placement follow.

Frontal. We all have identifying characteristics of voice: soft, melodic, harsh, or grating, as the case may be. Such characteristics, or sets, are with all of us. One of the easiest sets to accomplish is the so-called frontal, or metallic, voice. It is frontal because the oral space is used while the pharyngeal areas are constricted. It is metallic because the quality is brittle, sharp, and hard. To achieve this vocal placement, attempt the following:

1. Broaden the lips to a grin.
2. Tighten the muscles of the throat (pharynx).
3. Draw the tongue back toward the soft palate and attempt to maintain it there but not to the extent that your phonemes are not clear.
4. In a psychological sense, attempt to "speak at your teeth."
5. Read several sentences from your next acting unit in the extreme metallic placement.
6. Find a character in drama who might very well have some metallic characteristics in his voice.

Medial. The medial placement is more natural. The muscles which were constricted to achieve the metallic voice are, in this case, more relaxed. To produce the medial vocal placement, attempt the following:

1. Allow the labial articulators to be slightly more exaggerated than they are in normal speech. That is, allow them to be more widely separated in the open vowel sounds, allow their forward thrust on plosives to be slightly exaggerated, and permit them to protrude as required in certain fricative sounds.
2. Strive to separate the jaws as much as possible. This will help to eliminate much of the tight, metallic sound.
3. Do not give any particular attention to the muscles of the throat, other than allowing them to be relaxed.
4. Use the tongue with precision and form each sound clearly. However, allow the tongue to lie in a relaxed position as often as possible. Doing so will be natural to you when you

expand the opening of the mouth and the distance between the jaws.
5. Relax the walls of the cheeks as much as possible.
6. In a psychological sense, speak in a full voice. (This placement might be reminiscent of "Full Tone" concepts which are prevalent in the study of singing.)

Such oral placement ought not to carry with it the extremity of muscular manipulation as in the case of the metallic voice.

Pharyngeal. This vocal set is sometimes referred to as throaty. What is meant, of course, is that the dominance of resonation tends to take place in the throat, or pharynx. When you have achieved this placement, it will seem throaty.

To affect the pharyngeal placement, attempt the following:

1. Depress the tongue as much as you can. Affect this depression chiefly at the posterior section. There will be a tendency to draw the lower jaw downward. This is permissible, but strive to maintain the jaw in an essentially normal position.
2. In a psychological sense, speak with a big tone. You will find that if you lower your voice pitch and perhaps hold your shoulders back, you will be assisted in executing this vocal set.

The pharyngeal voice may seem muffled. It is unlikely that one would ever affect such a voice in the extreme, except for the portrayal of a character.

Nasal. Nasality embodies two vocal conditions. One is an abundance of nasality and the other is an abuse of it. Each of these may be a natural or an acquired vocal characteristic.

Denasal. Denasality is characterized by the voice which occurs with a head cold. One is prevented from "speaking through the nose." This condition may be simulated in the following manner. Close the mouth and actually have air emit through the nostrils. Then stop the flow of air abruptly by arching the soft palate across the opening between the mouth and the nasal cavity, damming the breath.

Once you have mastered denasality, recite several lines in this vocal extreme. You usually discover that, while this vocal placement seems to produce muffling, certain speech sounds tend to emerge more clearly than you might expect. Denasality may actually have a place in the actor's repertory of voices as he develops unusual characterizations. More likely than not, segments of it, coupled with the metallic, medial, and pharyngeal, will help to develop clarity, tone, and flexibility.

Nasality in the extreme can be experienced quickly by the utterance of the three phonemes [m], [n], and [ing]. The production of nasality with other speech sounds may not be so simple. Usually, an abundance of nasality can be more easily realized if one attempts to speak at a low level of intensity. This will permit the relaxation of the velum which is needed to produce nasal resonance. Doing this while speaking in bursts of breath will also aid in training the groups of muscles which must be relaxed in order to produce nasality.

Actually, one seldom evolves a voice which is not substantially modified by one's own normal speech pattern. As a matter of fact, the careful actor will cultivate a given set which he intends to use in building a character through a knowledge of the musculature and the ability to produce modifications in resonation. Subsequently, he will eliminate his own awareness as such a set becomes natural to his character. Moreover, the manipulation of these several voices should reveal to the actor through tape recording exercises that new color and shading are available to him for vocal effects.

Breathy. The breathy voice is just as the term implies. It is characterized by the emission of more breath than is really necessary to execute speech. One can affect this by simply forcing oneself to emit more breath than needed, or by allowing insufficient vibration of the vocal folds. Except as it relates to the character or is justified by the situation (a news report by a highly overwrought person), breathiness is usually a fault. It can be eliminated by a greater control over the release of the breath and by a greater tension of the vocal folds. By so doing, a full vibration of the speech sounds will replace the partial vibration of breathiness.

Harsh. The production of the harsh or strident sound is caused by overtense vocal folds. The throat muscles are tight and the sound is squeezed through the vocal mechanism. This tendency may be overcome by a relaxation of the neck and throat muscles and by practicing such open throat sounds as "ah."

Hoarse. We have all experienced hoarseness. It may have resulted from an attack of laryngitis, a common cold, or excessive yelling out of doors. These conditions produce hoarseness because the membranes of the vocal mechanism, most notably those in the laryngeal area, have become swollen and coated with secretions which are not present in the normal speech condition. Hoarseness can be affected by tensing the muscles around the laryngeal area and by tightening the muscles around the glottis. One can do this by first affecting a breathy tone. While producing it, begin to constrict the muscles until a hoarse quality emerges.

Experimentation to achieve harshness and hoarseness should be combined with the warning that too much exertion in producing these voices may induce the quality not only momentarily but also to a point beyond control. All of these manipulations are valuable only insofar as they make the actor the master of his voice. At no time should any of the placements or secondary vibration techniques produce strain or involuntary qualities in the voice.

PROJECTION

The concept of projection is frequently ambiguous. It is seldom defined and one can properly assume that it may convey various meanings. Stage directors invariably mean, "I can't hear you." The coach or teacher means that the size of the "visible" speech is not "coming through." To be sure, a louder voice is certainly the result of projection. The contention here is that projection is achieved by a careful control of the musculature and by a clarity in the utterance of each phoneme. The serious student of acting and the accomplished actor know that both mental and muscular control are at the core of artistic attainment. While some actors seem to possess the attributes for projection without considerable expenditure of time in learning, this does not mean that other actors do not need to involve themselves in exercises. Indeed, the lethargic actor would do well to invest time in perfecting more subtle controls than he seems to achieve naturally.

Pitch

The principal considerations that the student of acting should give to the study of pitch involve the finding of his range or level, and the examination of the way pitch can be used effectively for variety and inflection. Of fundamental importance is that pitch control is directly proportionate to the actor's ability to hear himself. When he begins to experiment with pitch as an artistic tool, he must simultaneously cultivate an ability to hear the vocal production of such experimentation. The musical keyboard of the piano is usually a point of reference in distinguishing pitch. It is advisable for all actors to test their natural pitch level with that of the piano. An actor does not have to sing well but he should be able to pitch his voice with the note being struck on the piano and to discover for himself the variation available to him by playing up and down the scale.

Without attempting to vocalize, the actor should maintain a state of utterance somewhere between singing and speaking. He should practice hitting a note struck well within his pitch range. When he has found his own level of pitch, it is then advisable to experiment going above and below this level. It is important that he discover for himself where the outside margins of his pitch range lie. He will find rather quickly that he can cultivate a falsetto voice, but it is difficult to issue much intensity in such a vocal register. This exercise which helps to make an actor aware of his ranges of pitch will be useful in his acting scenes.

As a test of pitch variability, one can attempt the following exercise. Tape record a short segment from an acting scene. Make every attempt to record it in the manner of your planned presentation. Play back the recording and find the extremities of pitch on the piano. What is the range? Reinterpret the same segment of the scene with the deliberate thought of cultivating a wide variation of pitch scale.

One may notice in the recording what is commonly referred to as monotone. Such a phenomenon is not really tone but pitch. A characteristic of this kind is more properly identified as *monopitch* which tends to produce two highly undesirable characteristics in voice. One is the fact that the individual uses only a few pitch variations. The other is that he tends to be unaware of natural harmonic structure. In effect, he speaks off key. Although this condition is often referred to as tone deaf it is more accurately termed pitch deaf. While we do not speak in a prescribed harmonic key, we do develop a prescribed harmonic set which in turn produces a pleasant speech melody.

When the actor is amply aware of his own level, has experimented with pitch variation in his own voice, and has sampled the melodic concept of key, he is ready to involve himself in another variation of pitch: inflection and emphasis.

An inflection is a modulation in pitch executed during the production of any phoneme. Naturally, such inflections fall on the phonation of a vowel or voice sound. There is usually a variation in pitch after a pause within the dialogue. This is commonly referred to as a *shift*, and logically falls within the discussion of inflection.

The best way to come to an understanding of inflection is to manipulate pitch modulations with your current acting script. Attempt the following exercises:

1. Choose a series of short sentences and preface each one by some simple exclamation, such as, "well," "my," "say," "oh," etc. Then recite each of these newly composed phrases with an upward inflection of the exclamatory word. Repeat, with a downward inflection. You will discover from this simple exercise that the meaning of the sentence will vary somewhat. By such exercises and experimentation you may discover more satisfactory patterns than the ones you originally intended.

2. Speak five to ten sentences from your acting scene into a tape recorder. When you listen to these sentences, indicate the inflections by arrows on your script. Read these sentences back into the tape recorder, only this time change the inflection to the opposite of what was used before. Again, you will discover that new meanings begin to emerge.

It is by this knowledge of musculature and by execution of frequent vocal exercises that the actor can become a master of pitch variety without seeming to be arbitrary or affected. One rarely is conscious of pitch variation while acting a role on the stage. The technique of variation in flexibility is part of the rehearsal process. *

Intensity

In order to have a loud voice, an actor must have enough breath control to support an intense utterance. Preferably, he should be in his medium pitch range. There is a danger, though, in assuming that projection is synonymous with intensity. The stage director is perhaps the most fallible in calling for loudness when phrasing, breath support, and clearness of articulation might actually give the effect he is seeking. Keep this in mind when reading the following discussion that is concerned primarily with intensity.

It is desirable for each actor to find some tool or measurement which can determine his intensity. He would be wise to consult speech correction clinics or speech scientists who have audiometric measuring devices. If these tools are not available, he must rely upon his ability to hear variations of intensities.

Variability of intensity can contribute to the general variety of an acting performance as well as save the actor from undue stress upon his vocal mechanism. He quite naturally evolves, either systematically or subconsciously, the kind of stress he intends to give the phrases in his dialogue. Ordinarily, the emphasis on phonemes or syllables calls for only a mild variation in the general level of intensity.

The actor may take from his next acting exercise a group of phrases in which a single word or group of words demands a certain stress. Read these phrases and give considerable emphasis to the important word or group of words. Then read them again, diminishing the amount of stress.

---

* A further discussion of pitch is presented in Chapter 7, Line Interpretation.

Phrasing

While phrasing sometimes refers to the cycle of breathing one cultivates in speech, it more fully implies the subtle relationship of speech rhythm to the ideas expressed. There are many techniques and suggestions that can be made with reference to phrasing. Some are highly mechanical and involve an elaborate system of diacritical marking. There are also a number of subjective tools of phrasing. Their applicability varies with their relevance to any given dramatic interpretation. Consequently, only six phrasing techniques are discussed here. They are in no way meant to be definitive. In executing these phrasing techniques, the actor should discover how to vary his use of the devices for better interpretation.

The techniques will be illustrated by referring to a single passage from Shakespeare in Act III, Scene 2 of *Romeo and Juliet*. In this scene, Juliet is speaking to her nurse who has just brought word of Tybalt's death at the hand of Romeo. The speech is rich in illustrations of phrasing, because it contains direct questions, reflection, the confrontation of another character, some exposition, a reference to one's own active involvement in the dramatic situation, and an evaluation of attitudes in action.

"Shall I speak ill of him that is my husband?
Ah, poor my lord, what tongue shall smooth thy name,
When I, thy three-hours wife, have mangled it?
But wherefore, villain, didst thou kill my cousin?
That villain cousin would have kill'd my husband:
Back, foolish tears, back to your native spring;
Your tributary drops belong to woe,
Which you mistaking offer up to joy.
My husband lives, that Tybalt would have slain;
And Tybalt's dead, that would have slain my husband:
All this is comfort; wherefore weep I then?
Some word there was, worser than Tybalt's death,
That murder'd me: I would forget it fain;

But, O, it presses to my memory,
Like damned guilty deeds to sinners' minds:
'Tybalt is dead, and Romeo banished;'
That 'banished,' that one word 'banished,'
Hath slain ten thousand Tybalts. Tybalt's death
Was woe enough, if it had ended there:
Or, if sour woe delights in fellowship,
And needly will be rank'd with other griefs,
Why follow'd not, when she said 'Tybalt's dead,'
Thy father, or thy mother, nay, or both,
Which modern lamentation might have moved?
But, with a rear-ward following Tybalt's death,
'Romeo is banished:' to speak that word,
Is father, mother, Tybalt, Romeo, Juliet,
All slain, all dead. 'Romeo is banished!'
There is no end, no limit, measure, bound,
In that word's death; no words can that woe sound.
Where is my father, and my mother, nurse?"

Forethought. The concept of forethought is as the term implies, that is, a character must conjure up the idea he is about to speak in dialogue. Obviously, a particular dramatic pause is called for. For example, Juliet says, "My husband lives, that Tybalt would have slain. . . ." At this moment Juliet realizes the irony of what has formulated in her mind. She reads up to the word "slain" and stops momentarily. Then, with such an interpretation in mind, she completes the phrase: "And Tybalt's dead, that would have slain my husband." It is this momentary realization which causes a pause and allows for a continuity of the thought prevailing in the utterance. The same technique might be applicable when she says, "But, O, it presses to my memory,/Like damned guilty deeds to sinners' minds." Here it is possible that the comparative phrase was thought of at a split moment, following the word "memory" or the word "like." If one interprets the speech with this attitude of forethought, the acceleration should be affected in the remainder of the phrase, "damned guilty deeds to sinners' minds." This technique should be used sparingly even though it does have a virtue in maintaining the continuity of thought during a pause.

Afterthought. The technique of afterthought is comparable to forethought in that it tends to leave the actor in a state of concentration while pausing. Logically, it comes at the end of a phrase which is highly revealing, profound, or ironic. By this device of afterthought, a dramatic suggestion, an implied answer, or greater shades of meaning may be realized. One profound thought in Juliet's mind might be borne out following the phrase, "All slain, all dead." Here the intrinsic interpretation could easily be that, when Juliet says, " 'Romeo is banished:' to speak that word,/Is father, mother, Tybalt, Romeo, Juliet . . .", it means that her life and everything she loves is dead if, indeed, Romeo is banished. At first she might think of this as being simply an excessive comparison to Romeo's banishment, but after having said it, she has an afterthought which produces a recognition in her of the reality of his banishment. It is a terrifying realization which she experiences and the capable actress will reveal in the pause this feeling of afterthought prior to speaking, " 'Romeo is banished!' " Such an attitude of mind should aid the actress in phrasing both the parallel structure preceding, "All slain, all dead," and the phrase which follows, "There is no end, no limit, measure, bound,/In that word's death; no words can that woe sound."

Take. Most actors are aware of the concept of "take" when it refers to the comic take and double take, that is, a delayed awareness of an ironic or comic idea. The notion of take as it relates to phrasing is similar but not necessarily applicable, except in the comic circumstance. Because the take can help point up a particularly rich phrase or idea, it is equally applicable in serious drama. When one uses such technique it will often affect the interpretation in ways not considered in usual explicative design.

Usually, when one employs take for phrasing, one requires some sort of concomitant physical gesture. One place in Juliet's speech where such a technique is applicable is when she says, "Hath slain ten thousand Tybalts." If the actress interprets the concept of banishment as being of supreme severity and feels that Tybalt's death is meaningless in relationship to the lover who has been banished, then the character can develop a mental attitude of finality at that point. Juliet might even move to leave the stage and then, by a take, make new reference to the entire concept of Tybalt's death and Romeo's banishment. This technique allows for a considerable variation in phrasing because if Juliet uses the concept of take, she will give herself sufficient time to develop a new mental attitude for the several sentences which follow.

Oral focus. Most actors are aware, or are made aware, of physical focus on the stage, that is, pointing to a given area, object, or person on the stage at a given moment. Such physical focus is used to achieve a heightened dramatic effect or to center the attention of the audience. Oral focus attempts to accomplish a similar pointing of word or phrase which otherwise might not be readily evident or meaningful to the listener. Oral focus is particularly needed in poetic and nonrealistic dramatic forms. This can be illustrated by the phrase which Juliet utters, "Some word there was, worser than Tybalt's death,/That murder'd me. . . ." It is perfectly evident that Juliet is not murdered; therefore, the phrase must imply the destruction of spirit rather than actual death. To make this metaphor clear, certain concepts within the phrase must be set apart, or focused. The simplest interpretation is that the word which is about to be uttered is, of course, the oft repeated "banished." It is this state imposed upon Romeo which, to Juliet's mind, forbodes spiritual death. Therefore she develops a phrasing for "Some word there was," which expresses the foreshadowing of the "word" which murdered her. The actress must phrase this sentence in such a way as to focus on "word" and "murdered." She can set the idea apart by heightened vocal intensity, pausing, intonation, or elongation of words. Such techniques of oral focus should not, however, be overly obvious.

Parenthetical thought. The previous illustration can also illustrate the notion of parenthetical thought. This term is nearly self-evident. If a phrase within the text is an adjunct, reflective, or secondary thought to the primary idea, it is parenthetical. An example of this kind of phrase is "worser than Tybalt's death." The audience is led to believe that there is something more important than the death of Tybalt which has moved Juliet. Juliet must read the three-part sentence with a phrasing which sets apart, or makes parenthetical, "worser than Tybalt's death." The actress or actor who is competent in phrasing will isolate such obvious references to parenthetical thought. Some may even pencil in actual parentheses for phrases which are in fact embellishments of the main idea. Such a practical use of the technique will be helpful in the early readings of the script.

The questioning concept. One of the mysteries of phrasing is the actor's use of the interrogative. Stage directors are frequently dismayed at actors who read the question as a declarative sentence or as if they were begging an obvious answer. It is advisable that all interrogatives be read with an "illusion of the first time" so that the audience and fellow actors will interpret the speaker as if he genuinely wished an answer. For some mysterious reason actors tend not to do this naturally or intuitively.

Several illustrations of this concept are evident in Juliet's speech. When Juliet responds to the nurse's question by asking a question, her request must be genuine. If she reads, "Shall I speak ill of him that is my husband?" her attitude and phrasing will cause her, almost unwittingly, to use the forethought technique before saying, "Ah, poor my lord." The emotional level of the utterance of the question is a problem for director and actress alike.

The actress is well advised to use the genuine question-asking concept in her initial readings. When Juliet says, "When I, thy three-hours wife, have mangled it?" it is evident that she is speaking largely to herself. Still, she should ask the question as if she expected a direct answer. Notice how another question cascades on top of it, "But wherefore, villain, didst thou kill my cousin?" The phrasing will heighten the dramatic intensity of the first four lines of Juliet's speech, if they carry with them an illusion of the first time.

Intonation

This term refers to the melodic pattern of a sentence. The position of the individual word on the melody scale is determined by its importance and by the meaning of the sentence. The intonation pattern is also influenced by the character's national or regional origin and by his cultural background.*

To illustrate intonation, write out a number of sentences which contain some natural alternation of phrases, such as the following: "Are you coming in or are you staying out?" "What difference does it make to you, you weren't there?" Read each alternative phrase with different inflections. Did any particular pattern of inflection and intonation seem the most comfortable and natural? What effect did the different intonation patterns have on the meaning of the sentence?

---

* These aspects of intonation are given further discussion in Chapters 6, Stage Dialects, and 7, Line Interpretation.

Pronunciation

The pronunciation of English words varies with geography. One naturally pronounces words as other people in one's original environment do. A problem arises for the actor when the dialogue for a character differs from that to which the actor is accustomed. Sometimes it is difficult for him to determine the correct pronunciation of a particular English word, since common usage often dictates a variation from one period of time to another. Accepting the influence of time and geographical regions on pronunciation, one can generalize that, for citizens of the United States, the so-called "northern standard" pronunciation is most suitable. This should be employed except for those occasions when a character has a precise regional dialect.

Stage
Dialects*

Thy speech bewrayeth thee.

St. Matthew 26:73

DIALECT

Dialect, broadly defined, denotes variations in language or speech. These variations can be quite legitimate or formalized, if one refers to the accepted standard differences within a language, such as in Chinese. It is well known that the Cantonese dialect differs greatly from that which is spoken in the north of China. While not strictly accents, both may be the accepted so-called dictionary languages of their respective areas.

For present purposes, however, the actor uses a more specific definition of dialect as he is concerned only with the variations in the English language. Moreover, he is focusing primarily on those variations which occur either as a result of a bilingual complication (the speech of a person who has learned English as a second language) or those regional variations in countries where English is the principal language. Moreover, he studies a dialect in terms of its theatrical effectiveness rather than from a scientific or purely linguistic point of view.

It is important to state clearly at the outset that it is not the author's intention to undertake a thorough analysis of dialect or to present a detailed, comprehensive listing of the changes which occur in each of the identifiable variants of English speech. There are a number of books which do this quite well and to which the student is referred for more extensive study. The purpose here is (1) to call attention to the importance of the subject, (2) to cite some general guidelines of approach, and (3) to provide a number of suggestions for certain of the major dialects which are most likely to be encountered by the actor.

Proficiency in the use of stage dialects is a skill which, for most people, does not come naturally. It must be learned. Even those who seem to have a natural facility or ear for dialect must practice and study to become truly proficient. It is a technique which the actor must

* This chapter was written by William R. McGraw, Ohio University.

acquire through conscious effort and training. It is a skill which will assist him in the development of the character and in its effective presentation before an audience. For these reasons, a discussion of dialect seems most appropriate in this text.

Since it is important for an actor to be familiar with the common dialects of the stage, it is surprising that some individuals consider dialect an extraneous subject that is of use only to a relatively small number of character actors. In many cases, an actor may avoid the subject because, in his first attempt, he has had little success in acquiring skill for a specific dialect. One need only point out that with considerable regularity actors encounter roles that require, to some degree, a knowledge of dialect and it has been proved repeatedly that, with diligence and study, they are able to acquire a knowledge of dialect sufficient to assist them in the portrayal of their characters.

Furthermore, a study of dialect tends to make the actor more conscious of his total voice and speech skills. As he develops a knowledge of the variations in dialect, he becomes more acutely aware of the differences in normal or standard speech. His ear becomes better trained and he learns to master voice and articulatory control. There also comes the added appreciation of people, with their multitude of differences, as reflected in their peculiarized speech.

The means

Of course it is a great advantage to inherit an "ear" for dialect, but this facility is rarely sufficient unto itself. In one way or another, the natural aptitude must be developed and supplemented. The traditional methods usually include (1) instruction from an authority, (2) exposure to authentic dialect speech, (3) recordings, and most important, (4) practice. All of these are utilized to attain an ear which can recognize the differences in speech sounds as they relate to dialects and to help develop the ability to execute these sounds.

Acquiring proficiency in the use of stage dialects is not a simple or mechanical process. Its ultimate purpose is to help recreate in the theater living characters of depth and dimension. The achievement of such a goal demands a keen awareness of the character's complexity and an ability to recreate this intricacy, in part, through peculiarized speech. Each dialect has its special rhythm, vowel and consonant changes, syntax, and melody pattern, all of which the actor must at one time or another consciously or unconsciously master.

Crocker, Fields, and Broomall state that learning a dialect is very much like studying a new language except that, for the most part, the meaning of the words is known.* Anyone who has attempted the mastery of a second language is aware of the futility of confining his study to the grammar and vocabulary. Rarely is he understood unless he pays particular attention to the details of quality, intonation, stress, and rhythm.

Perhaps the most useful device to employ throughout is the magnetic tape recorder. The individual actor should use it to compare his speech with models of the best dialect, just as the director may use the recorder to assist the entire cast in achieving consistency.

This raises the question of authenticity. As was indicated earlier, stage dialect is not an end in itself. It is essentially a device by which the actor completes the role and adds dimension to the character. If at any time the device interferes with the essential projection of that character, it is self-defeating. Such a problem may develop

---

* Charlotte Crocker, Victor A. Fields, and Will Broomall, *Taking the Stage*. New York: Pitman, 1939, p. 204. Despite the early publication of this particular text, the section on dialects remains one of the few really helpful sources for the actor who seeks to acquire a working knowledge of the subject.

if a truly authentic dialect is employed. The solution lies in compromise: the actor learns to master a consistent suggestion of the dialect, realizing that his primary concern is to be understood. This concern, shared with the director, is for deviations from the authentic to be consistent throughout the cast.

What, then, is the procedure the actor follows in mastering a dialect? To begin with, he studies the play to discover just how his particular character fits into the total scheme, all the while consciously assessing the character's speech. He experiments with the dialect, bearing in mind its relationship to the character and paying particular attention to the choice of words and phrase patterns of the dialogue.

At the same time, he avails himself of every external aid. He listens to examples of the particular dialect from an instructor, from records, or best of all, from someone who naturally speaks the authentic dialect. Throughout this process he trains his ear to recognize the characteristics of pronunciation, rhythm, intonation, and quality which distinguish the dialect from standard English. He uses the tape recorder to listen to his speech not only in isolation, but also as part of the ensemble. Finally, he recognizes the importance of practice, since it is only through continuous work that his ear will become attuned to recognize subtle peculiarities in the dialect. All of this is aimed at creating the most appropriate speech for the role, speech which is individually tailored to a particular character in a particular production.

BRITISH DIALECT

Paradoxically, although it is heard often, British dialect poses a major problem for the actor. The prevalence of British films since World War II has helped educate American audiences to a point where poor imitations are readily perceived. To speak of "British" is, of course, generalizing for, as any subject of England will quickly point out,

there are many variations within Britain beyond the obvious differences between upper class British, Cockney, and Scottish.* There is a sharp contrast, for instance, between the speech of a Yorkshireman and a resident of Cornwall, a Manchester factory worker and a London dockhand. For our purposes, probably the greatest number of roles call for the "educated Englishman," ranging roughly from the upper middle-class professional man to and including the traditional aristocracy. A firm grasp of the major characteristics, coupled with consistent execution, is the actor's goal. Anything less will elicit justifiable criticism.

A knowledge of British dialect is helpful, too, for another reason. Historically, most American actors have striven to imitate the speech of their British colleagues. This fact, plus the interchange of individual actors and casts between London and New York, has resulted in what has come to be called "stage English." This, of course, is neither British nor standard American speech. However, most authorities, including our leading actors and directors, agree that it probably comes the closest to an ideal form of spoken English, particularly for an Elizabethan drama.

The American actor, therefore, attempting to train his voice and improve his speech, especially for work in the classical plays, learns that his knowledge of the British dialect helps considerably in acquiring the best stage English. There will be no attempt here to set standards for ideal stage English, nor is it contended that British actors are generally better speakers because of their dialects. (There is, however, no question of the seriousness with which they pursue the training of their voices.) The point at issue is that

---

* One is reminded of Shaw's Higgins, who in Act I of *Pygmalion* says, "I can place any man within six miles. I can place him within two miles in London. Sometimes within two streets."

a knowledge of British dialect helps the American actor to improve his general stage speech, particularly as he confronts plays in the classical repertory.

Important in this consideration is the greater clarity of enunciation found in the British, the tendency toward more precise pronunciation, a steadier rhythm and flow of words, and the softening of [r] when it is followed by a consonant or is in the final position, as for example, *fahm* (farm) and *cah* (car). The following are just a few changes but ones which are representative of stage English.

Consonants:

[r] is flapped (single trill) when preceded or followed by a vowel, as in *veddy* (very) or *sittious* (serious).

[r] sometimes becomes a vowel glide when in final position, such as *beh-ah* (bear).

Double consonants are often articulated more carefully, as in *fak-tu-al* rather than *fakchual* (factual); or the single vowel is isolated as in *sit-yu-ashun* (situation).

Vowels:

[ă] becomes [ĕ] in many words, as in *flet* (flat).

[ă] becomes [ah] as in *chawnce* (chance). (This should be used sparingly and only when one is certain of its appropriateness.)

[ee] becomes [ĭ] as in *prittĭ*, rather than *prittee* (pretty).

[o] becomes [ĕ-ou] as in *ĕ-ou-pen* (open).

Practice the following lines with the suggested pattern of intonation and make the necessary consonant and vowel changes.

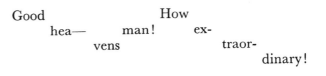

Good   How
    hea—   man!   ex-
        vens   traor-
                          dinary!

         He
Pity!   should   have   sec-
              really   a   ond
                              chance.

Practice Selection

LADY WINDERMERE'S FAN

by Oscar Wilde / excerpt from Act I

LORD DARLINGTON   (*Takes chair and goes across* L. C.) I am quite miserable, Lady Windermere. You must tell me what I did. (*Sits down at table* L.)

LADY WINDERMERE   Well, you kept paying me elaborate compliments the whole evening.

LORD DARLINGTON   (*Smiling*) Ah, now-a-days we are all of us so hard up, that the only pleasant things to pay *are* compliments. They're the only things we *can* pay.

LADY WINDERMERE   (*Shaking her head*) No, I am talking very seriously. You mustn't laugh, I am quite serious. I don't like compliments, and I don't see why a man should think he is pleasing a woman enormously when he says to her a whole heap of things that he doesn't mean.

LORD DARLINGTON	Ah, but I did mean them. (*Takes tea which she offers him.*)
LADY WINDERMERE	(*Gravely*) I hope not. I should be sorry to have to quarrel with you, Lord Darlington. I like you very much, you know that. But I shouldn't like you at all if I thought you were what most other men are. Believe me, you are better than most other men, and I sometimes think you pretend to be worse.
LORD DARLINGTON	We all have our little vanities, Lady Windermere.
LADY WINDERMERE	Why do you make that your special one? (*Still seated at table* L.)
LORD DARLINGTON	(*Still seated* L. C.) Oh, nowadays so many conceited people go about Society pretending to be good, that I think it shows rather a sweet and modest disposition to pretend to be bad. Besides, there is this to be said. If you pretend to be good, the world takes you very seriously. If you pretend to be bad, it doesn't. Such is the astounding stupidity of optimism.
LADY WINDERMERE	Don't you *want* the world to take you seriously then, Lord Darlington?
LORD DARLINGTON	No, not the world. Who are the people the world takes seriously? All the dull people one can think of, from the Bishops down to the bores. I should like *you* to take me very seriously, Lady Windermere, *you* more than anyone else in life.
LADY WINDERMERE	Why—why me?
LORD DARLINGTON	(*After a slight hesitation*) Because I think we might be great friends. Let us be great friends. You may want a friend some day.
LADY WINDERMERE	Why do you say that?
LORD DARLINGTON	Oh! — we all want friends at times.
LADY WINDERMERE	I think we're very good friends already, Lord Darlington. We can always remain so as long as you don't —
LORD DARLINGTON	Don't what?
LADY WINDERMERE	Don't spoil it by saying extravagant, silly things to me. You think I am a Puritan, I suppose? Well, I have something of the Puritan in me. I was brought up like that. I am glad of it. My mother died when I was a mere child. I lived always with Lady Julia, my father's eldest sister, you know. She was stern to me, but she taught me, what the world is forgetting, the difference that there is between what is right and what is wrong. *She* allowed of no compromise. *I* allow of none.
LORD DARLINGTON	My dear Lady Windermere!

LADY WINDERMERE	(*Leaning back on the sofa*) You look on me as being behind the age. — Well I am! I should be sorry to be on the same level as an age like this.
LORD DARLINGTON	You think the age very bad?
LADY WINDERMERE	Yes. Nowadays people seem to look on life as a speculation. It is not a speculation. It is a sacrament. Its ideal is love. Its purification is sacrifice.
LORD DARLINGTON	(*Smiling*) Oh, anything is better than being sacrificed.
LADY WINDERMERE	(*Leaning forward*) Don't say that.
LORD DARLINGTON	I do say it. I feel it — I know it.

Other Sources for Scenes of British Dialect

The collected plays of Noel Coward, George Bernard Shaw, and Oscar Wilde can be used.

IRISH DIALECT

Irish dialect is less difficult to master than British. By the same token, since it is easier for most people to imitate, a tendency to reproduce little more than the broadest aspects of "Pat and Mike" is characteristic of many actors. This, of course, is to be avoided, unless the role calls for such a stereotype.

There is a definite musical effect with Irish speech, due largely to the wide pitch fluctuation and its marked rhythmic flow. These factors, coupled with a fairly rapid rate and an obvious emotionalism in delivery, result in a dialect of wide coloration and beauty. One immediately thinks of how the speech directly reflects the Irish character. Conviviality, sentimentality, and anger are rarely concealed, but rather are manifested continuously in word and action. Consequently, the dialect lends itself extremely well to the theater where outward expression of inner feeling is paramount.

The fact that the major Irish plays are written by dramatists supremely conscious of syntax and idiomatic speech no doubt makes the portrayal of this dialect less difficult in the theater. O'Casey and Synge, for instance, are poets who rely heavily on the highly imagistic speech of the people. The result is that in reading a typical line of dialogue from one of their plays, with little attention paid to the other aspects of the dialect, a distinct flavor comes through because of word choice alone. This fact, of course, highlights a very important rule with respect to this and any other dialect in the drama: hold precisely to the wording given by the playwright. Paraphrasing or "improving" on the written dialogue, a habit many actors fall into, is never advisable and is particularly disastrous in a dialect play.

Other characteristics which one should remember are (1) the tendency to place considerable stress at the beginning of sentences, particularly those which start emotionally; (2) a thrusting of the breath forward and backward in the mouth; and (3) the deliberate addition of the aspirate [h] in such words as *hwhat* (what) and *afther* (after).

Just as important as any of these, however, are the key vowel and consonant changes. The most prominent of the consonant changes is the trilled [r]. In a word such as fair, a diphthong is almost derived, with *fay-ur* the result. In other instances, the [r] is not actually trilled but serves somewhat like a vowel, as in hard, which becomes *har-r-r-d*.

Other consonant changes are:

[th] becomes [t] as in *t'ing* (thing).

[t] often becomes [th] as in *thrust* (trust).

[s] becomes [sh] before consonants as in *shtick* (stick).

Of the vowel changes, the following are the most helpful.

[i] becomes [oi] as in *oice* (ice).

[a] is softened to [ä] as in *ädd* (add).

[ā] becomes [ĕ-uh] as in *ge-uht* (gate).

[ē] often becomes ā as in *tay* (tea).

[ŭ] becomes [oo] as in *yoong* (young).

Try the following intonation patterns, making the necessary vowel and consonant changes.

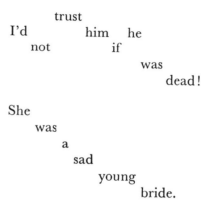

```
            trust
I'd             him   he
    not              if
                        was
                            dead!

She
    was
        a
          sad
              young
                   bride.
```

Practice Selections

THE PLAYBOY OF THE WESTERN WORLD

by John Millington Synge | excerpt from Act III*

CHARACTERS   PEGEEN and CHRISTY.

(*In* The Playboy of the Western World, *Synge is spoofing romanticism. When* CHRISTY *tells the townspeople that he has killed his father, they accept him as a hero and he responds by strutting like one. It is not surprising that* PEGEEN *has fallen in love with him and he with her.*)

SCENE   *Country public-house or shebeen, very rough and untidy.*

---

* John Millington Synge, *The Playboy of the Western World.* Reprinted by permission of Bruce Humphries, Boston. (Note the intimate bond of feeling and the casual informality in the scene from *The Playboy of the Western World,* Plate 22.)

PEGEEN   (*Radiantly, wiping his face with her shawl*) Well, you're the lad, and you'll have great times from this out when you could win that wealth of prizes, and you sweating in the heat of noon!

CHRISTY   (*Looking at her with delight*) I'll have great times if I win the crowning prize I'm seeking now, and that's your promise that you'll wed me in a fortnight, when our banns is called.

PEGEEN   (*Backing away from him*) You're right daring to go ask me that, when all knows you'll be starting to some girl in your own townland, when your father's rotten in four months, or five.

CHRISTY   (*Indignantly*) Starting from you, is it? (*He follows her.*) I will not, then, and when the airs is warming in four months, or five, it's then yourself and me should be pacing Neifin in the dews of night, the times sweet smells do be rising, and you'd see a little shiny new moon, maybe, sinking on the hills.

PEGEEN   (*Looking at him playfully*) And it's that kind of a poacher's love you'd make, Christy Mahon, on the sides of Neifin, when the night is down?

CHRISTY   It's little you'll think if my love's a poacher's, or an earl's itself, when you'll feel my two hands stretched around you, and I squeezing kisses on your puckered lips, till I'd feel a kind of pity for the Lord God is all ages sitting lonesome in his golden chair.

PEGEEN   That'll be right fun, Christy Mahon, and any girl would walk her heart out before she'd meet a young man was your like for eloquence, or talk, at all.

CHRISTY   (*Encouraged*) Let you wait, to hear me talking, till we're astray in Erris, when Good Friday's by, drinking a sup from a well, and making mighty kisses with our wetted mouths, or gaming in a gap or sunshine, with yourself stretched back unto your necklace, in the flowers of the earth.

PEGEEN   (*In a lower voice, moved by his tone*) I'd be nice so, is it?

CHRISTY   (*With rapture*) If the mitred bishops seen you that time, they'd be the like of the holy prophets, I'm thinking, do be straining the bars of Paradise to lay eyes on the Lady Helen of Troy, and she abroad, pacing back and forward, with a nosegay in her golden shawl.

PEGEEN   (*With real tenderness*) And what is it I have, Christy Mahon, to make me fitting entertainment for the like of you, that has such poet's talking, and such bravery of heart?

CHRISTY	(*In a low voice*) Isn't there the light of seven heavens in your heart alone, the way you'll be an angel's lamp to me from this out, and I abroad in the darkness, spearing salmons in the Owen, or the Carrowmore?
PEGEEN	If I was your wife, I'd be alone with you those nights, Christy Mahon, the way you'd see I was a great hand at coaxing bailiffs, or coining funny nick-names for the stars of night.
CHRISTY	You, is it? Taking your death in the hailstones, or in the fogs of dawn.
PEGEEN	Yourself and me would shelter easy in a narrow bush, (*With a qualm of dread*) but we're only talking, maybe, for this would be a poor, thatched place to hold a fine lad is the like of you.
CHRISTY	(*Putting his arm round her*) If I wasn't a good Christian, it's on my naked knees I'd be saying my prayers and paters to every jackstraw you have roofing your head, and every stony pebble is paving the laneway to your door.
PEGEEN	(*Radiantly*) If that's the truth, I'll be burning candles from this out to the miracles of God that have brought you from the south to-day, and I, with my gowns bought ready, the way that I can wed you, and not wait at all.
CHRISTY	It's miracles, and that's the truth. Me there toiling a long while, and walking a long while, not knowing at all I was drawing all times nearer to this holy day.
PEGEEN	And myself, a girl, was tempted often to go sailing the seas till I'd marry a Jew-man, with ten kegs of gold, and I not knowing at all there was the like of you drawing nearer, like the stars of God.
CHRISTY	And to think I'm long years hearing women talking that talk, to all bloody fools, and this the first time I've heard the like of your voice talking sweetly for my own delight.
PEGEEN	And to think it's me is talking sweetly, Christy Mahon, and I the fright of seven townlands for my biting tongue. Well, the heart's a wonder; and, I'm thinking, there won't be our like in Mayo, for gallant lovers, from this hour, to-day. (*Drunken singing is heard outside.*) There's my father coming from the wake, and when he's had his sleep we'll tell him, for he's peaceful then. (*They separate.*)

JUNO AND THE PAYCOCK

by Sean O'Casey / opening scene from Act III*

SCENE

It is about half-past six on a November evening; a bright fire is burning in the grate; MARY, *dressed to go out, is sitting on a chair by the fire, leaning forward, her hands under her chin, her elbows on her knees. A look of dejection, mingled with uncertain anxiety, is on her face. A lamp, turned low, is on the table. The votive light under the picture of the Virgin gleams more redly than ever.* MRS. BOYLE *is standing front of table, looking anxiously at* MARY.

MRS. BOYLE

An' has Bentham never even written to you since — not one line for the past month?

MARY

(*Tonelessly*) Not even a line, mother.

MRS. BOYLE

That's very curious. . . . What came between the two of yous at all? To leave you so sudden, an' yous so great together. (*She goes back round* R. *of table, and takes up coat and hat from bed in alcove.*) To go away t' England, an' not to even leave you his address. The way he was always bringin' you to dances, I thought he was mad afther you. Are you sure you said nothin' to him?

MARY

No, mother — at least nothing that could possible explain his givin' me up.

MRS. BOYLE

You know you're a bit hasty at times, Mary, an' say things you shouldn't say.

MARY

I never said to him what I shouldn't say, I'm sure of that.

MRS BOYLE

(*Coming back to front of table*) How are you sure of it?

MARY

Because I love him with all my heart and soul, mother. Why, I don't know; I often thought to myself that he wasn't the man poor Jerry was, but I couldn't help loving him, all the same.

MRS. BOYLE

But you shouldn't be frettin' the way you are; when a woman loses a man, she never knows what she's afther losin', to be sure, but, then, she never knows what she's afther gainin', either. You're not the one girl of a month ago — you look like one pinin' away. It's long ago I had a right to bring you to the doctor, instead of waitin' till to-night.

MARY

There's no necessity, really, mother, to go to the doctor; nothing serious is wrong with me — I'm run down and disappointed, that's all.

---

* Sean O'Casey, *Juno and the Paycock.* Copyright, 1925 (A–814996), by Macmillan. Reprinted by permission of St. Martin's Press and Macmillan.

MRS. BOYLE	I'll not wait another minute; I don't like the look of you at all. . . . I'm afraid we made a mistake in throwin' over poor Jerry. . . . He'd have been betther for you than that Bentham.
MARY	Mother, the best man for a woman is the one for whom she has the most love, and Charley had it all.
MRS. BOYLE	(*Putting on her hat and coat*) Well, there's one thing to be said for him — he couldn't have been thinkin' of the money, or he wouldn't ha' left you . . . it must ha' been somethin' else.
MARY	(*Wearily*) I don't know . . . I don't know, mother . . . only I think . . .
MRS. BOYLE	What d'ye think?
MARY	I imagine . . . he thought . . . we weren't . . . good enough for him.
MRS. BOYLE	(*Indignantly*) An' what was he himself, only a school teacher? Though I don't blame him for fightin' shy of people like that Joxer fella an' that oul' Madigan wan — nice sort o' people for your father to introduce to a man like Mr. Bentham. You might have told me all about this before now, Mary; I don't know why you like to hide everything from your mother; you knew Bentham, an' I'd ha' known nothin' about it if it hadn't bin for the Will; an' it was only to-day, afther long coaxin', that you let out that he'd left you.
MARY	It would have been useless to tell you — you wouldn't understand.
MRS. BOYLE	(*Hurt*) Maybe not. . . . Maybe I wouldn't understand. . . . Well, we'll be off now.

Other Sources for Scenes of Irish Dialect

The Collected Plays of Brendan Behan, Paul Vincent Carroll, Lady Gregory, Lennox Robinson, Sean O'Casey, and John Millington Synge can be used.

COCKNEY DIALECT

There is considerable demand for the Cockney dialect just as there is for the standard British and Irish. In fact, a knowledge of these three, plus Scottish, could serve the actor in perhaps half of the plays in which a knowledge of some particular dialect might be required.

Technically, Cockney is spoken only by the lower-class Londoner, although its influence has been felt in other cities. A Cockney enjoys talking and is rarely at a loss for words. He is willing to express an opinion on any subject and, although his erudition is limited, we note in his oratory that prevalent characteristic of all unsophisticated people, a basic common sense. Although somewhat less so, the dialect is similar to the Irish in its use of imagery—especially in its references to the physical world, the senses, and the basic appetites.

Probably the most outstanding characteristic is the great use of diphthongs and triphthongs (*ble-ook* — bloke. *Thets raw-eet-suh* — That's right, sir). Another is the presence of an extreme pitch fluctuation. Despite the predominantly high pitch, the result is a singularly melodic effect. The smoothness of flow, however, is frequently interrupted by the glottal stop which, when it occurs repeatedly, counters the glide that prevails in using the elongated vowels. Apostrophes indicate the glottal stop in the last two words of this sentence: *Thet's uh deh'ee bah'ul.* (That's a dirty bottle.)

Other important points to remember are (1) the overall rate is relatively slow; (2) like the standard British, the sound appears to be projected forward in the mouth and is decidedly nasal in timbre; and (3) the overall effect, in contrast to standard British, is the lack of precision in articulation — a definite slovenliness. But remember, only the effect of such indistinctness can be conveyed. An authentic Cockney would be unintelligible to the average American audience.

The major consonant changes in Cockney:

[h] drop the [h] in most words such as hold and hate, which become *'old* and *'ate,* and

[h] add the [h] when the preceding word ends in a vowel. The former change occurs more often than the latter. For example, changes would result in: *an 'ouse; H'it should be an 'ome.*

[r] is often introduced thus: *abart* (about,) or *ort* (ought).

[r] is often softened: *wuth* (worth).

[th] may, on occasion, become [f] or [v] as in *wiv* (with) and *froat* (throat).

The major vowel changes are:

[ā] becomes [i] as in *tike* (take).

[ī] becomes [awee] as *saw-eet* (sight).

[ou] becomes [a-oo] as in *a-oot* (out) or the [r] is added as in *art* (out).

[ō] becomes [eh-oop] (hope).

Try the following, making the proper vowel and consonant adjustments.

All   Any-
        Governor.   thing   say.
    right   you

Out
    of   heathen!
        my   ruddy
            sight! You

Plate 22. *The Playboy of the Western World* by John Millington Synge. Scene depicting informality and warm intimacy. Denison Summer Theater. Director: William Brasmer.

Practice Selection

THE OLD LADY SHOWS HER MEDALS

*by James M. Barrie / a one-act play**

MRS. DOWEY	Just one more winkle, Mrs. Mickleham? (*Indeed there is only one more.*) (*But* MRS. MICKLEHAM *indicates politely that if she took this one it would have to swim for it. The* HAGGERTY WOMAN *takes it long afterwards when she thinks, erroneously, that no one is looking.*) (MRS. TWYMLEY *is sulky. Evidently someone has contradicted her. Probably the* HAGGERTY WOMAN.)
MRS. TWYMLEY	I say it is so.
THE HAGGERTY WOMAN	I say it may be so.
MRS. TWYMLEY	I suppose I ought to know: me that has a son a prisoner in Germany. (*She has obviously scored that all good feeling seems to call upon her to end here. But she continues rather shabbily.*) Being the only lady present that has that proud misfortune. (*The others are stung.*)
MRS. DOWEY	My son is fighting in France.
MRS. MICKLEHAM	Mine is wounded in two places.
THE HAGGERTY WOMAN	Mine is at Salonaiky. (*The absurd pronunciation of this uneducated person moves the others to mirth.*)
MRS. DOWEY	You'll excuse us, Mrs. Haggerty, but the correct pronunciation is Salonikky.
THE HAGGERTY WOMAN	(*To cover her confusion*) I don't think. (*She feels that even this does not prove her case.*) And I speak as one that has War Savings Certificates.
MRS. TWYMLEY	We all have them. (*The* HAGGERTY WOMAN *whimpers and the other guests regard her with unfeeling disdain.*)
MRS. DOWEY	(*To restore cheerfulness*) Oh, it's a terrible war.
ALL	(*Brightening*) It is. You may say so.

---

* James M. Barrie, *The Old Lady Shows Her Medals.* Copyright, 1918, by Charles Scribner's. Copyright renewal, 1946, by Lady Asquith and Peter L. Davies. Reprinted by permission of Hodder and Stoughton, and Charles Scribner's.

MRS. DOWEY	(*Encouraged*) What I say is, the men is splendid, but I'm none so easy about the staff. That's your weak point, Mrs. Mickleham.
MRS. MICKLEHAM	(*On the defence, but determined to reveal nothing that might be of use to the enemy*) You may take it from me, the staff's all right.
MRS. DOWEY	And very relieved I am to hear you say it. (*It is here that the* HAGGERTY WOMAN *has the remaining winkle.*)
MRS. MICKLEHAM	You don't understand properly about trench warfare. If I had a map —
MRS. DOWEY	(*Wetting her finger to draw lines on the table*) That's the river Sommy. Now, if we had barrages here —
MRS. TWYMLEY	Very soon you would be enfilided. Where's your supports, my lady? (MRS. DOWEY *is damped.*)
MRS. MICKLEHAM	What none of you grasps is that this is a artillery war —
THE HAGGERTY WOMAN	(*Strengthened by the winkle*) I say that the word is Salonaiky. (*The others purse their lips.*)
MRS. TWYMLEY	(*With terrible meaning*) We'll change the subject. Have you seen this week's *Fashion Chat*? (*She has evidently seen and devoured it herself, and even licked up the crumbs.*) The gabardine with accordion pleats has quite gone out.
MRS. DOWEY	(*Her old face sparkling*) My sakes! You tell me?
MRS. TWYMLEY	(*With the touch of haughtiness that comes of great topics*) The plain smock has come in again, with silk lacing, giving that charming chic effect.
MRS. DOWEY	Oho!
MRS. MICKLEHAM	I must say I was always partial to the straight line (*Thoughtfully regarding the want of line in* MRS. TWYMLEY's *person*) though trying to them as is of too friendly a figure. (*It is here that the* HAGGERTY WOMAN's *fingers close unostentatiously upon a piece of sugar.*)
MRS. TWYMLEY	(*Sailing into the Empyrean*) Lady Dolly Kanister was seen conversing across the railings in a dainty *de jou*.
MRS. DOWEY	Fine would I have liked to see her.
MRS. TWYMLEY	She is equally popular as maid, wife, and munition-worker. Her two children is inset. Lady Pops Babington was married in a tight tulle.
MRS. MICKLEHAM	What was her going-away dress?

MRS. TWYMLEY	A champagny cream velvet with dreamy corsage. She's married to Colonel the Hon. Chingford — "Snubs," they called him at Eton.
THE HAGGERTY WOMAN	(*Having disposed of the sugar*) Very likely he'll be sent to Salonaiky.
MRS. MICKLEHAM	Wherever he is sent, she'll have the same tremors as the rest of us. She'll be as keen to get the letters wrote with pencils as you or me.
MRS. TWYMLEY	Them pencil letters.
MRS. DOWEY	(*In her sweet Scotch voice, timidly, afraid she may be going too far*) And women in enemy lands gets those pencil letters and then stop getting them, the same as ourselves. Let's occasionally think of that. (*She has gone too far. Chairs are pushed back.*)

Other Sources for Scenes of Cockney Dialect

A Night at an Inn by Lord Dunsany, *The Emperor Jones* by Eugene O'Neill, *Pygmalion* by George Bernard Shaw, *Outward Bound* by Sutton Vane, and *Philadelphia, Here I Come* by Brian Friel.

SCOTTISH DIALECT

Scottish dialect is considered more difficult to master than the other British Isles accents, but with some diligence and concentration at the outset on four or five major characteristics, the feel can be acquired and the details mastered with no greater difficulty than for other dialects. Certainly there is less demand for a knowledge of Scottish dialect than for British, Irish, or Cockney; but by the same token, when it is required, there are fewer actors available who can execute it. This gives an advantage to those who can.

The prime concerns in Scottish dialect are (1) the "glottal stop" combined with an overall staccato rhythm, (2) a narrow pitch range, (3) an inhibited tongue, (4) the burred [r], and (5) the key vowel changes.

The glottal stop is executed by simply using the glottis (the aperture in the vocal folds of the larynx) as a modifier of sound in place of the lips or tongue. In the word "bottle," for instance, instead of the tongue breaking the air after the first syllable, the glottis performs the task alone. This use of the glottis tends to create an overall staccato effect and is consistent with the clipped or inhibited tongue factor. The latter characteristic has been described as "hot potato speech" which, incidentally, is a clue to one of the best ways of getting initially attuned to the sound of the dialect.

In many ways the Scottish contrasts sharply with the Irish, most notably in the realm of pitch. In fact, the intonational pattern of the Scottish is so conservative that one considers it monotonous, especially as compared with the Irish or the Romance dialects. It is probably more accurate to say that the musical effect is simply more subtle, which may account in part for the difficulty some actors have in mastering it.

The trilled [r] is especially important when combined with certain vowel sounds. The [er] in the word "term", for instance, becomes "air", so that the effect is *tairm* and *sairtun* (certain).

Another change is the use of [na] in place of "not" or the contraction [n't] in such cases as *woud na* (would not) or *coud na* (could not). *I woud-na go*, for example.

A consonant change which may be used sparingly is the [ch] sound for [gh] in such words as weight and light so that the effect is *weicht* and *licht*.

The key vowel changes are:

[ă]   becomes [à] as in *ànd*(and).

[ĭ]   becomes [ee] as in *eece* (ice). Use sparingly.

[oo] The [oo] sound (as in good) becomes [ōō] as in food; thus the word "put" becomes *poot*.

[ou] (as in out) becomes [ōō] as in *aboot* (about).

Try the following:

He's
   a
     fuhrst   rate   män.

I'm shoo-urr   its   aboot   time   to   tuh'rrn
   oot the
     licht.

Practice Selection

THE OLD LADY SHOWS HER MEDALS

by James M. Barrie / a one-act play*

DOWEY

Do you recognise your loving son, missis? ("*Oh, the fine Scotch tang of him,*" *she thinks.*)

MRS. DOWEY

(*Trembling*) I'm pleased I wrote so often. ("*Oh, but he's raised,*" *she thinks.*)
(*He strides toward her, and seizes the letters roughly.*)

DOWEY

Let's see them.
(*There is a string round the package, and he unties it, and examines the letters at his leisure with much curiosity. The envelopes are in order, all addressed in pencil to* MRS. DOWEY, *with the proud words "Opened by Censor" on them. But the letter paper inside contains not a word of writing.*)

DOWEY

Nothing but blank paper. Is this your writing in pencil on the envelope?
(*She nods, and he gives the matter further consideration.*)
The covey told me you were a charwoman; so I suppose you picked the envelopes out of waste-paper baskets, or such like, and then changed the addresses?

(She nods again; still she dares not look up, but she is admiring his legs. When, however, he would cast the letters into the fire, she flames up with sudden spirit. She clutches them.)

MRS. DOWEY   Don't burn them letters, mister.

DOWEY   They're not real letters.

MRS. DOWEY   They're all I have.

DOWEY   *(Returning to irony)* I thought you had a son?

MRS. DOWEY   I never had a man nor a son nor anything. I just call myself Missis to give me a standing.

DOWEY   Well, it's past my seeing through.
(He turns to look for some explanation from the walls. She gets a peep at him at last. Oh, what a grandly set-up man. Oh, the stride of him. Oh, the noble rage of him. Oh, Samson had been like this before that woman took him in hand.)

DOWEY   *(Whirling round on her)* What made you do it?

MRS. DOWEY   It was everybody's war, mister, except mine. *(She beats her arms.)* I wanted it to be my war too.

DOWEY   You'll need to be plainer. And yet I'm d —— d if I care to hear you, you lying old trickster.
(The words are merely what were to be expected, and so are endurable; but he has moved towards the door.)

MRS. DOWEY   You're not going already, mister?

DOWEY   Yes, I just came to give you an ugly piece of my mind.

MRS. DOWEY   *(Holding out her arms longingly)* You haven't gave it to me yet.

DOWEY   You have a cheek.

MRS. DOWEY   *(Giving further proof of it)* You wouldn't drink some tea?

DOWEY   Me. I tell you I came here for the one purpose of blazing away at you.
(It is such a roaring negative that it blows her into a chair. But she is up again in a moment, is this spirited old lady.)

MRS. DOWEY   You could drink tea while you was blazing away. There's winkles.

DOWEY   Is there?
(He turns interestedly toward the table, but his proud Scots character checks him, which is just as well, for what she should have said was that there had been winkles.)

Not me. You're just a common rogue. (*He seats himself far from the table.*) Now, then, out with it. Sit down! (*She sits meekly; there is nothing she would not do for him.*) As you char, I suppose you are on your feet all day.

MRS. DOWEY   I'm more on my knees.

DOWEY   That's where you should be to me.

MRS. DOWEY   Oh, mister, I'm willing.

DOWEY   Stop it. Go on, you accomplished liar.

MRS. DOWEY   It's true that my name is Dowey.

DOWEY   It's enough to make me change mine.

MRS. DOWEY   I've been charring and charring and charring as far back as I mind. I've been in London this twenty years.

DOWEY   We'll skip your early days. I have an appointment.

MRS. DOWEY   And then when I was old the war broke out.

DOWEY   How could it affect you?

MRS. DOWEY   Oh, mister, that's the thing. It didn't affect me. It affected everybody but me. The neighbors looked down on me. Even the posters, on the walls, of the woman saying, "Go, my boy," leered at me. I sometimes cried by myself in the dark. You won't have a cup of tea?

DOWEY   No.

MRS. DOWEY   Sudden like the idea came to me to pretend I had a son.

DOWEY   You depraved old limmer. But what in the name of Old Nick made you choose me out of the whole British Army?

MRS. DOWEY   (*Giggling*) Maybe, mister, it was because I liked you best.

Other Sources for Scenes of Scottish Dialect

The Little Minister by James M. Barrie, *What Every Woman Knows* by James M. Barrie, and *The Hasty Heart* by John Patrick.

FRENCH DIALECT

French dialect, like the French language itself, is very pleasing to hear. As with the other dialects, it is a direct reflection of the character of the people. Although they pride themselves on their logic, which emerges consistently in their conversation, such rational thought does not always preclude excitable or emotional behavior. This quite naturally leads to animated speech, generously accompanied by hand gestures. It should be quite obvious that, as in the case of the Irish and the Italian, the French dialect lends itself extremely well to the stage.

There tends to be a fairly wide fluctuation on the scale with the dominant pitch essentially high. Unlike English speech, there is a rise in pitch as the sentence progresses. This is consistent with the tendency to place the emphasis on the last syllable of words, as in the following:

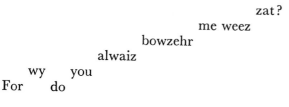

Another characteristic is that, although stress tends to fall toward the end of polysyllabic words, each syllable is heard distinctly and is given full valuation in terms of time. Overall tempo is fast. Try the following at a brisk rate:

Just as important, too, is the characteristic nasal timbre. This is definitely a hypernasal effect where resonance is permitted in the nose, coupled with a peculiar additional resonance in the mouth and head. It is not to be confused with the constricted nasality of a head cold (hyponasality). The key to an acceptable nasal quality lies in the use of the soft palate. In the words *Mon Cheri* let the resonance occur for the first word in the rear of the nasal cavities (do not sound the [n]). In the second word, twist the [r] with the back of the tongue and the soft palate. The latter is often termed the uvular [r]. *Mõ' Cheh-ree'*, for example.

In making all vowel changes, remember that there are no diphthongs in the French language and thus none in the dialect.

Crucial changes include:

[ĭ] becomes [ee] as in *eet* (it).
[ā] becomes [eh] as in *gret* (great).
[ă] becomes [à] as in *fàt* (fat).

Important consonant changes, in addition to the uvular or rolled [r], include:

[th] becomes [z] when voiced, as in *zees* (this).
[th] becomes [s] when unvoiced, as in *sink* (think).
[h] is eliminated, as in *'arm* (harm).
[d] and [t] are eliminated when in the final position, as in *an'* (and); *firs'* (first).

Practice Selection

FASHION

by Anna Cora Mowatt / excerpt from Act III, Scene 2

CHARACTERS   MILLINETTE, *a French Lady's maid*
COUNT JOLIMAITRE, *a fashionable European importation*
GERTRUDE, *a governess*

SCENE   *Housekeeper's Room. Enter* MILLINETTE, R.

MILLINETTE   I have set zat *bête*, Adolph, to watch for him. He say he would come back so soon as Madame's voiture drive from ze door. If he not come — but he will — he will — he *bien étourdi*, but he have *bon coeur*.

Enter COUNT, L.

COUNT   Ah! Millinette, my dear, you see what a good-natured dog I am to fly at your bidding —

MILLINETTE   Fly? Ah! *trompeur!* What for you fly from Paris? What for you leave me — and I love you so much? When you sick — you almost die — did I not stay by you — take care of you — and you have no else friend? What for you leave Paris?

COUNT   Never allude to disagreeable subjects, *mon enfant!* I was forced by uncontrollable circumstances to fly to ze land of liberty —

MILLINETTE   What you do with all ze money I give you? The last sou I had — did I not give you?

COUNT   I dare say you did, *ma petite* — wish you'd been better supplied! (*Aside*) Don't ask any questions here — can't explain now — the next time we meet —

MILLINETTE   But, ah, when shall we meet — ven? You do not deceive me, not any more.

COUNT   Deceive you! I'd rather deceive myself — I wish I could! I'd persuade myself you were once more washing linen in the Seine! (*Aside*)

MILLINETTE   I will tell you when we shall meet — On Friday night Madame give one grand ball — you come *sans doute* — Zen when ze supper is served — ze Americans tink of nothing else when ze supper come — zen you steal out of ze room, and you find me here — and you give me one grand *explanation!*

Enter GERTRUDE, R., *unperceived.*

COUNT	Friday night — while supper is serving — *parole d'honneur* I will be there — I will explain everything — my sudden departure from Paris — my — demme, my countship — everything! Now let me go — if any of the family should discover us —
GERTRUDE	(*Who during the last speech has gradually advanced,* L.) They might discover more than you think it advisable for them to know!
COUNT	The devil!
MILLINETTE	*Mon dieu!* Mademoiselle Gertrude!
COUNT	(*Recovering himself*) My dear Miss Gertrude, let me explain — aw — aw — nothing is more natural than the situation in which you find me —
GERTRUDE	I am inclined to believe that, Sir.
COUNT	Now — 'pon my honor, that's not fair. Here is Millinette will bear witness to what I am about to say —
GERTRUDE	Oh, I have not the slightest doubt of that, Sir.
COUNT	You see, Millinette happened to be lady's-maid in the family of — of — the Duchess Chateau D'Espagne — and I chanced to be a particular friend of the Duchess — *very particular* I assure you! Of course I saw Millinette, and she, demme, she saw me! Didn't you, Millinette?
MILLINETTE	Oh! oui — Mademoiselle, I knew him ver' well.
COUNT	Well, it is a remarkable fact that — being in correspondence with this very Duchess — at this very time —
GERTRUDE	That is sufficient, Sir — I am already so well acquainted with your extraordinary talents for improvisation, that I will not further tax your invention —
MILLINETTE	Ah! Mademoiselle Gertrude do' not betray us — have pity!
COUNT	(*Assuming an air of dignity*) Silence, Millinette! My word has been doubted — the word of a nobleman! I will inform my friend, Mrs. Tiffany, of this young person's audacity. (*Going*)
GERTRUDE	His own weapons alone can foil this villain! (*Aside*) Sir — Sir — Count! (*At the last word the* COUNT *turns*) Perhaps, Sir, the least said about this matter the better!
COUNT	(*Delightedly*) The least said? We won't say anything at all. She's coming round — couldn't resist me. (*Aside*) Charming Gertrude —

MILLINETTE	*Quoi?* What zat you say?
COUNT	My sweet, adorable Millinette, hold your tongue, will you? (*Aside to her*)
MILLINETTE	(*Aloud*) No, I will not! If you do look so from out your eyes at her again, I will tell all!
COUNT	Oh, I never could manage two women at once, — jealousy makes the dear creatures so spiteful. The only valor is in flight! (*Aside*) Miss Gertrude, I wish you good morning. Millinette, *mon enfant*, adieu (*Exit, L.*)
MILLINETTE	But I have one word more to say. Stop, Stop! (*Exit after him.*)

Other Sources for Scenes of French Dialect

The Happy Time and *Sabrina Fair* by Samuel Taylor.

ITALIAN DIALECT

Since both are Romance languages, there are certain similarities between the French and Italian dialects. For instance, the tempo is fast in both, and each tends to reflect directly the emotionalism of the speaker. Certain vowel and consonant changes are the same, such as:

[ĭ]   becomes [ee] as in *heet* (hit).

[ă]   becomes [à] as in *àsk* (ask).

The Italian tends to roll his [r], although it is more of a tongue-tip trill than uvular.

For the purposes of reproducing the dialect, however, it is the differences with which the actor must be primarily concerned. For instance, the Italian usually varies his pitch in steps rather than slides, that is, the intonation changes are sharp rather than gradual. This often creates a rather abrupt or explosive effect, as may be noted in the following:

Wats a
    da
      mat? (What's the matter?)

or

      much-a
We gotta   trub. (We have much trouble.)

The above phrases also illustrate two other characteristics which the actor should bear in mind: (1) the tendency to add the unstressed [uh] sound following consonant word endings and (2) apocope, the tendency to cut off syllables, particularly at the end of phrases or sentences. It has been pointed out that this characteristic is derived from the widely practiced "troncamento" in the native language "to serve the purposes of euphony."* Another sentence illustrating this would be:

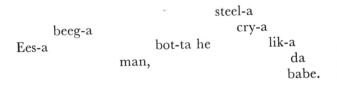

---

* Crocker, Fields, and Broomall, *Taking the Stage*, p. 267.

Other changes include:

[th] (voiced) becomes [d] as in *dere* (there).

[d] and [t] are executed with the tongue touching the upper front teeth.

[wh] is rarely given except with the [h] unvoiced — what becomes *wat*.

[ĕ] becomes [a] as in *frand* (friend).

[ŭ] becomes [o] as in *op* (up).

Practice Selection

THEY KNEW WHAT THEY WANTED

by Sidney Howard / excerpt from Act I*

SITUATION   TONY, *a prosperous man of sixty years, is about to marry a young woman whom he has wooed by correspondence.*

FATHER MCKEE   Why didn't you get married forty years ago?

TONY   I think you know verra good w'y. Ees because I'm no dam' fool. . . . W'en I'm young, I got nothing. I'm broke all da time, you remember? I got no money for havin' wife. I don' want no wife for mak' her work all da time. Da's no good, dat. Da's mak' her no more young, no more prett'. Evrabody say Tony is crazy for no' havin' wife. I say Tony is no dam' fool. W'at is happen? Pro'ibish' is com'. Salute! (*A glass of wine.* AH GEE *has returned to his kitchen.*) An' wat I say? I say, "Ees dam' fool law. Ees dam' fool fellas for bein' scare' an' pullin' up da grape' for tryin' growin' som'thing different." W'at I'm doin'? I'm keep the grape, eh? I say, "I come in dees country for growin' da grape! God mak' dees country for growin' da grape! Ees not for pro'ibish' God mak' dees country. Ees for growin' da grape!" Ees true? Sure ees true! (*Another glass of wine*) An' w'at happen? Before pro'ibish' I sell my grape' for ten, maybe twelve dollar a ton. Now I sell my grape' some'time one hundra dollar' da ton. Pro'ibish' is mak' me verra rich. (*Another glass of wine*) I got fine house. I got Joe for bein' foreman. I got two men for helpin' Joe. I got one Chink for cook. I got one Ford car. I got all I want, evrathing, excep' only wife. Now I'm goin' have wife. Verra nice an' young an' fat. Not for work. No! For sit an' holdin' da hands and havin' kids. Three kids. (*He demonstrates the altitude of each.*) Antonio . . . Giuseppe . . . Anna . . . . Da's like trees an' cows an' all good people. Da's fine for God an' evrabody! I tell you, Padre, Tony know w'at he want!

FATHER MCKEE   Whatever made you think a man of your age could have children? (*This staggers* TONY.) I tell you, it ain't possible.

---

* Sidney Howard, *They Knew What They Wanted.* Copyright, 1925, by Sidney Howard. Reprinted by permission of Charles Scribner's.

TONY	Eh? Tony is too old for havin' kids? I tell you, Tony can have twent' kids if he want! I tell you, Tony can have kids w'en he is one hundra year' old. Dio mio! From da sole of his feet to da top of his hat, Tony is big, strong man! I think I ondrastan' you verra good, Padre. Tony is not too old for havin' kids, He's too rich, eh? (*This rather strikes home.*) Yah! Tony is rich an', if he don' have no kids, den da church is gettin' all Tony's money an' da Padre is gettin' Tony's fine house all fix' up good for livin' in, eh?
FATHER MCKEE	(*A very severe shepherd*) Tony!
TONY	(*The horns of the devil with his fingers*) Don' you go for puttin' no evil eye on Tony an' his Amy!
FATHER MCKEE	You're givin' way to ignorant superstition, which ain't right in no good Cath'lic.
TONY	(*On his feet in a panic*) Dio mio! My Amy is comin' on dat train an' here you keep me, sittin', talkin' . . .

Other Sources for Scenes of Italian Dialect

A View from the Bridge by Arthur Miller, *The Rose Tattoo* by Tennessee Williams, and *Golden Boy* by Clifford Odets.

GERMAN DIALECT

For several reasons, German dialect is comparatively easy for the American actor to grasp. Germans tend to employ stress in the same manner as Americans do, both within a sentence and in the polysyllabic word. Also, the melody pattern tends to be quite similar to that of the English language, although the fluctuation on the scale is somewhat greater.

One of the noticeable differences in the German dialect is the extension of vowel sounds, whether it be monothong or diphthong. This can be exemplified in such words as around, which becomes *ara-oond*, and like, which becomes *la-eek*.

Another characteristic often overdone, but nonetheless significant, is the guttural quality which pervades both vowel and consonant sounds. Try the following sentence: *Ach ya, ma-ee nay-eem iss Schna-ee-duh.* (Oh yes, my name is Schneider.)

The most helpful consonant changes are the following:

[b] and [p], [g] and [k], and [d] and [t] are often interchanged. For example, *Pring id hee-r.* (Bring it here.) *He vas goingk?* (He was going?)

[w] becomes [v]. *Vee shell ko avay.* (We shall go away.)

[sp] becomes [shp] as in *shpeak* (speak). Also, stick becomes *shtick*.

A peculiarly Germanic sound is the [ich] which is produced by driving the breath stream with audible friction through a narrow aperture between the tongue and the roof of the mouth. This sound is employed often when the [ch] occurs as in *buch*, *Reich*. Another characteristic of the

Germanic language is the *umlaut*. Visually this is indicated by placing two dots over the vowels [ä], [ö], and [ü]. These umlaut vowels have the following variations:

[ä] Long has the sound of [e] as in there.
   Short has the sound of short [e] as in met.
[ö] Long is pronounced like long [e] with rounded lips.
   Short sounds like short [e] with rounded lips.
[ü] Long is pronounced long [i] with rounded lips.
   Short is pronounced short [i] with rounded lips.

Naturally, the German carries over these sounds from his mother tongue in his attempt to master the English language. These are typical melodic patterns of the German dialect:

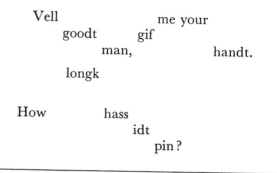

Practice Selection

STALAG 17

by Donald Bevan and Edmund Trzcinski / excerpt from Act I, Scene 1*

SCENE *The interior of a barracks in a German prisoner of war camp.*

STOSH (*Comes to* C. *of room, speaks loud as though he didn't know* SHULTZ *was coming.*) Hey, Harry, come here, it's Shultz. (*German corporal* SHULTZ *enters* C. *He bustles with efficient Teutonic good humour and cheerfulness which almost conceal his innate cruelty and arrogance.*) So this guy says to me that Shultz is always snooping around and playing Pratt Boy for the Commandant just to keep from going to combat. But I told him that I know Shultz wasn't doing it just to keep from going to combat.

SHULTZ (*Slaps* STOSH *on back, laughs.*) You're such a joker.

STOSH Shultz!

SHULTZ How is everybody today? What's the matter, you seem restless?

STOSH Yeah, Shultz, we were passing out guns when you came in.

HARRY	(*Going up to* SHULTZ) Hey, Shultz!
SHULTZ	(*Jovially*) Ja! (*Turns to* HARRY.)
HARRY	(*Sitting on stool*) Drop dead!
SHULTZ	You will drop dead.
STOSH	Hey, Shultz, Harry tells me you lived in New York before the war.
SHULTZ	Harry tells you I lived in New York . . . every time you see me, you tell me Harry tells you I lived in New York. You know I lived in New York . . . I had a luggage store in Radio City. A real first class shop. You know I sold two suitcases to Clark Gable once. . . . I'm like Harry . . . I'm a New Yorker.
HARRY	(*Seated on stool* D. R.) Hey, Shultz, how would you like to be back there, now? (*Intimately*) Broadway?
SHULTZ	(*Almost fondly*) Ja, Broadway!
HARRY	Times Square?
SHULTZ	Ja, Times Square, Central Park, Yorkville — I know all those places. Don't worry. I'll be there before you.
HARRY	(*Going up to* SHULTZ *confidentially*) Hey, Shultz, why don't you help us escape? We'll go home and have your luggage store open and waiting for you.
SHULTZ	You Americans! I couldn't understand you. You complain . . . for you the war is over. You don't work. You don't have duty . . .
STOSH	(*Crosses to him, imitating accent*) We don't eat.
SHULTZ	You got it good!
HARRY	You should live so long! (*Men laugh.*)
SHULTZ	Drop dead. (*Reaching in his jacket*) Would you like to see a picture of my shop? (*Pulls out pictures from pocket, hands them to* HARRY.) That's me in front. (HARRY *takes pictures.*)
HARRY	(*Excited over new pictures*) These are all right. Where did you get them, Shultz? In Paris? (*Men crowd around.*)
STOSH	Naw, these are Jerry broads. See how hefty they are?
DUKE	Hey, this is *real* art.

HARRY	Real art! You ever see statues with garters on?
STOSH	These are old pictures, there ain't no plastics in them bodies!
HOFFY	Look at the beer belly on that one.
STOSH	Imagine taking a dame like that home to Mother!
HARRY	Are you kidding — that *is* mother. Hey, Stosh, here's one for you.
STOSH	(*Crosses to* SHULTZ.) Who's this? She's got clothes on.
SHULTZ	That's my wife. Give them back. They are no good for you. You should not arouse yourself.

Other Sources for Scenes of German Dialect

Watch on the Rhine by Lillian Hellman, *Rip van Winkle* by Joseph Jefferson, and *There Shall Be No Night* by Robert E. Sherwood.

YIDDISH DIALECT

There are many variations and exceptions in the Yiddish dialect which, to a degree, negate precise, general rules. These variations are the result of a carryover from the individual's particular national origin since each country lends coloring to the language of its inhabitants. However, there are general characteristics which, if consistently followed, will provide a satisfactory flavor of Yiddish dialect. It is suggested, therefore, that the actor give particular attention to the following:

1. The Yiddish lilt has a singsong, almost monotonous pattern.

    Look   talk-
        whose   ing.

    It   be   eas-
      vould   so   y.

2. There are variations in syntax.
Didn't you had no dinner? (Didn't you have any dinner?)

3. There is substitution of certain vowels and consonants.

a) Vowels:
The long [ā] as in bake is shortened to the [ĕ] as in get. *meibi* (maybe).

[a] as in ask is changed to short [ĕ]. *glens* (glance).

Short [ă] as in mad is changed to short [ĕ] as in met. *'mej'n* (imagine).

Long [ē] is changed to short [ĭ] as in hit. *krim* (cream).

The short [ĕ] sound of set is changed to the short [ă] sound of had. *sal* (sell).

Short [ĭ] as in bit is changed to long [ē] as in heat. *les'n* (listen).

b) Consonants:
Medial [d] is sometimes changed to [t].
Final [d] is often dropped or changed to [t] as in *bet* (bad).

[k] sound varies greatly in Yiddish dialect. The medial or final [g] often has the sound of [k] as in *bekitch* (baggage).

[r] in the medial or final position is usually dropped as in *bä* (bar).

[s] is sometimes given a [z] sound as in *zoop* (soup).

[t] in the medial position is changed to [d] as in *fedü'* (feather).

[t] in the final position is usually dropped as in *fek* (fact).

[w] is usually changed to [v] as in *ve* (we).

[th] when voiced is changed to [d] as in *děĭ* (they).

Practice Selection

ABIE'S IRISH ROSE

by Anne Nichols / excerpt from Act I *

CHARACTERS	MRS. ISAAC COHEN SOLOMON LEVY ROSE MARY MURPHY
SITUATION	SOLOMON'S *son,* ABIE, *has brought his sweetheart,* ROSE MARY, *home to meet his father. But he has not revealed that they are married or that* ROSE MARY *is Irish.*

(MRS. COHEN *enters Right Center. She is a tall good-looking woman, very well dressed.*)

MRS. COHEN   Hello, Mr. Levy. Abie gave me the key and told me to walk right in.

SOLOMON   (*Rises, goes to her.*) Mrs. Cohen — I vant you to know Rosie. Miss Rosie Murpheski.

MRS. COHEN   (*Crosses to her.* ROSE MARY *rises.*) Miss Murpheski! I am glad to know anybody what iss a friend of Abie's.

SOLOMON   Sid down, Mrs. Cohen. Make yourself homely. (MRS. COHEN *sits on davenport.*) Oh, won't you lay off your furs for a minute?

MRS. COHEN   No thanks, I have to be goink in a few minutes.

SOLOMON   (*Center*) You von't feel the good of it. What's the use of havin' furs if you can't feel them when you go oud. (*Gets chair at back.*)

---

*Anne Nichols, *Abie's Irish Rose*. Copyright, 1924, by Anne Nichols. Copyright, 1927 (Novel), by Anne Nichols. Copyright, 1937 (Acting Edition), by Anne Nichols. Copyright, 1952 (In renewal), by Anne Nichols. Reprinted by permission of Samuel French.

MRS. COHEN	I always wear something around me in the house, ever since my operation — (SOLOMON *drops chair*.) don't I, Solomon?
SOLOMON	(*Puts chair Center, facing davenport. Paying no attention*) Yes. Yes — just think, Mrs. Cohen, Abie has known Rosie ever since the Var.
MRS. COHEN	Ve can blame a lod of things on the Var, can't ve.
ROSE MARY	I hope you won't blame the War for me.
MRS. COHEN	Vat a nize pleasant blame. Did you go over?
SOLOMON	Dod's vhere she met Abie.
MRS. COHEN	Oh, you poor dear, what a lot of suffering you must have seen.
ROSE MARY	I did.
SOLOMON	Abie got shot in the Argonne. He laid in the hospital for weeks.
MRS. COHEN	I can sympathize with anybody in a hospital.
SOLOMON	(*Trying to stop her*) Yes ve know, your appendix was amputated.
MRS. COHEN	You know, Miss Murpheski, it started with a little pain, right here. (*Indicating her abdomen*) Or was it here —
SOLOMON	Make up your mind.
MRS. COHEN	Now come to think of it —
SOLOMON	Don'd think of it, Mrs. Cohen. Forged it!

Other Sources for Scenes of Yiddish Dialect

A Majority Of One by Leonard Spigelgass and *The Tenth Man* by Paddy Chayefsky.

SCANDINAVIAN DIALECT

Although there are certain variations in Scandinavian dialect, the general characteristics should in most cases adequately serve the actor, whether he is playing a Danish, Norwegian, or Swedish character. The prevailing characteristics listed below should provide the actor with the means of achieving a believable Scandinavian dialect.

The melodic pattern. There is a definite singsong effect with almost uniform stress on the words and a rising inflection at the end of the sentence.

```
       name  Yon-  Yohn-    from      con-    n.
                                               i
My     iss    ny    son      Vis-             s


                                      y.
yust       beck         old          r
                                     t
I     come        from the      coun-
```

Vowel changes. The following vowel changes are particularly helpful in acquiring an authentic Scandinavian dialect.

[a] The long [ā] as in name is changed to short [ĕ] as in *ne:m* (name). (The [:] indicates a lengthening of the vowel sound.)
     The [à] as in mask is changed to short [ĕ] as in *le:fi:ng* (laughing).
     The short [ă] as in sad is changed to an elongated short [ĕ] as in *be:t* (bad).

[e] The short [ĕ] as in met is changed to the [à] in ask as in *fra:nt* (friend).

[oo] The long double [oo] is given an umlaut sound. This is made by rounding the lips while making the sound of [e] as in *skö:l* (school).
     The short double [oo] is changed to umlaut [ü] as in *kü:k* (cook).

Consonant changes. Most consonants in the Scandinavian dialect are pronounced the same as in American speech. The following consonants are characteristic differences.

[j] In the initial and medial position [j] is changed to [y] as in *Yonny* (Johnny) or *mayor* (major).
     In the final position [j] is changed to [sh] as in *be:gi:sh* (baggage).

[w] This is given the sound of [v] as in *vish* (wish).

[z] The American [z] sound is not used in the Scandinavian dialect. It is substituted with the sibilant [s] as in *ashüre* (azure), *ye:s* (jazz).

[th] When voiced, [th] is changed to [d] as in *be:d* (bathe). The unvoiced [th] is changed to [t] as in *tin* (thin).

Practice Selection

I REMEMBER MAMA

by John van Druten / excerpt from Act II*

KATRIN	Why aren't you having a soda, too?
MAMA	Better I like coffee.
KATRIN	When can I drink coffee?
MAMA	When you are grown up.

---

* John van Druten, *I Remember Mama*. Copyright, 1944, 1945, by John van Druten. Reprinted by permission of Harcourt, Brace & World.

KATRIN	When I'm eighteen?
MAMA	Maybe before that.
KATRIN	When I graduate?
MAMA	Maybe. I don't know. Comes the day you are grown up, Papa and I will know.
KATRIN	Is coffee really nicer than a soda?
MAMA	When you are grown up, it is.
KATRIN	Did you used to like sodas better . . . before you were grown up?
MAMA	We didn't have sodas before I was grown up. It was in the old country.
KATRIN	(*Incredulous*) You mean they don't have sodas in Norway?
MAMA	Now, maybe. Now I think they have many things from America. But not when I was little girl. (*The* SODA CLERK *brings the soda and the coffee.*) (*He sets them and departs.*)
KATRIN	(*After a good pull at the soda*) Mama, do you ever want to go back to the old country?
MAMA	I like to go back once to look, maybe. To see the mountains and the fjords. I like to show them once to you all. When Dagmar is big, maybe we all go back once . . . one summer . . . like tourists. But that is how it would be. I would be tourist there now. There is no one I would know any more. And maybe we see the little house where Papa and I live when we first marry. And . . . (*Her eyes grow misty and reminiscent.*) something else I would look at.
KATRIN	What is that? (MAMA *does not answer.*) What would you look at Mama?
MAMA	Katrin, you do not know you have brother? Besides Nels?
KATRIN	No! A brother? In Norway? Mama. . . .
MAMA	He is my first baby. I am eighteen when he is born.
KATRIN	Is he there now?
MAMA	(*Simply*) He is dead.
KATRIN	(*Disappointed*) Oh. I thought you meant . . . I thought you meant a real brother. A long-lost one, like in stories. When did he die?
MAMA	When he is two years old. It is his grave I would like to see again. (*She is suddenly near tears, biting her lip and stirring her coffee violently, spilling a few drops on her*

suit. She gets her handkerchief from her pocketbook, dabs at her skirt, then briefly at her nose, then she returns the handkerchief and turns to KATRIN *again.*)
(*Matter-of-factly*) Is good, your ice-cream soda?

KATRIN   (*More interested now in* MAMA *than in it*) Yes. Mama . . . have you had a very *hard* life?

MAMA   (*Surprised*) Hard? No. No life is easy all the time. It is not meant to be.

KATRIN   But . . . rich people . . . aren't *their* lives easy?

MAMA   I don't know, Katrin. I have never known rich people. But I see them sometimes in stores and in the streets, and they do not *look* as if they were easy.

KATRIN   Wouldn't you like to be rich?

MAMA   I would like to be rich the way I would like to be ten feet high. Would be good for some things — bad for others.

KATRIN   But didn't you come to America to *get* rich?

MAMA   (*Shocked*) No. We come to America because they are all here — all the others. Is good for families to be together.

KATRIN   And did you like it right away?

MAMA   Right away. When we get off the ferry boat and I see San Francisco and all the family, I say: "Is like Norway," only it is better than Norway. And then you are all born here, and I become American citizen. But not to get rich.

KATRIN   *I* want to be rich. Rich and famous. I'd buy you your warm coat. When are you going to get that coat, Mama?

MAMA   Soon now, maybe — when we pay doctor, and Mr. Hyde pay his rent. I think now I *must* ask him. I ask him tomorrow, after Dagmar comes home.

KATRIN   When I'm rich and famous, I'll buy you lovely clothes. White satin gowns with long trains to them. And jewelry. I'll buy you a pearl necklace.

MAMA   We talk too much! (*She signs to the* SODA CLERK.) Come, finish your soda. We must go home.

Other Sources for Scenes of Scandinavian Dialect

Anna Christie by Eugene O'Neill and *There Shall Be No Night* by Robert Sherwood.

OTHER FOREIGN DIALECTS

The dialects that have been discussed are, of course, simply representative of a wide range of language variations that occur in the written drama. Some knowledge of them is required if the actor is to fulfill his role. Strong argument can be given also for the need to know the Spanish, Greek, Russian, Chinese, and Japanese dialects. In addition, there are the less popular European dialects, such as Czech, Jugoslav, Polish, and Hungarian. Most of these are covered well in *Manual of Foreign Dialects*, *Taking the Stage*, and *Applied Phonetics.** These sources also give a comprehensive coverage of the other dialects.

AMERICAN DIALECTS

It goes without saying that even before the actor encounters a foreign dialect, he is likely to face the need to employ one of the American dialects. Of these probably the most critical is the one identified as southern white. Ample evidence of this can be found if one looks no further than the works of Tennessee Williams. It is just as evident, too, that directors and actors alike take for granted the requirements of southern speech. Native southerners rightfully point out that cursory attention to this problem often leads not only to poor imitation of southern speech, but also to jarring inconsistencies among the characters of the play. Just as the Englishman demands accuracy in the variations of British dialect, so the American audience demands an accurate demonstration of differences in the regional speech of the United States.

The major points to be remembered in southern speech are:

1. The comparatively slow and even tempo, resulting in a distinct drawl.
2. The predominant extension of vowel sounds often leading to diphthongization and tryphthongization. *Ah fe-aund it* (I found it) or *Yee-oo ma-id it, awl ra-eet* (You made it, all right).
3. The consistent softening of the medial and final [r] sound: *bannuh* (banner), *faltuh* (falter), *awdeh* (order).
4. The general avoidance of harsh or strident sounds. Foreigners consistently remark that southern dialect is more pleasant to hear than any other regional speech of the United States.

Most consonants in southern dialect, with the exception of the [r], are given a standard pronunciation; but the major point to remember is that at one time or another, all the vowels are extended and often diphthongized. Particular attention is called to the detailed aids given in the *Manual of American Dialects* by Herman and Herman† which also points out the peculiar differences between tidewater, mountain, and general southern speech. This reference work also cites the significant similarities and differences between southern and Negro dialect.

The following examples are typical of southern white dialect:

Ah

    cain't

          go   theah!

             ovuh

Y'all   ne-

    know   buh ow.

        thet

---

* Lewis Helmar Herman and Marguerite Shalett Herman, *Manual of Foreign Dialects*. Chicago: Ziff-Davis, 1943; Crocker, Fields, and Bromall, *Taking the Stage* (Part III); and Claude M. Wise, *Applied Phonetics*. Englewood Cliffs, N.J.: Prentice-Hall, 1957.

† Lewis Helmar Herman and Marguerite Shalett Herman, *Manual of American Dialects*. Chicago: Ziff-Davis, 1947.

Practice Selections

IN ABRAHAM'S BOSOM

by Paul Green / a play in one act*

CHARACTERS ABRAHAM MCCRANIE, *a Negro*
COLONEL MCCRANIE, *a white man*
LONNIE MCCRANIE, *his son*
BUD GASKINS ⎱   *Negro turpentine hands*
PUNY AVERY ⎰   *for the Colonel*

PLACE   *A turpentine woods in eastern North Carolina.*

TIME   *Noon on a summer day late in the Nineteenth Century.*

COLONEL   . . . You the first nigger I ever see so determined. But then you're uncommon! (*The* COLONEL *moves on.*) Come on, Lonnie.

ABE   (*Following somewhat timidly after him*) Colonel Mack, did di — you — what'd dey say over dere 'bout dat little school business?

COLONEL   Bless my soul, 'bout to forget it. I talked it over with the board and most of 'em think maybe we'd better not try it yet.

ABE   (*His face falling*) When dey say it might be a good time? I gitting right 'long wid dat 'rithmatic and spelling and reading. I kin teach de colored boys and gals a whole heap right now, and I'll keep studying.

COLONEL   (*Impatiently*) Oh, I dunno. Time'll come mebbe. Mebbe the time won't come. (*He moves on.*)

ABE   Cain't you git 'em to let me try it awhile? Reckon —

COLONEL   I don't know, I tell you. Got my business on my mind now.

LONNIE   He's done told you two or three times, can't you hear?

ABE   (*His eyes flashing and his voice shaking with sudden uncontrollable anger*) Yeh, yeh, I hear 'im. Dem white folks don't keer — dey —

* Paul Green, *In Abraham's Bosom*. Copyright, 1926, by Paul Green and Robert M. McBride. All Rights Reserved. Reprinted by permission of Paul Green.

LONNIE	(*Stepping before him*) Look out! None of your sass. Pa's already done more for you than you deserve. He even stood up for you and they laughing at him there in Lillington.
ABE	(*Trembling*) Yeh, yeh, I knows. But dem white folks don't think, — I going to show 'em, I —
LONNIE	(*Pushing himself before him*) Dry up. Not another word.
ABE	(*His voice almost breaking into a sob*) Don't talk to me lak dat, Mr. Lonnie. Stop him, Colonel Mack, 'fore I hurt him. (*The other Negroes draw off into a knot by the pine tree, mumbling in excitement and fear.*)
COLONEL	Stop, Lonnie! Abe, don't you talk to my son like that.
LONNIE	By God, I'm going to take some of the airs off'n him right now. You've gone around here getting sorrier and more worthless every day for the last year. What you need is a good beating, and I'm gonna give it to you. (*He steps backward and snatches the whip from his father's hand.*)
COLONEL	Stop that, Lonnie!
LONNIE	Keep out of this, Pa. (*He comes towards* ABE.) I'll beat his black hide off'n him.
ABE	Keep 'im back dere, Colonel Mack. I mought kill him! Keep 'im off.
LONNIE	Kill him! All right, do it. There, damn your dirty soul! (*He strikes* ABE *across the face with his whip. With a snarl* ABE *springs upon him, tears the whip from his hands and hurls him headlong into the thicket of briars and brushes. Then he stands with his hands and head hanging down, his body shaking like one with the palsy.*)
PUNY	(*Screaming*) You done kilt Mr. Lonnie! Oh, Lawdy, Lawdy!
COLONEL	(*Running to* LONNIE *who is crawling up out of the mud with his clothes and skin torn. He is sobbing and cursing.*) Are you hurt? How bad are you hurt?
LONNIE	Let me git at that son of a bitch and I'll kill him dead. (*Moaning*) Oh, I'll beat his brains out with one o' them axes.
COLONEL	If you ain't dead, you'd better keep your hands off'n him. I'll fix him. (*He reaches down and picks up the whip. Thundering*) Git down on your knees, Abe McCranie! Git down! you slave, I'm gonna beat you. (ABE *jerks his head up in defiance, but before the stern face of the* COLONEL *his strength goes out of him. He puts out his hands in supplication.*)
ABE	Don't beat me, Colonel Mack, don't beat me wid dat whip!

COLONEL	Git down on your knees! I've beat many a slave, and I'll beat you, you fool! (*He strikes him several blows.*)
ABE	(*Falling on his knees*) Oh, Lawd, have muhcy upon me! (*The* COLONEL *begins to beat him blow upon blow.* PUNY *and* BUD *stand near the pine in breathless anxiety.*)
PUNY	De Colonel 'll kill 'im!
BUD	(*Seizing his arm*) Shet dat mouf, nigger!
COLONEL	(*As he brings the whip down*) Let this be a lesson to you to the end of your life!
ABE	(*His back twitching under the whip, his voice broken*) Muhcy, Colonel Mack, Muhcy!
COLONEL	You struck a white man; you struck my son.
ABE	(*Raising his tear-stained face*) I yo' son, too; you my daddy. (*He throws himself down before him, embracing his feet. The* COLONEL *lowers the whip, then throws it behind him.*)

AUNTIE MAME

by Jerome Lawrence and Robert E. Lee / excerpt from Act I, Scene 12*

SITUATION	BEAUREGARD JACKSON PICKETT BURNSIDE, AUNTIE MAME's *fiancé, has invited* AUNTIE MAME *down to his southern home to meet his kinfolks. Naturally, she wants to make a good impression.*
AUNTIE MAME	I cain't tell you how chowmin' it is to meet all of you-all! (*This doesn't sound quite right to her, but she carries it off nicely.*)
	(SALLY *swoops up, taking* MAME's *hands with a gush of affection.*)
SALLY	And I'm Sally Cato MacDougal. I could just tell from the first *instant* I set eyes on you that we was gonna be the *closest* of bosom friends, Mame. May I call you Mame?
AUNTIE MAME	Please do.

SALLY	You call me "Sally Cato," heah? — All my most intimate friends *do*. (*Several glances are exchanged.* AUNTIE MAME *is completely taken in.*)
AUNTIE MAME	Why, that's awfully kind of you, Sally Cato.
SALLY	Was it *horses* brought you and Beauregard together?
AUNTIE MAME	(*Blankly*) Horses?
SALLY	Well, I can't imagine Beau even *lookin'* at a lady who wasn't practically *bawn* on a horse.
AUNTIE MAME	(*Laying it on*) Oh, I just love riding. Up in New York hardly a day goes by that I don't have the sadd — the *boots* on. Up every morning at the crack of dawn for a brisk canter through Central Park.
SALLY	Well, now — that settles it. Here I've been wrackin' my poor brain tryin' to figure what *special* I could do to let you know how I feel about your bein' down here. And what could be better than a *hunt*!
AUNTIE MAME	(*Paling a little*) A hunt? ? ?
SALLY	(*Raising her voice*) Listen, evabodeh! Beauregard's gone and *surprised* us all! It seems Miz Dennis here is a prominent North'n horsewoman.
AUNTIE MAME	(*Trying to put the brakes on this*) Well, I wouldn't say *prominent* — No, I'm not prominent.
SALLY	(*Barreling on*) So natcherly we'll have to have a hunt! Dawn, tomorrow morning! And evabody's invited! (*She turns brightly to* AUNTIE MAME.) Won't we have the lark, all of us — at sunup — leapin' over those hedges, jumpin' over those river gaps, the hounds yappin' around those boulders — (AUNTIE MAME *steadies herself against one of the columns.*) I tell you, Mame, every eye in this county is going to be on you tomorrow mornin'!
AUNTIE MAME	(*Thinking fast*) If I'd only *known*. You see, I didn't bring down any of my ridin' togs.
SALLY	Don't worry, Mame child. I've got *dozens* of things you could wear. What's your shoe size? (MAME *tries to draw her feet under her skirt.*)
AUNTIE MAME	(*Lying*) Three-B.
SALLY	Marvelous. Same as I wear. I can even fit you out with boots.
AUNTIE MAME	(*Weakly*) I don't know if Beau would want to —
SALLY	(*Barreling on*) You *do* ride astride, Mame dear?

AUNTIE MAME	(*A hopeful gleam in her eyes*) No, no. Sidesaddle — always. Daddy, the Colonel, insisted that I learn it. He said it was the only way for a true lady to ride. So gracefully. Silly of him, of course, because *nobody* rides sidesaddle these days, but it's the only way I know how. (*She sighs, pleased with herself.*)
SALLY	(*Purring*) Now, isn't that grand! I just happen to have a little old sidesaddle that'll do you *fine*.
	(BEAU *comes out on the lawn again, carrying a trayful of punch glasses. Graciously he passes them around to the guests.*)
BEAU	Refreshment, ladies? (MAME *drinks a whole punch cup at one gulp.*)
SALLY	Beau darlin', we're havin' ourselves a hunt! At dawn tomorrow! And you want to hear somethin' fantastic? Your sweet little Yankee girl is gonna ride sidesaddle.
BEAU	I won't allow it! It's too dangerous.
SALLY	But, darlin', she's insisted.
BEAU	Well, anything Mame says she can do, she can do. I tell you — this is an amazing woman. (MAME *quickly downs a second drink.*)
SALLY	Oh, Mame sugah — I'm just goin' to *hold my breath* until dawn tomorrow.
AUNTIE MAME	Do that, honey. (*The lights fade.*)

Other Sources for Scenes of Negro and Southern Dialect

The Green Pastures by Marc Connelly, *The Little Foxes* by Lillian Hellman, *The Emperor Jones* by Eugene O'Neill, and *The Glass Menagerie* by Tennessee Williams.

Pennsylvania Dutch

The Pennsylvania Dutch people have retained many sounds, words, and expressions which reflect their German origin. Typical of these expressions are the following:

Make the window open.

I don't care even.

If I leave you the door open, will you lock it after?

The intonation pattern. Although there is a rising inflection on the accented syllable followed by a falling inflection, the intonation, like the home-spun habits of the Pennsylvania Dutch people, tends to be plain and lacking in the musical cadences of such dialects as the Irish or the Romance languages.

| Yah, | set | good | troub- | Em- |
| you're | for a | much | le | ma. |

Vowel changes. There are not many radical vowel changes in the Pennsylvania Dutch dialect. Occasionally, in a carry-over from the German, vowels are given the umlaut sound. Some of the variants are as follows:

The [à] in ask is changed to the [ä] in palm.

Short [ŏ] as in odd may be changed to the [ä] of arm.

Short [ŭ] as in tub is changed to the sound of [ä] as in father.

Consonant changes. More important than the variants in the vowel sounds are the changes in the consonants which reflect the German origins of these people.

[b] receives a slight [p] sound. *ribp* (rib).

[f] commonly takes the sound of [v] as in *stavf* (staff).

[g] is colored with the sound of [k]. *gkoingk* (going).

[j] is usually changed to [tch] as in *tchä:tch* (judge).

[p] is given a [b] coloring. *ca:bp* (cap).

[t] is given a slight [d] sound. *madt* (mad).

[th] is often changed to [t]. *trow* (throw).

[v] in some instances is given the [f] sound, while in other cases, a sound of [w]. *salf* (salve) or *walue* (value).

[w] is generally changed to [v]. *vish* (wish).

[z] is usually given the sibilant [s] sound. *jass* (jazz).

Practice Selection

PAPA IS ALL

by Patterson Greene / excerpt from Act I*

("*Papa is All is the story of a Pennsylvania Dutch mother, daughter, and son who rebel against a tyrannical father.* PAPA *misuses the Mennonite tradition for purposes of his own, suppressing, in the name of religion, the simple pleasures and recreations of every day life. . . .*") *He has just demanded that the lamps be extinguished because there is still some daylight. (The room is not quite dark, because the late twilight is aided by the full moon. . . . The door to* EMMA's *room is opened carefully, and* EMMA, *carrying a lighted candle, sidles into the room.*)

EMMA I heard him go upstairs —

MAMA (*Contemplating her absently*) He's gone to bed a while.

* Patterson Greene, *Papa is All.* Copyright, 1942, by Patterson Greene. Reprinted by permission of Patterson Greene.

EMMA	(*Tremulously*) My dress — he tore it bad, but I mended it some — and then I hadn't no more — any more thread. Have you got some — to match?
MAMA	(*Startled out of her revery*) Such thread it is in the needle now. (*Goes to the Left Center chair, sits.*) Come here oncet. (EMMA *goes to her.*) On the footstool — (EMMA *draws up the footstool, sits on it so that her left sleeve is accessible to* MAMA's *needle. She holds the candle so as to light the sleeve, which* MAMA *begins to mend deftly.*)
EMMA	Mama —
MAMA	Yes, well —
EMMA	I'm going to him.
MAMA	(*Her needle halts, but she makes no other gesture.*) Yes, well —
EMMA	I — I can't help it —
MAMA	Yah. Is he a good man?
EMMA	If he's a good man? I think so — I don't know. I don't care, even! What is it but such a little thing only — a ride to Lancaster and back in a Ford-car, and a picture to look at! Other girls do it — every night — The roads are full of cars with girls in them, and their young men driving — (*Her voice has taken on an intensity which belies her words, and* MAMA *has quietly resumed her stitches.*) If I talk a little and ride a little only, is it any difference if he's a good man or a bad man? Is it, Mama?
MAMA	If you ain't too much *for* him, maybe —
EMMA	I'm not so much *for* him! It's just I — I — Oh, I *am* for him! It seems now I know him, I can't let him go ever. I don't *care* if he's bad or good — if I can be *with* him only!
MAMA	(*Regretfully, but resigned*) Yah, you're set for a good much trouble, Emma. You're so warm in the head always.
EMMA	(*Impulsively*) Mama — if you say so, I won't go —
MAMA	(*Breaking off the thread*) I don't say you should go, and I don't say you should don't. But — (*Practically; taking the candle from* EMMA) If I leave you the door open, will you lock it good after?
EMMA	(*Jumping up*) Mama! (*In an unaccustomed display of affection, she stoops and kisses* MAMA. *She darts to the rear door, hesitates, and turns back.*) Mama — are you afraid?
MAMA	I don't rightly know.

EMMA   You needn't be —

MAMA   Ach, Emma, I don't mean for *you*, any. It's Papa, that way — if it's sinful, maybe, to go agin' him —

EMMA   (*Earnestly*) It don't *feel* anyways sinful, Mama —

MAMA   Yah. (*Wistfully*) If you had a nice new coat only!

EMMA   (*A little tremulously again*) It — it isn't needful any — (*Turns, opens the door, looks out into the night. Her head lifts and all worry leaves her.*) It's coming summer on — (*Drifts hopefully through the door, and on to the stile.*)
(MAMA, *candle in hand, looks after* EMMA *a moment, then moves towards* EMMA's *room.*)

Line
Interpretation

Speak the speech, I pray you, as I pronounced it to you, trippingly on the tongue; but if you mouth it, as many of your players do, I had as lief the town crier spoke my lines.

Shakespeare

The actor who has an expressive body and possesses a harmoniously modulated voice may be able to capture the fancy of an audience momentarily. He cannot, however, hope to give a completely satisfying performance if he does not concern himself with conveying the thought of the lines he is saying. This infinitely important aspect of the art of acting is termed line interpretation.

AN APPROACH TO LINE INTERPRETATION

Understanding the script

The logical approach to line interpretation must begin with a complete understanding of the script. One cannot give to others something which one does not possess. Until the thought and emotional content of the author's lines have been absorbed, the actor cannot adequately convey the author's meaning to the audience. Herein lies one of the most common difficulties for beginning actors: lines are often spoken with little communication of

their logical and emotional content. Since the original thinking has been done by the author, the actor may repeat parrot-like the lines of the script with little or no thinking. To avoid this error, the actor should ask himself a number of provocative questions:

1. What is the character really saying?
2. What is the overall meaning of the play?
3. How does each scene contribute to the meaning of the play?
4. What seems to be the mood of the entire play and mood of each scene?
5. How does the character contribute to the play as a whole, as well as to the particular scene?
6. What is the character's objective?
7. How does the character plan to achieve his goal?

These and other similar questions will stimulate the actor's thinking to a point where the intellectual and emotional content of the lines becomes his own.

The basic tenet of this approach to interpretation is that any true expression of thought or feeling must come from within. External or mere vocal manifestation of feeling may appear to be hollow and false. Although the natural expression of dialogue may not meet all the exigencies of the actor's varied roles, it forms a logical base on which to build. The actor is well advised to find the natural expression of a line before he proceeds to the technical nuances of interpretation.

Subtext

In addition to the logical, literal meaning of a line, there is embodied in dramatic dialogue a quality Stanislavski terms subtext. He explains the term as "the inwardly felt expression of a human being in a part, which flows uninterruptedly beneath the words of the text, giving them life and a basis for existing."* It is the subtext which gives depth and poignancy to the character's thoughts and emotions, for a line of dialogue usually embodies much more than literal information. When Eliza asks, "What's to become of me?" in Shaw's *Pygmalion*, she is expressing much more than a casual thought to be satisfied by a simple answer. It is the troubled cry of a displaced human being. She cannot return to her former life as a flower girl, nor has she the means to continue her life as a lady in high society. Thus, as Stanislavski further points out, the subtext supplies the character not only with the appropriate words and actions but also with the truth of their expression.

The norm of conversation

All line interpretation is based on the pattern of good conversation. The actor must use the conventions of speech which are current and acceptable to the cultured members of the society in

---

* Constantin Stanislavski, *Building a Character*. New York: Theatre Arts Books, 1949, p. 108.

which he lives. This does not mean that he should copy the all too prevalent dull and colorless conversation of *real* life. Acting is an art; consequently, it is not a photographic copy of *actual* life. The dramatic import of the scene often requires an intensification, a coloring or pointing of the lines for proper interpretation. In no case, however, should there be a distortion or falsification of the conversational mode of expression, except when a trait of the character. To depart from or ignore this principle will, in some degree, impair the effectiveness of the actor's communication.

FACTORS INFLUENCING LINE INTERPRETATION

Type of play

Basically, all plays may be divided into two groups, the comic and the serious. Although there are many gradations in each category, the actor must first of all sense the author's viewpoint of life and evaluate the overall mood of the play. Not infrequently, a director is obliged to remind the actors of the type of play they are rehearsing. In the case of comedy, in order to achieve the proper mood the cast may need to play with a lighter touch, more vocal variety, a faster pace, or greater inclusion of comic business. Comedy, and to an even greater extent farce, demands that the actor approach his role with a high degree of intellectual objectivity and a mastery of the various techniques of playing comedy. Conversely, greater emotional involvement, intensity, and depth of feeling are required of the actor in a serious drama.

Style of play

Each style of writing demands special treatment by the actor. The idealized poetic language of a classic or romantic play must be treated in a different manner from the earthy prose of a naturalistic play such as *Tobacco Road*. Even out of context, the following excerpts suggest a great variation in the manner of line interpretation.

EBEN: Ain't he a devil out o' hell? It's jest t' spite us — the damned old mule!

> Eugene O'Neill, *Desire Under the Elms*

CYRANO: My hat I toss lightly away:
From my shoulders I slowly let fall
The cloak which conceals my array,
And my sword from my scabbard I call,
Like Celadon, graceful and tall,
Like Scaramouche, quick hand and brain, —
And I warn you, my friend, once for all,
I shall thrust when I end the refrain.

> Edmond Rostand, *Cyrano de Bergerac*

PIERROT: My only love,
You are *so* intense . . . Is it Tuesday,
Columbine? —
I'll kiss you if it's Tuesday.

> Edna St. Vincent Millay, *Aria Da Capo*

A more detailed treatment of the principles and techniques of acting in various types and styles of plays is presented in Part Two.

Character

Before an actor can interpret his lines adequately, he must thoroughly understand and visualize the character he is playing. Although all the factors which go to make up a characterization have a bearing on line interpretation, mention is made here of only the more important elements.

The general type of character, his humor, and his attitude toward life. Each of these factors colors the expression of the character's thoughts and any change of attitude is reflected in the character's manner of speech. Consider, for example, "Merry Christmas" as said by Scrooge and by Bob Cratchit. As the character of Scrooge finally mellows, there is a corresponding change in his voice from harshness to kindliness.

Variations in the character's attitude toward other characters. As in real life, each stage character has a different manner with each person he meets depending on his degree of liking or disliking. An actor cannot properly interpret a character's lines until he understands how the character feels toward the others in the play. In Act II, Scene 5 of *Romeo and Juliet* the lines of the Nurse, which at first glance seem harsh and cantankerous, should in delivery be mellowed by the fact that she is very fond of Juliet and is only teasing.

It would be impossible to list here all the various psychological attitudes which color and shade the interpretation of a character's lines in relation to the other characters in the scene. It is the actor's responsibility to determine his character's attitude and relationship toward other characters and then to modify the interpretation of his lines as the situation requires.

Background. More is revealed through an individual's speech than he may realize. A man's origin as well as his cultural and social background is often revealed through his speech. As Higgins so aptly states in Shaw's *Pygmalion*, "Men begin in Kentish Town with £80 a year and end in Park Lane with a hundred thousand. They want to drop Kentish Town; but they give themselves away every time they open their mouths."

Actually, speech reveals a man's background by both the choice of words and the manner of delivery. But since the playwright has made the word selection, we are concerned here only with the manner of expression. In general, the cultured person speaks with more concern for pronunciation and articulation than the untrained individual, whose unstudied habits and manners are often carried over into careless and faulty speech. In *Pygmalion* Eliza has to learn both the thoughts of cultured people and their manner of expression.

The unpleasant sounds of the flower girl are replaced by the pleasant, well modulated speech of the "duchess."

Nationality and locale. Each nation and geographical area has its own particular characteristics of speech commonly called dialects. These differences in speech were discussed in the preceding chapter. When a particular dialect is essential to the character's interpretation, the actor must familiarize himself with it in order to acquire acceptable vocal expression.

Age, health, and general physical condition. The effect of age on speech is indicated in Jaques' discourse on the seven ages of man in Shakespeare's *As You Like It* (Act II, Scene 7).

> "The sixth age shifts
> Into the lean and slipper'd pantaloon
> With spectacles on nose and pouch on side,
> His youthful hose, well saved, a world too wide
> For his shrunk shank; and his big manly voice,
> Turning again toward childish treble, pipes
> And whistles in his sound."

Obviously, the age and the general health of a character may be revealed by a great variety of characteristics. When the appropriate alterations in the manner of line reading are combined with the physical characteristics of a particular age or state of health, greater believability will be achieved. For example, rapid line delivery and run-on sentences may convey impetuous youth as contrasted with the slow, halting, and confused delivery often characteristic of old age. Each character must be evaluated for his individuality so that the actor may achieve a truthful portrayal without relying on the familiar vocal clichés of old age.

The situation

The actor should examine the scene to determine how the situation may influence the interpretation of the lines. He may ask himself: (1) Where is the action taking place? (2) Is the scene indoors or out in the open? (3) Is the character talking to a crowd or to one or two persons? (4) Is there a quality of secrecy? (5) Is the mood one of gaiety and abandon? (6) Is the scene pervaded by a mood of sadness or solemnity? The answers to these and similar questions should provide clues as to how the lines may best be interpreted.

In the following excerpt from *The Fall of the City,** the Orator is speaking from a plaza to a vast throng of people. This situation would require a maximum amount of force and projection. The open throat type of delivery similar to that which is used in calling to someone at a distance would be appropriate in this scene.

> "Freemen of this nation!
> The persuasion of your wills against your wisdom
> is not dreamed of.
> We offer themes for your consideration.
> What is the surest defender of liberty?
> Is it not liberty?
> A free people resists by Freedom:
> Not locks! Not blockhouses!
>
> The future is a mirror where the past
> Marches to meet itself. Go armed toward arms!
> Peaceful toward peace! Free and with music
> toward freedom!
> Face tomorrow with knives and tomorrow's a
> knife-blade.
> Murder your foe and your foe will be murder! —
> Even your friends suspected of false-speaking:
> Hands on the door at night and the floor boards
> squeaking."

In the following scene (Act V, Scene 1) of Shakespeare's *Macbeth*, the speeches are delivered with a minimum of volume since the two characters are near to each other and do not wish to

---

* Archibald MacLeish, *The Fall of the City*, pp. 8–9. Copyright, 1937, by Archibald MacLeish. Reprinted by permission of Houghton Mifflin.

disturb Lady Macbeth. The projection of the voice should be just enough to carry to the audience. If this scene were played with absolute naturalness and with no regard for the theater, the audience would probably not hear a single line.

GENTLEWOMAN: Lo, you, here she comes! This is her very guise, and, upon my life, fast asleep. Observe her; stand close.

DOCTOR: How came she by that light?

GENTLEWOMAN: Why, it stood by her: she has light by her continually; 'tis her command.

DOCTOR: You see, her eyes are open.

GENTLEWOMAN: Ay, but their sense is shut.

DOCTOR: What is it she does now? Look, how she rubs her hands.

GENTLEWOMAN: It is an accustomed action with her, to seem thus washing her hands: I have known her to continue in this a quarter of an hour.

Subject matter

The manner of interpreting lines in the script varies with the importance or magnitude of each line's content. We normally use a big voice, with more volume, in speaking of important matters and a small voice for tiny or inconsequential things. People instinctively use a tiny voice in speaking to an infant. The actor must evaluate his material, line by line, to determine how the subject matter in each case may affect his portrayal.

In the following excerpts, consider how the subject matter may influence the manner of interpretation.

(SISTER JOANNA *of the* CROSS *talks to and plays with the newly arrived child in the basket.*)

SISTER JOANNA: Pretty one! Pretty one! Do you love me, sweetheart? Do you love me? Little one! Little one! Whom do you love?

Gregorio Martinez Sierra, *The Cradle Song*

POLONIUS: What do you read, my lord?

HAMLET: Words, words, words.

POLONIUS: What is the matter, my lord?

HAMLET: Between who?

POLONIUS: I mean, the matter that you read, my lord.

Shakespeare, *Hamlet*

PORTIA: The quality of mercy is not strain'd,
It droppeth as the gentle rain from heaven
Upon the place beneath: it is twice blest;
It blesseth him that gives, and him that takes:
'Tis mightiest in the mightiest: it becomes
The throned monarch better than his crown;
His scepter shows the force of temporal power,
The attribute to awe and majesty,
Wherein doth sit the dread and fear of kings;
But mercy is above this sceptred sway;
It is enthroned in the hearts of kings,
It is an attribute to God himself;
And earthly power doth then show likest God's
When mercy seasons justice. Therefore, Jew,
Though justice be thy plea, consider this,
That, in the course of justice, none of us
Should see salvation: we do pray for mercy;
And that same prayer doth teach us all to render
The deeds of mercy. I have spoke thus much
To mitigate the justice of thy plea;
Which if thou follow, this strict court of Venice
Must needs give sentence 'gainst the merchant
    there.

Shakespeare, *The Merchant of Venice*

"Awake, awake!
Ring the alarum-bell. Murder and treason!
Banquo and Donalbain! Malcolm! awake!
Shake off this downy sleep, death's counterfeit,
And look on death itself! up, up, and see
The great doom's image! Malcolm! Banquo!
As from your graves rise up, and walk like sprites,
To countenance this horror. Ring the bell."

Shakespeare, *Macbeth*

Line values

The interpretation of lines should vary according to line values. If we examine a character's lines in a scene, we find that they vary considerably in significance. Some lines, such as greetings or responses to offerings of refreshments, are often included (particularly in realistic plays) to give the scene a true-to-life quality. These lines are usually spoken casually or are underplayed. Other lines have a bearing on the plot or theme and are essential to the understanding of the play. A line of this type is Mrs. Pearce's question regarding Eliza in Shaw's *Pygmalion*: "But what's to become of her?" This same thought is repeated by Eliza in Act IV after returning from the garden party: "What's to become of me? What's to become of me?" Obviously this question is important to the theme and should be stressed.

Emphasis may be given to a line of dialogue in a variety of ways: increasing the volume and raising the pitch, using greater vocal intensity and projection, decreasing the rate of delivery, or pausing before the line is given.

Intellectual versus emotional content

The actor should examine each line to determine if it is chiefly intellectual or emotional in content. Intellectual lines are usually interpreted with more individual word stress and wider pitch pattern than lines which are basically emotional. The following informational lines would normally be delivered with strong stress on the important words and a rather wide pitch pattern.

WIFE: (*Calling to her husband, upstairs*) A letter just came from Susan. She says that she will arrive on Friday at 10:35 A.M., TWA Flight 417. Did you hear? Don't forget.

In contrast, the following emotional lines would be interpreted with a minimum of individual word stress and pitch variation.

"I hate you. You are detestable."

"I love you."

"Oh, my dear, I'm so sorry."

A study of Hamlet's soliloquy (Act II, Scene 2) will further illustrate how pitch, word stress, and melodic pattern vary in relation to the intellectual and emotional content of the line. The first two-thirds of the speech is basically emotional, and the emotional intensity varies considerably. One emotional climax, for example, occurs on the words, "O, vengeance!"

"O, what a rogue and peasant slave am I!
Is it not monstrous that this player here,
But in a fiction, in a dream of passion,
Could force his soul so to his own conceit
That from her working all his visage wan'd;
Tears in his eyes, distraction in's aspect,
A broken voice, and his whole function suiting
With forms to his conceit? And all for nothing!
For Hecuba?
What's Hecuba to him or he to Hecuba,
That he should weep for her? What would he do,
Had he the motive and cue for passion
That I have? He would drown the stage with
    tears
And cleave the general ear with horrid speech,
Make mad the guilty, and appal the free;
Confound the ignorant, and amaze, indeed,
The very faculties of eyes and ears.
Yet I,
A dull and muddy-mettled rascal, peak,
Like John-a-dreams, unpregnant of my cause,
And can say nothing; no, not for a king,
Upon whose property and most dear life
A damn'd defeat was made. Am I a coward?
Who calls me villain? breaks my pate across?
Plucks off my beard and blows it in my face?
Tweaks me by the nose? gives me the lie i' the
    throat,
As deep as to the lungs? who does me this, ha!
'Swounds, I should take it: for it cannot be
But I am pigeon-liver'd, and lack gall

To make oppression bitter, or ere this
I should have fatted all the region kites
With this slave's offal: — bloody, bawdy villain!
Remorseless, treacherous, lecherous, kindless
  villain!
O, vengeance!
Why, what an ass am I! This is most brave,
That I, the son of a dear father murder'd
Prompted to my revenge by heaven and hell,
Must, like a whore, unpack my heart with words,
And fall a-cursing like a very drab,
A scullion!
Fie upon't! foh!"

The next line of the soliloquy, "About, my brain!", indicates that Hamlet realizes his emotional outburst is futile. He now decides to rationalize his problem. For the remainder of the soliloquy intellectual control is evident.

"About, my brain! Hum, I have heard
That guilty creatures, sitting at a play,
Have by the very cunning of the scene
Been struck so to the soul that presently
They have proclaim'd their malefactions;
For murder, though it have no tongue, will speak
With most miraculous organ. I'll have these
  players
Play something like the murder of my father
Before mine uncle: I'll observe his looks;
I'll tent him to the quick: if he but blench,
I know my course. The spirit that I have seen
May be the devil; and the devil hath power
To assume a pleasing shape; yea, and perhaps
Out of my weakness and my melancholy,
As he is very potent with such spirits,
Abuses me to damn me: I'll have grounds
More relative than this: — the play's the thing
Wherein I'll catch the conscience of the king."

Shakespeare, *Hamlet*

This latter portion lends itself to stronger word stress and consequently a wider and more varied melodic pattern.

Obviously, the actor should not attempt to interpret the soliloquy until he has a thorough understanding of the situation and of Hamlet's thoughts and feelings.

Word imagery

Words vary greatly in the mental pictures which they conjure up. They may suggest such qualities as beauty, ugliness, repulsiveness, or harshness. Normally the voice reflects the mental image or thought to be expressed, revolting or pleasant as the case may be. The actor must have the proper *mental* image in order for the vocal cords and the other modifiers of sound to produce the proper *vocal* image. In the following examples try to capture the mental images suggested by the words.

"How sweet the moonlight sleeps upon this bank!
Here will we sit, and let the sounds of music
Creep in our ears: soft stillness and the night
Becomes the touches of sweet harmony."

Shakespeare, *The Merchant of Venice*

"Come, thick night,
And pall thee in the dunnest smoke of hell,
That my keen knife see not the wound it makes,
Nor heaven peep through the blanket of the dark,
To cry 'Hold, hold!' "

Shakespeare, *Macbeth*

"Her waggon-spokes made of long spinners' legs;
The cover, of the wings of grasshoppers;
Her traces, of the smallest spider's web;
Her whip, of cricket's bone; the lash, of film."

Shakespeare, *Romeo and Juliet*

"O, look! methinks I see my cousin's ghost
Seeking out Romeo, that did spit his body
Upon a rapier's point."

Shakespeare, *Romeo and Juliet*

"Where bloody Tybalt, yet but green in earth,
Lies festering in his shroud; . . ."

Shakespeare, *Romeo and Juliet*

"They came to the evil-smelling tannery and the frog pond just behind it, stretching cold and still in the moonlight and covered with a noxious, slimy scum."

Edward Pepel, *A Night Out*

"Ah, you smell so good. Sweat, onions, wine. You have all the smells a man should have."

Lillian Hellman, *The Lark**

"Gee, it's beautiful tonight . . . as if it were a special night . . . for me and Muriel . . . Gee, I love tonight . . . I love the sand, and the trees, and the grass, and the water and the sky, and the moon . . . it's all in me and I'm in it . . . God, it's so beautiful!"

Eugene O'Neill, *Ah, Wilderness!*†

TECHNIQUES OF LINE INTERPRETATION

Thus far in this chapter we have stressed the importance of gaining an understanding of the import of the lines. It is only by this approach that the actor's lines will have the ring of truth. However, since the drama presents an intensified and often idealized representation of life, the actor cannot rely entirely on an actual lifelike

---

* Jean Anouilh, *The Lark*. Adapted by Lillian Hellman. Copyright as an unpublished work, 1955, by Lillian Hellman. Copyright, 1956, by Lillian Hellman. Reprinted by permission of Random House.

† Eugene O'Neill, *Ah, Wilderness!* Copyright, 1933, by Eugene O'Neill. Renewed, 1960, by Carlotta Monterey O'Neill. Reprinted by permission of Random House.

portrayal. He must, in short, present not actual life but an illusion of life, modified and adapted to the conditions of the theater.

Although the understanding of a line is the proper approach to its interpretation, it is helpful if the actor knows the methods whereby the meaning and the emotional content of the line may be given greater distinctness and poignancy. The thought content is conveyed chiefly by emphasizing the important or key words and by grouping words that are closely related. First to be considered are the techniques and principles of emphasis.

Emphasis

By means of emphasis the listener's attention is called to a particular syllable, word, phrase, or sentence. The normal or conversational method of emphasis is to raise the pitch and increase the volume of the important element. Important words or phrases must not be dropped to a lower level or uttered with less force than the unimportant words in the sentence. If this is done, it distorts the normal conversational pattern of speech and belies the meaning. This, of course, should be avoided. The following sentence illustrates the principle of emphasis.

```
                                          devil.
       spirit
                              seen
              I                       be
The       that   have      may    the
```

This sentence may be read with varying degrees of word emphasis and inflection. It is impossible to give an exact graphic representation of the melodic pattern. However, the most important word, "devil," should occupy the highest pitch position and receive the greatest emphasis. The pitch position of words must correspond with their relative importance to the thought.

Not only must the proper words be emphasized but each must be stressed to the proper degree. Emphasis is a matter of contrast. If one tries to emphasize everything one emphasizes nothing. Unimportant items must be suppressed or shoved into the background. In conversational speech such unimportant words as prepositions, conjunctions, articles, and the like are passed over lightly and not given a complete articulation. The articles *a* and *the* usually receive a weak stress. In like manner, *and* often becomes *'nd* or *'n'* and *will* is shortened to *w'l* or *'l*. Although unimportant words are shortened or clipped in conversational speech, this device should in no sense be applied to the important words in the sentence. Careless articulation is an all too common fault in American speech.

In general, we give emphasis to a new element or modification of a previously expressed idea. For example, "Today we honor a *hero*; a *beloved*, *national*, hero." On the other hand, we do not emphasize words which express ideas that are understood or taken for granted. We do not need to stress the idea, for instance, that water *flows*, birds *fly*, or that the temperature is expected to go down to ten *degrees*. Unless a contrast is implied, we do not emphasize personal or relative pronouns for the simple reason that the person referred to is generally understood. For example, Eliza should say, "What's to *become* of me?" not "What's to become of *me*?"

In addition to giving the important word a higher pitch level and an increase of stress there are a number of other ways of achieving emphasis. One of the most useful for the actor is the dramatic pause. A break in the established tempo or rhythm of the sentence calls attention to or emphasizes the next word or phrase. Note how the pause may point up the thought in the following lines.

ALICE: You said you had something to tell me.

STEVE: (*Pause*) You promise not to be upset?

ALICE: (*Pause*) I'll try not to.

STEVE: (*Pause*) I must go away — tomorrow.

ALICE: But, why?

STEVE: I can't tell you now. (*Pause*) Perhaps later.

ALICE: Oh, Steve. I'll miss you — so terribly!

Another method of emphasis is a change in the rate of delivery. Normally, important thoughts are expressed in a slower or more deliberate tempo than the normal rate, as in the following:

"Come on, let's hurry or we'll be late for the party. (*Pause, followed by a slower tempo*) I'm sorry. I forgot. She'll be there and that would spoil everything for you."

A slower rate for the last line adds to its significance.

A change in the quality of voice for a particular word, phrase, or sentence is likely to draw the listener's increased attention. For example, a man reading his newspaper may be quite unaware of conversation in the room. But should his companions suddenly change from a normal voice to a whisper, his attention is immediately drawn to their conversation.

Word grouping

Closely related to word emphasis in the communication of meaning is the matter of proper word grouping. We normally speak in word phrases. The communication of meaning is enhanced when words which form a unit of thought are grouped together with a slight pause preceding and following the unit. A pause in the wrong place or a faulty grouping of words may confuse the meaning or convey a thought which was not intended by the author. Note how grouping may change the meaning of the following line:

"The teacher / says the principal / is a fool."
"The teacher says / the principal is a fool."

The word groups in the opening lines of Lincoln's Gettysburg Address might be as follows:

Four score and seven years ago / our fathers brought forth on this continent a new nation, //

conceived in Liberty / and dedicated to the proposition / that all men are created equal. // Now we are engaged in a great civil war, / . . .

Some actors believe that marking the script for word emphasis and word grouping is a helpful device in communication. This is a matter for each actor to decide. The important consideration is which approach will be most helpful in producing the best results.

Uses of the pause

In addition to its function in emphasis and word grouping, the pause has a number of other uses which, properly applied, aid in the effectiveness of line interpretation. The trained actor inserts slight pauses into the natural breaks of the sentence to give the impression that he is thinking of what he has to say. This technique avoids the appearance of memorized lines and gives a more natural quality to the interpretation. It also aids in maintaining what has been termed "the illusion of the first time." The actor spends weeks in rehearsal in order to acquire perfect memorization. But the performance must seem to the audience unrehearsed and unmemorized. Although the actor could easily toss off the following line in one breath, he should, for the sake of illusion and truth, make several pauses.

"Well, / I don't know. / I suppose / I could."

A pause before responding to another character's speech may indicate reflection, indecision, perplexity, or any number of mental and emotional adjustments to the line. In such instances, the character must pause before he can with justifiable believability respond. In like manner, pauses of varying duration are inserted into a telephone conversation to give the illusion that the character is listening and responding to what the other person is saying. For instance:

"Hello. / Bill! It's wonderful to hear your voice. / Where are you speaking from? // Can't you come out to the house? /// Fine. / Then we'll expect you in about an hour. // Good. / Goodbye."

Another use of the pause is to give the punch to a laugh line. The pause usually comes just before the word or phrase that brings the laugh. This technique is illustrated by the following lines from Kesselring's *Arsenic and Old Lace.**

(JONATHAN BREWSTER *and* DR. EINSTEIN *are in the process of disposing of the corpse of one of their victims when* ELAINE HARPER, *a neighbor girl, inadvertently comes into the house. Not knowing who she is and fearing that she might expose them causes* JONATHAN *to hold and threaten her. At this moment* TEDDY BREWSTER, *who thinks he is Theodore Roosevelt, enters from the cellar.*)

ELAINE: Teddy! Teddy! Tell these men who I am.

(TEDDY *turns and looks at her a moment.*)

TEDDY: That's my daughter, // Alice.

Since the number of pauses in a speech is influenced by the complexity of the thought, difficult passages should be broken into relatively small units. Observe the necessity for pauses and small word groups in this speech by Brutus (Act I, Scene 2).

"That you do love me, I am nothing jealous;
What you would work me to, I have some aim:
How I have thought of this and of these times,
I shall recount hereafter; for the present,
I would not, so with love I might entreat you,
Be any further moved. What you have said
I will consider; what you have to say
I will with patience hear, and find a time
Both meet to hear and answer such high things.
Till then, my noble friend, chew upon this:
Brutus had rather be a villager

---

* Joseph Kesselring, *Arsenic and Old Lace.* Copyright, 1942, by Dramatists Play Service. Copyright, 1941, by Random House. Reprinted by permission of Random House.

Than to repute himself a son of Rome
Under these hard conditions as this time
Is like to lay upon us.''

Shakespeare, Julius Caesar

In contrast, Petruchio's discourse (Act IV, Scene 1) on how to tame a shrew may be delivered in larger word groups and fewer pauses.

"Thus have I politicly begun my reign,
And 'tis my hope to end successfully.
My falcon now is sharp and passing empty;
And till she stoop she must not be full-gorged,
For then she never looks upon her lure.
Another way I have to man my haggard,
To make her come and know her keeper's call,
That is, to watch her, as we watch these kites
That bate and beat and will not be obedient.
She eat no meat to-day, nor none shall eat;
Last night she slept not, nor to-night she shall not;
As with the meat, some undeserved fault
I'll find about the making of the bed;
And here I'll fling the pillow, there the bolster,
This way the coverlet, another way the sheets:
Ay, and amid this hurly I intend
That all is done in reverend care of her;
And in conclusion she shall watch all night:
And if she chance to nod, I'll rail and brawl,
And with the clamour keep her still awake.
This is a way to kill a wife with kindness;
And thus I'll curb her mad and headstrong
    humour.
He that knows better how to tame a shrew,
Now let him speak: 'tis charity to show.''

Shakespeare, The Taming of the Shrew

The duration of a pause is governed by (1) the overall tempo of the play, (2) the emotional intensity, and (3) the dramatic import of the line or the significance of the plot action. If the tempo of the play is fast, as in the case of farce or light comedy, then the pauses are generally of shorter duration. Conversely, pauses are generally longer in tragedies and serious drama. In these the magnitude of the thought and the intensity of the emotion justify a longer break in the flow of dialogue. In the following excerpt from Act I of *The Father* by Strindberg,* not only is the emotional intensity very high, but also the scene contains certain lines which state the theme of the play. Study the scene for the location and duration of pauses which may contribute to effectiveness in playing the scene.

LAURA: Is Bertha to leave home now?

CAPTAIN: Yes, she is to start in a fortnight.

LAURA: That is your decision?

CAPTAIN: Yes.

LAURA: Then I must try to prevent it.

CAPTAIN: You cannot.

LAURA: Can't I? Do you really think I would trust my daughter to wicked people to have her taught that everything her mother has implanted in her child is mere foolishness? Why, afterward, she would despise me all the rest of her life!

CAPTAIN: Do you think that a father should allow ignorant and conceited women to teach his daughter that he is a charlatan?

LAURA: It means less to the father.

CAPTAIN: Why so?

LAURA: Because the mother is closer to the child, as it has been discovered that no one can tell for a certainty who the father of a child is.

CAPTAIN: How does that apply in this case?

LAURA: You do not know whether you are Bertha's father or not.

CAPTAIN: I do not know?

LAURA: No; what no one knows, you surely cannot know.

CAPTAIN: Are you joking?

---

* August Strindberg, *The Father*. Copyright, 1912, by L. E. Bassett. Reprinted by permission of Bruce Humphries, Boston.

LAURA: No; I am only making use of your own teaching. For that matter, how do you know that I have not been unfaithful to you?

CAPTAIN: I believe you capable of almost anything, but not that, nor that you would talk about it if it were true.

LAURA: Suppose that I was prepared to bear anything, even to being despised and driven out, everything, for the sake of being able to keep and control my child, and that I am truthful now when I declare that Bertha is my child, but not yours. Suppose —

CAPTAIN: Stop now!

LAURA: Just suppose this. In that case your power would be at an end.

CAPTAIN: When you had proved that I was not the father.

LAURA: That would not be difficult! Would you like me to do so?

CAPTAIN: Stop!

LAURA: Of course I should only need to declare the name of the real father, give all details of place and time. For instance — when was Bertha born? In the third year of our marriage.

CAPTAIN: Stop now, or else —

LAURA: Or else, what? Shall we stop now? Think carefully about all you do and decide, and whatever you do, don't make yourself ridiculous.

CAPTAIN: I consider all this most lamentable.

LAURA: Which makes you all the more ridiculous.

CAPTAIN: And you?

LAURA: Oh, we women are really too clever.

CAPTAIN: That's why one cannot contend with you.

LAURA: Then why provoke contests with a superior enemy?

CAPTAIN: Superior?

LAURA: Yes, it's queer, but I have never looked at a man without knowing myself to be his superior.

CAPTAIN: Then you shall be made to see your superior for once, so that you shall never forget it.

LAURA: That will be interesting.

The pause is an effective device for heightening the suspense of a scene. Note how the pauses dramatize the shooting of Candy's old dog in Act II, Scene 1 of Steinbeck's *Of Mice and Men*.*

SLIM: (*As* CANDY *looks toward him for help*) Better let him go, Candy.

CANDY: (*Looks at each person for some time.* WHIT *makes a gesture of protest and then resigns himself. The others look away, to avoid responsibility. At last, very softly and hopelessly*) All right. Take him. (*He doesn't look down at the dog at all. Lies back on his bunk and crosses his arms behind his head and stares at the ceiling.* CARLSON *picks up the string, helps the dog to its feet.*)

CARLSON: Come, boy. Come on, boy. (*To* CANDY, *apologetically*) He won't even feel it. (CANDY *does not move or answer him.*) Come on, boy. That's the stuff. Come on. (*He leads the dog toward the door.*)

SLIM: Carlson?

CARLSON: Yeah.

SLIM: (*Curtly*) Take a shovel.

CARLSON: Oh, sure, I get you.
(*Exit* CARLSON *with the dog.* GEORGE *follows to the door, shuts it carefully and sets the latch.* CANDY *lies rigidly on his bunk. The next scene is one of silence and quick staccato speeches.*)

SLIM: (*Loudly*) One of my mules got a bad hoof. Got to get some tar on it. (*There is a silence.*)

GEORGE: (*Loudly*) Anybody like to play a little euchre?

---

* John Steinbeck, *Of Mice and Men*. Copyright, 1965, by John Steinbeck. Reprinted by permission of Viking Press, and McIntosh and Otis.

WHIT: I'll lay out a few with you. (*They take places opposite each other at the table but* GEORGE *does not shuffle the cards. He ripples the edge of the deck. Everybody looks over at him. He stops. Silence again.*)

SLIM: (*Compassionately*) Candy, you can have any of them pups you want. (*There is no answer from* CANDY. *There is a little gnawing noise on the stage.*)

GEORGE: Sounds like there was a rat under there. We ought to set a trap there. (*Deep silence again*)

WHIT: (*Exasperated*) What the hell is takin' him so long? Lay out some cards, why don't you? We ain't gonna get no euchre played this way. (GEORGE *studies the backs of the cards. And after a long silence there is a shot in the distance. All the men start a bit, look quickly at* CANDY. *For a moment he continues to stare at the ceiling and then rolls slowly over and faces the wall.* GEORGE *shuffles the cards noisily and deals them.*)

As an example of how pauses, combined with deliberate line interpretation, may change the mood and connotation of the lines, note the following short scene. Two men meet and a casual conversation takes place.

FIRST MAN: Good morning. How are you?

SECOND MAN: Fine.

FIRST MAN: Where are you going?

SECOND MAN: I'm going downtown.

FIRST MAN: I'll see you later.

SECOND MAN: Yes. You certainly will.

If the above lines are spoken rapidly without definite pauses, a light, casual, conversational effect is produced. If you then deliver the lines slowly, deliberately, with little melody and intermixed with pauses, you will find that the scene takes on a sinister connotation.

FIRST MAN: (*Pause, looking the other over*) Good morning. (*Pause*) How are you?

SECOND MAN: (*Pause*) Fine.

FIRST MAN: (*Pause, deliberately*) Where are you going?

SECOND MAN: (*Pause, deliberately*) I'm going downtown.

FIRST MAN: (*Pause*) I'll — see — you – later.

SECOND MAN: (*Pause*) Yes. (*Pause*) You — certainly — will.

VOCAL ELEMENTS IN LINE INTERPRETATION

Although, as stated earlier, the natural approach to acting provides a sound foundation on which to build a believable character, it is essential that the actor acquire skill in his use of the elements of sound—pitch, volume, quality, and rate—in order to acquire proficiency in line interpretation.

Pitch

It goes without saying that the actor must have a controlled pitch range. In addition, he must understand not only the relationship of pitch to the content of the lines but also what pitch variations may connote to the listener. The three elements of pitch—key or level, interval or step, and inflection—have been discussed in the chapter on the actor's voice. Here we are concerned with the application of pitch to line interpretation.

Key or level. Although each individual is limited in his pitch range — approximately one and one-half to two octaves on the musical scale — the actor must learn to vary his voice level to conform to the requirements of each line, shifting his voice up or down as the line changes in importance or emotional content. The middle level is used for most conversational situations where no unusual intellectual stimulation or emotional feeling is evident. The expository scenes at the opening of most dramas are usually played in the middle range. The low pitch level suggests depth of emotional feeling, quietude, or serenity. In this speech the low-keyed voice seems most appropriate.

"O God of battles! steel my soldiers' hearts;
Possess them not with fear; take from them now
The sense of reckoning, if the opposed numbers
Pluck their hearts from them."

Shakespeare, Henry V

The high-keyed voice indicates tension, excitement, fear, or hysteria, particularly when combined with more than the normal vocal force. The high voice without exaggerated volume is conducive to a feeling of gaiety, revelry, or fantasy. In the following examples, find the pitch level which seems most appropriate to the character, the situation, and the mood.

LADY MACBETH: The thane of Fife had a wife; Where is she now? What, will these hands ne'er be clean? No more o' that, my lord, no more o' that; you mar all with this starting.

Shakespeare, Macbeth

HAMLET: Come, come, and sit you down; you shall not budge;
You go not till I set you up a glass
Where you may see the inmost part of you.

QUEEN: What wilt thou do? thou wilt not murder me? Help, help, ho!

POLONIUS: (*Behind*) What, ho! help, help, help!

Shakespeare, Hamlet

In the following speech (Act I, Scene 5), observe how pitch change on the part of Lady Macbeth may indicate a shift from prose to poetry and also a change from reading the letter to expressing her own thoughts.

" 'They met me in the day of success; and I have learned by the perfectest report, they have more in them than mortal knowledge. When I burned in desire to question them further, they made themselves air, into which they vanished. Whiles I stood rapt in the wonder of it, came missives from the King, who all-hailed me "Thane of Cawdor;" by which title, before, these weird sisters saluted me, and referred me to the coming-on of time, with "Hail, King that shalt be!" This have I thought good to deliver thee, my dearest partner of greatness, that thou mightst not lose the dues of rejoicing, by being ignorant of what greatness is promised thee. Lay it to thy heart, and farewell.'

Glamis thou art, and Cawdor, and shalt be
What thou art promised: yet do I fear thy nature;
It is too full o' the milk of human kindness
To catch the nearest way: thou wouldst be great,
Art not without ambition, but without
The illness should attend it: what thou wouldst
    highly,
That wouldst thou holily; wouldst not play false,
And yet wouldst wrongly win: thou'ldst have,
    great Glamis,
That which cries 'Thus thou must do, if thou have
    it;
And that which rather thou dost fear to do
Than wishest should be undone.' Hie thee hither,
That I may pour my spirits in thine ear,
And chastise with the valour of my tongue .
All that impedes thee from the golden round,
Which fate and metaphysical aid doth seem
To have thee crown'd withal."

Shakespeare, Macbeth

Interval or step. The variation of pitch between words or syllables is called pitch interval or step. As mentioned earlier in this section, the lifting of a word or syllable in pitch is the primary method of emphasis. However, the interval has many other uses and connotations. When used properly, the interval adds variety and melody to the dialogue. Too little use of the interval or a repetitious pattern tends to make the speech monotonous. This lack of pitch variety is often the case when an untrained actor reads poetry. The pattern is often similar to the following:

Haste   Nymph,   bring   thee
   thee,   and   with

Jest   youth-   Jol-   ty.
   and   ful   li-

This singsong tendency may be avoided by a more varied melodic pattern, pitch level, and phrasing.

Consider the possible pitch variation and melody in these lines spoken by Portia (Act III, Scene 2).

"I pray you, tarry: pause a day or two
Before you hazard; for, in choosing wrong,
I lose your company: Therefore forbear awhile.
There's something tells me, but it is not love,
I would not lose you; and you know yourself,
Hate counsels not in such a quality."

Shakespeare, The Merchant of Venice

When the interval between words or syllables is large, the effect is one of mental vigor or alertness. The following speech by Brutus (Act III, Scene 2) is that of an alert, vigorous mind. This mental state, as well as the thought content of the speech, demands a style of delivery using wide intervals.

"Romans, countrymen, and lovers! Hear me for my cause, and be silent, that you may hear: believe me for mine honour, and have respect to mine honour, that you may believe: censure me in your wisdom, and awake your senses, that you may the better judge. If there be any in this assembly, any dear friend of Caesar's, to him I say that Brutus' love to Caesar was no less than his. If then that friend demand why Brutus rose against Caesar, this is my answer: not that I loved Caesar less, but that I loved Rome more. Had you rather Caesar were living, and die all slaves, than that Caesar were dead, to live all freemen? As Caesar loved me, I weep for him; as he was fortunate, I rejoice at it; as he was valiant, I honour him. But

as he was ambitious, I slew him. There is tears for his love; joy for his fortune; honour for his valour; and death for his ambition. Who is here so base that would be a bondman? If any, speak; for him have I offended. Who is here so rude that would not be a Roman? If any, speak; for him have I offended. Who is here so vile that will not love his country? If any, speak; for him have I offended. I pause for a reply."

Shakespeare, Julius Caesar

In contrast to the mental vigor indicated in the previous example, the speech of Macbeth (Act V, Scene 5), just after he has been informed of Lady Macbeth's death, suggests mental weariness and depression of spirit. This mood is best conveyed by small intervals or a somewhat flat, horizontal melody pattern.

"She should have died hereafter;
There would have been a time for such a word.
To-morrow, and to-morrow, and to-morrow,
Creeps in this petty pace from day to day,
To the last syllable of recorded time;
And all our yesterdays have lighted fools
The way to dusty death. Out, out, brief candle!
Life's but a walking shadow, a poor player
That struts and frets his hour upon the stage
And then is heard no more: it is a tale
Told by an idiot, full of sound and fury,
Signifying nothing."

Shakespeare, Macbeth

In a similar vein is the expression of a wife's grief at her husband's grave, from the Requiem scene of Arthur Miller's Death of a Salesman.*

LINDA: Forgive me dear. I can't cry. I don't know what it is, but I can't cry. I don't understand it. Why did you ever do that? Help me,

---

* Arthur Miller, Death of a Salesman, p. 139. Copyright, 1949, by Arthur Miller. Reprinted by permission of Viking Press.

Willy, I can't cry. It seems to me that you're just on another trip. I keep expecting you. Willy, dear, I can't cry. Why did you do it? I search and search and I search, and I can't understand it, Willy. I made the last payment on the house today. Today, dear. And there'll be nobody home. (*A sob rises in her throat.*) We're free and clear. (*Sobbing more fully, released*) We're free . . . We're free . . . We're free . . . .

In the following example from the final scene of Eugene O'Neill's *Bound East for Cardiff** Yank is lying on his bunk, near to death because of a fall on board ship. He is talking to his friend Driscoll.

(DRISCOLL *reaches out and grasps* YANK's *hand. There is a pause, during which both fight to control themselves.*)

YANK: My throat's like a furnace. (*He gasps for air.*) Gimme a drink of water, will yuh, Drisc? (DRISCOLL *gets him a dipper of water.*) I wish this was a pint of beer. Oooohh! (*He chokes, his face convulsed with agony, his hands tearing at his shirt-front. The dipper falls from his nerveless fingers.*)

DRISCOLL: For the love ov God, what is ut, Yank?

YANK: (*Speaking with tremendous difficulty*) S'long, Drisc! (*He stares straight in front of him with eyes starting from their sockets.*) Who's that?

DRISCOLL: Who? What?

YANK: (*Faintly*) A pretty lady dressed in black. (*His face twitches and his body writhes in a final spasm, then straightens out rigidly.*)

Because of Yank's weakened physical condition and hazy mental state, his speech will lack strong emphasis and, consequently, the pitch interval will be slight. There will be only a very moderate lifting of the voice for each important word. This principle of raising the voice for important words must be followed regardless of the physical and mental state of the character.

---

* Eugene O'Neill, *Bound East for Cardiff*. Copyright, 1920, by Eugene O'Neill. Reprinted by permission of Random House.

Any variations in the use of interval for line interpretation are variations of degree.

Inflection. As mentioned earlier, the glide of the voice from one pitch level to another is called inflection. This is similar to the slur on the music score. This glide may occur on words or on syllables within words. The important point for the actor is that he must not only have his voice under sufficient control for the proper execution of inflections but he must also know when and why inflections are to be used.

Inflections convey a number of connotations to the listener. (1) The inflection may convey a satiric or sarcastic attitude. For example, "Oh, yea?" when said with an upward glide of the voice may mean "Oh, no." (2) The upward glide at the end of a statement may mean a falsehood, doubt, insecurity, or uncertainty, as illustrated by, "Perhaps I'll learn to love him, after a while." (3) The inflection may convey something more than the literal wording. There is more in the line than meets the eye. An example of this use of inflection is Mae West's famous line, "Come up and see me sometime."

Inflection may add a gay, merry, or lyrical quality to the dialogue. The following verse spoken by Touchstone (Act III, Scene 2) seems to require a great deal of inflection to catch the gay, lyrical, comic note.

"If a hart do lack a hind,
Let him seek out Rosalind.
If the cat will after kind,
So be sure will Rosalind.
Winter garments must be lined,
So must slender Rosalind.
They that reap must sheaf and bind;
Then to cart with Rosalind.
Sweetest nut hath sourest rind,
Such a nut is Rosalind.
He that sweetest rose will find,
Must find love's prick and Rosalind."

Shakespeare, *As You Like It*

An exaggerated use of inflection may heighten the artificial, nonsensical, or farcical quality of the dialogue. In the scene from Oscar Wilde's *The Importance of Being Earnest* at the end of this chapter, an exaggerated use of inflection is important, particularly for Lady Bracknell's lines.

In summary, varying degrees of inflection may change the meaning of the line, the attitude of the character, or the mood of the scene.

Force

The late Milne Kibbee, a well-known actor during the period between the two World Wars, is said to have given his daughter, Lois, three basic rules for acting: "learn your lines, face the audience, and speak loud." Obviously, these simple rules are far from adequate to meet the requirements of the actor's art. Plainly, the last two rules would require a great deal of modification. But in our contemporary theater, even more than in Mr. Kibbee's day, many professional actors fail to project the author's lines clearly and forcefully. Such faulty delivery not only irritates the audience but also is inexcusable for anyone who calls himself a professional. This deficiency in the case of some actors is probably the result of insufficient voice training. More often it is a misuse of style; it is an attempt to give an actual lifelike delivery. Such an approach ignores the basic nature of the theater and, to a degree, negates acting as an art form. In addition to the basic requirement that the actor speak his lines loudly enough to be heard, there are a number of factors which have a bearing on the degree of force or volume in the delivery.

Attack. Various writers, in discussing voice production, have used the terms *effusive, expulsive,* and *explosive* to describe the form of attack or application of force to a word or line. The effusive form of attack refers to an even distribution of vocal force. There is no sudden release of air over the vocal bands. Many situations and moods (meditative, peaceful, serene,) seem to be best served by this use of force.

DUKE: If music be the food of love, play on;
Give me excess of it, that, surfeiting,
The appetite may sicken, and so die.
That strain again! It had a dying fall:
Oh, it came o'er my ear like the sweet sound
That breathes upon a bank of violets,
Stealing and giving odour!

Shakespeare, *Twelfth Night*

In the expulsive form of attack there is a vigorous, but not extreme, release of air over the vocal bands. Air pressure is controlled or held and then suddenly released with strong attack on the important words. A keyed-up or disturbed character often employs this form of vocal attack.

IAGO: Awake! what, ho, Brabantio! thieves! thieves! thieves! Look to your house, your daughter and your bags! Thieves! thieves!

Shakespeare, *Othello*

The explosive form of attack is self-descriptive. It is a violent and extreme use of vocal force. It results from high muscular pressure causing a loud, sharp sound when the air is suddenly released over the vocal bands.

"Stop! stop! Don't come near me!
Help! help!"

Although these terms for the use of force may be helpful to the actor, they obviously do not cover all the variations in volume. In the following excerpts, test the application of vocal force which seems most appropriate in each instance.

Look Homeward, Angel, by Ketti Frings, is based on the novel by Thomas Wolfe. This scene is from Act III.*

(MRS. GANT *has just heard that her son,* EUGENE, *is planning to marry* LAURA. ELIZA *appears at the door*

---

* Ketti Frings, *Look Homeward, Angel.* Copyright, 1958, by Edward C. Aswell. Reprinted by permission of Ketti Frings.

of LAURA's *room.* LAURA *is dressed and is packing her suitcase on the bed.*)

LAURA: Oh, Mrs. Gant. I've been expecting you. Come in. (*As* ELIZA *enters*)

ELIZA: I should think you would.

LAURA: Mrs. Gant, before you say anything —

ELIZA: I'll vow I can't believe a mature woman — at a time of trouble like this — would take advantage of a child, a mere child —

LAURA: Mrs. Gant, will you please listen?

ELIZA: (*Tossing a nightgown from head of bed into suitcase*) I will listen to nothing. You just pack your things and get out of this house. I should have known what you were from the first minute I set eyes on you . . . "I'm looking for a room, Mrs. Gant . . ." Why, butter wouldn't melt in your mouth —

LAURA: (*Slowly, distinctly*) Mrs. Gant, I am not marrying Eugene. I'm not. I wish with all my heart I could!

ELIZA: (*Turning to dresser*) You can't lie out of it. Gene just told me.

LAURA: I am engaged to be married to a young man in Richmond.

ELIZA: What kind of a wicked game are you playing with my child?

LAURA: (*Sits on bed.* ELIZA *sits chair Left.*) Mrs. Gant, this isn't easy. I should have told Gene long ago — but I didn't. A girl about to get married suddenly finds herself facing responsibilities. I never liked responsibilities. Gene knows how I am. I like music, I like to walk in the woods, I like — to dream. I know I'm older than Gene, but in many ways I'm younger. The thought of marriage frightened me. I told my fiancé I needed time to think it over. I fell in love with Eugene. I found the kind of romance I'd never known before, but I've also found that it isn't the answer. Gene is a wonderful boy, Mrs. Gant. He must go to college. He must have room to

expand and grow, to find himself. He mustn't be tied down at this point in his life. He needs the whole world to wander in — and I know now that I need a home, I need children — I need a husband. (*Rises, closes bag.*) For people like me there are rules, very good rules for marriage and for happiness — and I've broken enough of them. I telephoned Philip last night. He's arriving at the depot on that early train. We're going on to Charleston together, and we'll be married there. He loves me, and I will love him too after a while. (*Takes note from desk.*) I left this note for Eugene. I couldn't just tell him. (*Gives it to* ELIZA. *Crosses for bag, puts it Down Left of head of bed. Gets hat and purse from bureau.*) Will you say good-bye to Mr. Gant for me, and tell him I hope he feels better? And my good-byes to Mr. Clatt and the others? And to Helen. Especially to Helen. She works so hard. (*Looks around.*) Good-bye, little room. I've been happy here. (*Picks up suitcase, faces* ELIZA.) Some day you're going to have to let him go, too. Good-bye, Mrs. Gant. (*She exits.*)

This speech of Capulet is from Act III, Scene 5.

"God's bread! it makes me mad:
Day, night, hour, tide, time, work, play,
Alone, in company, still my care hath been
To have her match'd: and having now provided
A gentleman of noble parentage,
Of fair demesnes, youthful, nobly train'd,
Stuff'd, as they say, with honourable parts,
Proportion'd as one's thought would wish a man;
And then to have a wretched puling fool,
A whining mammet, in her fortune's tender,
To answer 'I'll not wed; I cannot love,
I am too young; I pray you, pardon me.'
But, an you will not wed, I'll pardon you:
Graze where you will, you shall not house with me:
Look to 't, think on 't, I do not use to jest.
Thursday is near; lay hand on heart, advise:
An you be mine, I'll give you to my friend;
An you be not, hang, beg, starve, die in the streets,
For, by my soul, I'll ne'er acknowledge thee,

Nor what is mine shall never do thee good:
Trust to 't, bethink you; I'll not be forsworn."

Shakespeare, *Romeo and Juliet*

Volume in relation to character. Mention has been made of the use of varying degrees of force as a means of suggesting the situation and of indicating the gravity of the subject matter. The type of character the speaker is also influences the volume of delivery. Sometimes a character is referred to as a "loud mouth." This type of individual speaks with more than the normal use of volume, regardless of the occasion or the content of his speech. Typical of this group is the midway barker or the "con" man. In the following excerpt from Act I of *The Rainmaker,** Starbuck must combine winsome traits with his aggressiveness.

STARBUCK: And then I look up and there's a herd of white buffalo stampedin' across the sky. And then, sister-of-all-good-people, down comes the rain! Rain in buckets, rain in barrels, fillin' the lowlands, floodin' the gulleys. And the land is as green as the valley of Adam.

In contrast with Starbuck, Mr. Pim is an indecisive willy-nilly. He has thoughtlessly and erroneously told the Mardens that on the boat from Australia to England he met a Mr. Telworthy. This was the name of Mrs. Marden's former husband, who, supposedly, had long since died. In this scene from Act III of *Mr. Pim Passes By,*† Mr. Pim returns to apologize and make amends for his error. His delivery would lack assertiveness and assurance.

PIM: (*In a whisper*) Er — may I come in, Mrs. Marden?

---

* N. Richard Nash, *The Rainmaker.* Copyright, 1955, by N. Richard Nash. Reprinted by permission of N. Richard Nash, and Random House.

† A. A. Milne, *Mr. Pim Passes By.* Copyright, 1931, by Alfred A. Knopf. Reprinted by permission of Curtis Brown, London.

OLIVIA: (*In surprise*) Mr. Pim!

PIM: (*Anxiously and again looking around at staircase*) Mr. Marden is — er — not here?

OLIVIA: (*Getting up*) No! Do you want to see him? I will —

PIM: (*Another look around at staircase and moving down center*) No, no, no! Not for the world. There is no immediate danger of his returning, Mrs. Marden?

OLIVIA: (*Surprised*) No, I don't think so, Mr. Pim. But . . . what is it? You —

PIM: I took the liberty of returning by the window in the hope of finding you alone.

OLIVIA: Yes?

PIM: (*Still rather nervous and throwing up his arms in distress*) Mr. Marden will be so angry with me, and very rightly. Oh, I blame myself. I blame myself entirely. I don't know how I can have been so stupid.

Emotional intensity. Strong feeling or high emotional tension, as in the Capulet speech, is usually accompanied by use of extreme volume. In the case of uncontrolled emotion the use of force is accompanied by a higher than normal pitch of the voice, as in the final stages of a quarrel. In controlled emotion the pitch is often low, the loudness restrained, and the attack on the words sharp and firm. Consider how a man might express the following line.

"You get out of my house, Sir, or I'll throw you out!"

Volume, combined with an increase of pitch and tempo, is an effective device for building to the high dramatic peak of a speech or scene. Conversely, a drop in pitch level and a decrease in volume and tempo are often used to convey a drop in the emotional intensity, or a return to the norm. Usually there is a succession of "builds" and "drops" within a scene. It is the duty of the actor to study his script in order to determine where they occur. It can be readily observed that the following speech by King Henry (Act III, Scene 1) begins with a strong attack, drops to a more quiet yet intense use of force, and then builds to a climax at the end.

"Once more unto the breach, dear friends, once
    more;
Or close the wall up with our English dead.
In peace there's nothing so becomes a man
As modest stillness and humility:
But when the blast of war blows in our ears,
Then imitate the action of the tiger;
Stiffen the sinews, summon up the blood,
Disguise fair nature with hard-favoured rage;
Then lend the eye a terrible aspect;
Let it pry through the portage of the head
Like the brass cannon; let the brow o'erwhelm it
As fearfully as doth a galled rock
O'erhand and jutty his confounded base,
Swilled with the wild and wasteful ocean.
Now set the teeth and stretch the nostril wide,
Hold hard the breath and bend up every spirit
To his full height. On, on, you noblest English,
Whose blood is fet from fathers of war proof!
Fathers that, like so many Alexanders,
Have in these parts from morn till even fought,
And sheathed their swords for lack of argument:
Dishonour not your mothers; now attest
That those whom you called fathers did beget you.
Be copy now to men of grosser blood,
And teach them how to war. And you, good
    yeomen,
Whose limbs were made in England, show us here
The mettle of your pasture; let us swear
That you are worth your breeding; which I doubt
    not;
For there is none of you so mean and base,
That hath not noble luster in your eyes.
I see you stand like greyhounds in the slips,
Straining upon the start. The game's afoot:
Follow your spirit, and upon this charge
Cry 'God for Harry, England, and Saint
    George!' "

                Shakespeare, *Henry V*

Frequently a build in emotional intensity can be effected by each character "topping" the lines of the previous character, that is, by heightening the intensity, volume, and pitch as the lines progress. This excerpt from Shakespeare's *Julius Caesar* (Act IV, Scene 3) might involve topping.

BRUTUS: When Marcus Brutus grows so covetous,
To lock such rascal counters from his friends,
Be ready, gods, with all your thunderbolts,
Dash him to pieces!

CASSIUS: I denied you not.

BRUTUS: You did.

CASSIUS: I did not: he was but a fool
That brought my answer back. Brutus hath
    rived my heart:
A friend should bear his friend's infirmities,
But Brutus makes mine greater than they are.

BRUTUS: I do not, till you practice them on me.

CASSIUS: You love me not.

BRUTUS: I do not like your faults.

CASSIUS: A friendly eye could never see such faults.

BRUTUS: A flatterer's would not, though they do
    appear
As huge as high Olympus.

CASSIUS: Come, Antony, and young Octavius,
    come,
Revenge yourselves alone on Cassius,
For Cassius is aweary of the world;
Hated by one he loves; braved by his brother;
Check'd like a bondman, all his faults observed,
Set in a notebook, learned and conn'd by rote,
To cast into my teeth. O, I could weep
My spirit from mine eyes! There is my dagger,
And here my naked breast; within, a heart
Dearer than Plutus' mine, richer than gold;
If that thou be'st a Roman, take it forth;
I, that denied thee gold, will give my heart:
Strike, as thou didst at Caesar; for I know
When thou didst hate him worst, thou lovedst him
    better
Than ever thou lovedst Cassius.

BRUTUS: Sheathe your dagger:
Be angry when you will, it shall have scope;
Do what you will, dishonor shall be humour.
O Cassius, you are yoked with a lamb,
That carries anger as the flint bears fire,
Who, much enforced, shows a hasty spark
And straight is cold again.

CASSIUS: Hath Cassius lived
To be but mirth and laughter to his Brutus,
When grief and blood ill-temper'd vexeth him?

BRUTUS: When I spoke that, I was ill-temper'd too.

CASSIUS: Do you confess so much? Give me your
        hand.

BRUTUS: And my heart too.

CASSIUS: O Brutus!

BRUTUS: What's the matter?

CASSIUS: Have not you love enough to bear with
        me,
When that rash humor which my mother gave me
Makes me forgetful?

BRUTUS: Yes, Cassius, and from henceforth,
When you are over-earnest with your Brutus,
He'll think your mother chides, and leave you so.

Another example which requires a careful use
of vocal force is the scene between Elizabeth and
Mary in Schiller's *Mary Stuart*, which is included
in the exercises at the end of this chapter.

Tempo

When properly used, the rate of speech is a most
effective tool for an actor. The connotations
which various tempos may convey are closely
linked with our physiological and psychological
makeup and our social conditioning. In moments
of high tension and excitement, there is a quicken-
ing of the heartbeat and respiration. We normally associate a rapid tempo as being more
appropriate for occasions of gaiety and a slow
tempo for occasions of solemnity. Although
tempo may exert a dominant control over the mood
of the scene, its use in conveying clarity of thought,

character delineation, and the overall unity of the
play's rhythm cannot be overestimated. It is not
implied here that rate should be used as an
obviously arbitrary device but rather that the
appropriate tempo should develop out of the
exigencies of the script. In the search for an
appropriate tempo in the scene, the actor has no
exact guides comparable to those available to the
musician. The musical score has such time indi-
cators as the basic rhythm, $\frac{3}{4}$, $\frac{4}{4}$, note duration,
rests, retards, the metronome time rate, and such
descriptive terms as andante, largo, and vivace.
Except for an occasional descriptive word such as
thoughtfully, hurriedly, and the like, supplied by
the author, the actor has little to guide him in
determining how slowly or rapidly a line or scene
should be played. He must derive the appropriate
tempo from a thorough understanding of the
subject matter, the character, and the mood.

As the subject matter becomes more profound, solemn, or complex, the tempo must be
reduced to correspond with it. Conversely, a
rapid tempo must be reached for light, trivial, or
commonplace material. It is the subtle variations
of tempo in relation to the material which test the
actor's dramatic sensitivity and artistry.

A constant awareness of the appropriate
tempo for a given scene must be accompanied by
an equally important concern for rapid cue pickup. Regardless of what tempo has been established, the actor should respond immediately to
the line which precedes his, unless there is good
reason for a delayed reply. Such response may
be more than mere vocal reply, since physical
reaction to what has been said usually precedes
vocal response. Even if a pause is indicated by the
script or desired for the effective relaying of
emotions, the actor must be aware that the pause
is also a part of the technique of cue pickup. In
many situations the character should say the
initial words of his speech before the previous
speech has been completed. In such cases the
technique of "overlapping" must be put to use.

This usually involves an increase of intensity, volume, and pitch, in addition to the basic task of interrupting the previous speaker.

Opportunities for topping and overlapping may be found in this scene (Act I, Scene 1) from *The Doctor in Spite of Himself* by Molière.*

(*Situation: The universal battle of the sexes, a domestic quarrel.*)

MARTINE: (*Off stage*) You wretch, (*crash*) come back here and fix this table!

SGANARELLE: Correct me if I'm wrong, my dear, but I seem to recall that you broke the leg off that table.

MARTINE: I needed it to beat some sense into that head of yours.

SGANARELLE: How dare you address me in such language? Who do you think is boss around here? (*Enter from* R.)

MARTINE: I am and don't you forget it. (*Hurls shoe at him.*) Now come back here and fix that table. (*Enter from* R.)

SGANARELLE: I won't!

MARTINE: You will!

SGANARELLE: I won't!

MARTINE: You will!

SGANARELLE: No; I tell you that I'll do nothing of the kind. You listen to me. I'm master here.

MARTINE: And I tell you that I'll have you live as I plan. I didn't marry you to put up with your pranks.

SGANARELLE: Oh! What a monstrous plague it is to have a wife!

MARTINE: Oh! What a nuisance it is to have a husband!

SGANARELLE: Aristotle was perfectly right in saying that a woman is worse than a devil!

MARTINE: Look at Master Clever, with his silly Aristotle!

---

* Adapted by Everett M. Schreck.

SGANARELLE: Yes, Master Clever. Find me another chopper of wood who can argue upon things as I can. Why, I served a famous physician for six years.

MARTINE: He tended the furnace.

SGANARELLE: When only a boy of five, I could speak Greek and Latin and knew five of Shakespeare's plays by heart. Ingratitude, thy name is woman.

MARTINE: A plague on the silly fool.

SGANARELLE: A plague on the saucy slut.

MARTINE: Cursed be the hour and the day when I took it into my head to say "yes."

SGANARELLE: Cursed be the cuckold of a notary that made me sign my own ruination.

MARTINE: It ill becomes you to complain on that score. You ought to thank Heaven every minute of the day that you have me for a wife. Did you deserve to marry a woman like me?

SGANARELLE: It's true you did me too much honor, and I had great occasion to be satisfied with my wedding night! Zounds! Let's not get on that subject. I might say certain things . . .

MARTINE: What? What could you say?

SGANARELLE: Enough; let's drop the subject. It's enough that we know what we know, and that you were very lucky to meet with me.

MARTINE: Lucky? What do you call "very lucky to meet with you?" A fellow who will drive me to the hospital — a debauched, deceitful wretch, who eats up all I have!

SGANARELLE: That's a lie, I drink part of it.

MARTINE: Who sells piece by piece everything that's in the house!

SGANARELLE: That's called living on one's means.

MARTINE: Who has taken the very bed from under me!

SGANARELLE: (*Aside*) Now she doesn't sleep so late in the morning!

MARTINE: In short, who does not leave me a stick of furniture in the whole house.

SGANARELLE: There will be less trouble in moving.

MARTINE: And who, from morning to night, does nothing but gamble and drink!

SGANARELLE: I have to keep my spirits up!

MARTINE: And what am I to do all the while with my family?

SGANARELLE: Whatever you like.

MARTINE: I have got four, poor, little children on my hands.

SGANARELLE: Put them down.

MARTINE: — Who keep asking me every moment for bread.

SGANARELLE: Whip them. When I've had enough to eat and drink, everyone in the house ought to be satisfied.

MARTINE: And do you mean to tell me, you sot, that things can go on like this?

SGANARELLE: Wife, let us proceed gently, if you please.

MARTINE: That I am to bear forever with your insolence and your debauchery?

SGANARELLE: Let's not get into a passion, wifie.

MARTINE: How can one avoid it with you for a husband?

SGANARELLE: My dear, you know that I am not very patient and that my arm knows how to wield a club!

MARTINE: Ha! I laugh at your silly threats.

SGANARELLE: My little chickadee, your hide is itching as usual.

MARTINE: I'll let you see that I'm not afraid of you.

SGANARELLE: My dearest better half, you have set your heart upon a thrashing.

MARTINE: Do you think I'm afraid of your talk?

SGANARELLE: Sweet object of my affections, I shall box your ears for you.

MARTINE: Sot that you are!

SGANARELLE: I shall thrash you.

MARTINE: Walking wine-cask!

SGANARELLE: I shall pummel you.

MARTINE: Infamous wretch!

SGANARELLE: I shall curry your skin.

MARTINE: Wretch! villain! deceiver! cur! scoundrel! gallows-bird! churl! rogue! drunkard! scamp! thief! . . .

SGANARELLE: You will have it, will you? (*Takes a stick and beats her.*)

MARTINE: (*Shrieking*) Help! help! help! help!

SGANARELLE: This is the real way of quieting you.

In these excerpts and in those at the end of this chapter, the actor may experiment with various tempos in order to discover the one which seems most appropriate to the material and the situation.

Quality

During the rehearsal period the actor should give careful consideration to the quality of voice to be used in interpreting his lines. In general, the type of character dictates the quality of voice to be used. For example, a hard, avaricious character would in all probability have a harsh, unpleasant voice. On the other hand, we think of a gentle, kindly person as having a soft, pleasing voice. But there are many variations or combinations of character types, each with an individual manner of speech. Each character must vary his particular voice quality in response to the inner thoughts and feelings he has for the other characters.

In order to acquire the appropriate voice quality, the actor may find a dual approach helpful. (1) Acquire, as completely as possible, the character's inner thoughts and feelings. This should, to a degree at least, indicate a tonal quality which is appropriate. (2) Heighten and intensify the voice quality by technically controlling the placement and formation of the sounds. To acquire control over the quality of voice often requires much patience and practice. However, most individuals are capable of variations in vocal quality, as evidenced by vocal changes that occur automatically in response to their emotions.

This scene (Act I, Scene 3) with Shylock, Antonio, and Bassanio, from Shakespeare's *The Merchant of Venice*, illustrates the need for changes in voice quality, particularly on the part of Shylock.

SHYLOCK: (*Aside*) How like a fawning publican he
   looks!
I hate him for he is a Christian;
But more for that in low simplicity
He lends out money gratis and brings down
The rate of usance here with us in Venice.
If I can catch him once upon the hip,
I will feed fat the ancient grudge I bear him.
He hates our sacred nation; and he rails,
Even there where merchants most do congregate,
On me, my bargains, and my well-won thrift,
Which he calls interest. Cursed be my tribe,
If I forgive him!

BASSANIO: Shylock, do you hear?

SHYLOCK: I am debating of my present store;
And, by the near guess of my memory,
I cannot instantly raise up the gross
Of full three thousand ducats. What of that?
Tubal, a wealthy Hebrew of my tribe,
Will furnish me. But soft! How many months
Do you desire? (*To Antonio*) Rest you fair, good
   signior;
Your Worship was the last man in our mouths.

. . . .

ANTONIO: Well, Shylock, shall we be beholding to
   you?

SHYLOCK: Signior Antonio, many a time and oft
In the Rialto you have rated me
About my moneys and my usances:
Still have I borne it with a patient shrug;

For sufferance is the badge of all our tribe.
You call me misbeliever, cut-throat dog,
And spit upon my Jewish gaberdine,
And all for use of that which is mine own.
Well then, it now appears you need my help:
Go to, then, you come to me and you say
"Shylock, we would have moneys." You say so;
You that did void your rheum upon my beard,
And foot me as you spurn a stranger cur
Over your threshold; moneys is your suit.
What should I say to you? Should I not say,
"Hath a dog money? Is it possible
A cur can lend three thousand ducats?" Or
Shall I bend low and in a bondman's key,
With bated breath and whispering humbleness,
Say this, —
"Fair sir, you spit on me on Wednesday last;
You spurned me such a day, another time
You called me dog, and for these courtesies
I'll lend you thus much moneys"?

ANTONIO: I am as like to call thee so again,
To spit on thee again, to spurn thee too.
If thou wilt lend this money, lend it not
As to thy friends; for when did friendship take
A breed for barren metal of his friend?
But lend it rather to thine enemy;
Who if he break, thou mayst with better face
Exact the penalty.

SHYLOCK: Why, look you how you storm!
I would be friends with you, and have your love,
Forget the shames that you have stain'd me with,
Supply your present wants, and take doit
Of usance for my moneys, and you'll not hear me:
This is kind I offer.

PUNCTUATION MARKS A GUIDE TO LINE INTERPRETATION

Punctuation marks are an aid to the reader in acquiring both the intellectual and emotional content of the printed page. A knowledge of what the markings signify will not only help the actor to gain the proper understanding of the script but will also help him to communicate more completely the author's meaning.

The period

The period at the end of a sentence usually indicates finality or completeness of thought. This concept is generally conveyed by a falling inflection (⌐). However, when the line suggests meditation, doubt, or uncertainty, the voice may be sustained on a level, or even raised. The actor should guard against the all too common fault of using a descending scale in reading the line. This tendency is called "running down to the period." The line begins high and strong but the voice decreases in pitch and volume as it nears the period. The melodic pattern is similar to this:

$$\text{The}\quad{}^{\text{quality}}\quad{}_{\text{of}}\quad{}^{\text{mercy}}\quad\text{is}\quad{}_{\text{not}}\quad{}_{\text{strain'd.}}$$

Although this descending scale often occurs in normal conversation, its use on the stage should be purposeful rather than habitual. A faulty melodic pattern may be due to a lack of breath control or to a mere saying of words without regard to the meaning. One serious result of the descending melody is that the main point of the sentence may be lost since the last word, often the most important one, is not emphasized. To avoid this, the last or important word is usually given increased stress and a higher pitch. The melodic pattern might be similar to the following:

$$\text{The}\quad \text{q}^{\text{u}}{}^{\text{a}}{}^{\text{i}}{}^{\text{l}\cdot}{}_{\text{t}}\text{y}\quad {}_{\text{of}}\quad \text{m}^{\text{e}}{}^{\text{r}}{}^{\text{c}}\text{y}\quad \text{is}\quad \text{not}\quad \text{s}^{\text{t}}{}^{\text{rai}}\text{n'd.}$$

The repetitious descending scale of line reading not only inhibits the communication of thought but also produces monotony and a generally depressed feeling.

The comma

Commas are used to separate words in a series, and for parenthetical expressions and nonrestrictive clauses. They do not necessarily indicate pauses. Although we sometimes pause for a comma, we frequently do not pause for a comma; often we pause where there is no comma when the sense of the sentence requires it. In the following example there should be no pause for the commas.

No, no, no, I wouldn't say that.

Frequently, as in the next example, there must be pauses even though there are no punctuation marks.

James had used had had where John had used had. Had had made the best sense.

When pausing within the sentence for either commas or sense, the voice level should be sustained and the definite falling inflection should be avoided.

Colons and semicolons

These markings indicate the ending of a unit of thought. Depending on the thought or emotion to be conveyed, a falling voice inflection or a sustained level is normally used for these markings. In addition to a proper interpretation of the line, the colon or semicolon offers the actor an opportunity for a breath intake.

The dash

This mark indicates a break in thought or feeling, or an abrupt change in sentence structure. It usually requires a pause with sustained pitch. Note the use of the dash for conveying the thought and emotion in Vanzetti's conversation as recorded by reporter Philip D. Strong.*

---

* Robert P. Weeks, ed., *Commonwealth vs. Sacco and Vanzetti*, p. 226. Copyright, 1958. Reprinted by permission of Prentice-Hall.

"If it had not been for these thing, I might have live out my life, talking at street corners to scorning men. I might have die, unmarked, unknown, a failure. Now we are not a failure. This is our career and our triumph. Never in our full life could we hope to do so much work for tolerance, for joostice, for man's understanding of man, as now we do by accident.

"Our words — our lives — our pains — nothing! The taking of our lives — lives of a good shoemaker and a poor fishpeddler — all! That last moment belongs to us — that agony is our triumph!"

The exclamation point

This punctuation mark denotes strong feeling or emphasis. It usually requires the actor to use a higher pitch, more volume, and greater intensity, although the proper effect may also be achieved by a strong attack without an increase in pitch or volume. As stated elsewhere, however, the actor should be guided by inner motivation for the proper expression of his thoughts and emotions.

Notice how the punctuation marks aid the understanding of content and the interpretation of Hamlet's soliloquy (Act I, Scene 2). Although many of these markings have been added since Shakespeare's day by various editors and publishers, their help to the interpreter is beyond question.

"Oh, that this too too solid flesh would melt,
Thaw, and resolve itself into a dew!
Or that the Everlasting had not fix'd
His canon 'gainst self-slaughter! O God! God!
How weary, stale, flat, and unprofitable
Seem to me all the uses of this world!
Fie on't! ah fie! 'tis an unweeded garden,
That grows to seed; things rank and gross in
    nature
Possess it merely. That it should come to this!
But two months dead! Nay, not so much, not two:
So excellent a king; that was, to this,

Hyperion to a satyr: so loving to my mother,
That he might not beteem the winds of heaven
Visit her face too roughly. Heaven and earth!
Must I remember? Why, she would hang on him,
As if increase of appetite had grown
By what it fed on: and yet, within a month —
Let me not think on't. — Frailty, thy name is
    woman! —
A little month, or ere those shoes were old
With which she follow'd my poor father's body,
Like Niobe, all tears: — why she, even she, —
O God! a beast that wants discourse of reason
Would have mourn'd longer, — married with my
    uncle,
My father's brother, but no more like my father
Than I to Hercules: within a month;
Ere yet the salt of most unrighteous tears
Had left the flushing in her galled eyes,
She married. O, most wicked speed, to post
With such dexterity to incestuous sheets!
It is not, nor it cannot come to good:
But break, my heart, for I must hold my tongue!

Shakespeare, *Hamlet*

The question mark

The question mark causes difficulty for many beginning actors. Due to early grade school training, they are inclined to end every question with a rising inflection. The continued use of a rising inflection for questions not only makes for monotony but also, when improperly used, gives an unnatural melodic pattern to the sentence. The rising inflection is proper and natural only for certain questions. Many questions which we ask every day are said with a falling inflection. For example:

How do you do?

Is this yours or mine?

What time is it?

How far is it to the station?

Other questions are normally said with a rising inflection.

Are you ready?

Are you going?

Is this your bag?

Will your uncle be waiting at the station?

In each group of questions there is a common element. In the second group each question could be answered by a yes or no. In the first group the questions could not be answered by yes or no. Although there may be some exceptions to the rule, in general, questions which require a yes or no answer have a rising inflection. Other questions end with a falling inflection. This is characteristic of American speech.

COMMON FAULTS OF LINE INTERPRETATION

Emphasis placed on the wrong word. This fault usually results from a misunderstanding of the meaning of the sentence.

Overemphasis. In his desire to be heard, the actor sometimes puts too much emphasis on every word. This produces a strained and stilted effect. Moreover, when unimportant words are stressed, it takes the listener's attention from the key words in the sentence and communication of the meaning is impaired.

Faulty melody pattern. This may take the form of improper emphasis, descending scale, or an imposed, arbitrary, or repetitious pattern. In general, this fault may be corrected by a more thorough understanding of the script and by absorbing the author's thoughts and feelings.

Faulty phrasing or grouping. This stems from too much attention to individual words. Meaning is best expressed when closely related words are grouped, with slight pauses between each group.

Monotony. This very serious fault may relate to any or all the vocal elements: pitch, volume, rate, or quality. Its correction may require greater identification with the character and involvement in the situation, as well as extensive vocal training.

Lack of vocal projection. This fault may be due to a lack of vitality in the actor or by his misguided sense of what is appropriately natural to acting. Assuming there is no speech impediment, the fault may also be attributed to deficiency in enunciation, articulation, or breath control.

Faulty pitch level. Sometimes the actor assumes a voice level which is too high or too low for the best expression of the mood of the scene. The natural approach based on inner truth should, in most cases, correct this fault.

Practice Selections

JOHN BROWN'S BODY

by Stephen Vincent Benét

JOHN BROWN'S SPEECH*

I have, may it please the Court, a few words to say.

In the first place I deny everything but what I have all along admitted: of a design on my part to free slaves. . . .

Had I interfered in the matter which I admit, and which I admit has been fairly proved . . . had I so interfered in behalf of the rich, the powerful, the intelligent, or the so-called great . . . it would have been all right.

I see a book kissed which I suppose to be the Bible, . . . which teaches me to remember them that are in bonds as bound with them. I endeavored to act up to that instruction. . . . I believe that to have interfered as I have done . . . in behalf of His despised poor, I did no wrong, but right. Now, if it is deemed necessary that I should forfeit my life . . . and mingle my blood . . . with the blood of millions in this slave country whose rights are disregarded by wicked, cruel and unjust enactments, I say, let it be done.

HENRY VIII

by William Shakespeare / Queen's plea in Act II, Scene 4

(*The* QUEEN *makes no answer, rises out of her chair, goes about the court, comes to the* KING, *and kneels at his feet; then speaks.*)

QUEEN KATHARINE

Sir, I desire you do me right and justice,
And to bestow your pity on me; for
I am a most poor woman, and a stranger,
Born out of your dominions; having here
No judge indifferent, nor no more assurance
Of equal friendship and proceeding. Alas, sir,

---

* *Selected Works of Stephen Vincent Benét*, published by Holt, Rinehart & Winston, pp. 48–49. Copyright, 1927, 1928, by Stephen Vincent Benét. Copyright renewed © 1955, by Rosemary Carr Benét. Reprinted by permission of Brandt & Brandt.

In what have I offended you? What cause
Hath my behavior given to your displeasure,
That thus you should proceed to put me off,
And take your good grace from me? Heaven witness,
I have been to you a true and humble wife,
At all times to your will conformable,
Ever in fear to kindle your dislike,
Yea, subject to your countenance, glad or sorry
As I saw it inclined: when was the hour
I ever contradicted your desire,
Or made it not mine too? Or which of your friends
Have I not strove to love, although I knew
He were mine enemy? what friend of mine
That had to him derived your anger, did I
Continue in my liking? nay, gave notice
He was from thence discharged? Sir, call to mind
That I have been your wife, in this obedience,
Upward of twenty years, and have been blest
With many children by you; if in the course
And process of this time you can report,
And prove it too, against mine honour aught,
My bond to wedlock or my love and duty,
Against your sacred person, in God's name,
Turn me away, and let the foul'st contempt
Shut door upon me, and so give me up
To the sharp'st kind of justice. Please you, sir,
The king, your father, was reputed for
A prince most prudent, of an excellent
And unmatch'd wit and judgment: Ferdinand,
My father, king of Spain, was reckon'd one
The wisest prince that there had reign'd by many
A year before: it is not to be question'd
That they had gather'd a wise council to them
Of every realm, that did debate this business,
Who deem'd our marriage lawful: wherefore I humbly
Beseech you, sir, to spare me, till I may
Be by my friends in Spain advised, whose counsel
I will implore: if not, i' the name of God,
Your pleasure be fulfill'd!

MARY STUART

by Friedrich Schiller / excerpt from Act III, Scene 4*

ELIZABETH   How, my lords? Which of you announced to me a prisoner bow'd down by woe? I see a haughty person, not one humbled by calamity.

MARY   So be it! — To this I will submit. (*She turns toward the* QUEEN.) Heaven has decided for you, sister. Your happy head is now with triumph crowned. I bless the Divine Power which thus has raised you. (*She kneels.*) But in your turn be merciful! Let me not lie thus disgraced before you! Stretch out your royal hand to raise me from the depth of my distress!

ELIZABETH   (*Stepping back*) You are where it becomes you, Lady Stuart. And I thankfully praise my God's protection who did not wish that I should kneel as a suppliant at your feet as you now kneel at mine.

MARY   (*With increased energy of feeling*) Oh! there are gods who punish haughty pride! Respect them, the dreadful ones, who thus before your feet have humbled me! Do not profane the royal Tudor blood, for in my veins it flows as pure as in your own. . . . My all, my life, my fortune now depends upon the influence of my words and tears; that I may move your heart. . . . If you regard me with those icy looks, my shuddering heart contracts itself, and frigid horror chains the words of supplication in my breast.

ELIZABETH   (*Cold and severe*) What have you to say to me, Lady Stuart? You wish'd to speak with me; and I, forgetting the Queen, and all the wrongs I have endured, fulfil the pious duty of the sister, and grant your request for my presence. Yet, in yielding to the generous feelings of magnanimity, I expose myself to rightful censure. For well you know, you would have had me murdered.

MARY   How shall I begin? O, Heaven! strengthen my words yet take from them whatever might offend. I cannot speak for myself without heavily accusing you and that I do not wish to do . . . I am a Queen, like you, yet you confined me in prison. I came to you as a suppliant, yet you scorned the holy law of hospitality, confined me in a dungeon; tore my friends and servants from me; I was exposed to unseemly want, and hurried to the bar of a disgraceful, insolent tribunal — no more of that! I will throw the blame of all on fate. 'Twas not your fault, no more than it was mine. An evil spirit rose from the abyss, to kindle in our hearts the flames of hate, by which our tender youth has been

---

* Friedrich Schiller, *Mary Stuart*. Translated by Everett M. Schreck.

divided. It grew with us, and evil men fanned the fatal fire with their breath. . . . No foreign tongue is now between us, sister. (*Approaching her confidently, and with a flattering tone*) Now we stand face to face; now sister, speak; name my crime, I'll give you satisfaction. . . .

ELIZABETH   Accuse not fate! It was your own deceitful heart and the wild ambition of your house. Your uncle, the proud, imperious priest, whose shameless hand grasps at all crowns, attacked me with unprovoked hostility. What arms did he not employ to storm my throne? . . . He fanned the flames of religious frenzy and civil insurrection. — But God was with me. . . . The blow was aimed at my head, but it is yours which falls!

MARY   I am in God's hand. You will never use your power to destroy me.

ELIZABETH   Who shall prevent me? Your uncle gave the example to all the kings of the world, how one makes a peace with his enemies. Mine shall be the school of Saint Bartholomew! I practice only what your priests have taught. . . . Say, with what lock can I secure your faith, which cannot be open'd by St. Peter's keys? No alliance can be concluded with a breed of serpents. Force is my only security.

MARY   O! this is but your wretched, dark suspicion! Had you declar'd me heir to your dominions, as is my right, then gratitude and love in me had procured for you a faithful friend and kinswoman.

ELIZABETH   Your friendship is abroad, Lady Stuart, your house is Papacy, the monk is your brother. Name *you* my successor! That in my life you might seduce my people —

MARY   O! sister, rule your realm in peace! I give up every claim to these dominions. Greatness no longer tempts me — You have done your worst on me; you have utterly destroyed me! But I cannot believe that you have come here to mock unfeelingly your hapless victim! Now speak the word, say, "Mary, you are free!" Say this, and I will take my life, my freedom, as a present from your hands. — I wait the word. — Woe to you if you do not grant this blessing, for then, sister, not for all this island's wealth, would I exchange my present lot for yours.

ELIZABETH   Do you confess at last that you are conquered? Are all your schemes run out? . . . Will no adventurer attempt for you again, the sad gallantry? Yes, it is finished, Lady Mary. . . . The world has other cares; no one is desirous of the dangerous honour of becoming your fourth husband! . . .

MARY   (*Starting angrily*) Sister, sister! — O, God! God! Grant me self-control!

ELIZABETH	(*Regards her long, with a look of proud contempt.*) Are these the charms, Lord Leicester, near which no woman may dare to stand? In truth, this honour has been cheaply gain'd; she who is common to all, may easily become the common object of applause.
MARY	This is too much!
ELIZABETH	(*Laughing insultingly*) Now you show your true face, till now it was only a mask.
MARY	(*Burning with anger, yet with a noble dignity*) My sins were human, and the faults of youth: superior force misled me. I have never denied or sought to hide it: I despised all false appearance as became a Queen. The worst of me is known, and I can say, that I am better than my reputation. But woe to you, when, in time to come, the world shall tear the robe of honour from your deeds. . . . Virtue was not your inheritance from your mother. We know full well what it was which brought the head of Anne Boleyn to the block.
SHREWSBURY	(*Stepping between both* QUEENS) Is this the moderation, the submission you promised, Lady Mary?
MARY	Moderation! I've endured what human nature can endure. Farewell, to lamb-hearted resignation and suffering patience!
SHREWSBURY	She is beside herself, my queen. Forgive her. (ELIZABETH, *speechless with anger, casts enraged looks at* MARY.)
MARY	(*Raising her voice*) If right prevail'd, you would now be kneeling before me for I'm your rightful queen. The English have been cheated by a juggler. A bastard — yes a bastard soils the English throne!

THE IMPORTANCE OF BEING EARNEST

by Oscar Wilde / excerpt from Act I

(LADY BRACKNELL *has inadvertently discovered* JACK WORTHING *proposing to her daughter* GWENDOLEN, *who is promptly and unceremoniously asked to leave and wait below in the carriage.*)

LADY BRACKNELL	(*Sitting down*) You can take a seat, Mr. Worthing. (*Looks in her pocket for notebook and pencil.*)
JACK	Thank you, Lady Bracknell, I prefer standing.

LADY BRACKNELL   (*Pencil and notebook in hand*) I feel bound to tell you that you are not down on my list of eligible young men, although I have the same list as the dear Duchess of Bolton has. We work together, in fact. However, I am quite ready to enter your name, should your answers be what a really affectionate mother requires. Do you smoke?

JACK   Well, yes, I must admit I smoke.

LADY BRACKNELL   I am glad to hear it. A man should always have an occupation of some kind. There are far too many idle men in London as it is. How old are you?

JACK   Twenty-nine.

LADY BRACKNELL   A very good age to be married at. I have always been of opinion that a man who desires to get married should either know everything or nothing. Which do you know?

JACK   (*After some hesitation*) I know nothing, Lady Bracknell.

LADY BRACKNELL   I am pleased to hear it. I do not approve of anything that tampers with natural ignorance. Ignorance is like a delicate exotic fruit: touch it and the bloom is gone. The whole theory of modern education is radically unsound. Fortunately in England, at any rate, education produces no effect whatsoever. If it did, it would prove a serious danger to the upper classes, and probably lead to acts of violence in Grosvenor Square. What is your income?

JACK   Between seven and eight thousand a year.

LADY BRACKNELL   (*Makes a note in her book*) In land, or in investments?

JACK   In investments, chiefly.

LADY BRACKNELL   That is satisfactory. What between the duties expected of one during one's lifetime, and the duties exacted from one after one's death, land has ceased to be either a profit or a pleasure. It gives one position, and prevents one from keeping it up. That's all that can be said about land.

JACK   I have a country house with some land, of course, attached to it, about fifteen hundred acres, I believe; but I don't depend on that for my real income. In fact, as far as I can make out, the poachers are the only people who make anything out of it.

LADY BRACKNELL   A country house! How many bedrooms? Well, that point can be cleared up afterwards. You have a town house, I hope? A girl with a simple, unspoiled nature, like Gwendolen, could hardly be expected to reside in the country.

JACK	Well, I own a house in Belgrave Square, but it is let by the year to Lady Bloxham. Of course, I can get it back whenever I like, at six months' notice.
LADY BRACKNELL	Lady Bloxham? I don't know her.
JACK	Oh, she goes about very little. She is a lady considerably advanced in years.
LADY BRACKNELL	Ah, now-a-days that is no guarantee of respectability of character. What number in Belgrave Square?
JACK	149.
LADY BRACKNELL	(*Shaking her head*) The unfashionable side. I thought there was something. However, that could easily be altered.
JACK	Do you mean the fashion, or the side?
LADY BRACKNELL	(*Sternly*) Both, if necessary, I presume. What are your politics?
JACK	Well, I am afraid I really have none. I am a Liberal Unionist.
LADY BRACKNELL	Oh, they count as Tories. They dine with us. Or come in the evening, at any rate. Now to minor matters. Are your parents living?
JACK	I have lost both my parents.
LADY BRACKNELL	Both? To lose one parent may be regarded as a misfortune — to lose both seems like carelessness. Who was your father? He seems to have been a man of wealth. Was he born in what the Radical papers call the purple of commerce, or did he rise from the ranks of the aristocracy?
JACK	I am afraid I really don't know. The fact is, Lady Bracknell, I said I had lost my parents. It would be nearer the truth to say that my parents seem to have lost me . . . I don't actually know who I am, by birth. I was . . . well, I was found. (*Rises.*)
LADY BRACKNELL	Found!
JACK	The late Mr. Thomas Cardew, an old gentleman of a very charitable and kindly disposition, found me, and gave me the name of Worthing, because he happened to have a first-class ticket for Worthing in his pocket at the time.
LADY BRACKNELL	*Where* did the charitable gentleman who had a first-class ticket for Worthing find you?
JACK	(*Gravely*) In a handbag.

LADY BRACKNELL	A handbag?
JACK	(*Very seriously*) Yes, Lady Bracknell. I was in a handbag — a somewhat large leather handbag, with handles to it — an ordinary handbag, in fact.
LADY BRACKNELL	In what locality did this Mr. Thomas Cardew come across this ordinary handbag?
JACK	In the cloakroom at Victoria Station. It was given to him in mistake for his own.
LADY BRACKNELL	(*Rising*) Mr. Worthing, I confess I feel somewhat bewildered by what you have just told me. To be born, or at any rate bred, in a handbag, whether it had handles or not, seems to me to display a contempt for the ordinary decencies of family life that remind one of the worst excesses of the French Revolution. And I presume you know what that unfortunate movement led to? As for the particular locality in which the handbag was found, a cloakroom at a railway station might serve to conceal a social indiscretion — has probably, indeed, been used for that purpose before now — but it can hardly be regarded as an assured basis for a recognized position in good society.
JACK	May I ask then what you would advise me to do? I need hardly say I would do anything in the world to insure Gwendolen's happiness.
LADY BRACKNELL	I would strongly advise you, Mr. Worthing, to try and acquire some relations as soon as possible, and to make a definite effort to produce, at any rate, one parent, of either sex, before the season is quite over.
JACK	Well, I don't see how I can possibly manage to do that. I can produce the handbag at any moment. It is in my dressing room at home. I really think *that* should satisfy you, Lady Bracknell.
LADY BRACKNELL	(*Crossing*) Me, sir? What has it to do with me? You can hardly imagine that I and Lord Bracknell would dream of allowing our only daughter — a girl brought up with the utmost care — to marry into a cloakroom, and form an alliance with a handbag. Good morning, Mr. Worthing. (*Exits.*)

Chapter eight
Characterization

It is the character that is the starting-point for everything.

Coquelin

"Time to smear on the paint and pretend I'm somebody else." Although John Barrymore's remark seems facetious, it strikes at the very essence of the art of acting. Creation of a believable character is the special domain of the actor. As Taubman states:

"A role in a drama to an actor, like the notes in a symphonic score to a conductor, is the basic source material, not the finished product. The speeches and instructions provided by the playwright, however precise, are the potter's clay. The task of shaping remains for the actor, guided by the director."*

The lighting designer may determine whether a scene will be played in dim or bright light, in a somber or fanciful atmosphere. The costume mistress may decide what clothes the actor will wear. The director may tell him where to play a scene on the stage, when and where to move during a speech, or otherwise guide him in the creative process. But when the performance day arrives, the director and all others who have been involved in the preparatory process must deliver the play into the hands of the actors and hope for the best. Each actor makes the final decisions about the character the audience is to see in the theater, since this is his responsibility. Whatever the characterization may be, it is conditioned by the mental, emotional, and physical resources of the individual actor.

If one were to ask a number of leading actors how they approach the problem of characterization, it is doubtful that two identical answers would be received. Each actor has his own working method. A good example of this is found in the way each of the Redgrave sisters, Lynn and Vanessa, develops her role:

"Vanessa's way of working is dead opposite to Lynn's. Where Lynn begins with imitation and ends with insight, Vanessa begins with the idea of

* Howard Taubman, *The New York Times*, 16 May 1965, sect. 2, p. 1.

the character and ends with an illustration of that idea in gestures."*

The process, moreover, may vary somewhat with the play at hand and the particular character in question. Despite such differences in approach, there are certain steps which actors generally follow: (1) analysis, (2) selectivity, (3) synthesis, and (4) projection.

Before the actor becomes too deeply engrossed in developing a characterization for his role, it is important that he thoroughly understand the play. A careful analysis of the script should aid in the discovery of a number of factors that will prove useful in the process of building his specific character. He may then turn his attention to the task of discovering the relationship of his character to others in the play and to the playwright's basic plot and theme.

When he has completed his analysis, the actor begins to select those aspects which are most dramatic and pertinent. Then he synthesizes these different elements into a consistent whole. Finally, the actor projects, in the most effective manner, this determined characterization to the audience. The emphasis that individual actors place on each step of this process varies greatly. Some tend to emphasize character analysis more than the techniques of acting. Others reverse this approach. While the emphasis varies with the working method of the individual, most actors would agree that the artistic goal is more important than the method or route which an actor employs to achieve his objective. As has been stressed in the preceding chapters, an actor must learn to develop and control his mind, voice, and body through constant drill and purposeful practice. If these tools are in good working order they can be at his command in the selection, synthesis, and projection of a character.

---

* "Cover Story," *Time*, 89 (17 March 1967): 82.

This chapter will be concerned primarily with an analysis of characterization. Since the other steps are greatly conditioned by the particular play in question, they are considered separately in Part Two which deals with specific types and styles of acting.

Before continuing our discussion of characterization, let us establish some guiding principles of acting. The success or failure of a production depends upon what the audience sees, feels, and thinks between the opening and final curtains. Everything an actor does in rehearsal is aimed at a final artistic effect on stage or on the screen before a live audience. The actor should remember, then, that the principles stated here are meant to be applied pragmatically. They provide an actor with an organized guide as he approaches the rehearsal period. The principles which the actor finds helpful should be followed. Those not proving helpful should be discarded. If it helps an actor to write a detailed analysis of his role, he should do so. If another actor can repeatedly achieve an artistic effect by retaining all ideas and feelings in his mind rather than on paper, he should do this. In any case, the actor should never allow principles to interfere with his creativity. Indeed, one can learn all the principles of acting and still not achieve an artistic effect. Principles are guides, not sure-fire methods. They may help the inexperienced actor to become competent. They may guide the experienced actor to a more organized and efficient approach to his characterization. For these reasons, principles are extremely important. However, one should remember to view them as a means to an end, not an end in themselves.

PLAY ANALYSIS

People come to see plays for various reasons. They may come to escape the worries and problems of the everyday world. They may come because it is the thing to do. They may come to find emotional release, or to share an aesthetic experience. Although audiences differ in many respects, they nonetheless have certain attitudes in common. They will not tolerate being bored or fooled. A theater audience rightfully expects an exciting experience, presented with honesty and free from chicanery. The audience enters the theater with a willing suspension of disbelief. In other words, it assumes a positive attitude. But the actor must so develop his character as to make believability possible. An audience will accept almost anything except inconsistency or triviality. Both of these insult the theatergoer's taste and intelligence. Everything an actor does or says on stage must be dramatically pertinent and meaningful.

The analysis of a character presupposes careful and sensitive readings of the script. The actor must know the theme of the play, the dominant mood, and the style. Before he can begin to examine his own particular part, he must possess a knowledge of the whole.

Type of play

The development of the character is strongly influenced by the type of the play. As Aristotle stated, "Tragedy depicts men as better than they are and comedy as worse than they are in real life." To this generalization, one might add that the contemporary genre, serious drama, portrays men as they seem to be in real life. The actor must, therefore, take cognizance of the various approaches to his dramatic character as it is presented in the different types of drama.

In pure tragedy the characters are more idealized and ennobled than in other forms of drama. Tragedy, since it deals with serious themes of significance, demands dignity by the performers. It also requires a greater emotional range and a more heightened and sustained emotional empathy with the audience than does comedy. There are many other factors in tragedy which the actor must take into consideration, such as more polished diction and the elimination of the mundane and trivial. In contrast, comedy, particularly high comedy, relies on an intellectual appeal to the audience. That is, the actor plays more from the head than the heart. Still another manner of playing is required in farce. The emotional empathy of the audience for the character is minimized. For example, the character may express the various emotions of fear, anger, or despair to the accompaniment of audience amusement and laughter. Both comedy and farce call for an increase in the amount of mirth-provoking action and character business. A character will of necessity be played in quite different manners depending on whether the play is a tragedy, drama, melodrama, comedy, or farce. (See Plates 23, 24, 25, 26 on pages 170–172.)

In like manner, the playing of a particular scene varies with the type of play. A comic scene in tragedy is tuned to the overall mood of the play and may not be played as broadly as a similar scene would be played in a comedy or farce. Usually, comic scenes in tragedies assume an ironic rather than a humorous character. Remembering this, the actor should constantly bear in mind the type of the play and should adjust his techniques and his manner of playing accordingly.

Elements of the play

In the *Poetics*, Aristotle listed six essential elements of a play: plot, character, dialogue, thought or theme, music or lyrical quality, and spectacle. It is said that Aristotle called tragedy "character shown through action." Modern playwrights, feeling deeply the frustrations and disordered conditions of life, have departed from many of Aristotle's precepts. An examination of plays written during the last century reveals that each one of the elements, in a particular instance, has received the primary or dominant importance. In contrast to the Aristotelian principle, one might say that

Plate 23. *The Emperor Jones* by Eugene O'Neill. The character depicts agony, extreme fear, and desperation. Ohio State University. Director: Everett M. Schreck. Photograph: Department of Photography, Ohio State University.

Plate 24. *The House of Bernarda Alba* by Federigo Garcia Lorca. Scene depicting a bitter, tragic conflict. Memphis State University. Director: Eugene Bence.

serious modern playwrights have "shown character through *inaction*." For instance, in the plays of Chekhov and Saroyan the characters are of primary importance and the plot is negligible. In certain of Shaw's plays, the idea or thesis is dominant. We are told that Oscar Wilde wrote *The Importance of Being Earnest* to prove that a play could be interesting for the sake of dialogue alone. As another instance, the melodramatic plays of the nineteenth century relied heavily on manipulated plots and spectacular effects to engage the interest of the audience.

It is not our purpose to enter into a discussion of the principles and practices of playwriting, but

Plate 25. *Uncle Vanya* by Anton Chekhov. Realistic scene of anger and frustration. University of Michigan. Director: Richard Burgwin.

rather to call the actor's attention to the fact that plays differ widely in the importance given to a particular element. Of what concern is this to an actor? He must know if he is dealing with a play in which the plot or character or dialogue or idea is dominant. For example, if the actor is playing a role in a typical melodrama with the usual emphasis on spectacle and plot at the expense of characterization, it would be futile to attempt to create three-dimensional characters from the two-dimensional types supplied by the playwright. The actor would instead concentrate his work on developing suspense and interest through business and varying tempos. However, if the actor is cast for a part in Chekhov's *The Sea Gull*, his problem is entirely different. Here, unquestionably, the interest in the play must be sustained through the appeal of the characters. This fact throws a heavy burden on the actor since he must draw on all his creative powers to develop his character with truth,

Plate 26. *The Rivals* by Richard Brinsley Sheridan. Character exaggeration for farce. University of Hawaii. Director: Edward Langhans. Photograph: Stan Rivera, Camera Hawaii.

style. Style, basically, is the manner of playing. Primarily, style determines the degree of actor-audience contact. In the realistic style, typical of most of our contemporary theater presentations, the actor seemingly ignores the presence of the audience. In a sense, the members of the audience are eavesdroppers and the actor must not break the illusion by overtly acknowledging their presence. However, in the nonrealistic style, exemplified by plays from historical periods, the actor not only recognizes the presence of the audience but often makes direct contact with it.

An actor must adjust his approach to the various styles of drama: naturalism, realism, classicism, romanticism, and expressionism. Naturalism requires a detailed representation of the character. In contrast, the characters in classicism and romanticism are cast in a more idealized and elevated mold. A still different approach is required for expressionism, which depicts characters as symbols or abstractions of human beings or human emotions.

It is our intent at this point merely to call the actor's attention to the influence of types and styles of dramas on his characterization. The manners of acting in the various styles and types of plays will be given a more detailed treatment under specific headings in Part Two.

depth, and enrichment. Or again, if the actor is dealing with a poetic or lyrical play, primary attention must be given to the interpretation of the dialogue and its melodic patterns, cadences, and inflections. It is evident that each play presents special problems for the actor and each characterization demands an individual and special point of view.

Style of the play

Closely allied to the type of the play as a factor in characterization is the importance of the play's

PRIMARY FACTORS INFLUENCING CHARACTER ANALYSIS

Once the actor has given careful time and consideration to a sensitive analysis of the script as a whole, he must concentrate his efforts on an analysis of the character he is to portray. The task of character analysis may be a painstaking one for the actor but invariably results in greater personal satisfaction as well as a more complete and meaningful experience for the audience. Character analysis may involve the following.

1. A search for the objectives which the character seeks in the play.
2. A concern for the basic motivations which guide the character in his attempt to fulfill his objectives.
3. A determination of the major factors which contribute to the total development of the character.
4. A discovery of the influence of other characters on the character being analyzed.
5. An awareness of the proper emotional response desired from the audience.

Let us examine in detail each of these factors.

Character objectives

What does the character want? What obstructs the achievement of his objective? How does he go about achieving his goal? Does the goal change during the play? What are his goals in particular scenes? How are they related to his long-range objective? These are simple questions, but frequently they are overlooked by the actor in preparing his characterization.

Let us consider a specific example from Patrick Hamilton's *Angel Street*. In this play Mr. Manningham's goal is to find the jewels which were left in the old house years before. His psychological intimidation of the new Mrs. Manningham, his mysterious forays into the night, and his sinister attitude all relate directly to this basic goal. At times he deviates from his objective, as in the case of his flirtation with the maid. This provides a further insight into what he has probably been doing while away from the house. However, this flirtation is momentary, for Manningham immediately returns to the business at hand when the maid leaves. Detective Rough, on the other hand, seeks as his goal to trap Manningham. Rough's methodical manner and his consolation of Mrs. Manningham contribute to his basic drive.

It is the goal for which a character strives that gives consistency and meaning to his actions, so the actor should determine at the beginning what goal the character seeks. He should keep this in mind as he probes other aspects of the characterization.

Character motivations

In considering the objectives of the character, the question is asked: What does the character want in the play? Other questions involving motivations are directly related to this one: Why does he desire to achieve his objective? Why does he employ certain methods to attain his goal?

The motivations for thoughts and actions are seldom simple. Characters in a play are complex and are moved to action by many different impulses. To act Hamlet effectively, the actor should not assume that there is only one motive guiding the character. The richness and depth of such a character as Hamlet demand sensitive probing of all the complexities of Hamlet's nature. We note that Hamlet maintains, as a primary objective, the revenge of his father's murder, but in the so-called mad scene, in which he feigns insanity, a secondary objective is apparent. Here his purpose is to confuse and foil Polonius and Claudius. By this action, Hamlet may achieve his primary objective. Therefore, the actor considers not only the character's primary objective for the entire play but also its departures from this objective for a given scene. In other words, why does the character act in a particular way at a given time? The answers to this question and the others mentioned will aid the actor in finding meaningful facets of the character.

Character development

In addition to the basic traits of the character, the actor must consider the many and often subtle changes experienced by a character during the play's evolution. It may be argued that fundamentally a character does not change, but rather modifies his objectives and changes the means by which he attempts to achieve them.

Even a change of attitude is not true of all characters. Sergeant Quirt is actually the same character at the end of *What Price Glory?* (by Maxwell Anderson and Laurence Stallings) as he is at the beginning. The action of the play has had little or no effect on him. However, this example is the exception rather than the rule. Most characters undergo some modification or development during the play's action. King Lear goes mad; Lady Macbeth suffers a mental breakdown; and in O'Neill's tragedy, *Beyond the Horizon*, Ruth goes through an almost complete metamorphosis. In Act I she is a young girl very much in love, tender and charming. In Act II she is disillusioned and embittered. Her hopes of fulfilled love, momentarily stimulated by Andy's return, are crushed again. In Act III she is resigned and beyond the normal feelings of love and hate. These changes in the character of Ruth comprise not only time (age) but also mood, attitude, and emotional expression. Consequently, the actor must study the play closely to discover the many variations in the character from act to act, scene to scene. These character variations may be revealed in physical condition, mental state, emotions, moods, or in the objectives and goals which motivate or influence the play's action.

The theater experience is an ongoing process, involving changes from moment to moment. The developments or changes create interest and suspense. The audience wonders what will happen next. How will a certain character react to a new situation? How will this new situation affect his future life? How will he cope with this new problem? What will become of him? And yet, there is a sustaining and consistent movement which keeps the play from disintegrating into chaos. This movement contributes to the establishment and development of a meaningful characterization. It should be borne in mind that a man's reactions to the momentous events of his life are often the most revealing indicators of his nature. This statement is also true of characters in a play. Consequently, the actor must probe deeply into the play to find the often subtle but meaningful interplay which will give added consistency to the development of his character.

Character relationships

A character is not a fixed entity. What he is or how he reacts is conditioned to a great degree by the other characters. In real life, a man's attitude and behavior pattern may be quite different with his wife, his favorite daughter, his son, his best friend, or his bitterest enemy. Yet in no sense would such variations of attitude be considered abnormal or inconsistent. Rather, such behavior patterns are the norm.

For the sake of good manners or status, men and women often try to hide their true feelings. The actor, of dramatic necessity, must clearly exhibit those feelings which are within the character he is portraying. Consider Hamlet's relationship with Ophelia, Gertrude, Claudius, Horatio, Polonius, Osric, Rosencrantz, and Guildenstern. His manner should be quite different with each. Even subtle variations in character relationship should not only be understood by the actor but should also be clearly projected to the audience. A character's attitude may be revealed by various combinations of physical and vocal expressions (aloofness, haughtiness, harshness, intimacy, tenderness) which are conditioned by what is appropriate to the character and the situation at the moment. Such expressions should be individually perfected so that they do not appear as stereotyped manifestations of attitude. The attitudes must always be considered in light of the basic goals sought by the character at the moment. Proper communication of character relationships not only heightens the overall meaning and dramatic values of the play but also contributes to the truth and believability of the characters.

Desired emotional response

True theater provides an emotional-intellectual experience and evokes a response from the audience. An individual seated in the audience feels differently toward Othello than he does toward Iago. The desired empathic response of the audience toward a character is generally not revealed specifically by the author, nor is the kind and degree of audience response for each character easily and readily determined. But the script's core of meaning and its dominant dramatic values should reveal how the actor must perform to achieve the proper empathic and sympathetic response from the audience.

Empathy. Dolman defines empathy as "the tendency to respond to any object by assuming an imitative motor attitude toward it — by feeling ourselves into it, consciously or unconsciously."* When watching a football game the members of the crowd, both inwardly and overtly, react to the physical actions on the field. When a group of men are standing on a bench watching a game, the man on the end is sometimes pushed off as the others empathically move with the charge of the offensive line and the ball carrier.

Another example of empathic response is revealed in the motion picture version of Shakespeare's *As You Like It.* During the wrestling scene between Orlando and Charles, the camera is turned on Touchstone who, in face and body, reveals the physical strain, torture, and agony of the wrestlers. In like manner, the members of an audience often experience unpleasant tensions of the throat after listening for some time to a speaker who continually uses a high-pitched or husky voice. It is not uncommon for individuals to try empathically to clear the speaker's throat. Also, an actor who is nervous, ill at ease, overly tense, or physically awkward in movement produces a detrimental empathy in the audience.

It is evident that achieving the proper empathic audience response is of vital concern to the actor. He may, consciously or unconsciously, convey to the audience his physical state of awkwardness, nervousness, or tension and evoke a correspondingly unfavorable audience reaction. The important point here is that the actor should determine the desired empathic response and, through proper control, arouse it in the audience. This can only be determined by an understanding of the particular character, his relationship to the other characters, and his contribution to the whole play.

Furthermore, the actor must analyze the audience. He should try to determine how the audience may react to certain types, to certain emotions, to certain uses of language. He must continually ask himself, How will the audience react if I do or say this? Is this the proper reaction when the play is viewed as a whole? These questions may not form the criteria for judging the artistic effectiveness of the actor's creation, but they should play an integral part in developing his characterization.

Sympathy. Closely related to empathy, yet distinctly different, is the matter of audience sympathy. In order for a play to achieve its intended dramatic impact, each character must have its proper degree of audience sympathy. To use the standard example of melodrama, the audience should love the hero and hate the villain. A reversal of this audience reaction, in any degree, does serious damage to the play's meaning and effectiveness. Moreover, it is imperative that the audience understand, either in terms of ordinary life or idealized life, why the character acts the way he does. It would be ludicrous to say that

---

* John Dolman, Jr., *The Art of Acting.* New York: Harper, 1949, p. 27.

every protagonist should be sympathetic in order for the play to be artistically effective. Richard III provides a notable example. And yet, knowing what motivates the Duke of Gloucester may bring about a closer identification of the audience with him.

A major criticism leveled at many modern tragedies is that they tend to emphasize the weaknesses of men without revealing their strengths or showing the reasons why they are weak. They often present a partial, distorted, or fragmentary view rather than a true picture of man. Individual characters in a play usually do have strengths as well as weaknesses. These the actor must find. He must find out what a character is willing to die for. Conversely, he must discover what a character believes is unworthy of self-sacrifice.

As mentioned earlier, arousing misplaced sympathy may injure the production by misrepresenting the character's true nature. In the play *Rain*, to portray Sadie Thompson as the heroine and Reverend Davidson as the villain weakens and distorts the play. A more powerful and meaningful production is achieved if each of these characters, one representing worldliness and the other extreme spirituality, is represented with honesty and sincerity of purpose, no matter how misguided or overzealous each character may appear to be. If Reverend Davidson is represented as a hypocrite and charlatan, the scene in which Sadie is converted becomes farcical. If Davidson is interpreted as a hypocrite, his final act of suicide, presumably motivated by remorse, can hardly be explained or justified. There is, of course, also the question of a play's meaning. Should the audience leave a production of *Rain* with the idea that prostitutes are "the beautiful people" and that all missionaries are fanatical, hypocritical joy-killers? The actor might ask, as he contemplates a character, What kind and degree of audience reaction should he receive? If the sympathy of the audience is misplaced, lacking, or faulty in degree and kind,

the play's meaning and dramatic impact are impaired.

Although the character's emotional appeal may be carefully woven into the fabric of the play, the playwright's concept of what that appeal is or should be is not always easy to determine or interpret. The actor may be misled by what the character says and does specifically, thinking that either sympathetic or unsympathetic audience reaction must follow certain actions or dialogue. The important point to remember is that the actor can, to a considerable extent, control the audience reaction to his character by his physical manner and the way in which he delivers his lines. To quote a familiar expression, "It is not what you say but how you say it." One also often hears the statement, "Smile when you say that." A smile would change the reaction to the remark.

The question may be asked: How does the actor determine the proper sympathetic appeal required for the character? There are several answers to this question. Of primary importance is what seems to be the playwright's intention as evidenced in the play. How will the attitude of a particular audience to a character contribute to or detract from the author's purpose? If, as in some cases, the playwright's objective is difficult to determine, the actor may ask himself, What interpretation of the character makes the play more universal, more poignant, or more dramatic, or best serves its total theatrical effectiveness?

It is clearly evident that creating a character is most intricate and complicated and is far from being a simple task. It demands that the actor know how and why people act as they do. It further demands that he be able to present the character in an artistic manner, and in a way meaningful to the audience. In the process of shaping and adapting the character to the requirements of the play and to the audience, the actor must often rely on his director's judgment as well as his own.

OTHER FACTORS INFLUENCING CHARACTERIZATION

Physical condition

Age has an important bearing on the character's physical condition and, consequently, on the manner of playing the role. Frequently the age of the character is given in the cast list or in the character description within the text of the play, but whether the age of the character is specifically given or not, the actor must strive to arrive at a close approximation. Usually, in a well-written play, what a character says and does is indicative of his age. Sometimes the answer to the question of age may be found in the comments of other characters in the play who casually describe a character as an old roué, a young blade, a spinster, or may refer to age-oriented qualities such as senility. In other instances, the approximate age of a character is expressed in the dialogue. In Maxwell Anderson's *The Star Wagon* the wife remarks, "We've been married thirty-five years, Steve." From this we can infer that she is well past middle age.

Equally important in its bearing on proper interpretation is the character's state of health, strength, and physical vigor. This information can usually be obtained directly or indirectly from a careful study of the text of the play.

Personal appearance

Closely related to physical condition is the character's personal appearance, his peculiarities and habits. Here we are concerned with such matters as posture, carriage, characteristic movement, mannerisms, features, and habits of dress.* All of

---

* See *The Crown Bride* by August Strindberg, Plate 27. The picture is notable for its mood and the makeup of the characters, who are played by graduate students.

Plate 27. *The Crown Bride* by August Strindberg. Realistic characterization achieved by expert makeup. University of Minnesota. Director: Robert Moulton.

these characteristics would require consideration by an actor playing such characters as Malvolio in *Twelfth Night*, Cyrano de Bergerac, or the role of Eugene Gant in *Look Homeward, Angel*.

Educational and social background. Important clues to a character result from knowing his educational background and social status. This information has an important bearing on how he speaks and whether his diction is slovenly or polished and refined. Although the character's cultural status is often revealed in his choice of words and the sentence structure of his lines, the articulation and melodic patterns are left to the discretion of the actor. In addition to speech, the character's behavior and his observance of the rules of etiquette, courtesy, and social graces usually indicate his education and social background.

Psychological type

This aspect of the character may or may not be specified by the author. However, a careful study of the script should indicate whether the character might best be portrayed as a shy, retiring, inhibited introvert, an egocentric extrovert, or some other variation of these two psychological types. The actor must also discover the character's attitude toward life. Is he happy, cheerful, and buoyant in spirit? Or is he pessimistic and cynical? Does he believe that life has some meaning?

Moreover, the actor should determine the character's emotional stability. Is he even-tempered? Is he easily aroused to anger? Howard Lindsay's comment relative to playing the character of Clarence Day is pertinent here. "I still recall with deep gratitude a remark Dorothy made to me as we were driving home after a performance. 'You know, Howard, I don't think Father is so much bad-tempered as hot-tempered.' This thought switched me back upon the track from which I had become derailed."*

All types and degrees of emotional behavior applicable to the character must be fully conceived by the actor before a meaningful and proper characterization can be realized.

Economic status

This aspect of the character is, as a rule, clearly indicated by the playwright. We generally know if the character is of royal lineage, a member of the idle rich, or a day laborer. However, there are many variations of characters within each economic class. This phase of characterization assumes particular importance in modern American dramas. In our society it is not uncommon to find the uncultured and newly rich, the indigent

intellectual, or an uncouth tycoon, like the junk dealer in Kanin's *Born Yesterday*. One cannot draw characters in such plays as Odets' *Waiting for Lefty* without direct and immediate reference to the economic conditions of the time. A knowledge of the economic status, although helpful, is not by itself a reliable guide to the interpretation of the character. It is the duty of the actor to discover how the economic status of the character may influence the characterization and to indicate this by the various techniques at his disposal in order to add further clarity and enrichment to the interpretation.

Nationality and locale

It seems appropriate here to sound a note of warning. There has been a tendency in the theater to stereotype certain national, racial, and religious groups. One has only to be reminded of how the Negro, the Jew, and the Irishman have been consistently misrepresented on the American stage. Fortunately, during recent years there has been a gradual breaking away from these rigid national, racial, and religious concepts. Admittedly, there are certain characteristics which distinguish one race or nationality from another, but each group (racial, national, or religious) is made up of widely dissimilar individuals. In creating his characterization, the actor should take individual differences into consideration and avoid fixed generalities.

It is obvious that certain nationalities look at life differently from others. The tragic perspective of the Russian writers, notably Tolstoy, Gorki, and Chekhov, although not all-inclusive, is yet significant.

In the realm of comedy, the dry wit of the English is well known. Even more to the point, the Irish writers provide excellent examples of an individualized comic spirit. Synge's *The Playboy of the Western World* has seldom had successful productions in the United States because the wit

---

* Toby Cole and Helen Kritch Chenoy, *Actors on Acting*. New York: Crown, 1959, p. 550.

and humor of the play are frequently lost. Much of the difficulty is due to a lack of understanding of the Irish character and temperament. To perform such plays as *The Playboy* or *The Tinker's Wedding* effectively, one must see the world through the rather unique vision of the Irish. If a certain nationality looks at life in a consistently different manner from other peoples, the actor should take cognizance of this and adjust his playing accordingly.

As an aid to the actor in his analysis of the character's personality, a work sheet is provided below. The chart presents him with a convenient reference to certain particularities which may be applied to a development of his characterization. By checking the various personality traits, the actor may be able to find some concrete suggestions of general attributes appropriate to the character he is playing. To show how to use the work sheet, we have selected the character of Willy Loman from Arthur Miller's *Death of a Salesman*. The items checked indicate how we have envisioned the character. Our interpretation would seem to suggest a man of average

date _____

Arthur Miller _____   *Death of a Salesman* _____
playwright   playbook

CHARACTER WORK SHEET
(individual form)

director/actor _____

Willy Loman _____
character

ANALYSIS OF THE CHARACTER IN THE PLAYBOOK
Personality of the Character (what the character is like)
Profile: check each scale; then draw connecting lines.

	Traits	Rating Scale					General Characteristics
Physical	*Sex*	virile	male ✓		female	feminine	attraction: medium
	Age	18–25	25–35	35–45	45–55	over 55 ✓	race: white
	Features	handsome	good looking	average ✓	homely	ugly	coloring: ruddy
	Figure	perfect	good	average	poor ✓	malformed	oddity: none
	Vitality	dynamic	active	average ✓	sedentary	listless	drives: success
	Coordination	very skilled	graceful	handy ✓	clumsy	uncoordinated	skills: handwork
Mental	*I.Q.*	genius	brilliant	average ✓	dull	moron	
	Education	scholar	student	schooled	unschooled ✓	illiterate	fields: selling
	Pri. capability	artistic	philosophic	scientific	social ✓	mechanical	interests: gardening
	Creative abil.	genius	talented	average	unoriginal ✓	barren	accomplishments:
	Background	very happy	happy	average	unhappy ✓	very unhappy	
Emotional	*E. type*	extrovert ✓	extroambivert	ambivert	introambivert	introvert	fixed attitudes: yes
	E. depth	life-long	lasting	average	passing ✓	momentary	loves: family—money
	E. strength	consuming	strong	normal	weak ✓	feeble	desires: success
	E. control	complete	good	average	poor ✓	no control	weaknesses: false values
	Pers. security	com. security	much security	some	little ✓	no security	family: wife, 2 sons
Social	*Social type*	extrovert ✓	extroambivert	ambivert	introambivert	introvert	
	Ego	objective	out'd* directed	balanced	inw'd* directed ✓	subjective	prejudices: yes
	Social abil.	leader	suggester	average	imitator ✓	follower	
	Sociability	many friends	numerous	some	few friends ✓	no friends	group: none
	Econ. status	wealthy	independent	salaried	laborer	poor ✓	occupation: salesman
	Religion	devout	orthodox	conventional ✓	agnostic	atheist	church: none
	Politics	fascist	oligarchist	democrat ✓	socialist	communist	
	Moral viewp'.	uncompromising	strict	conventional	liberal	none ✓	

*outwardly   *inwardly

physical, emotional, and mental stature with certain traits appearing at extremes. The column headed "General Characteristics" provides further indications of Willy Loman's character and personality.

The chart is intended as a guide and not a set of rules. Since the authors feel that characterization is effective only when it possesses individuality, there has been no attempt to include in the foregoing discussion dogmatic principles or magical short cuts to aid the actor in finding specific physical actions and vocal qualities appropriate to each type of character. Even to suggest the existence of such rules or to advocate their mechanical application would merely negate the primary concern of characterization believability.

In the development of his characterization during the rehearsal period and also in the performances, the actor should bear in mind the principles of the dual nature of acting which are discussed in Chapters 1 and 9. In a sense, the actor and the character are one. Each is absorbed in the other. Although the character seems to motivate the actor in physical action and vocal expression, the actor must maintain at all times an intellectual detachment and control. However, he should not let his knowledge of the play's ending influence or color the way in which the character plays a particular scene.

The character lives from moment to moment. He is aware of his objective because of the opposing forces which make up the drama, but he is not confident of its achievement. The character is no more assured of the plot action in succeeding scenes than an individual in real life knows with certainty what will happen tomorrow. Yet actors occasionally lose the anxiety and deep concern which is necessary for the character in a particular scene because, as actors, they know that in the end of the play all is well. To illustrate, throughout the court scenes of *The Caine Mutiny Court-Martial* the cast should give the impression that Lt. Maryk's life is at stake, that he may be hanged for his crime of mutiny. In other words, the actor must not allow *his* knowledge of the plot to divert the *character* from a normal behavior.

On the other hand (and this is the other side of acting), the actor must at all times be in complete control. He should use his knowledge of the play in its entirety as a guide to the complete development of the character. This knowledge should lead him to an understanding of which character trait to reveal at a particular time and which to hold in abeyance. A thorough study of the play should also aid him in locating the "big scenes" with their technical demands and in determining the essential psychological foreshadowing for later plot action.

Plate 28. *Hedda Gabler* by Henrik Ibsen. Hedda shows haughty disinterest in Tesman's morning-shoes. University of Iowa. Director: Jean Scharfenberg.

Exercises

1. Put on a mask of the Halloween type and study its facial characteristics in a mirror. Evolve a characterization based on the facial characteristics.
2. Choose a well-known character. Learn as much as possible about the character's habits, mannerisms, and eccentricities. Build a characterization based on the sum of your knowledge.
3. After reading the entire play, use the character work sheet to aid in the analysis of the characters in the following scenes.

Practice Selections

HEDDA GABLER

by Henrik Ibsen / final scene of Act III

SITUATION

HEDDA *has broken off her romance with* EILERT LÖVBORG *and married* GEORGE TESMAN, *a rather undistinguished scholar who seems to be in line for a coveted professorship at the university.* LÖVBORG *arrives in the city with a scholarly manuscript which he has written with the help and inspiration of* MRS. ELSTED. *The work may be the deciding factor in securing the professorship for* LÖVBORG *instead of* TESMAN. LÖVBORG *takes his manuscript to a party with* TESMAN *and* JUDGE BRACK. *After drinking to excess,* LÖVBORG *loses the manuscript on the way home. It is recovered by* TESMAN *and given to* HEDDA. LÖVBORG *returns to the* TESMAN *house in utter despair, believing that his manuscript is lost beyond recovery.*

HEDDA

I don't know what else happened last night. But is it so absolutely irretrievable?

LÖVBORG

It is not merely last night. I know that perfectly well. But it is *this*, that I don't want to live that kind of life either. Not now over again. It is courage of life and the defiance of life that she has snapped in me.

HEDDA

(*Looking in front of her*) The sweet little simpleton has had her fingers in the destinies of a man. (*Looks at him.*) But how could you be so heartless to her, all the same?

LÖVBORG

Oh, don't say that it was heartless!

* Henrik Ibsen, *Hedda Gabler*. Translated by Edmund Gosse. Reprinted by permission of Walter H. Baker (Baker's Plays). (Note the realistic setting and the austere, disdainful attitude of Hedda toward Tesman and Miss Juliana Tesman in Plate 28.)

HEDDA	Go and destroy what has filled her thoughts for such a long, long time! You don't call that heartless?
LÖVBORG	To you I can speak the truth, Hedda.
HEDDA	The truth?
LÖVBORG	Promise me first — give me your word upon it, that what I now confide to you, you will never let Thea know.
HEDDA	You have my word upon it.
LÖVBORG	Good. Then I will tell you that that was not true which I stood here and declared.
HEDDA	That about the sheets?
LÖVBORG	Yes. I have not torn them into fragments. I have not thrown them into the fjord either.
HEDDA	No, no — But — where are they, then?
LÖVBORG	I have destroyed them all the same! To all intents and purposes, Hedda.
HEDDA	I don't understand that.
LÖVBORG	Thea said that what I had done was the same to her as murdering a child.
HEDDA	Yes, that's what she said.
LÖVBORG	But, to kill one's child — that is not the worst thing you can do to it.
HEDDA	*That* not the worst?
LÖVBORG	No. That is the worst which I wished to shield Thea from hearing about.
HEDDA	And what then is this worst?
LÖVBORG	Suppose now, Hedda, that a man — about such an hour in the morning as this — after a wild night of carouse, came home to the mother of his child and said: Listen — I have been here and there. In this place and that place. And I have taken your child with me. To this place and that place. I have lost the child. Utterly lost it. The Devil knows into whose hands it has fallen. Who may have had their fingers in it.
HEDDA	Ah! but, after all — this was nothing more than a book —
LÖVBORG	The pure soul of Thea was in that book.

HEDDA Yes, I understand that.

LÖVBORG And therefore you understand also that between her and me there is no future henceforward.

HEDDA And which way will you go?

LÖVBORG No way. Merely see how I can make an end altogether. The sooner the better.

HEDDA (*A step nearer*) Eilert Lövborg — now listen to me. Could you not contrive — that it should be done beautifully?

LÖVBORG Beautifully? (*Smiles*) With vine-leaves in my hair, as you used to fancy —

HEDDA Oh, no! The vine-leaf — I don't think anything more about that! But beautifully, all the same! Just for once — Good-by! You must go now. And don't come here any more.

LÖVBORG Good-by, Mrs. Tesman. And give a message to George Tesman from me. (*He is going.*)

HEDDA No, wait! You shall take with you a keepsake from me. (*She goes to the writing-table and opens the drawer and pistol case. Comes back to* LÖVBORG *with one of the pistols.*)

LÖVBORG (*Looking at her*) This? Is *this* the keepsake?

HEDDA (*Nods slowly*) Do you recollect it? It was aimed at you once.

LÖVBORG You should have used it then.

HEDDA Look here! *You* use it now.

LÖVBORG (*Puts the pistol into his breast pocket.*) Thanks!

HEDDA And do it beautifully, Eilert Lövborg. Only promise me that!

LÖVBORG Good-by, Hedda Gabler. (*He goes out through the hall door.*)
(*She then goes to the writing table and takes out the packet with the manuscript, peeps into the envelope, pulls one or two of the leaves half out, and glances at them. She then takes the whole of it and sits down in the armchair by the stove. She holds the packet in her lap. After a pause, she opens the door of the stove, and then the packet also.*)

HEDDA (*Throws one of the sheets into the fire and whispers to herself.*) Now I am burning your child, Thea! You with your curly hair! (*Throws several sheets into the fire.*) Your child and Eilert Lövborg's child. (*Throws the rest in.*) Now I am burning — am burning the child.

Analysis of the Characters

1. What is Hedda's objective?
2. What are her motivations?
3. Why does she wish to destroy Lövborg and his manuscript?
4. Why does Lövborg confide in Hedda?
5. Why does he wish to take his own life?
6. Is Hedda emotionally unbalanced?
7. What might be the audience's reaction to Hedda?
8. Are these characters three-dimensional?
9. How closely should the interpretation of the lines approximate the conversation of actual life?
10. What emotional key seems most effective for this scene?

THE IMPORTANCE OF BEING EARNEST

by Oscar Wilde / scene from Act II

CHARACTERS   REV. CANON CHASUBLE, MISS PRISM, *governess, and* JOHN WORTHING.

SITUATION   *In order to have an excuse to get away from his estate in the country,* JACK WORTHING *has invented a younger brother by the name of* ERNEST, *whom he must see occasionally. But since his fiancée,* GWENDOLEN, *has insisted that she can only marry a man of the name of* ERNEST, *it now seems advisable to "dispose" of his brother and be christened with the name of* ERNEST.

MISS PRISM   You are too much alone, dear Dr. Chasuble. You should get married. A misanthrope I can understand — a womanthrope, never!

CHASUBLE   (*With a scholar's shudder*) Believe me, I do not deserve so neologistic a phrase. The precept as well as the practice of the Primitive Church was distinctly against matrimony.

MISS PRISM   (*Sententiously*) That is obviously the reason why the Primitive Church has not lasted up to the present day. And you do not seem to realize, dear Doctor, that by persistently remaining single, a man converts himself into a permanent public temptation. Men should be more careful; this very celibacy leads weaker vessels astray.

CHASUBLE   But is a man not equally attractive when married?

MISS PRISM   No married man is ever attractive except to his wife.

CHASUBLE   And often, I've been told, not even to her.

MISS PRISM	That depends on the intellectual sympathies of the woman. Maturity can always be depended on. Ripeness can be trusted. Young women are green. (DR. CHASUBLE *starts*.) I spoke horticulturally. My metaphor was drawn from fruits. But where is Cecily?
CHASUBLE	Perhaps she followed us to the schools. (*Enter* JACK *slowly from the back of the garden. He is dressed in the deepest mourning, with crepe hatband and black gloves.*)
MISS PRISM	Mr. Worthing!
CHASUBLE	Mr. Worthing?
MISS PRISM	This is indeed a surprise. We did not look for you till Monday afternoon.
JACK	(*Shakes* MISS PRISM'S *hand in a tragic manner.*) I have returned sooner than I expected. Dr. Chasuble, I hope you are well?
CHASUBLE	Dear Mr. Worthing, I trust this garb of woe does not betoken some terrible calamity?
JACK	My brother.
MISS PRISM	More shameful debts and extravagance?
CHASUBLE	Still leading his life of pleasure?
JACK	(*Shaking his head*) Dead!
CHASUBLE	Your brother Ernest dead?
JACK	Quite dead.
MISS PRISM	What a lesson for him! I trust he will profit by it.
CHASUBLE	Mr. Worthing, I offer you my sincere condolence. You have at least the consolation of knowing that you were always the most generous and forgiving of brothers.
JACK	Poor Ernest! He had many faults, but it is a sad, sad blow.
CHASUBLE	Very sad indeed. Were you with him at the end?
JACK	No. He died abroad; in Paris, in fact. I had a telegram last night from the manager of the Grand Hotel.
CHASUBLE	Was the cause of death mentioned?
JACK	A severe chill, it seems.

MISS PRISM	As a man sows, so shall he reap.
CHASUBLE	(*Raising his hand*) Charity, dear Miss Prism, charity! None of us are perfect. I myself am peculiarly susceptible to draughts. Will the interment take place here?
JACK	No. He seemed to have expressed a desire to be buried in Paris.
CHASUBLE	In Paris! (*Shakes his head.*) I fear that hardly points to any very serious state of mind at the last. You would no doubt wish me to make some slight allusion to this tragic domestic affliction next Sunday. (JACK *presses his hand convulsively.*) My sermon on the meaning of the manna in the wilderness can be adapted to almost any occasion, joyful, or, as in the present case, distressing. (*All sigh.*) I have preached it at harvest celebrations, christenings, confirmations, on days of humiliation, and festal days. The last time I delivered it was in the Cathedral, as a charity sermon on behalf of the Society for the Prevention of Discontent among the Upper Orders. The Bishop, who was present, was much struck by some of the analogies I drew.
JACK	Ah! that reminds me, you mentioned christenings, I think, Dr. Chasuble? I suppose you know how to christen all right? (DR. CHASUBLE *looks astounded.*) I mean, of course, you are continually christening, aren't you?
MISS PRISM	It is, I regret to say, one of the Rector's most constant duties in this parish. I have often spoken to the poorer classes on the subject. But they don't seem to know what thrift is.
CHASUBLE	But is there any particular infant in whom you are interested, Mr. Worthing? Your brother was, I believe, unmarried, was he not?
JACK	Oh, yes.
MISS PRISM	(*Bitterly*) People who live entirely for pleasure usually are.
JACK	But it is not for any child, dear Doctor. I am very fond of children. No! the fact is, I would like to be christened myself, this afternoon, if you have nothing better to do.
CHASUBLE	But surely, Mr. Worthing, you have been christened already?
JACK	I don't remember anything about it.
CHASUBLE	But have you any grave doubts on the subject?
JACK	I certainly intend to have. Of course, I don't know if the thing would bother you in any way, or if you think I am a little too old now.

CHASUBLE	Not at all. The sprinkling, and, indeed, the immersion of adults is a perfectly canonical practice.
JACK	Immersion!
CHASUBLE	You need have no apprehensions. Sprinkling is all that is necessary, or indeed I think advisable. Our weather is so changeable. At what hour would you wish the ceremony performed?
JACK	Oh, I might trot around about five if that would suit you.
CHASUBLE	Perfectly, perfectly! In fact I have two similar ceremonies to perform at that time. A case of twins that occurred recently in one of the outlying cottages on your own estate. Poor Jenkins, the carter, a most hard-working man.
JACK	Oh! I don't see much fun in being christened along with other babies. It would be childish. Would half-past five do?
CHASUBLE	Admirably! Admirably! (*Takes out watch.*) And now, dear Mr. Worthing, I will not intrude any longer into a house of sorrow. I would merely beg you not to be too much bowed down by grief. What seem to us bitter trials are often blessings in disguise.
MISS PRISM	This seems to me a blessing of an extremely obvious kind.

Part Two

Styles of
Acting

Style in the Theater

Every play must be regarded as a unique phenomenon, for which a unique style of production must be found.

Mordecai Gorelik

INFLUENCES ON STYLE

Theater is a living, everchanging artistic medium of expression. In its 2500 years of existence, the theater of the western world has employed varying forms and styles, in both play script and methods of staging, to achieve its artistic objectives. These objectives are to delight, instruct, and persuade, to probe for the meaning of life, or to reveal man's relationship to man and God.

There are many underlying factors which contribute to the changing patterns of theater art. Among them are the following:

1. The ideological, social, or religious philosophy of a particular society may impose a characteristic style on its theater. For instance, in modern Russia the style of theater is harnessed to a philosophy of socialist realism.

2. The form and style of the drama may be influenced by the contemporary architecture of the theater and its technical facilities. The tragedies of Aeschylus, Sophocles, and Euripides were adapted, quite understandably, to the facilities of the open-air theaters of the fifth century B.C. In like manner, the plays of Shakespeare conformed to the physical conditions of the Globe Theatre.

3. The drama may mirror the manners and customs of its period. Notably, the style of Restoration comedies reflects the artificiality and sophistication of the aristocratic class of that time.

4. The style of drama may express a particular author's viewpoint or philosophy of life: optimism, pessimism, or negation of life, as the case may be. As an example, Jean-Paul Sartre's *No Exit* is notable for its existential philosophy.

5. Theater style may be the expression of the artistic philosophy of a producer, director, or designer, as exemplified by the constructive style of Meierhold, the theatricalism of Max Reinhardt, or the symbolistic styles of Gordon Craig and Adolphe Appia.

For an appreciation of theater styles, the aspiring actor must, of necessity, be a connoisseur of theater as a whole, its dramatic literature, its types and styles of staging, and the techniques of acting applicable to each. Although the director and the actor must reach a cooperative agreement on the stylistic approach to the play, in the actual performance the responsibility for an effective and appropriate interpretation of the playwright's script falls upon the actor.

Style is the sine qua non of theater art. Rarely does a critic review a play without mentioning the effect of style on some phase of the production. In certain instances, it is quite discernible that style has contributed to the dramatic effectiveness of the production. In other cases, the misuse of style has contributed to the artistic or financial failure of the play. Unquestionably, the success or failure of a production stems directly from the stylistic treatment given the play and the manner and quality of the staging. A case in point is O'Neill's *The Iceman Cometh*, which failed in its original production but later was produced with notable success. Undoubtedly, the artistic and financial success of *The Three-Penny Opera* at the Théâtre de Lys, which established a performance record, was due in large measure to its unified, charming style. It is the actor's task to discover, through a penetrating study of the script and from the comments of the director, the style which seems most appropriate and dramatically effective.

DEFINITIONS OF STYLE

The term *style* has a variety of meanings. Basically, style is the mode or manner of expression, the way in which the artist manipulates the material of his art to achieve the desired creation. It is the particular personal stamp which the artist puts on his work. We frequently refer to the individual style of a painter or musician. When artists employ a characteristic uniformity in their mode of expression, they are grouped as belonging to a particular school. For example, the term *impressionism* was applied to a school of painting that began to be manifest in the latter half of the nineteenth century in the works of Monet, Manet, and Cézanne. The term was also applied to the musical compositions of Debussy and Ravel. Yet within the general characteristics of a particular stylistic school there are marked individual differences that each artist puts into his creation. One trained in the art of music can easily detect a difference in the impressionistic compositions of Debussy and Ravel. Similarly, the individual styles of designers, directors, and actors are often clearly evident.

The late Alexander Dean defined style as the degree and kind of lifelike quality which the artist incorporates into his work, or, in other words, the various departures from a true-to-life representation. A glance at the comic sheet of a newspaper reveals sundry departures from a true, or actual, life representation. The most obvious variations are in the degree of abstraction, distortion, exaggeration, and selectivity. Although these various ways of depicting life cannot be neatly circumscribed, they have, for convenience and point of reference, been given terms. The nearest approach to a photographic representation of life is termed naturalism. Other styles which, in various ways and degrees, depart from actual life are realism, symbolism, classicism, romanticism, expressionism, and epic. These terms apply both to the written script and to the manner of staging. The actor, of course, must be able to sense the style of the script and develop an appropriate acting style in his character portrayal.

In comparison to the graphic arts, acting style is very much restricted in the degree to which it can depart from lifelike representation. This is because we are dealing with a real human being, the actor. Only to a limited degree may he be exaggerated, distorted, or abstracted. Limitation is particularly true of his voice, with its restricted range of pitch, volume, and quality. It follows that, in all theater styles, there must be a degree of realism to conform to the reality of the living actor. Moreover, there must be a degree of reality in the stage presentation in order to orient the audience and to satisfy its universal desire to relate the dramatic action to its own actual world. Theater styles may be likened to a tethered animal with the stake to which he is tied representing actual life. The actor, like the tethered animal, may wander in various directions and distances from actual life, but he cannot completely escape. So we see that acting styles are more modified, less clear-cut and distinct, more closely related to actual life than corresponding styles in the graphic arts.

STYLISTIC FORMS OF DRAMATIC PRODUCTION

The production of a play in all its phases (acting, directing, lighting, setting, and costuming) generally assumes one or the other of two stylistic forms. We are indebted to Alexander Bakshy for the terms *representational* and *presentational* to designate these two forms of dramatic production.*

Representational production

There has been a gradual and almost continuous trend toward greater verisimilitude from the fifth century B.C. to the present day. Euripides was more realistic than either of his predecessors, Aeschylus and Sophocles. In the realm of settings, the perspective vistas of the Teatro Olimpico stage and the Serlian wings and backcloth of the six-teenth century, depicting tragic, comic, and satiric scenes, were attempts to achieve greater reality. In the art of acting, which seemed more reluctant to break with tradition, the trend toward realism was less obvious until the eighteenth and, more particularly, the nineteenth centuries. In spite of the fact that Garrick's style of acting was considered realistic as compared to that of his predecessors, it would not be so labeled by the acting standards of today. Granting that significant advances toward realism in the total production of the play were made by Charles Kean and Tom Robertson, the first revolutionary advance toward realism was made by the Duke of Saxe-Meiningen whose philosophy and principles of staging were adopted by André Antoine, Stanislavski, and Otto Brahm.

In the realistic, representational style of production, the spectacle is treated "as a true image of life existing outside, and quite independent of the theatre."† The setting represents, in certain degrees, the *actual* locale of the dramatic action. Such staging, in either the realistic or naturalistic style, negates the theatrical aspects of the production and seeks to establish and enhance the illusion of reality. The audience, whose presence is overtly ignored, views the performance through a seeming fourth wall in the proscenium arch. Except for certain concessions to stage convention such as facing stage furniture in some degree toward the audience, every attempt is made to give the stage setting the appearance of a real room or actual exterior as the case may be.

Gassner states that "duality of experience exists to some degree in every theatre and for both the performer and his audience: action in the theatre is both make-believe and actual for them."‡ Usually the spectator keeps this duality

---

* Alexander Bakshy, *The Theatre Unbound*. London: Cecil Palmer, 1923, p. 92.

† *Ibid.*, p. 92.

‡ John Gassner, *Form and Idea in Modern Theatre*. New York: Holt, Rinehart and Winston, 1956, p. 210.

in balance. He accepts the illusion, believes in and is moved by the action, yet maintains his awareness that he is sitting in a theater and that the play is make-believe. The representational style, by various illusion-furthering devices, swings the pendulum from the experience of make-believe to the experience of the actual. It is doubtful whether this experience of the actual is wholly achieved with most spectators. However, there are many instances which attest to the fact that, in representational productions, spectators may lose their aesthetic distance, become completely involved in the action, and forget for a period of time that they are in a theater seeing a play.

In like manner, the actor is both character and performer. This duality, which must be kept in proper balance, varies in each style of production. In the representational style, the actor becomes more the character and less the performer. In the further refinement to a naturalistic style, he attempts, as far as possible, to obliterate his own personality and become the actual character.

In all phases of the representational style, an attempt is made to achieve verisimilitude and an illusion of the actual. The most striking nonrealistic element in this style of production is that one wall of the real room is removed so that the audience may see the action. This nonillusionistic part of the setting the audience accepts or agrees to ignore.

Presentational production

In contrast to the representational style, presentational is nonillusionistic. It does not seek to represent a spectacle which is apart from and independent of the theater and its audience. Rather, it accepts the theater as a place for the presentation of drama and frankly recognizes the presence of the audience. The focus of this style of production is on the audience, not, as in the representational style, on the stage.

This style of theater has existed in various forms since antiquity, until supplanted by the representational style in the latter half of the nineteenth century. The presentational style of theater encompasses the great dramas of the past: Greek tragedy and comedy, Elizabethan drama, Molière comedy, and English Restoration comedy. Although the architecture of the theater and the manner of staging varied from one period to the other, the basic concept of the drama and its presentation remained the same, "an image of life existing in the theatre and finding its expression in the forms of the theatre."* Granting that various illusion-furthering devices are used in presentational staging (Sophocles supposedly introduced painted scenery), the illusion of reality is actually created in the mind of the spectator, not, as in the representational style, on the stage by the designer, scene builder, costumer, and electrician. A spectator sitting in the theater of Dionysus in broad daylight in front of the permanent proscenium was undoubtedly moved with pity and fear by the tragedy of Oedipus Rex, yet was, because of the manner of the presentation, fully aware that he was seeing a theatrical production. The nonillusionistic elements of the production were accepted by the audience.

In like manner, the limitations of the formal, nonillusionistic Elizabethan stage were fully realized by Shakespeare. To compensate for the limitations, he frequently indicated the imagined locale in the dialogue. For example, "This is the coast of Illyria," or, "Now we are in Arden." His dependence on the imagined rather than the actual illusionistic scene is evident in the lines from the Prologue in *Henry V*.

"O, pardon? since a crooked figure may
Attest in little place a million;

---

* Bernard Hewitt, *Art and Craft of Play Production.* New York: J. B. Lippincott, 1940, p. 66.

And let us, ciphers to this great accompt,
On your imaginary forces work.

. . . .

Piece out our imperfections with your thoughts;
Into a thousand parts divide one man,
And make imaginary puissance;
Think, when we talk of horses, that you see them
Printing their proud hoofs i' the receiving earth;
For 'tis your thoughts that now must deck our
  kings,
Carry them here and there; jumping o'er times,
Turning the accomplishment of many years
Into an hour-glass: . . ."

In general, for this style, the actor recognizes the presence of an audience. He accepts the physical elements of the theater and the production for what they actually are: stage, scenery, properties, costumes, and lights. He is no longer confined behind the proscenium arch but may now take the play through this barrier to the audience. In his dual role mentioned previously, he now becomes less the actor-character and more the actor-performer while, at the same time, he maintains sufficient reality to achieve believability. When an eighteenth century playgoer went to see Garrick in the role of Hamlet, he accepted the nonillusionistic, presentational style of the production. Although he may have believed in and been moved by the dramatic action, his belief was of the theater, of make-believe. Much of his enjoyment in the presentation no doubt came from observing how Garrick played the part and comparing his manner with that of other famous actors of the day.

Representational-presentational production

Certain plays have a mixture of illusionistic (representational) and nonillusionistic (presentational) elements and, consequently, are so treated in production. In Thornton Wilder's *Our Town*, for example, the overall treatment is non-illusionistic. The stage is obviously a stage and not a representation of the locale of the action. Usually in a production of this play, nonrepresentational masking units are used at down right and down left while the rear wall of the stagehouse is visible to the audience. Nonrealistic set properties are used, such as a board on the backs of two chairs serving as a soda fountain. The stage manager communicates directly with the audience, leaning against the proscenium arch or moving about as he "sets" the stage in the imagination of the audience. However, individual scenes within the play are acted in a representational style. The characters play to each other and seemingly ignore the presence of the audience.

The representational (illusionistic) and the presentational (nonillusionistic) styles of production have been equally successful in providing audiences with satisfying and exciting theatrical experiences. The many successful productions of *Our Town* attest to the fact that the illusion of reality resides more in the characters than in the setting. A real kitchen with hot and cold running water is of little illusion-furthering value unless the characters who inhabit the room are true and real.

INFLUENCES ON THE STYLE OF ACTING

Style is inherent in the play script and therefore is not a mode which may be arbitrarily imposed. The appropriate manner of acting in a particular play stems directly from the author's mood and his treatment of the play's elements. Although certain plays have been produced in different styles, it does not follow that all these treatments are artistically justified or are equally successful in communicating the play's highest values. It seems obvious that for a particular script one style will be more appropriate than another. It is the obligation of every theater artist to acquire an understanding of the stylistic qualities of the play and adapt his contribution to the furthering of the author's concept. This is particularly true of the actor who, more than any other contributor to the production, establishes and controls the basic style and communicates the author's meaning.

Direct influence of the playwright

Viewpoint of life. Every playwright approaches his task of representing life with a definite point of view. He may see life in terms of the grandiose, heroic, romantic, nostalgic, fanciful, whimsical, or pessimistic. With the notable exception of *Ah, Wilderness!*, there is a strain of pessimism or negation of life which permeates the plays of Eugene O'Neill. The plays of Tennessee Williams reveal a preoccupation with the sordid, the sensational, and the disintegrated elements of life. In contrast, the plays of Sir James Barrie and A. A. Milne emphasize life's whimsical and sentimental aspects. With each play, an actor must assess the author's point of view and modify his manner of playing to conform with the author's concept.

Closely related to the playwright's viewpoint of life is the play's prevailing mood. This important quality is sometimes difficult to evaluate and one must determine, within the general categories of serious and comic, how seriously or comically the play should be presented. The problem must be resolved jointly by the director and the actor, based on their decision as to what, in their best judgment, seems to be the author's intention, and what mood treatment may be most effective in achieving that intention.

Treatment of dialogue. Here, of course, is one of the most definitive elements in determining the style of a play. A careful examination of the dialogue reveals whether a play is basically naturalistic, realistic, symbolic, classic, romantic, or expressionistic. In trying to determine the style, the actor may pose these questions: Is the dialogue sporadic, nonsequential, and lacking in selectivity? (If so, it suggests a naturalistic style of writing.)

Is the dialogue an obvious departure from what the characters might actually say in the given situation? Does the dialogue reveal the author's cleverness or wit? Is there an economy of words to convey the ideas? (Such a treatment is characteristic of highly selected realism.) Is the dialogue poetic, adorned, and emotionally restrained? (This is typical of the classic style.) Is the dialogue poetic, richly embellished, and surcharged with emotional words? (If so, the play suggests the romantic style.)

Each playwright employs dialogue in his own individualistic way for a particular purpose and effect. Shakespeare used poetic dialogue for the principal characters and prose for servants and minor characters. This treatment was obviously intentional, since he could, with equal mastery, have written prose for the nobility and poetry for the lowly born. Not only is dialogue an important factor in determining the style of the play, but it also imposes on the actor the need for a careful consideration of appropriate line interpretation. To speak Shakespeare's poetic dialogue as if it were prose or to poetize the prose is to misappropriate the style of the play and the author's intention. The different styles of delivery required for various inherent style characteristics of each play is treated under the appropriate headings in the succeeding pages.

Treatment of character. Just as with dialogue, the author's treatment of the characters is a revealing indicator of the play's style. In considering the bearing of the characters on the style of the play, the actor may again ponder certain questions. Are the characters true to life, commonplace, the kind one might meet on the street or know as neighbors? (If so, the play is probably in either the naturalistic or realistic category.) Are the characters larger than life, noble, heroic, or statuesque? (If such is the case, a classic or romantic play is suggested.) Or again, are the characters symbolistic, representing groups, classes, or ideas?

(This treatment is characteristic of symbolic or expressionistic drama.) Characters in drama are quite diverse; they may be true to life, grandiose, symbolic, three-dimensional, type, or cartoon, with many variations within each group. Each particular character bears the stamp of the play's style and necessitates an individual approach by the actor.

Treatment of plot. As with dialogue and character, the element of plot is given a variety of treatments by individual playwrights. Each treatment, although not definitive, has some bearing on the play's style. The manipulation of plot is an artistic device. The more obviously the plot is contrived, the less the play represents actual life, which is in reality plotless. When playwrights seek to portray a photographic image of life, they generally minimize the plot and give dominance to other elements, such as character, dialogue, or the environmental conditions. Plays of the naturalistic style are notable for their formlessness and weakness in plot structure. In contrast, the Greek classic tragedies, of which *Oedipus Rex* is a supreme example, are models of tight, interrelated plot structure. Plot treatment in romantic dramas is complex, involved, loosely constructed, and melodramatic. In addition, it often contains insufficiently motivated action, and mixed moods with emphasis on the sensational, sentimental, and pathetic.

As has been indicated, an overemphasis on plotting for its own sake may foster artificiality or only a surface reality. This was the chief criticism leveled against the well-made plays of Scribe and Sardou. Space does not permit the enumeration and analysis of all the many plot devices. Suffice it to say, a study of the play's plot will guide an actor toward a better understanding of the play and its inherent style.

Treatment of theme. Subject matter and theme per se are not reliable guides to either the type of play or its style. The same general theme or subject may be treated from a variety of viewpoints. *Journey's End*, by Sheriff, and *What Price Glory?* both deal with war but the former is serious and tragic, the latter is comic and depreciates the glories of war. More important, then, to our discussion is the manner in which the theme or subject is treated. For example, is the author's treatment of his material serious, straightforward, sympathetic, or is it facetious, light, or definitely "tongue in cheek"? In any case, the actor must be aware of the author's approach to his material.

The theme or idea of the play may be given a direct or indirect presentation by the playwright, and may be adapted to the representational or presentational style. The direct presentation, commonly used in propaganda plays, is generally offensive, particularly to those who do not subscribe to the ideas which the play expounds. Generally more acceptable and of a higher artistic level is the indirect presentation in which the message of the play is implied. It is important that the author's manner in treating his central idea should be taken into account in determining the style of the play's performance.

Treatment of rhythm and lyrical element. Although rhythm is present in various natural phenomena, such as the surge and ebb of waves on the shore and the human heartbeat, there is a less definite rhythm or recurring accent in the human actions of real life. Characteristically, normal human speech, although pulsating with word phrases, is devoid of definite rhythmic patterns. Consequently, when the playwright arbitrarily infuses rhythm into the dialogue, it is an artistic device which automatically removes the play, in some degree, away from a true-to-real-life representation. It is not surprising, then, that we find rhythm constituting a dominant element in the classic and romantic plays while noticeably absent in slice-of-life naturalism. Rhythm has a universal appeal. Its diverse patterns constitute dominant factors in the aesthetic and sensory pleasures of both the visual and auditory arts.

Keenly aware of the sensory appeal of rhythm, writers of expressionistic dramas frequently resort to rhythmic speech to heighten the emotional and theatrical effectiveness of the play. When rhythm is present in a play, it should be accepted and augmented. To do otherwise is to thwart the playwright's intention and impair the artistic quality of the play's presentation.

Closely related to rhythm is the lyrical element which is an obvious and dominant quality in all poetic plays. This element is also found, though less easily discernible, in many prose plays. The dramas of William Saroyan give notable examples of this quality. A lyrical quality is prominent also in the speech pattern of certain nationalities, such as the Irish. It is undoubtedly this lyrical quality of speech and the weather vane-like shifts of mood which make the performing of Irish plays difficult for anyone except a native Irishman. However, if a lyrical element is present, subtle as it may be, it must be captured in order to achieve an artistically successful production.

Period of the production

In a contemporary production, it is perhaps futile to attempt to reproduce with historical accuracy any past period. Even if one were able to reproduce the original architecture of the theater and the spectacle, it would be impossible to recapture the audience participation and certain other environmental factors of the original production. Yet a flavor and spirit of the period is highly desirable. Indeed, the success of a production is often determined by the degree to which the manners of the period and the theatrical conditions become an integral part of the stylistic approach. For example, it is very important in presenting a Restoration comedy to capture the artificiality, affectation, and sophistication of the period. In like manner, the courtly graces and mannerisms of the Louis XIV period, in the seven-

teenth century, seem highly appropriate for the playing of Molière's comedies.

Costumes

Period costumes automatically impose a style of playing. Voluminous clothing, corseted bodices, and other characteristics of a particular period will frequently impede or determine the amount and kind of action in which the actor may engage. Not the least important part of a period costume is the footwear. Since this item imposes a style of movement, it should not be ignored even though the feet are concealed by the clothing. To illustrate, the extremely long-toed shoes of the thirteenth century caused the wearer to turn his feet to the side, inducing a characteristic manner of walking. Each period costume dictates its own particular style characteristics. The actor should determine what these distinctive features are and how they will affect his actions. Needless to say, the actor should wear his period costume, or an approximate facsimile, in rehearsals so that he may become adjusted to its peculiarities and limitations. It is highly important that the actor adjust himself to the costume, wearing it with ease and with a manner appropriate to the period.

Physical aspects of the theater and production

Down through the centuries, the physical characteristics of the theater and the production facilities have had a dominant effect on the style of acting. The Greek theaters of the fifth century B.C., in many instances comparable in size to stadiums of the present day, imposed a style of acting peculiar to their physical conditions. Another contributing factor was the mask which precluded facial expressions. Undoubtedly the mask, which the actor changed for each character, took on lifelike characteristics which, due to the enlarged features, conveyed the character's dominant emotions to the farthest part of the theater. It is interesting to note that in the extant Greek tragedies there is very little physical contact between the characters and no violent action is indicated as taking place on stage. This may have been a matter of decorum or it may have been imposed by the cothurnus, masks, and long, flowing robes which in some degree limited the actor in his freedom of action. In contrast, the short overgarments of the comic characters permitted great freedom of movement, in keeping with the exaggerated action required in the plays of Aristophanes.

In a modern production of a Greek tragedy, it is appropriate to make certain modifications. The masks are usually eliminated, thus allowing for the increased effectiveness of facial expressions in our comparatively small theaters. On the other hand, the dignity, restraint, and grandeur of the original production should be retained.

As another example of the influence of the physical characteristics of the theater on the style of acting, one might cite the original Abbey Theatre in Dublin. This small, intimate theater was ideally adapted to the naturalistic plays of O'Casey. In this theater facial expressions, detailed pantomimic business, and the subtleties of conversational delivery could be conveyed with dramatic effectiveness. The same intimate, naturalistic style of acting would be little short of a complete failure if transferred to a mammoth stage and auditorium.

In order to achieve an authentic style, the total production characteristics of the play's original period should be taken into consideration: the size of the stage and the auditorium, the available playing areas, the placement of entrances and exits, and the use of stage furniture, period properties, and costumes. All of these influence the style of acting in a vital way. Even though it is important to capture the basic style and spirit of a period, the actor must modify his stylistic approach in order to conform to the modern production of the play, the physical conditions of the theater in which the play is being presented, and his director's interpretation.

FACTORS IN THE MANNER OF PLAYING

Style in acting is derived from a combination of many factors. By unifying and blending these factors in varying proportions, a specific style emerges. Each of the following topics is a vital factor in achieving a style of acting.

Actor-audience relationship

The degree of the actor's contact with the audience has varied from period to period in theatrical history and, to some extent, within individual plays of a particular period. As mentioned previously, the actor in presentational styles of production recognizes the presence of the audience and often plays directly to it; the actor in representational styles avoids obvious recognition of the audience's presence. However, there are variations in the degree and kind of audience contact within the presentational manner of playing.

It is not an uncommon practice in the contemporary theater, perhaps at the director's request, for actors to err by making direct contact with the audience in a production of an obviously realistic play. The actor must consider how his audience relationship will conform to the inherent style of the script and contribute to the overall effectiveness of the production. When direct contact with the audience is intended by the playwright, it should be accepted rather than evaded. There is a tendency in certain modern productions of historical plays to approach such stylistic devices as asides and soliloquies with seeming apology and embarrassment, with a muttering of the lines, and with delivery of the dialogue to the floor, the ceiling, or the wings. Such an approach is a travesty of the author's intended effect.

Actor-character versus actor-performer

This is a determining characteristic of the representational and the presentational styles. Within the two approaches there are variations in the character-actor duality. Each style requires an individual approach, one shifting the balance more toward the character, another toward the performer side of the duality. Of the various styles, naturalism swings the pendulum furthest toward character, while a Restoration comedy emphasizes the performer and minimizes the character side of the duality. The balance in this duality must be decided by the actor and director for each play. They must base their judgment on the play's inherent style and the most effective manner of its realization.

Degree of selectivity

Each artist selects from the available materials only those which are useful to his purpose. The degree to which he applies this principle has an important bearing on the style of his art product. The naturalistic playwright, who represents life in a more or less photographic manner, is less selective than the classic poet who portrays life in terms of the ideal and the universally significant. Thus, by degrees of selectivity, we move from naturalism through realism, symbolism, classicism, and romanticism to abstract expressionism. It would seem that since the playwright has established the style through his selectivity and treatment of the play's elements, there is little left for the actor to do in this matter except to conform to the dictates of the script. Yet the actor has considerable freedom in terms of movement, gesture, and pantomimic business, which generally are not indicated in the script. Consequently, he may have to invent business for the naturalistic play and eliminate all but the most significant actions for the classic drama. A very effective bit of business in *Tobacco Road* is Jeeter Lester's washing himself at the well in the morning. A similar mundane action would be out of place for Hamlet or Oedipus. The actor himself must exercise a selectivity in keeping with the style of the play.

Use of body positions

Until the revolutionary change in theater style during the latter half of the nineteenth century, it was common practice for the actor to play almost entirely in the open, or audience-facing, position. But a radical change in acting style came on the night of March 30, 1887, in a little, inconspicuous hall in the back streets of Paris where André Antoine presented *Jacques Damour*, adapted from a story by Emile Zola, as the pièce de résistance in a bill of one-acts. On this memorable night Antoine played the part of Jacques, a French Enoch Arden. As the play unfolded a rare magic gripped the audience members. They forgot that they were sitting on uncomfortable, closely packed chairs. The stage was no longer a stage but the back room of a Paris butcher shop. The players were not actors but vivid Parisian types. Jacques seemed unaware of the presence of the audience. He even played whole scenes with his back turned to the audience. The curtain closed amid an uproar of cheers and applause. On this night naturalism was born in Paris.*

Despite the reactions of many artisans in contemporary theater against extreme naturalism, its main tenets—truth, verisimilitude, lifelike characters, and ensemble playing—have remained dominant factors in our theater. Due to this naturalistic tradition, there remains a tendency to modify the full-front body position in present day productions of historical dramas. Yet the body position of the actor remains a useful device in establishing the style of the performance. Naturalism utilizes the quarter, profile, three-quarter, and full-back positions while it generally minimizes the full-front position. Realism employs the full-front and full-back positions to a limited degree and relies mainly on the one-quarter, profile, and to some extent the three-quarter positions. The open positions, full-front and one-quarter, are dominant in the romantic and classic styles. The specific use of body positions as a stylistic device will be treated later in connection with each particular style.

---

* Mordecai Gorelik, *New Theatres for Old*. New York: Samuel French, 1948, p. 124 ff.

Use of stage areas

As is true of the character's body positions, the use of the stage areas, particularly on the proscenium stage, contributes to the establishment of style. Although Shakespeare undoubtedly used many playing areas in the Globe Theatre, for centuries the center of the stage has been the traditional dominant area for the play's action. This was particularly true in the eighteenth and early nineteenth centuries when the center of the stage was reserved for the star performer and considered a "no-man's land" by the other members of the cast. It remained for such pioneers of the theater as the Duke of Saxe-Meiningen, Andrè Antoine, Otto Brahm, and Stanislavski to demonstrate the effective use of all the stage areas. They discovered that, in addition to providing variety, a particular area of the stage enhanced the interpretation of the scene by reason of its relative connotation, denotation, and strength values. The use of various stage areas, as exemplified in productions of naturalism and realism, has modified the earlier overuse of stage center in modern productions of historical plays. Yet if the actor is concerned with the establishment of the style and flavor of the play's original period, he would do well to consider the use of the stage areas of that time. Since we are told that in the classic Greek theater the principal characters entered by the central door of the scene house, we may assume that their playing was confined largely to the central portion of the stage, leaving the side areas to the minor characters who entered from the side doors or from the *parodi*. Although each *parodus* served as an entrance for the audience, it also functioned as the place of entrance and exit for the chorus, and, on occasion, for the entrance or departure of a principal character.

During the seventeenth and eighteenth centuries in England, the actors entered from either side through the proscenium doors, hurried to the center of the stage near the front, and played the scene openly to the audience. If the general format and playing areas of the original produc-

tion are followed, it is quite likely that the style and the audience appreciation of the play will be enhanced.

Degree and kind of movement

Movement on the stage is used in a variety of ways and fulfills many functions. Our primary concern here is how movement may be useful in establishing the type and style of a production. We are well aware that in real life, in moments of great solemnity (funerals, state occasions, weddings), the tempo and the amount of action are diminished while on festive occasions the tempo and actions are increased. Correspondingly, the tempo and action of a tragedy are diminished, while the action in comedy is accelerated. In the case of farce, an extremely rapid tempo, additional action, and stage business are superimposed. One has only to compare the small list of properties for a tragedy with the extensive requirements for a comedy or farce to realize the relative amount of physical action and business which each type requires.

As in the case of the type of play, movement may contribute to the play's style. Briefly, the following variations of movement indicate the stylistic possibilities: dignified, formal, sedate (classic style); large, flowing movements and gestures (romantic); delicate, precise, detailed, mannered (Molière or Restoration period); highly motivated movement combined with detailed pantomimic business (naturalism). A more detailed consideration of the application of movement to the type and style of the play is given under the appropriate headings in succeeding pages.

Use of the vocal elements

Granting the vocal limitations mentioned earlier, the subtle variations in the use of pitch, volume, quality, and rate are important contributing factors in establishing both the type of drama and its particular style. For example, the low-keyed, narrow, melodic pattern seems most appropriate for serious drama and tragedy. In contrast, the high-keyed, wide, melodic pattern is conducive to the mood of comedy and farce. In like manner, the varying applications of the four vocal elements, both in degree and kind, contribute to the establishment of the various styles of acting: earthy naturalism; lofty, grandiose romanticism; ethereal symbolism; or abstract, mechanized expressionism. The particular application of the vocal elements to the types and styles of drama is treated under each type and style category.

Stylistic Forms of
Dramatic Production

Drama is not a flat mirror of life, giving a faithful but colorless image of reality. It is a focussing mirror, which condenses the colored rays and transforms a gleam into a light and a light into a flame.

Victor Hugo

Section one/Representational style of acting

Since the bulk of contemporary plays falls into the category of representational style, this is the form most familiar to students of the theater. In view of the fact that characters in this style of drama (naturalism, realism, and symbolism) are, in general, more closely identified with actual life, it seems logical to begin with naturalism and gradually proceed to the less familiar styles.

NATURALISM

This style developed as a revolt against romanticism but, more generally, it is in opposition to all that is false, artificial, and pretentious in the theater. The aim of naturalism is to present life on the stage truthfully, accurately, scientifically, and with objectivity. It attempts to represent "a slice of life" with, in so far as stage conventions permit, photographic reality. Since the characters, dialogue, atmosphere, background, and mood of the drama are more important than the plot, there is a tendency to avoid climaxes and theatricality per se. (See Plate 29.)

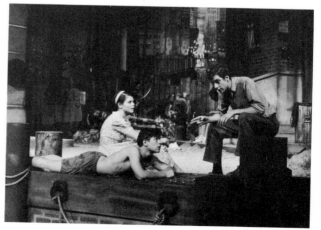

Plate 29. *Dead End* by Sidney Kingsley. Scene depicting naturalism. San Jose State College. Director: Hal J. Todd.

General Principles of Naturalistic Acting

1. Ensemble playing is of great importance.
2. The actor gives the illusion of living the character.
3. Acting is subjective.
4. The actor plays and reacts to other characters in the scene.
5. There is much use of pantomimic business reflecting the mundane aspects of life.
6. Much attention is given to such stage business as is appropriate to the character and the situation.
7. With the exception of the arena and the thrust stages, the actor plays within the proscenium frame.
8. The character's actions are motivated by his thoughts and emotions.
9. There is little or no movement for its own sake.
10. There is no obvious recognition of the presence of the audience.
11. Line interpretation closely approximates the characteristics of real life speech.
12. Highly polished, cultivated, and pointed speech is generally avoided, except as it relates to a particular character.
13. There is great emphasis on dialect.
14. All the stage areas may be used with approximate facility.
15. All stage body positions are used, although the full-front position is minimized.
16. The mood of the play, with its subtle variations, should be sustained.
17. It is essential that the emotions of the characters be communicated to the audience.
18. The tempo, although varied, is medium to slow.
19. The opportunities for effective dramatic pauses should be noted.
20. The climactic builds and drops, when present, must be well motivated and unhurried.
21. Sharp breaks in the tempo or rhythm are best avoided.
22. The norm in voice and action should be maintained.
23. Truth and believability in all aspects of the characterization are highly important.

Practice Selection

THE SEA GULL

by Anton Chekhov | excerpt from Act IV*

CHARACTERS	CONSTANTINE TREPLIEFF, *a young, struggling writer* NINA ZARIETCHNAYA, *a young girl, the daughter of a rich landowner*
SITUATION	TREPLIEFF *is desperately in love with* NINA. *But she is enchanted with the debonair novelist,* TRIGORIN. *She runs away with him to the city, bears him a child and becomes an actress. She returns and again rejects* TREPLIEFF.

(TREPLIEFF *goes out, and is heard walking quickly along the terrace. In a few minutes he comes back with* NINA ZARIETCHNAYA)

TREPLIEFF	Oh, Nina, Nina! (NINA *lays her head on* TREPLIEFF's *breast and stifles her sobs.*)
TREPLIEFF	(*Deeply moved*) Nina, Nina! It is you — you! I felt you would come; all day my heart has been aching for you. (*He takes off her hat and cloak.*) My darling, my beloved has come back to me! We musn't cry, we mustn't cry.
NINA	There is someone here.
TREPLIEFF	No one is here.
NINA	Lock the door, someone might come.
TREPLIEFF	No one will come in.
NINA	I know your mother is here. Lock the door. (TREPLIEFF *locks the door on the right and comes back to* NINA.)
TREPLIEFF	There is no lock on that one. I shall put a chair against it. (*He puts an armchair against the door.*) Don't be frightened, no one shall come in.
NINA	(*Gazing intently into his face*) Let me look at you. (*She looks about her.*) It is warm and comfortable in here. This used to be a sitting-room. Have I changed much?

---

* Anton Chekhov, *The Sea Gull.* Translated from the Russian, with an Introduction by Marian Fell. Copyright, 1912, by Charles Scribner's. Reprinted by permission of Charles Scribner's.

TREPLIEFF	Yes, you have grown thinner, and your eyes are larger than they were. Nina, it seems so strange to see you! Why didn't you let me go to you? Why didn't you come sooner to me? You have been here nearly a week, I know. I have been several times each day to where you live, and have stood like a beggar beneath your window.
NINA	I was afraid you might hate me. I dream every night that you look at me without recognizing me. I have been wandering about on the shores of the lake ever since I came back. I have often been near your house, but I have never had the courage to come in. Let us sit down. (*They sit down.*) Let us sit down and talk our hearts out. It is so quiet and warm in here. Do you hear the wind whistling outside? As Turgenieff says, "Happy is he who can sit at night under the roof of his home, who has a warm corner in which to take refuge." I am a sea gull — and yet — no. (*She passes her hand across her forehead.*) What was I saying? Oh, yes, Turgenieff. He says, "and God help all houseless wanderers." (*She sobs.*)
TREPLIEFF	Nina! You are crying again, Nina!
NINA	It is all right. I shall feel better after this. I have not cried for two years. I went into the garden last night to see if our old theatre were still standing. I see it is. I wept there for the first time in two years, and my heart grew lighter, and my soul saw more clearly again. See, I am not crying now. (*She takes his hand in hers.*) So you are an author now, and I am an actress. We have both been sucked into the whirlpool. My life used to be as happy as a child's; I used to wake singing in the morning; I loved you and dreamt of fame, and what is the reality? To-morrow morning early I must start for Eltz by train in a third-class carriage, with a lot of peasants, and at Eltz the educated tradespeople will pursue me with compliments. It is a rough life.
TREPLIEFF	Why are you going to Eltz?
NINA	I have accepted an engagement there for the winter. It is time for me to go.
TREPLIEFF	Nina, I have cursed you, and hated you, and torn up your photograph, and yet I have known every minute of my life that my heart and soul were yours for ever. To cease from loving you is beyond my power. I have suffered continually from the time I lost you and began to write, and my life has been almost unendurable. My youth was suddenly plucked from me then, and I seem now to have lived in this world for ninety years. I have called out to you, I have kissed the ground you walked on, wherever I looked I have seen your face before my eyes, and the smile that had illumined for me the best years of my life.
NINA	(*Despairingly*) Why, why does he talk to me like this?

TREPLIEFF	I am quite alone, unwarmed by any attachment. I am as cold as if I were living in a cave. Whatever I write is dry and gloomy and harsh. Stay here, Nina, I beseech you, or else let me go away with you. (NINA *quickly puts on her coat and hat.*)
TREPLIEFF	Nina, why do you do that? For God's sake, Nina! (*He watches her as she dresses. A pause.*)
NINA	My carriage is at the gate. Do not come out to see me off, I shall find the way alone. (*Weeping*) Let me have some water. (TREPLIEFF *hands her a glass of water.*)
TREPLIEFF	Where are you going?
NINA	Back to the village. Is your mother here?
TREPLIEFF	Yes, my uncle fell ill on Thursday, and we telegraphed for her to come.
NINA	Why do you say that you have kissed the ground I walked on? You should kill me rather. (*She bends over the table.*) I am so tired. If I could only rest — rest. (*She raises her head.*) I am a sea gull — no — no, I am an actress. (*She hears* ARKADINA *and* TRIGORIN *laughing in the distance, runs to the door on the left and looks through the keyhole*) He is there too. (*She goes back to* TREPLIEFF) Ah, well — no matter. He does not believe in the theatre; he used to laugh at my dreams, so that little by little I became downhearted and ceased to believe in it too. Then came all the cares of love, the continual anxiety about my little one, so that I soon grew trivial and spiritless, and played my parts without meaning. I never knew what to do with my hands, and I could not walk properly or control my voice. You cannot imagine the state of mind of one who knows as he goes through a play how terribly badly he is acting. I am a sea gull — no — no, that is not what I meant to say. Do you remember how you shot a sea gull once? A man chanced to pass that way and destroyed it out of idleness. That is an idea for a short story, but it is not what I meant to say. (*She passes her hand across her forehead.*) What was I saying? Oh, yes, the stage. I have changed now. Now I am a real actress. I act with joy, with exaltation, I am intoxicated by it, and feel that I am superb. I have been walking and walking, and thinking and thinking, ever since I have been here, and I feel the strength of my spirit growing in me every day. I know now, I understand at last, Constantine, that for us, whether we write or act, it is not the honour and glory of which I have dreamt that is important, it is the strength to endure. One must know how to bear one's cross, and one must have faith. I believe, and so do not suffer so much, and when I think of my calling I do not fear life.

TREPLIEFF	(*Sadly*) You have found your way, you know where you are going, but I am still groping in a chaos of phantoms and dreams, not knowing whom and what end I am serving by it all. I do not believe in anything, and I do not know what my calling is.
NINA	(*Listening*) Hush! I must go. Good-bye. When I have become a famous actress you must come and see me. Will you promise to come? But now — (*She takes his hand.*) It is late. I can hardly stand. I am fainting. I am hungry.
TREPLIEFF	Stay, and let me bring you some supper.
NINA	No, no — and don't come out, I can find the way alone. My carriage is not far away. So she brought him back with her? However, what difference can that make to me? Don't tell Trigorin anything when you see him. I love him — I love him even more than I used to. It is an idea for a short story. I love him — I love him passionately — I love him to despair. Have you forgotten, Constantine, how pleasant the old times were? What a gay, bright, gentle, pure life we led? How a feeling as sweet and tender as a flower blossomed in our hearts? Do you remember, — (*She embraces* TREPLIEFF *impetuously and runs out onto the terrace.*)

Playing the Scene

1. What seems to be the mood of the scene?
2. To what degree is this scene a real life situation?
3. Is this scene devoid of what one might term theatricality?
4. Are there instances where the actor must pause in his delivery although no pause is indicated in the text?
5. How would Treplieff's suicide, shortly after this scene, affect the actor's playing of the character?

Other Sources for Scenes of Naturalism

Awake and Sing by Clifford Odets

Dead End by Sidney Kingsley

Desire Under the Elms by Eugene O'Neill

Street Scene by Elmer Rice

The Lower Depths by Maxim Gorky

REALISM

This form of drama differs from naturalism in degree more than in kind. Although realism seeks to present an illusionistic representation of life, there is more selectivity, arrangement, order, and control in each of the play's elements than there is in naturalism.

The dialogue is seemingly lifelike but is not what the character actually might say in the given situation. Rather, in many instances, the dialogue is obviously what the author wishes the character to say for dramatic, comic, or theatrical effect.

The realists do not shun theatricality, even for its own sake. Although the characters in realism are seemingly complete, there is less emphasis on the psychological and environmental factors than in naturalism. In the realistic play we find that the play elements—plot, character, and idea—are integrated and balanced. The realistic playwright is less concerned with the inner psychology of his characters and gives greater emphasis to their outward actions.

The plot in realistic drama is generally compact, with many climaxes and changes of mood often included for sheer theatricality. Realism is concerned, not with real life, but with what *seems* to be real life, given an artistic and theatrical treatment. (See Plate 30.)

General Principles

1. Within the framework of realism, the basic factors which motivate and determine the character's action should be found.
2. Truth and believability in the given situation should be sought.
3. Playing should be to the other characters in the scene and only indirectly to the audience.
4. Only significant and meaningful business which is appropriate to the character should be included.
5. Line interpretation is conversational but heightened and intensified.
6. Vocal techniques for the pointing of meaning and comedy may be used but with restraint.
7. Some arbitrary movement may be imposed.

SERIOUS DRAMA

As everyone who has made a thorough study of drama knows, there is no sharp dividing line between tragedy and comedy. Not infrequently, plays include both tragic and comic characteristics, yet it is possible in most instances to differentiate one category of drama from the other.

Serious drama lacks the high solemnity, universality, and larger-than-life characters of tragedy. But like tragedy the ending is, in varying degrees, unhappy. The characters are personalities rather than types and since they are not un-

like ourselves, they arouse our sympathies over their misfortunes.

General Principles

1. The serious mood should be established and sustained.
2. Mood variations should be blended and toned to the overall level.
3. The melodramatic portrayal of emotions is best avoided.
4. Characterizations should be complete and the reactions well motivated.
5. It is usually wise to underplay comic implications.

Plate 30. *The Little Foxes* by Lillian Hellman. Scene representing realism. Ohio State University. Director: Charles Ritter. Photograph: Leo M. Wilhelm.

Practice Selection

A DOLL'S HOUSE

*by Henrik Ibsen | excerpt from Act II**

(*To avoid blackmail,* NORA *is trying to persuade* HELMER *not to dismiss* KROGSTAD *from his position in* HELMER's *bank.*)

NORA	Torvald.
HELMER	Yes.
NORA	If your little squirrel were to ask you something very, very prettily — ?
HELMER	What then?
NORA	Would you do it?
HELMER	I should like to hear what it is, first.
NORA	Your squirrel would run about and do all her tricks if you would be nice, and do what she wants.
HELMER	Speak plainly.
NORA	Your skylark would chirp about in every room, with her song rising and falling —
HELMER	Well, my skylark does that anyhow.
NORA	I would play the fairy and dance for you in the moonlight, Torvald.
HELMER	Nora — you surely don't mean that request you made of me this morning?
NORA	(*Going near him*) Yes, Torvald, I beg you so earnestly —
HELMER	Have you really the courage to open up that question again?
NORA	Yes, dear, you *must* do as I ask; you *must* let Krogstad keep his post in the bank.
HELMER	My dear Nora, it is his post that I have arranged Mrs. Linde shall have.

---

* Henrik Ibsen, *A Doll's House.* Translated by William Archer. Copyright, 1890, by John W. Lovell. Reprinted by permission of Walter H. Baker. (See Plate 17.)

NORA	Yes, you have been awfully kind about that; but you could just as well dismiss some other clerk instead of Krogstad.
HELMER	This is simply incredible obstinacy! Because you chose to give him a thoughtless promise that you would speak for him, I am expected to —
NORA	That isn't the reason, Torvald. It is for your own sake. This fellow writes in the most scurrilous newspapers; you have told me so yourself. He can do you an unspeakable amount of harm. I am frightened to death of him —
HELMER	Ah, I understand; it is recollections of the past that scare you.
NORA	What do you mean?
HELMER	Naturally you are thinking of your father.
NORA	Yes — yes, of course. Just recall to your mind what these malicious creatures wrote in the papers about papa, and how horribly they slandered him. I believe they would have procured his dismissal if the Department had not sent you over to inquire into it, and if you had not been so kindly disposed and helpful to him.
HELMER	My little Nora, there is an important difference between your father and me. Your father's reputation as a public official was not above suspicion. Mine is, and I hope it will continue to be so, as long as I hold office.
NORA	You never can tell what mischief these men may contrive. We ought to be so well off, so snug and happy here in our peaceful home, and have no cares — you and I and the children, Torvald! That is why I beg you so earnestly —
HELMER	And it is just by interceding for him that you make it impossible for me to keep him. It is already known at the Bank that I mean to dismiss Krogstad. Is it to get about now that the new manager has changed his mind at his wife's bidding —
NORA	And what if it did?
HELMER	Of course — if only this obstinate little person can get her way! Do you suppose I am going to make myself ridiculous before my whole staff, to let people think that I am a man to be swayed by all sorts of outside influence? I should very soon feel the consequences of it, I can tell you! And besides, there is one thing that makes it quite impossible for me to have Krogstad in the bank as long as I am manager.
NORA	Whatever is that?
HELMER	His moral failings I might have overlooked, if necessary —

NORA	Yes, you could — couldn't you?
HELMER	And I hear he is a good worker too. But I knew him when we were boys. It was one of those rash friendships that so often prove an incubus in after life. I may as well tell you plainly, we were once on very intimate terms with one another. But this tactless fellow lays no restraint on himself when other people are present. On the contrary, he thinks it gives him the right to adopt a familiar tone with me, and every minute it is "I say, Helmer, old fellow" and that sort of thing. I assure you it is extremely painful for me. He would make my position in the bank intolerable.
NORA	Torvald, I don't believe you mean that.
HELMER	Don't you? Why not?
NORA	Because it is such a narrow-minded way of looking at things.
HELMER	What are you saying? Narrow-minded? Do you think I am narrow-minded?
NORA	No, just the opposite, dear — and it is exactly for that reason.
HELMER	It's the same thing. You say my point of view is narrow-minded, so I must be so too. Narrow-minded! Very well — I must put an end to this. (*Goes to the hall door and calls.*) Helen!
NORA	What are you going to do?
HELMER	(*Looking among his papers*) Settle it. (*Enter* MAID.) Look here; take this letter and go downstairs with it at once. Find a messenger and tell him to deliver it and be quick. The address is on it, and here is the money.
MAID	Very well, sir. (*Exit with the letter.*)
HELMER	(*Putting his papers together*) Now then, little Miss Obstinate.
NORA	(*Breathlessly*) Torvald — what was that letter?
HELMER	Krogstad's dismissal.
NORA	Call her back, Torvald! There is still time. Oh Torvald, call her back! Do it for my sake — for your sake — for the children's sake! Do you hear me, Torvald? Call her back! You don't know what that letter can bring upon us.
HELMER	It's too late.
NORA	Yes, it's too late.

HELMER	My dear Nora, I can forgive the anxiety you are in, although really it is an insult to me. It is, indeed. Isn't it an insult to think that I should be afraid of a starving quill-driver's vengeance? But I forgive you nevertheless, because it is such eloquent witness to your great love for me. (*Takes her in his arms.*) And that is as it should be, my own darling Nora. Come what will, you may be sure I shall have both courage and strength if they be needed. You will see I am man enough to take everything upon myself.
NORA	(*In a horror-stricken voice*) What do you mean by that?
HELMER	Everything, I say —
NORA	(*Recovering herself*) You will never have to do that.
HELMER	That's right. Well, we will share it, Nora, as man and wife should. That is how it shall be. (*Caressing her*) Are you content now? There! there! — not these frightened dove's eyes! The whole thing is only the wildest fancy! — Now, you must go and play through the Tarantella and practice with your tambourine. I shall go into the inner office and shut the door, and I shall hear nothing; you can make as much noise as you please. (*Turns back at the door.*) And when Rank comes, tell him where he will find me. (*Nods to her, takes his papers and goes into his room, and shuts the door after him.*)
NORA	(*Bewildered with anxiety, stands as if rooted to the spot, and whispers.*) He was capable of doing it. He will do it. He will do it in spite of everything. — No, not that! Never, never! Anything rather than that! Oh, for some help, some way out of it! (*The door bell rings.*) Doctor Rank! Anything rather than that — anything, whatever it is! (*She puts her hands over her face, pulls herself together, goes to the door and opens it.*)

Playing the Scene

1. What dominant traits should be revealed in each character?
2. What should be the attitude or response of the audience to each character?
3. What is the actor-audience relationship?
4. Which lines of dialogue are particularly significant?
5. Is there a steady progression of the story?
6. Is there any seemingly irrelevant dialogue?

Other Sources for Scenes of Realistic Serious Drama

The Dark at the Top of the Stairs by William Inge

The Little Foxes by Lillian Hellman

The Wild Duck by Henrik Ibsen

Plate 31. *Death of a Salesman* by Arthur Miller. Modern tragedy depicting family conflict. Ohio State University. Director: Everett M. Schreck. Photograph: Leo M. Wilhelm.

MODERN TRAGEDY

Modern tragedy, generally, lacks the artistic qualities which critics have ascribed to high tragedy. The themes are contemporary and are frequently lacking in magnitude and universal significance. The characters are commonplace, without noble birth, and often without nobility of spirit. With certain exceptions, such as the tragedies of Maxwell Anderson, the dialogue employs unadorned prose.

Manner of Playing

1. The actor should determine what is the core of the destroying forces or conflict, whether it is within or external to the protagonist.

2. The steps which contribute to the protagonist's downfall should be underscored.

3. The effectiveness of the play is generally heightened if the actor points up the ennobling qualities of such characters as the "spine" of the play may require.

4. It is important to establish and communicate the dominant, serious mood.

5. In general, the actor should underplay comic elements or tone the comic scenes to the dominant mood of the play as a whole. (See scene from *Death of a Salesman*, Plate 31.)

Practice Selections

DEATH OF A SALESMAN

by Arthur Miller / excerpt from Act II*

SITUATION	WILLY LOMAN, *a failure in the declining years of his life, appeals to his friend and neighbor,* CHARLEY, *for financial assistance.*
CHARLEY	. . . There's some money — fifty dollars. I got an accountant inside.
WILLY	Charley, look . . . (*With difficulty*) I got my insurance to pay. If you can manage it — I need a hundred and ten dollars. (CHARLEY *doesn't reply for a moment; merely stops moving.*)
WILLY	I'd draw it from my bank but Linda would know, and I . . .
CHARLEY	Sit down, Willy.
WILLY	(*Moving toward the chair*) I'm keeping an account of everything, remember. I'll pay every penny back. (*He sits.*)
CHARLEY	Now listen to me, Willy.
WILLY	I want you to know I appreciate . . .
CHARLEY	(*Sitting down on the table*) Willy, what're you doin'? What the hell is goin' on in your head?
WILLY	Why? I'm simply . . .
CHARLEY	I offered you a job. You can make fifty dollars a week. And I won't send you on the road.
WILLY	I've got a job.
CHARLEY	Without pay? What kind of a job is a job without pay? (*He rises.*) Now, look, kid, enough is enough. I'm no genius but I know when I'm being insulted.
WILLY	Insulted!
CHARLEY	Why don't you want to work for me?

---

* Arthur Miller, *Death of a Salesman.* Copyright, 1949, by Arthur Miller. Reprinted by permission of Viking Press and Elaine Green.

WILLY	What's the matter with you? I've got a job.
CHARLEY	Then what're you walkin' in here every week for?
WILLY	(*Getting up*) Well, if you don't want me to walk in here —
CHARLEY	I am offering you a job.
WILLY	I don't want your goddam job!
CHARLEY	When the hell are you going to grow up?
WILLY	(*Furiously*) You big ignoramus, if you say that to me again I'll rap you one! I don't care how big you are!
	(*He's ready to fight.*)
	(*Pause*)
CHARLEY	(*Kindly, going to him*) How much do you need, Willy?
WILLY	Charley, I'm strapped, I'm strapped. I don't know what to do. I was just fired.
CHARLEY	Howard fired you?
WILLY	That snotnose. Imagine that? I named him. I named him Howard.
CHARLEY	Willy, when're you gonna realize that them things don't mean anything? You named him Howard, but you can't sell that. The only thing you got in this world is what you can sell. And the funny thing is that you're a salesman, and you don't know that.
WILLY	I've always tried to think otherwise, I guess. I always felt that if a man was impressive, and well liked, that nothing —
CHARLEY	Why must everybody like you? Who liked J. P. Morgan? Was he impressive? In a Turkish bath he'd look like a butcher. But with his pockets on he was very well liked. Now listen, Willy, I know you don't like me, and nobody can say I'm in love with you, but I'll give you a job because — just for the hell of it, put it that way. Now what do you say?
WILLY	I — I just can't work for you, Charley.
CHARLEY	What're you, jealous of me?
WILLY	I can't work for you, that's all, don't ask me why.

CHARLEY (*Angered, takes out more bills*) You been jealous of me all your life, you damned fool! Here, pay your insurance. (*He puts the money in* WILLY's *hand.*)

WILLY I'm keeping strict accounts.

CHARLEY I've got some work to do. Take care of yourself. And pay your insurance.

WILLY (*Moving to the right*) Funny, y'know? After all the highways, and the trains, and the appointments, and the years, you end up worth more dead than alive.

CHARLEY Willy, nobody's worth nothin' dead. (*After a slight pause*) Did you hear what I said?
(WILLY *stands still, dreaming.*)

CHARLEY Willy!

WILLY Apologize to Bernard for me when you see him. I didn't mean to argue with him. He's a fine boy. They're all fine boys, and they'll end up big — all of them. Someday they'll all play tennis together. Wish me luck, Charley. He saw Bill Oliver today.

CHARLEY Good luck.

WILLY (*On the verge of tears*) Charley, you're the only friend I got. Isn't that a remarkable thing? (*He goes out.*)

Playing the Scene

1. What are the tragic flaws in Willy's character?
2. Do you find in this scene a foreshadowing of Willy's suicide?
3. What are the ennobling qualities in the character of Willy?
4. How may sympathy for Willy be heightened?
5. What manner of playing this scene will achieve the highest dramatic values?
6. Why does Willy refuse to take a job with Charley?
7. What is Willy's objective?
8. What is Charley's objective?

RAIN

by John Colton and Clemence Randolph | excerpt from Act II*

CHARACTERS

REVEREND DAVIDSON, *a missionary to the South Pacific Islands*
SADIE THOMPSON, *a prostitute*

(SADIE *appears on the veranda. The change in her is extraordinary. Her hair is disheveled and her eyes glare with fear. The tears stream down her face. She stands waiting patiently until* REVEREND DAVIDSON *has finished saying grace for the evening meal.*)

DAVIDSON

(*Lifting his head and seeing* SADIE — *speaking in a pleasant cordial voice*) Can I do something for you, Miss Thompson?
(SADIE *comes toward* DAVIDSON *with a horrible cringing movement.*)

SADIE

I'm sorry for what I said to you today — for everything that's happened — I ask pardon.

DAVIDSON

(*Smiling*) I guess my back's broad enough to bear a few hard words.

SADIE

You've got me beat, I'm all in — For God's sake don't make me go to 'Frisco. I'll go anywhere else you say.
(DAVIDSON'S *genial manner vanishes and his voice grows hard and stern. He leaves the table and comes to her.*)

DAVIDSON

Why don't you want to go back there?

SADIE

I guess my people live there. I don't want them to see me like this.

DAVIDSON

I understood you had no people.

SADIE

I've got a father.

DAVIDSON

You told me yourself your father did not live in San Francisco.

SADIE

Yes.

DAVIDSON

That isn't the reason you do not want to go back — what is the reason?

SADIE

I've told you.

DAVIDSON	No, you have not told me.
SADIE	(*Craftily*) It's this way, Rev. Davidson. I'm trying to go straight now. If I go back to San Francisco, I can't go straight.
DAVIDSON	What will prevent you from going straight — if you really want to?
SADIE	There's a man in San Francisco, who won't let me.
DAVIDSON	Why won't he let you?
SADIE	He just won't. (*More furtively, cautiously, feeling her way carefully but not carrying conviction*) It's this way. I'm afraid he'll get me again.
DAVIDSON	Who is this man?
SADIE	(*At random*) Sort of a politician.
DAVIDSON	And you fear his influence?
SADIE	Yes — that's it. — He's a bad man — I'm scared of him.
DAVIDSON	Does he need to know you have returned?
SADIE	Oh, he'll know all right.
DAVIDSON	San Francisco is a big place, it should not be difficult to keep out of his way — if you want to.
SADIE	(*Groping her way*) I'll have to get help once I get back. The only folks who'll help me are in with him.
DAVIDSON	If you earnestly desire to go straight, there will be no necessity of going to your former friends for help. My mission will look after you until you are on your feet. This man you fear will never know you are in the city.
SADIE	(*Wildly*) He'll know, though — He'll know! All the boats coming in are being watched.
DAVIDSON	Do you mean to tell me that every boat coming into the port will be watched, on the chance you are on it?
SADIE	Yes — Yes!
DAVIDSON	(*In a terrible voice*) Come, Miss Thompson, these evasions are getting you nowhere. Why are you afraid to return to San Francisco?
SADIE	I've told you — I can't go straight there.

DAVIDSON   (*Rising and towering over* SADIE *who puts her hands up to her face and cringes*)
Shall I tell you why you are afraid to go back? (*She cowers before him.*)
You have told me lies. Now I shall tell you the truth. This politician you fear
is a politician in uniform — and he wears a badge!
(*He takes her by the shoulders, and his great shining eyes seem to bore into her soul.*)
What you fear is — the penitentiary.
(*She gives a sudden cry, then weakens at the knees and falls, clasping his legs.*)

SADIE   Don't send me back there. I swear to you before God, I'll be a good woman.
I'll give all this up.

(DAVIDSON *leans over her, lifts her face, forces her to look at him.*)

DAVIDSON   Is that it — the penitentiary?

SADIE   (*Faintly*) I was framed! But I got away before they caught me. They'll nab me
the moment I step off the ship, and it's three years for mine — three years —
three years — three years.
(DAVIDSON *lets go of* SADIE *and she falls in a heap on the floor, sobbing bitterly.*)
(*After a second, between her sobs*) Give me a chance — one chance.

DAVIDSON   (*With shining eyes*) I'm going to give you the finest chance you've ever had.

SADIE   (*Taking hope, half rises*) I don't have to go back — you mean?

DAVIDSON   Yes, you'll have to go back, you will sail for San Francisco Tuesday as the
Governor has ordered.
(SADIE *gives a groan of horror, sinks on the floor again and bursts into low, hoarse moans,
scarcely human.*) If you are truly repentent you will gladly accept this punish-
ment — you will offer it to God as the atonement for your sins.
(*The missionary's lips move silently in prayer.*)
(*Finishing his prayer. Gently*) When you want me, Sadie Thompson, call for
me — I will come. (DAVIDSON *is extraordinarily moved. Tears run down his cheeks.*)
At any hour — day or night — when you need me I will come — I shall be
waiting for your call.
(*He turns and slowly starts toward the stairs.* SADIE's *shuddering moans become fainter.
They are now deep, tortured sighs*)
(DAVIDSON *begins to mount the stairs.* SADIE *rouses herself. She gives a little cry.*
DAVIDSON *pauses.*)

SADIE   (*Struggling to her feet*) Reverend Davidson — wait a minute! (*A flicker of craft
comes into* SADIE's *eyes — the craft is desperation. Her expression indicates her mind is working rapidly. She crosses to* DAVIDSON *and clasps her hands.*) Reverend Davidson —
you're right. — I am a bad woman, but I want to be good, only I don't know
how. — So you let me stay here with you, then you can tell me what to do, and
no matter what it is I'm going to do it for you.

DAVIDSON   (*Shaking his head*) No, you can't stay here. — You've got to go back to San Francisco — you've got to serve your time.

SADIE   (*Looking at him astonished after her offer*) You mean to say if I repent and I want to be good — I still have to go to the penitentiary?

DAVIDSON   Yes — you've got to go.

SADIE   All right then — you send me back there and that's my finish.

DAVIDSON   No — it will be your beginning!

SADIE   (*Turning to him and throwing her last plea*) But I was framed, I tell you! — I was framed!

DAVIDSON   (*Standing, arms folded*) Innocent or guilty, you must serve your sentence! It's the only way you can prove to God that you are worthy of His mercy.

SADIE   Innocent or guilty? What kind of a God are you talking about? — Where's your mercy? Ah, no, Rev. Davidson, I guess that repentance stuff is off.

DAVIDSON   Was it ever on, Miss Thompson?

SADIE   Whether it was or not, it's off now! The way you figure out God, he's nothing but a Cop.

DAVIDSON   You've got to go back to San Francisco.

SADIE   (*Throwing discretion to the winds*) Straight orders from your private heaven, eh? Ah, no, Rev. Davidson, your God and me could never be shipmates, and the next time you talk to Him — (*She steps up to him and shouts in his face.*) You tell Him this from me — Sadie Thompson is on her way to Hell!

DAVIDSON   (*Drawing himself up to full height and shouting back at her*) Stop! This has gone far enough!

SADIE   (*In wild hysteria*) No! It hasn't gone far enough! You've been telling me what's wrong with me — Now I'll tell you what's wrong with you — you keep yelling to me — be punished! — Go back and suffer! How do you know what I have suffered? You don't know — you don't care — you don't even ask and you call yourself a Christian — you're nothing but a miserable witch burner — that's what you are — you believe in torture — you know you're big and you're strong and you've got the law on your side — and the power to hang me — all right! But I want to tell you this — I've got the power to stand here and say to you — Hang me and be damned to you! (*She stampedes into her room, sobbing hoarsely.*) DAVIDSON's *lips move in prayer as*
    The Curtain Falls.

Playing the Scene

1. What universal entity does each character represent?
2. What is the tragic flaw in Reverend Davidson's character?
3. Is Davidson a hypocrite, a fanatic, or a sincere, spiritual man of God? How would each of these interpretations of his character affect the meaning and dramatic impact of the play?
4. How much audience sympathy should each character receive?
5. Are there qualities of nobility in each character?
6. What are their noble qualities and how may they be portrayed?
7. How would a reading of the entire play affect the answers to the following questions?
a) How should the scene be played?
b) Why does Davidson go to Sadie's room?
c) Why does he take his life?
d) What bearing does his final act have on the interpretation of his character?

Other Sources for Scenes of Modern Tragedy

Ethan Frome by Owen David and Donald Davis
Of Mice and Men by John Steinbeck
Riders to the Sea by John Millington Synge

MODERN POETIC TRAGEDY

This type is similar to the tragedy described in the preceding section except that poetic dialogue is used. The problem for the actor in this type of drama is to achieve believability in commonplace characters who communicate in the medium of poetic language.

Manner of Playing

1. The extremely lofty or "grand" style is to be avoided.
2. A logical approach might well be to seek a balance between poetic diction and conversational prose, without a loss of meaning.
3. In order to enhance the beauty of the language, the actor should strive for sincerity, clear diction, and a pleasing melodic pattern.

Practice Selections

WINTERSET

by Maxwell Anderson / excerpt from Act I, Scene 3*

CHARACTERS   MIO, *about* 17
                     MIRIAMNE, *about* 15

SITUATION   MIO *is seeking to find the persons who were responsible for the death of his father in order to avenge the crime. He meets* MIRIAMNE *and the two are immediately drawn to each other.*

MIO

So now little Miriamne will go in
and take up quietly where she dropped them all
her small housewifely cares. — When I first saw you,
not a half-hour ago, I heard myself saying,
this is the face that launches ships for me —
and if I owned a dream — yes, half a dream —
we'd share it. But I have no dream. This earth
came tumbling down from chaos, fire and rock,
and bred up worms, blind worms that sting each other
here in the dark. These blind worms of the earth
took out my father — and killed him, and set a sign
on me — the heir of the serpent — and he was a man
such as men might be if the gods were men —
but they killed him —
as they'll kill all others like him
till the sun cools down to the stabler molecules,
yes, till men spin their tent-worm webs to the stars
and what they think is done, even in the thinking,
and they are the gods, and immortal, and constellations
turn for them all like mill wheels — still as they are
they will be, worms and blind. Enduring love,
oh gods and worms, what mockery! — And yet
I have blood enough in my veins. It goes like music,
singing, because you're here. My body turns
as if you were the sun, and warm. This men called love
in happier times, before the Freudians taught us
to blame it on the glands. Only go in
before you breathe too much of my atmosphere
and catch death from me.

MIRIAMNE

I will take my hands
and weave them to a little house, and there
you shall keep a dream —

MIO

God knows I could use a dream
and even a house.

MIRIAMNE

You're laughing at me, Mio!

MIO

The worms are laughing.
I tell you there's death about me
and you're a child! And I'm alone and half mad
with hate and longing. I shall let you love me
and love you in return, and then, why then
God knows what happens!

MIRIAMNE   Something most unpleasant?

MIO   Love in a box car — love among the children.
I've seen too much of it. Are we to live
in this same house you make with your two hands
mystically, out of air?

MIRIAMNE   No roof, no mortgage!
Well, I shall marry a baker out in Flatbush,
it gives hot bread in the morning! Oh, Mio, Mio,
in all the unwanted places and waste lands
that roll up into the darkness out of sun
and into sun out of dark, there should be one empty
for you and me.

MIO   No.

MIRIAMNE   Then go now and leave me.
I'm only a girl you saw in the tenements,
and there's been nothing said.

MIO   Miriamne.
(*She takes a step toward him.*)

MIRIAMNE   Yes.
(*He kisses her lips lightly.*)

MIO   Why, girl, the transfiguration on the mount
was nothing to your face. It lights from within —
a white chalice holding fire, a flower in flame,
this is your face.

MIRIAMNE   And you shall drink the flame
and never lessen it. And round your head
the aureole shall burn that burns there now,
forever. This I can give you. And so forever
the Freudians are wrong.

MIO   They're well-forgotten
at any rate.

MIRIAMNE   Why did you speak to me
when you first saw me?

MIO   I knew then.

MIRIAMNE

And I came back
because I must see you again. And we danced together
and my heart hurt me. Never, never, never,
though they should bind me down and tear out my eyes,
would I ever hurt you now. Take me with you, Mio,
let them look for us, whoever there is to look,
but we'll be away.

Playing the Scene

1. What manner of playing this scene will best serve the dramatic values of *Winterset*?
2. How may the poetic language of the characters be made more acceptable and believable?
3. How may the nobility of the characters be enhanced?
4. How much importance should be given to the rhythm of the language?
5. Which stage areas seem most appropriate for this scene?
6. What amount and kind of movement is inherent in the scene?

J. B.

by Archibald MacLeish | the Prologue*

(*Two broken-down actors venture to play the parts of* GOD *and* SATAN, *with surprising and unforeseen results.*)

(*Back to back the shadows of* MR. ZUSS *and* NICKLES *adjust their masks. The masked shadows turn to each other and gravely bow. Their gestures are the stiff formal gestures of pantomime. Their voices, when they speak, are so magnified and hollowed by the masks that they scarcely seem their own.*)

GODMASK

Whence comest thou?

SATANMASK

From going to and fro in the earth
(*There is a snicker of suppressed laughter.*)
And from walking up and down in it . . .
(*A great guffaw.* MR. ZUSS *tears off his mask.*)

MR. ZUSS

(*Shouting*) Lights!
(*The spotlight fades out. The dangling bulbs come feebly on.*)

---

* Archibald MacLeish, *J. B.* Copyright, 1958, by Archibald MacLeish. Reprinted by permission of the publisher, Houghton Mifflin. (See Plate 1.)

Nobody told you to laugh like that.
What's so funny? It's irreverent. It's impudent.
After all, you are talking to God.
That doesn't happen every Saturday
Even to kitchen kin like you.
Take that face off! It's indecent!
Makes me feel like scratching somewhere!
(NICKLES *painfully removes his mask.*)

NICKLES

Do I look as though I'd laughed?
If you had seen what I have seen
You'd never laugh again! . . .
(*He stares at his mask.*)
                            Weep either . . .

MR. ZUSS

You roared. I heard you.

NICKLES

                            Those eyes *see.*

MR. ZUSS

Of course they see — beneath the trousers
Stalking up the pulpit stair:
Under the skirts at tea — wherever
Decent eyes would be ashamed to.
Why should you laugh at that?

NICKLES

                            It isn't
That! It isn't that at all!
They see the *world.* They do. They see it.
From going to and fro in the earth,
From walking up and down, they see it.
I know what Hell is now — to *see.*
Consciousness of consciousness . . .

MR. ZUSS

                            Now
Listen! This is a simple scene.
I play God. You play Satan.
God is asking where you've been.
All you have to do is tell him:
Simple as that. "In the earth," you answer.

NICKLES

Satan answers.

MR. ZUSS

                        All right — Satan.
What's the difference?

NICKLES

Satan *sees.*
He sees the parked car by the plane tree.
He sees behind the fusty door,
Beneath the rug, those almost children
Struggling on the awkward seat —
Every impossible delighted dream
She's ever had of loveliness, of wonder.
Spilled with her garters to the filthy floor.
Absurd despair! Ridiculous agony!
(*He looks at the mask in his hands.*)
What has any man to laugh at!
The panting crow by the dry tree
Drags dusty wings. God's mercy brings
The rains — but not to such as he.

MR. ZUSS

You play your part, I'll say that for you.
In it or out of it, you play.

NICKLES

You really think I'm playing?

MR. ZUSS

Aren't you?
Somebody is. Satan maybe.
Maybe Satan's playing *you.*
Let's begin from the beginning.
Ready!
(*They take their places back to back.*)
Masks!
(*They raise their masks to their faces.*)
Lights!
(*The bulbs go out. Darkness. Silence. In the silence:*)

A DISTANT VOICE

Whence comest thou?

MR. ZUSS

That's my line.

NICKLES

I didn't speak it.

MR. ZUSS

You did. Stop your mischief, won't you?

NICKLES

Stop your own! Laughing. Shouting.

MR. ZUSS

Lights, I said!
(*The spotlight throws the enormous shadows on the canvas sky.*)

GODMASK

Whence comest thou?

SATANMASK	From going to and fro in the earth . . .
	(*A choked silence.*)
	And from walking up and down in it.
GODMASK	Hast thou considered my servant Job
	That there is none like him on the earth
	A perfect and an upright man, one
	That feareth God and escheweth evil?

Playing the Scene

1. What physical characteristics might differentiate the characters, Zuss and Nickles, from Godmask and Satanmask?
2. What vocal characteristics might be appropriate and effective for each character?

Other Sources for Scenes of Modern Poetic Tragedy

Anne of the Thousand Days by Maxwell Anderson

Mary of Scotland by Maxwell Anderson

The Masque of Kings by Maxwell Anderson

MODERN MELODRAMA

The late George P. Baker remarked that "melodrama is insufficiently motivated tragedy." If this statement is accepted, its implications for the actor are clear. The writer of melodrama seems more concerned with plot manipulation, situation, and startling effects than with the development of well-rounded characters. In tragedy the action seems to develop from the characters' free will, while in melodrama the characters are little more than pawns in the forward rush of events. As a result, the characters in melodrama are generally distinct types, either dominantly good or bad. Seldom, if ever, does one find in melodrama a mixture of moral qualities within any one character. In contemporary melodramas, however, one finds characters with more depth and psychological motivation than was the case in comparable plays of the nineteenth century.

Since the plot of melodrama is the dominant element and somewhat arbitrarily contrived, the actor should be on the alert for climaxes, heightened emotions, varied moods, exaggerated actions, and distinct changes of pace.

Manner of Playing

1. The dominant trait of the character must be determined.
2. The amount and kind of empathy the character should receive must be ascertained.
3. The actor should strive for believability within the context of the play.
4. Overacting or "hamming it up" should be avoided.

Practice Selection

ANGEL STREET

by Patrick Hamilton / excerpt from Act I*

CHARACTERS   MRS. MANNINGHAM *and* MR. MANNINGHAM

SCENE   *The scene is a living-room on the first floor of a four-storied house in a gloomy and un-fashionable quarter of London, in the latter part of the last century. . . . Fireplace Down Right. Door above fireplace leading to a little room. Settee Right, Left of fireplace with stool in front of it. Table Center with chairs Right and Left of it. Window at Left. Desk in front of window with chairs back and above it. Secretary against wall Up Right. Lamp on table Center. Sliding double doors at back Left Center leading to hall, to Left the front door, to Right the servants' quarters. A circular stair leading to the upper floors is at back up Right Center. Chairs Down Right and Left.*

(With seeming kindness, MR. MANNINGHAM *is diabolically driving his wife into insanity. He committed a murder fifteen years ago but failed to find his victim's valuable jewels. He is still searching.)*

MRS. MANNINGHAM   *(Crossing to him)* Jack — I'm going to make a last appeal to you. I'm going to make a last appeal. I'm desperate, Jack. Can't you see that I'm desperate? If you can't, you must have a heart of stone.

MR. MANNINGHAM   *(Turns to her.)* Go on. What do you wish to say?

MRS. MANNINGHAM   Jack, *(Crosses to front of settee.)* I may be going mad, like my poor mother — but if I am mad, you have got to treat me gently. Jack — before God — I never lie to you knowingly. If I have taken down that picture from its place I have not known it. *I have not known it.* If I took it down on those other occasions I did not know it, either. *(Turns and crosses to Center.)* Jack, if I steal your things — your rings — your keys — your pencils and your handkerchiefs, and you find them later at the bottom of my box, as indeed you do, then I do not know that I have done it — Jack, if I commit these fantastic, meaningless mischiefs — so meaningless — *(A step toward him)* Why should I take a picture down from its place? *(Pause)* If I do all these things, then I am certainly going off my head, and must be treated kindly and gently so that I may get well. *(Crosses to him.)* You must *bear* with me, Jack, *bear* with me — not storm and rage. God knows I'm trying, Jack, I'm trying! Oh, for God's sake believe me that I'm trying and be kind to me!

* Patrick Hamilton, *Angel Street.* Copyright, 1942, by Patrick Hamilton. Reprinted by permission of the Estate of the late Patrick Hamilton and of A. M. Heath.

MR. MANNINGHAM	Bella, my dear — have you any idea where that picture is now?
MRS. MANNINGHAM	Yes, yes, I suppose it's behind the cupboard.
MR. MANNINGHAM	Will you please go and see?
MRS. MANNINGHAM	(*Vaguely*) Yes — yes — (*Crosses below him, goes Right to upper end of secretary and produces it.*) Yes, it's here.
MR. MANNINGHAM	(*Reproachfully. As he crosses to the desk, places the Bible on it and crosses up Left.*) Then you did know where it was, Bella. (*Turns to her.*) You did know where it was.
MRS. MANNINGHAM	(*As she starts toward him*) No! No! I only *supposed* it was! I only supposed it was because it was found there before! It was found there twice before. Don't you see? I *didn't* know — I didn't!
MR. MANNINGHAM	There is no sense in walking about the room with a picture in your hands, Bella. Go and put it back in its proper place.
MRS. MANNINGHAM	(*Pause as she hangs the picture on wall — she comes back to the back of the chair Right of table.*) Oh, look at our tea. We were having our tea with muffins —
MR. MANNINGHAM	Now, Bella, I said a moment ago that we have got to face facts. And that is what we have got to do. I am not going to say anything at the moment, for my feelings are running too high. In fact, I am going out immediately, and I suggest that you go to your room and lie down for a little in the dark.
MRS. MANNINGHAM	No, no — not my room. For God's sake don't send me to my room! (*Grabbing chair*)
MR. MANNINGHAM	There is no question of sending you to your room, Bella. (*Crosses to her.*) You know perfectly well that you may do exactly as you please.
MRS. MANNINGHAM	I feel faint. Jack — (*He goes quickly to her and supports her.*) I feel faint —
MR. MANNINGHAM	Very well — (*Leading her to settee. She sinks down with her head to Left end.*) Now, take things quietly and come and lie down, here. Where are your salts? (*Crosses to secretary, gets salts and returns to her, back of settee.*) Here they are — (*Pause*) Now, my dear, I am going to leave you in peace —
MRS. MANNINGHAM	(*Eyes closed, reclining*) Have you got to go? Must you go? Must you always leave me alone after these dreadful scenes?
MR. MANNINGHAM	Now, no argument, please. I had to go in any case after tea, and I'm merely leaving you a little earlier, that's all. (*Pause, going into wardrobe and returning with undercoat on*) Now is there anything I can get for you?

MRS. MANNINGHAM	No, Jack dear, nothing. You go.
MR. MANNINGHAM	Very good — (*Goes toward his hat and overcoat which are on the chair above desk, and stops.*) Oh, by the way, I shall be passing the grocer and I might as well pay that bill of his and get it done with. Where is it, my dear? I gave it to you, didn't I?
MRS. MANNINGHAM	Yes, dear. It's on the secretary. (*Half rising*) I'll —
MR. MANNINGHAM	(*Crossing to secretary*) No, dear — don't move — don't move, I can find it. (*At secretary and begins to rummage.*) I shall be glad to get this thing off my chest. Where is it, dear? Is it in one of these drawers?
MRS. MANNINGHAM	No — it's on top. I put it there this afternoon.
MR. MANNINGHAM	All right. We'll find it — We'll find it — Are you sure it's here, dear? There's nothing here except some writing paper.
MRS. MANNINGHAM	(*Half rising and speaking suspiciously*) Jack, I'm sure it *is* there. Will you look carefully?
MR. MANNINGHAM	(*Soothingly*) All right, dear. Don't worry. I'll find it. Lie down. It's of no importance, I'll find it — No, it's not here — It must be in one of the drawers —
MRS. MANNINGHAM	(*She has rushed to the secretary*) It is not in one of the drawers! I put it out here on top! You're not going to tell me *this* has gone, are you?
MR. MANNINGHAM	(*Speaking at the same time*) My dear. Calm yourself. Calm yourself.

(Together)

MRS. MANNINGHAM	(*Searching frantically*) I laid it out here myself! Where is it? (*Opening and shutting drawers*) Where is it? Now you're going to say I've hidden this!
MR. MANNINGHAM	(*Walking away to Left end of settee*) My God! — What new trick is this you're playing upon me?
MRS. MANNINGHAM	(*At Right lower end of settee*) It was there this afternoon! I put it there! This is a plot! This is a filthy plot! You're all against me! It's a plot! (*She screams hysterically.*)
MR. MANNINGHAM	(*Coming to her and shaking her violently*) Will you control yourself! Will you control yourself! (*Pause until she calms down*) Listen to me, Madam, if you utter another sound I'll knock you down and take you to your room and lock you in darkness for a week. I have been too lenient with you, and I mean to alter my tactics.
MRS. MANNINGHAM	(*Sinks to her knees.*) Oh, God help me! God help me!

MR. MANNINGHAM	May God help you, indeed. Now listen to me. I am going to leave you until ten o'clock. (*He lifts her up.*) In that time you will recover that paper, and admit to me that you have lyingly and purposely concealed it — if not, you will take the consequences. (*Pause as he places her in the chair down Right and crosses Left to above desk.*) You are going to see a doctor, (*He stops and turns to* BELLA.) Madam, more than one doctor — (*Puts his hat on and throws his coat over his arm.*) and they shall decide what this means. Now do you understand me?
MRS. MANNINGHAM	Oh, God — be patient with me. If I am mad, be patient with me.
MR. MANNINGHAM	I have been patient with you and controlled myself long enough. It is now for you to control yourself, or take the consequences. Think upon that, Bella. (*Goes to Left Center doors and opens them.*)
MRS. MANNINGHAM	Jack — Jack — don't go — Jack — You're still going to take me to the theatre, aren't you?
MR. MANNINGHAM	What a question to ask me at such a time. No, Madam, emphatically, I am not. You play fair by me, and I'll play fair by you. But if we are going to be enemies, you and I, you will not prosper, believe me. (*Goes out.*)

Playing the Scene

1. Where are the high emotional climaxes in the above scene?

2. Where are the low points in the scene?

3. Should Mr. Manningham's words of endearment seem real to Mrs. Manningham?

4. Should Mr. Manningham's words of endearment seem real or false to the audience?

5. How might an actress playing Mrs. Manningham achieve the high emotional climaxes in this scene? Should she rely on (1) emotional memory and inner feelings, (2) vocal and physical techniques, or (3) a combination of 1 and 2?

Other Sources for Scenes of Modern Melodrama

Anastasia by Guy Bolton

Dial "M" for Murder by Frederick Knott

Ladies in Retirement by Edward Percy and Reginald Denham

Night Must Fall by Emlyn Williams

COMEDY

The generic term *comedy* embraces a great variety of dramatic forms, from the high, intellectual comedy of manners to the low comedy of physical action. In common parlance, comedy refers to a play with a happy ending, having as its dominant purpose the provocation of laughter. However, as Nicoll points out, a happy ending is not the distinguishing characteristic of comedy nor does this dramatic form depend upon laughter.* The fundamental and distinguishing characteristic of comedy (and this is of special interest to the actor) is that the characters of comedy are universalized types and not personalized individuals. They are the misers, the braggarts, the nitwits, and simpletons, types which are common to all periods and places. In the *Poetics*, Aristotle states that comedy represents men as worse than they are in real life. By this he undoubtedly meant that the foibles, failings, and idosyncrasies of the characters are exaggerated.

Another important characteristic of comedy is that it depends for its success upon insensibility on the part of the audience. Emotional involvement is detrimental to the comic spirit. We sometimes say that in comedy the actor must play from his head, not his heart, to the head of the audience. Comedy is intellectual pleasure and, as Henri Bergson indicated, as soon as we begin to sympathize, we lose the spirit of laughter.†

Theories of comedy

There have been many attempts to capture and analyze the comic spirit. George Meredith, in his well-known *An Essay on Comedy and the Comic Spirit*, maintains that comedy is one of the most wholesome and effectual ways of probing and purifying the ills of the world.‡ Bergson, in *Laughter*, develops at some length the idea that comedy evolves from "something mechanical encrusted on the living."§ Even though no one theory seems to satisfy all types and conditions of comedy, certain psychological conditions seem to prevail when the comic effect is achieved.

Although by no means exhaustive, the following factors are usually present in comedy.

1. Some illogical adjustment to the situation, either of thought or action, is evident. It is comic when the lady advises the migrating birds to take route 61 out of Memphis because we expect an individual to make logical, sensible adjustments to a given situation. If the normal behavior pattern is broken, as when the patient absentmindedly removes the thermometer from her mouth to stir her breakfast coffee, the effect is comic.

2. Some degree of exaggeration in language, character traits, or action is present.

3. Some form of incongruity in manner or dress is manifest. It is characteristic of comedy to depart from the norm or the conventional. When short dresses are the fashion, a long dress appears comic. It is this departure from the norm in voice (nasal, denasal, drawl) which has contributed to the comic effectiveness of certain comedians.

4. An opportunity for the sudden release of inhibitions or tensions is provided. This factor may account for the laughter which often accompanies profanity. It may also account for the unwonted and seemingly uncalled for laughter in a serious scene of high emotional tension.

5. A superiority complex in the audience is established. The comic effect is enhanced when members of the audience consider themselves to be wiser and better informed than the characters in the play.

The principle that all art must seem effortless is particularly true in the playing of comedy. Since

---

* Allardyce Nicoll, *The Theory of Drama*. New York: Benjamin Blom, 1931, pp. 187, 213.

† Henri Bergson, *Laughter*, trans. Cloudesley Berreton and Fred Rothwell. New York: Macmillan, 1913, p. 139.

‡ George Meredith, *An Essay on Comedy and the Uses of the Comic Spirit*. Westminster: Archibald Constable, 1898, pp. 88–97.

---

§ Bergson, *Laughter*, p. 37.

the comic Muse is delicate and elusive, the comic devices must be made to seem spontaneous, unplanned, and unlabored. A rollicking pace and a light touch invoke the comic spirit much more readily than a hammer and tongs method of playing.

Since a superiority complex on the part of the audience is a basic essential for the enjoyment of comedy, the actor should avoid obvious awareness of his own enjoyment of the comic lines and actions. Carol Channing remarked on one occasion, "To be funny, it must be serious." By this she meant that a situation or line which is comic to the audience must be serious to the character.

It is generally agreed that comedy is more difficult to play than serious drama. In playing comedy, a great deal of technical skill must be mastered, in devices such as preparation for a laugh, line pointing, topping, timing, duration of pauses, and holding. It is important to analyze the play in order to determine the dominant mood and spirit. If possible, the actor should find an approach to the character which brings out the best dramatic values and the greatest enjoyment to the audience. In general, the principal characters in a comedy must not be disliked by the audience.

Comedy-drama

This type of comedy is a mixture of the comic and the serious, with the scales weighted on the serious side. The play may deal with the evils of our society or the problems of an individual in an imperfect society. One facet of *The Time of Your Life* by William Saroyan (selected as a sample of

comedy-drama) presents the inhumane oppression of an individual by an officer of the law. In contrast, Joe, a compulsive drinker, has a boundless compassion for his fellow man. The scene between Joe and Kit Carson is one of the lighter, more comic scenes of the play. The characters should react from inner motivation and be sympathetic or unsympathetic as the particular role may require.

Plate 32. *The Time of Your Life* by William Saroyan. Scene showing Joe and the inveterate story teller, Kit Carson. Ohio State University. Director: Everett M. Schreck.

Practice Selection

THE TIME OF YOUR LIFE

*by William Saroyan / excerpt from Act II**

SCENE
Nick's Pacific Street Saloon, Restaurant, and Entertainment Palace at the foot of Embarcadero, in San Francisco.

CHARACTERS
JOE, *a young loafer with money and a good heart*
KIT CARSON, *an old Indian-fighter*

(An old man who looks like Kit Carson staggers in Right, looks around; edges to bar; reaction to NICK; *goes above to left and moves about aimlessly and finally goes to chair left of Center table.)*

KIT CARSON
Murphy's the name. Just an old trapper. Mind if I sit down?

JOE
Be delighted. What'll you drink?

KIT CARSON
(Sitting down) Beer. Same as I've been drinking. And thanks.

JOE
(To NICK*)* Glass of beer, Nick. (NICK *brings the beer to the table, and goes back of bar.* KIT CARSON *swallows it in one swig, wipes his big white mustache with the back of his right hand.)*

KIT CARSON
(Moving in) I don't suppose you ever fell in love with a midget weighing thirty-nine pounds?

JOE
Can't say I have, but have another beer.

KIT CARSON
(Intimately) Thanks, thanks. Down in Gallup twenty years ago. Fellow by the name of Rufus Jenkins came to town with six white horses and two black ones. Said he wanted a man to break the horses for him because his left leg was wood and he couldn't do it. Had a meeting at Parker's Mercantile Store and finally came to blows, me and Henry Walpal. Bashed his head with a brass cuspidor and ran away to Mexico, but he didn't die. *(Sailor enters Right and goes to bar.)*
Couldn't speak a word. Took up with a cattle-breeder named Diego, educated in California. Spoke the language better than you and me. Said, Your job,

* William Saroyan, *The Time of Your Life.* Copyright, 1939, by William Saroyan. Copyright, 1941 (Acting Edition), by Samuel French. Reprinted by permission of Samuel French and William Saroyan. (See Plate 32.)

Murph, is to feed them prize bulls. I said, Fine, what'll I feed them? He said, Hay, lettuce, salt, beer, and aspirin. Came to blows two days later over an accordion he claimed I stole. I had *borrowed* it. During the fight I busted it over his head; ruined one of the finest accordions I ever saw. Grabbed a horse and rode back across the border. Texas. Got to talking with a fellow who looked honest. Turned out to be a Ranger who was looking for me.
(KILLER *enters Right. Sits downstage of bar.*)

JOE

Yeah. You were saying, a thirty-nine–pound midget.

KIT CARSON

Will I ever forget that lady? Will I ever get over that amazon of small proportions?

JOE

Will you?

KIT CARSON

If I live to be sixty.

JOE

You look more than sixty now.

KIT CARSON

That's trouble showing in my face. Trouble and complications. I was fifty-eight three months ago.

JOE

That accounts for it, then. Go ahead, tell me more.

KIT CARSON

Told the Texas Ranger my name was Rothstein, mining engineer from Pennsylvania, looking for something worth while. Mentioned two places in Houston. Nearly lost an eye early one morning, going down the stairs. (*Rises.*) Ran into a six-footer with an iron claw where his right hand was supposed to be. Said, You broke up my home. Told him I was a stranger in Houston. The girls gathered at the top of the stairs to see a fight. Seven of them. Six feet and an iron claw. That's bad on the nerves.
(*Breaks Left.*) Kicked him in the mouth when he swung for my head with the claw. Would have lost an eye except for quick thinking. He rolled into the gutter and pulled a gun. Fired seven times. I was back upstairs. Left the place an hour later, dressed in silk and feathers, with a hat swung around over my face. Saw him standing on the corner, waiting. (*Crossing Left*) Said, Care for a wiggle? Said he didn't. I went on down the street and left town. I don't suppose you ever had to put a dress on to save your skin, did you?
(*Crosses to Left of Center table and sits.*)

JOE

(*Signals* NICK *for beer*) No, and I never fell in love with a midget weighing thirty-nine pounds. Have another beer?

KIT CARSON

Thanks.

Playing the Scene

1. Is there warmth in Joe's character?
2. Does he believe Kit Carson's story?
3. Does Kit Carson believe his own tales of adventure?

Other Sources for Scenes of Comedy-Drama

Ah, Wilderness! by Eugene O'Neill
The Hasty Heart by John Patrick

Pure comedy

Plays of this type lack the warmth and serious overtones of comedy-drama. Rarely, if ever, are the characters' deeper emotions conveyed to the audience. The audience, therefore, does not become emotionally involved in the problems of the characters.

Manner of Playing

1. The actor should strive for vocal variety and rapid pace.
2. In general, low key pitch and strong force for word emphasis should be avoided.

Practice Selection

HARVEY

by Mary Chase / excerpt from Act I, Scene 2*

SITUATION   ELWOOD P. DOWD, *a lovable drunk, whose constant companion is an invisible, white rabbit, has long since become a perpetual annoyance to his sister,* VETA, *and her daughter,* MYRTLE. *Their plan to put* ELWOOD *in an institution misfires.*

(*Enter* ELWOOD *from* C. *He doesn't see* BETTY *at first. He looks around the room carefully.*)

BETTY   Good evening.

ELWOOD   (*Removing his hat and bowing*) Good evening. (*Puts hat on desk. Walks over to her.*)

BETTY   I am Mrs. Chumley. Doctor Chumley's wife.

ELWOOD   I'm happy to know that. Dowd is my name. Elwood P. Let me give you one of my cards. (*Gives her one.*) If you should want to call me — call me at this one. Don't call me at that one, because that's (*Points at card.*) the old one. (*Starts one step. Looking.*)

---

* Mary Chase, *Harvey.* Copyright, 1953, by Mary Chase. Copyright, 1943, by Mary Chase (under the title, *The White Rabbit*). Copyright, 1944, by Mary Chase (under the title, *Harvey*). Reprinted by permission of Harold Freedman, Brandt & Brandt Dramatic Department.

BETTY	Thank you. Is there something I can do for you?
ELWOOD	(*Turns to her.*) What did you have in mind?
BETTY	You seem to be looking for someone.
ELWOOD	(*Walking*) Yes, I am. I'm looking for Harvey. I went off without him.
BETTY	Harvey? Is he a patient here?
ELWOOD	(*Turns.*) Oh, no. Nothing like that. (*Crosses to door down* L.)
BETTY	Does he work here?
ELWOOD	(*Looking out down* L. *door*) Oh, no. He is what you might call my best friend. He is also a pooka. He came out here with me and Veta this afternoon.
BETTY	Where was he when you last saw him?
ELWOOD	(*Behind chair* L. *of desk*) In that chair there — with his hat and coat on the table.
BETTY	There doesn't seem to be any hat and coat around here now. Perhaps he left?
ELWOOD	Apparently. I don't see him anywhere. (*Looks in* SANDERSON's *office.*)
BETTY	What was that word you just said — pooka?
ELWOOD	(*Crosses* C. *He is looking in hallway* C.) Yes — that's it.
BETTY	Is that something new? (*Looks in hallway.*)
ELWOOD	(*Coming down*) Oh, no. As I understand it, that's something very old.
BETTY	Oh, really? I had never happened to hear it before.
ELWOOD	I'm not too surprised at that. I hadn't myself, until I met him. I do hope you get an opportunity to meet him. I'm sure he would be quite taken with you. (*Down* C. *on a line with Betty*)
BETTY	Oh, really? Well, that's very nice of you to say so, I'm sure.
ELWOOD	Not at all. If Harvey happens to take a liking to people he expresses himself quite definitely. If he's not particularly interested, he sits there like an empty chair or an empty space on the floor. Harvey takes his time making his mind up about people. Choosey, you see. (*Crosses above table to door* R.)
BETTY	That's not such a bad way to be in this day and age.
ELWOOD	Harvey is fond of my sister, Veta. That's because he is fond of me, and Veta and I come from the same family. Now you'd think that feeling would be mutual,

wouldn't you? (*Looks in office* R. *Crosses to chair* R. *of table.*) But Veta doesn't seem to care for Harvey. Don't you think that's rather too bad, Mrs. Chumley?

BETTY

Oh, I don't know, Mr. Dowd. I gave up a long time ago expecting my family to like my friends. It's useless.

ELWOOD

But we must keep on trying. (*Sits chair* R. *of table.*)

BETTY

Well, there's no harm in trying, I suppose.

ELWOOD

Because if Harvey has said to me once he has said a million times — "Mr. Dowd, I would do anything for you." Mrs. Chumley —

BETTY

Yes —

ELWOOD

Did you know that Mrs. McElhinney's Aunt Rose is going to drop in on her unexpectedly tonight from Cleveland?

BETTY

Why no, I didn't —

ELWOOD

Neither does she. That puts you both in the same boat, doesn't it?

BETTY

Well, I don't know anybody named — Mrs. —

ELWOOD

Mrs. McElhinney? Lives next door to us. She is a wonderful woman. Harvey told me about her Aunt Rose. That's an interesting little news item, and you are perfectly free to pass it around.

BETTY

Well, I —

ELWOOD

Would you care to come downtown with me now, my dear? I would be glad to buy you a drink.

BETTY

Thank you very much, but I am waiting for Dr. Chumley and if he came down and found me gone he would be liable to raise — he would be irritated!

ELWOOD

We wouldn't want that, would we? Some other time, maybe? (*He rises.*)

BETTY

I'll tell you what I'll do, however.

ELWOOD

What will you do, however? I'm interested.

BETTY

If your friend comes in while I'm here I'd be glad to give him a message for you.

ELWOOD

(*Gratefully*) Would you do that? I'd certainly appreciate that. (*Goes up* C. *to top of desk for his hat.*)

BETTY

No trouble at all. I'll write it down on the back of this. (*Holds up card. Takes pencil from purse.*) What would you like me to tell him if he comes in while I'm still here?

ELWOOD

Ask him to meet me downtown — if he has no other plans.

BETTY	(*Writing*) Meet Mr. Dowd downtown. Any particular place downtown?
ELWOOD	He knows where. Harvey knows this town like a book.
BETTY	(*Writing*) Harvey — you know where. Harvey what?
ELWOOD	Just Harvey.
BETTY	(*Rises — crosses to desk*) I'll tell you what.
ELWOOD	What?
BETTY	(*Swings chair* R. *of desk in position.*) Doctor and I are going right downtown — to 12th and Montview. Dr. McClure is having a cocktail party.
ELWOOD	(*At* L. *of desk; he writes that down on a pad on desk.*) A cocktail party at 12th and Montview.
BETTY	We're driving there in a few minutes. We could give your friend a lift into town.
ELWOOD	I hate to impose on you — but I would certainly appreciate that.
BETTY	No trouble at all. Dr. McClure is having this party for his sister from Wichita.
ELWOOD	I didn't know Dr. McClure had a sister in Wichita.
BETTY	Oh — you know Dr. McClure?
ELWOOD	No.
BETTY	(*Puts* ELWOOD's *card down on desk.*) But — (*Sits chair* R. *of desk.*)
ELWOOD	You're quite sure you haven't time to come into town with me and have a drink?
BETTY	I really couldn't — but thank you just the same.
ELWOOD	Some other time, perhaps?
BETTY	Thank you.
ELWOOD	It's been very pleasant to meet you, and I hope to see you again.
BETTY	Yes, so do I.
ELWOOD	Good-night, my dear. (*Tips hat — bows — goes to door, turns.*) You can't miss Harvey. He's very tall — (*Shows with hands.*) Like that — (*Exits down L.*)

Playing the scene

1. What seems to be the best style for this scene?

2. What is the key to Elwood's character?

3. Is Veta justified in wanting to put Elwood in an institution?

4. Should the audience be induced to believe that Harvey exists?

Other Sources for Scenes of Pure Comedy

Come Blow Your Horn by Neil Simon

The Male Animal by James Thurber and Elliott Nugent

Any Wednesday by Muriel Resnik

Mary, Mary by Jean Kerr

Sentimental comedy

Sentimental plays lack the intellectual appeal and objectivity of pure comedy. The emotions of the characters are on the surface and are pleasingly delicate rather than violent and deep.

Manner of playing

1. The actor should avoid any appearance of insincerity.

2. A delicate, mellow vocal quality with a pleasing melodic pattern seems most appropriate.

3. The general style of acting for sentimental comedy is best described as a mixture of realism and romanticism.

4. Audience sympathy for the characters is exceedingly important.

Sources for Scenes of Sentimental Comedy

Alice Sit-by-the-Fire by J. M. Barrie

Quality Street by J. M. Barrie

Trelawny of the 'Wells' by A. W. Pinero

What Every Woman Knows by J. M. Barrie

Whimsical comedy

These plays are of delicate substance. The dominant quality is a combination of the capricious, humorous, fantastic, and quaint. There is usually a comic and surprising plot development, combined with quaint and unusual characters.

Manner of playing

1. The style of playing must be light with a touch of artificiality.

2. The principal characters must be warm and sympathetic.

3. Movement and business should be highly selected and precise.

Sources for Scenes of Whimsical Comedy

Dover Road by A. A. Milne

Mr. Pim Passes By by A. A. Milne (See excerpt in Chapter 7.)

The Glass Slipper by Ferenc Molnár

There's Always Juliet by John Van Druten

High comedy

In this type of comedy the intellectual appeal is paramount. For the most successful presentation, high comedy requires an audience with a marked degree of sophistication.

The characters in high comedy often border on the artificial. Their emotions tend to be largely on the surface, with a pseudo quality. They are not expressions of real and deep feeling. A good example of a comic scene showing exaggerated pseudo emotions is one from Molnar's *The Play's the Thing* (Plate 33, p. 240). Another scene showing exaggerated or melodramatic feeling is the one in Shaw's *Misalliance* (Plate 34, p. 240).

Plate 33. *The Play's the Thing* by Ferenc Molnár. Scene from high comedy, depicting exaggerated pseudo emotions. Ohio State University. Director: Everett M. Schreck. Photograph: Department of Photography, Ohio State University.

Plate 34. *Misalliance* by George Bernard Shaw. The scene depicts melodramatic action in a comic context as the "killer" is disarmed. University of Michigan. Director: William R. McGraw. Photograph: F. W. Ouradnik, Ann Arbor, Michigan.

Manner of Playing

1. Playing with a light touch and extreme vocal variety contributes to this style.

2. The tempo, although varied, is effortlessly rapid.

3. A wide, melodic vocal pattern in the middle and upper pitch levels is highly effective.

4. The excessive use of volume as a device for word emphasis is to be avoided.

Practice Selection

MAN AND SUPERMAN

by G. B. Shaw | excerpt from Act IV*

(*The aggressive* ANN *pursues the reluctant* JACK TANNER.)

ANN   Violet is quite right. You ought to get married.

TANNER   (*Explosively*) Ann: I will not marry you. Do you hear? I won't, won't, won't, won't, WON'T marry you.

ANN   (*Placidly*) Well, nobody asked you, sir she said, sir she said, sir she said. So that's settled.

TANNER   Yes, nobody has asked me, but everybody treats the thing as settled. It's in the air. When we meet, the others go away on absurd pretexts to leave us alone together. Ramsden no longer scowls at me: his eye beams, as if he were already giving you away to me in church. Tavy refers me to your mother and gives me his blessing. Straker openly treats you as his future employer: it was he who first told me of it.

ANN   Was that why you ran away?

TANNER   Yes, only to be stopped by a lovesick brigand and run down like a truant schoolboy.

ANN   Well, if you don't want to be married, you needn't be.
(*She turns away from him and sits down, much at her ease.*)

TANNER   (*Following her*) Does any man want to be hanged? Yet men let themselves be hanged without a struggle for life, though they could at least give the chaplain a black eye. We do the world's will, not our own. I have a frightful feeling that I shall let myself be married because it is the world's will that you should have a husband.

ANN   I daresay I shall, someday.

TANNER   But why me — me of all men! Marriage is to me apostasy, profanation of the sanctuary of my soul, violation of my manhood, sale of my birthright, shameful surrender, ignominious capitulation, acceptance of defeat. I shall decay like a

---

* G. B. Shaw, *Man and Superman*. Copyright, 1903, by G. B. Shaw. Reprinted by permission of Miss N. Wilson for The Society of Authors.

thing that has served its purpose and is done with; I shall change from a man with a future to a man with a past; I shall see in the greasy eyes of all the other husbands their relief at the arrival of a new prisoner to share their ignominy. The young men will scorn me as one who has sold out; to the young women I, who have always been an enigma and a possibility, shall be merely somebody else's property — and damaged goods at that; a second-hand man at best.

ANN   Well, your wife can put on a cap and make herself ugly to keep you in countenance, like my grandmother.

TANNER   So that she may make her triumph more insolent by publicly throwing away the bait the moment the trap snaps on the victim!

ANN   After all, though, what difference would it make? Beauty is all very well at first sight; but who ever looks at it when it has been in the house three days? I thought our pictures very lovely when papa bought them; but I haven't looked at them for years. You never bother about my looks: you are too well used to me. I might be the umbrella stand.

TANNER   You lie, you vampire: you lie.

ANN   Flatterer. Why are you trying to fascinate me, Jack, if you don't want to marry me?

TANNER   The Life Force. I am in the grip of the Life Force.

ANN   I don't understand in the least; it sounds like the Life Guards.

TANNER   Why don't you marry Tavy? He is willing. Can you not be satisfied unless your prey struggles?

ANN   (*Turning to him as if to let him into a secret*) Tavy will never marry. Haven't you noticed that that sort of man never marries?

TANNER   What! a man who idolizes women! who sees nothing in nature but romantic scenery for love duets! Tavy, the chivalrous, the faithful, the tenderhearted and true! Tavy never marry! Why, he was born to be swept up by the first pair of blue eyes he meets in the street.

ANN   Yes, I know. All the same, Jack, men like that always live in comfortable bachelor lodgings with broken hearts, and are adored by their landladies, and never get married. Men like you always get married.

TANNER   (*Smiting his brow*) How frightfully, horribly true! It has been staring me in the face all my life; and I never saw it before.

ANN	Oh, it's the same with women. The poetic temperament's a very nice temperament, very amiable, very harmless and poetic, I daresay; but it's an old maid's temperament.
TANNER	Barren. The Life Force passes it by.
ANN	If that's what you mean by the Life Force, yes.
TANNER	You don't care for Tavy?
ANN	(*Looking round carefully to make sure that* TAVY *is not within earshot*) No.
TANNER	And you do care for me?
ANN	(*Rising quietly and shaking her finger at him*) Now, Jack! Behave yourself.
TANNER	Infamous, abandoned woman! Devil!
ANN	Boa-constrictor! Elephant!
TANNER	Hypocrite!
ANN	(*Softly*) I must be, for my future husband's sake.
TANNER	For mine! (*Correcting himself savagely*) I mean for his.
ANN	(*Ignoring the correction*) Yes, for yours. You had better marry what you call a hypocrite, Jack. Women who are not hypocrites go about in rational dress and are insulted and get into all sorts of hot water. And then their husbands get dragged in too, and live in continual dread of fresh complications. Wouldn't you prefer a wife you could depend on?
TANNER	No, a thousand times no: hot water is the revolutionist's element. You clean men as you clean milk pails, by scalding them.
ANN	Cold water has its uses too. It's healthy.
TANNER	(*Despairingly*) Oh, you are witty: at the supreme moment the Life Force endows you with every quality. Well, I too can be a hypocrite. Your father's will appointed me your guardian, not your suitor. I shall be faithful to my trust.
ANN	(*In low siren tones*) He asked me who I would have as my guardian, before he made that will. I chose you!
TANNER	The will is yours then! The trap was laid from the beginning.
ANN	(*Concentrating all her magic*) From the beginning—from our childhood—for both of us—by the Life Force.

TANNER   I will not marry you. I will not marry you.

ANN   Oh, you will, you will.

TANNER   I tell you, no, no, no.

ANN   I tell you, yes, yes, yes.

TANNER   No.

ANN   (*Coaxing—imploring — almost exhausted*) Yes. Before it is too late for repentance. Yes.

TANNER   (*Struck by the echo from the past*) When did all this happen to me before? Are we two dreaming?

ANN   (*Suddenly losing her courage, with an anguish that she does not conceal*) No. We are awake; and you have said no: that is all.

TANNER   (*Brutally*) Well?

ANN   Well, I made a mistake: you do not love me.

TANNER   (*Seizing her in his arms*) It is false: I love you. The Life Force enchants me: I have the whole world in my arms when I clasp you. But I am fighting for my freedom, for my honor, for my self, one and indivisible.

ANN   Your happiness will be worth them all.

TANNER   You would sell freedom and honor and self for happiness?

ANN   It will not be all happiness for me. Perhaps death.

TANNER   (*Groaning*) Oh, that clutch holds and hurts. What have you grasped in me? Is there a father's heart as well as a mother's?

ANN   Take care, Jack: if anyone comes while we are like this, you will have to marry me.

TANNER   If we two stood now on the edge of a precipice, I would hold you tight and jump.

ANN   (*Panting, falling more and more under the strain*) Jack: let me go. I have dared so frightfully — it is lasting longer than I thought. Let me go: I can't bear it.

TANNER   Nor I. Let it kill us.

ANN   Yes: I don't care. I am at the end of my forces. I don't care. I think I am going to faint.

Playing the Scene

1. Are the thoughts strictly what the characters would say or what Shaw wishes them to say for comic and dramatic effect?
2. What is Shaw's purpose in this play?
3. Does Ann lose empathy by her aggressiveness?
4. Why is Tanner reluctant to marry Ann?
5. What seems to be the proper mood for playing this scene?

Other Sources for Scenes of High Comedy

The Play's the Thing by Ferenc Molnár.

The Guardsman by Ferenc Molnár.

Satiric comedy

The primary purpose of satire is to correct the ills or abuses in our society by exposing them to ridicule. The derision may be pointed at a person or circumstance which is in need of correction. In view of this purpose, it follows that *idea* is the dominant element in the play. More than in other forms of comedy, satire utilizes the devices of exaggeration and derision and appeals directly to the intellect of the spectator. Even though the plot action is dealing with material which is normally serious (example: the death of the artist in *The Doctor's Dilemma*), it is not taken seriously by the audience.

Manner of Playing

1. Avoid arousing the sympathetic emotions of the audience.
2. When possible, use pantomimic business to de-emotionalize the scene.
3. Nonrealistic properties may be used in certain instances to point up the satiric idea and play down the emotion of the scene. (Example: toy pistols in place of real weapons.)
4. The satiric ideas must be clearly pointed.
5. A light, gay mood should be maintained.

Practice Selection

ARMS AND THE MAN

by G. B. Shaw | excerpt from Act III*

(RAINA, *daughter of a Bulgarian General, has hidden an enemy, a Serbian officer,* BLUNTSCHLI, *in her bedchamber to prevent his being killed.*)

RAINA	You look ever so much nicer than when we last met. (*He looks up, surprised.*) What have you done to yourself?
BLUNTSCHLI	Washed; brushed; good night's sleep and breakfast. That's all.
RAINA	Did you get back safely that morning?
BLUNTSCHLI	Quite, thanks.

---

* G. B. Shaw, *Arms and the Man.* Copyright, 1898, by G. B. Shaw. Reprinted by permission of The Public Trustee and The Society of Authors.

RAINA	Were they angry with you for running away from Sergius's charge?
BLUNTSCHLI	No, they were glad; because they'd all just run away themselves.
RAINA	(*Going to the table, and leaning over it towards him*) It must have made a lovely story for them — all that about me and my room.
BLUNTSCHLI	Capital story. But I only told it to one of them — a particular friend.
RAINA	On whose discretion you could absolutely rely?
BLUNTSCHLI	Absolutely.
RAINA	Hm! He told it all to my father and Sergius the day you exchanged the prisoners. (*She turns away and strolls carelessly across to the other side of the room.*)
BLUNTSCHLI	(*Deeply concerned and half incredulous*) No! You don't mean that, do you?
RAINA	(*Turning, with sudden earnestness*) I do indeed. But they don't know that it was in this house that you hid. If Sergius knew, he would challenge you and kill you in a duel.
BLUNTSCHLI	Bless me! Then don't tell him.
RAINA	(*Full of reproach for his levity*) Can you realize what it is to deceive him? I want to be quite perfect with Sergius — no meanness, no smallness, no deceit. My relation to him is the one really beautiful and noble part of my life. I hope you can understand that.
BLUNTSCHLI	(*Sceptically*) You mean that you wouldn't like him to find out that the story about the ice pudding was a — a — a — You know.
RAINA	(*Wincing*) Ah, don't talk of it in that flippant way. I lied! I know it. But I did it to save your life. He would have killed you. That was the second time I ever uttered a falsehood. (BLUNTSCHLI *rises quickly and looks doubtfully and somewhat severely at her.*) Do you remember the first time?
BLUNTSCHLI	I! No. Was I present?
RAINA	Yes; and I told the officer who was searching for you that you were not present.
BLUNTSCHLI	True. I should have remembered it.
RAINA	(*Greatly encouraged*) Ah, it is natural that you should forget it first. It cost you nothing: it cost me a lie! — a lie!! (*She sits down on the ottoman, looking straight before her with her hands clasped on her knee.* BLUNTSCHLI, *quite touched, goes to the ottoman with a particularly reassuring and considerate air, and sits down beside her.*)

BLUNTSCHLI	My dear young lady, don't let this worry you. Remember: I'm a soldier. Now what are the two things that happen to a soldier so often that he comes to think nothing of them? One is hearing people tell lies. (RAINA *recoils.*) The other is getting his life saved in all sorts of ways by all sorts of people.
RAINA	(*Rising in indignant protest*) And so he becomes a creature incapable of faith and of gratitude.
BLUNTSCHLI	(*Making a wry face*) Do you like gratitude? I don't. If pity is akin to love, gratitude is akin to the other thing.
RAINA	Gratitude. (*Turning on him*) If you are incapable of gratitude you are incapable of any noble sentiment. Even animals are grateful. Oh, I see now exactly what you think of me! You were not surprised to hear me lie. To you it was something I probably did every day — every hour. That is how men think of women. (*She walks up the room melodramatically.*)
BLUNTSCHLI	(*Dubiously*) There's reason in everything. You said you'd told only two lies in your whole life. Dear young lady: isn't that rather a short allowance? I'm quite a straightforward man myself; but it wouldn't last me a whole morning.
RAINA	(*Staring haughtily at him*) Do you know, sir, that you are insulting me?
BLUNTSCHLI	I can't help it. When you get into that noble attitude and speak in that thrilling voice, I admire you; but I find it impossible to believe a single word you say.
RAINA	(*Superbly*) Captain Bluntschli!
BLUNTSCHLI	(*Unmoved*) Yes?
RAINA	(*Coming a little towards him, as if she could not believe her senses*) Do you mean what you said just now? Do you know what you said just now?
BLUNTSCHLI	I do.
RAINA	(*Gasping*) I! I!!! (*She points to herself incredulously, meaning*) "I, Raina Petkoff, tell lies!" (*He meets her gaze unflinchingly. She suddenly sits down beside him, and adds, with a complete change of manner from the heroic to the familiar*) How did you find me out?
BLUNTSCHLI	(*Promptly*) Instinct, dear young lady. Instinct, and experience of the world.
RAINA	(*Wonderingly*) Do you know, you are the first man I ever met who did not take me seriously?
BLUNTSCHLI	You mean, don't you, that I am the first man that has ever taken you quite seriously?

RAINA   Yes, I suppose I do mean that. (*Cosily, quite at her ease with him*) How strange it is to be talked to in such a way! You know, I've always gone on like that — I mean the noble attitude and the thrilling voice. I did it when I was a tiny child to my nurse. She believed in it. I do it before my parents. They believe in it. I do it before Sergius. He believes in it.

BLUNTSCHLI   Yes: he's a little in that line himself, isn't he?

RAINA   (*Startled*) Do you think so?

BLUNTSCHLI   You know him better than I do.

RAINA   I wonder — I wonder is he? If I thought that — ! (*Discouraged*) Ah, well, what does it matter? I suppose, now that you've found me out, you despise me.

BLUNTSCHLI   (*Warmly, rising*) No, my dear young lady, no, no, no a thousand times. It's part of your youth — part of your charm. I'm like all the rest of them: the nurse — your parents — Sergius. I'm your infatuated admirer.

RAINA   (*Pleased*) Really?

BLUNTSCHLI   (*Slapping his breast smartly with his hand, German fashion*) Hand aufs Herz! Really and truly.

RAINA   (*Very happy*) But what did you think of me for giving you my portrait?

BLUNTSCHLI   (*Astonished*) Your portrait! You never gave me your portrait.

RAINA   (*Quickly*) Do you mean to say you never got it?

BLUNTSCHLI   No. (*He sits down beside her, with renewed interest, and says, with some complacency*) When did you send it to me?

RAINA   (*Indignantly*) I did not send it to you. (*She turns her head away, and adds, reluctantly*) It was in the pocket of that coat.

BLUNTSCHLI   (*Pursing his lips and rounding his eyes*) Oh-o-oh! I never found it. It must be there still.

RAINA   (*Springing up*) There still! — for my father to find the first time he puts his hand in his pocket! Oh, how could you be so stupid?

BLUNTSCHLI   (*Rising also*) It doesn't matter: it's only a photograph: how can he tell who it was intended for? Tell him he put it there himself.

RAINA   (*Impatiently*) Yes, that is so clever — so clever! What shall I do?

BLUNTSCHLI   Ah, I see. You wrote something on it. That was rash!

RAINA	(*Annoyed almost to tears*) Oh, to have done such a thing for you, who care no more — except to laugh at me — oh! Are you sure nobody has touched it?
BLUNTSCHLI	Well, I can't be quite sure. You see I couldn't carry it about with me all the time: one can't take much luggage on active service.
RAINA	What did you do with it?
BLUNTSCHLI	When I got through to Peerot I had to put it in safe keeping somehow. I thought of the railway cloak room; but that's the surest place to get looted in modern warfare. So I pawned it.
RAINA	Pawned it! ! ?
BLUNTSCHLI	I know it doesn't sound nice; but it was much the safest plan. I redeemed it the day before yesterday. Heaven only knows whether the pawnbroker cleared out the pockets or not.
RAINA	(*Furious — throwing the words right into his face*) You have a low, shopkeeping mind. You think of things that would never come into a gentleman's head.
BLUNTSCHLI	(*Phlegmatically*) That's the Swiss national character, dear lady.
RAINA	Oh, I wish I had never met you. (*She flounces away and sits at the window fuming.*)

Playing the Scene

1. What is Shaw's dominant purpose in *Arms and the Man*?
2. How may the interpretation of the characters contribute to the meaning of the play?
3. Are there lines of dialogue in the above scene which should not be taken literally?
4. Does Raina really mean it when she says, "Oh, I wish I had never met you"?
5. How much empathy from the audience should each character receive?
6. Do you find in the dialogue a need for a special pointing of Shaw's ideas?

Other Sources for Scenes of Satiric Comedy

The Doctor's Dilemma by G. B. Shaw
The Women by Clare Boothe

FARCE

In this variation of the comic genre, the dominant emphasis is on situation. The characters often are mere pawns in an exaggerated plot action extending beyond the probable and, at times, even the possible. It is characteristic of farce that the plot is based on a possible but highly improbable premise. For example, in *The Importance of Being Earnest* the farcical premise is that neither Gwendolen nor Cecily will marry a man unless his name is Ernest. In the modern farce, *Three Men on a Horse*, the premise is that Erwin, under certain circumstances, can pick the winning horse in a race. By various devices, the audience is induced to accept the farcical premise.

The characters in farce react from emotional rather than intellectual motivations. If logic or reason were allowed to control the character's actions, the exaggerated, ridiculous plot would of necessity come to a standstill. It is also characteristic of farce that the emotions of the characters per se are not conveyed to the audience. The audience does not empathize with the character's plight. For instance, the audience may laugh while the character weeps.

Manner of Playing

1. The opening scene of a farce should be played in a manner similar to that of a realistic comedy.
2. It is advisable to increase and broaden the farcical playing gradually as the plot develops.
3. The actor must prepare the audience by steps to accept the exaggerated situations.
4. A great amount of pantomimic business and superimposed action is highly essential.
5. The overall tempo should be rapid. Slow pace is a bane to farce.
6. The central character should win the favor of the audience.
7. Laughter is the dominant objective of farce.
8. A gay and, at times, hilarious mood should be maintained throughout the play. (See Plate 35, *Three Men on a Horse*.)

Plate 35. *Three Men on a Horse* by Cecil Holm and George Abbott. Scene reflecting exaggeration in characterization and action, typical of farce. Denison Summer Theater. Director: E. A. Wright.

Practice Selections

THREE MEN ON A HORSE

by John Cecil Holm and George Abbott | excerpt from Act II, Scene 2*

(*Three Gamblers,* CHARLEY, FRANKIE, *and* PATSY, *discover that* ERWIN *can pick the horses in a race. They maroon him in their hotel so that he can fix the races for them.* PATSY's *girl friend,* MABEL, *is left in charge of* ERWIN *while they go out to recover* ERWIN's *verses, which they had given to a Mr. Liebowitz.*)

MABEL   Gee, it's awful nice of you to stay here and help Patsy like you been doin'.

* John Cecil Holm and George Abbott, *Three Men on a Horse*. Copyright, 1934, 1935, by John Cecil Holm. Copyright Renewed, 1962, 1963, by John Cecil Holm. Reprinted by permission of Dramatists Play Service.

ERWIN	I was desperate or I wouldn't have done such a thing.
MABEL	But if you know how much we liked to have you here — I don't mean just the boys, I mean more particularly just myself personally.
ERWIN	Give me back my pants.
MABEL	What's the matter?
ERWIN	I ought to call up my wife.
MABEL	Not just now, Erwin — I don't want you to get out of bed. You might faint again.
ERWIN	I ought to call her. I've punished her enough. She'll be worried.
MABEL	But listen now, pet, just wait till Patsy gets back, will you? 'Cause I promised I wouldn't let you call anybody.
ERWIN	Yes, but I haven't been home all night.
MABEL	She must be used to that.
ERWIN	Oh, no, she isn't.
MABEL	You're a good deal different than most men then. God knows Patsy's liable to disappear for a week at a time. But he's awfully good to me though — You ought to see all the swell things he gave me when I quit the Follies for him! . . . Two weeks later they tried a four horse parlay at Saratoga and we lost everything — I didn't have a nightgown left, to my name.
ERWIN	Oh! That must have been terrible.
MABEL	Well, it's just the breaks. Now, it looks as though things is brightening up again since you come into my life.
ERWIN	Where's my pencil — quick — (*He writes.*)
MABEL	What is it? You got the first race? (ERWIN *shakes his head.*) Let's see. (*She takes the paper and reads.*)

"My soul was sad as darkest night.
But now the world seems fair and bright
Because you came so true and fine.
Oh, stay and be my Valentine."

ERWIN	Valentine's Day Number One. It doesn't do any hurt to get ahead of schedule.
MABEL	Yeah. If you're ahead then you're a fast worker, is that it?

ERWIN	What?
MABEL	Never mind. (*Reads*.) "Stay and be my Valentine." Gee, that's wonderful! . . . I'm crazy about poetry.
ERWIN	I don't get much time to write real poetry. I've been so busy with my Mother's Day verses.
MABEL	Oh . . . gee, I haven't heard from Mom in a long time — of course I haven't written to her lately — maybe I ought to send her one of them . . . a verse . . . it might make her feel good . . . you see, I ain't sure she's my mother. (*Business of taking drink*)
ERWIN	Oh, but she'd feel good anyway.
MABEL	I guess so. I haven't seen her since I came to New York to go on the stage.
ERWIN	Did you really used to be on the stage?
MABEL	Yeah, I used to be in the Follies. I'd like to get back in show business but Patsy doesn't think I look as good as I used to. (*Stands up and pats her hips*.) Don't you think I could get back if I worked hard?
ERWIN	Sure, I'll bet you could. Of course, I've never seen a Follies girl close to before — only from the balcony. You look all right to me.
MABEL	Do I really, Erwin?
ERWIN	Why yes — yes — you're beautiful.
MABEL	Gee, I like you . . . just think — maybe I have read one of your poems in a magazine — like a movie magazine — and here I am standing talking to you . . . I guess that's what you call romantic. Gee, I'm pretty jealous of your wife, you know it.
ERWIN	You are? Why?
MABEL	Havin' you all to herself — I'm just thinkin, how wonderful it would be to travel around the country with you — listenin' to your poetry and helpin' you make a lot of money bettin' on the horses.
ERWIN	Oh, but I wouldn't bet — that would spoil everything.
MABEL	Well, I mean — just enough for a fur coat and stuff like that.
ERWIN	But I don't think I could tell what ones are going to win if I ever started betting on them.
MABEL	Well anyhow, you could make a lot of money if you wanted to, just with words for songs like they have in shows . . . lyrics.

ERWIN	You think so?
MABEL	Sure. Say, lots of times I sang words in the chorus that wasn't half as good as that.
ERWIN	Did you sing in the Follies?
MABEL	Yeah — I did a specialty once. Want me to show you? (*He nods.*) Say, I'd do anything for you. (*Goes to radio.*) 'Cause I'm crazy about poetry, that's why. (*Turns radio on. Tries a few steps.*) I may not be so good till I get limbered up. (*Radio begins to talk.*) I'll see if I can get my dress off — I guess among friends it's all right huh? (*Starts to take off her dress.*)
ANNOUNCER	Two tablets daily and assure yourself a perfect health and a happy old age — The Press Radio News Report will be brought to you at five P.M. At this time we present Ivan Aronson and his jazzy Cossacks in a program of dance music — "Take it away Ivan!" (*Music*)
ERWIN	What is? (MABEL *crosses right.*) Maybe I ought to telephone my wife.
MABEL	Don't you want to see my dance?
ERWIN	Yes, I do.
MABEL	(*Gets music.*) Here we go. Now, you're the audience. I come out, you see, with a big spot on me. (*Dances.*) The other girls are jealous 'cause I got a specialty — (*She kicks, exposing all.*) Of course this is just a rough idea —
ERWIN	Say, that's good!
MABEL	This is my finish. (*Whirls across stage. Turns off radio. Leans against bureau.*)
ERWIN	What's the matter?
MABEL	(*Breathless*) Out of practice . . . haven't done this for so long . . . got dizzy.
ERWIN	(*Jumps out of bed and helps* MABEL *to bed where she sits.*) I'll give you a drink. (*Pours drink.*)

Playing the Scene

1. What are the dominant traits in each character?
2. Is Mabel making a play for Erwin?
3. How will a rapid tempo contribute to the effectiveness of the scene?

THE PROPOSAL

by Anton Chekhov | excerpt (a one-act play) *

CHARACTERS	STEPAN STEPANOVITCH CHUBUKOV, *a landowner*
	NATALYA STEPANOVNA, *his daughter, twenty-five years old*
	IVAN VASSILEVITCH LOMOV, *a neighbour of Chubukov, thirty-five years old*
SCENE	*A drawing-room in* CHUBUKOV'S *house*
SITUATION	LOMOV *has called to make a proposal of narriage to* NATALYA. *But before he can get to the important question, they get into an argument over the ownership of a piece of land, Oxen Meadows.*

(*Enter* CHUBUKOV.)

CHUBUKOV   What's the matter? What are you shouting at?

NATALYA STEPANOVNA   Papa, please tell this gentleman who owns Oxen Meadows, we or he?

CHUBUKOV   (*To* LOMOV) Darling, the Meadows are ours!

LOMOV   But, please, Stepan Stepanitch, how can they be yours? Do be a reasonable man! My aunt's grandmother gave the Meadows for the temporary and free use of your grandfather's peasants. The peasants used the land for forty years and got as accustomed to it as if it was their own, when it happened that . . .

CHUBUKOV   Excuse me, my precious. . . . You forget just this, that the peasants didn't pay your grandmother and all that, because the Meadows were in dispute, and so on. And now everybody knows that they're ours. It means that you haven't seen the plan.

LOMOV   I'll prove to you that they're mine!

CHUBUKOV   You won't prove it, my darling.

LOMOV   I shall!

CHUBUKOV   Dear one, why yell like that? You won't prove anything by just yelling. I don't want anything of yours, and don't intend to give up what I have. Why should I? And you know, my beloved, that if you propose to go on arguing about it, I'd sooner give up the meadows to the peasants than to you. There!

---

* Anton Chekhov, *The Proposal*. Copyright, 1935, by Illustrated Editions. Reprinted by permission of World Publishing Company.

LOMOV	I don't understand! How have you the right to give away somebody else's property?
CHUBUKOV	You may take it that I know whether I have the right or not. Because, young man, I'm not used to being spoken to in that tone of voice, and so on: I, young man, am twice your age, and ask you to speak to me without agitating yourself, and all that.
LOMOV	No, you just think I'm a fool and want to have me on! You call my land yours, and then you want me to talk to you calmly and politely! Good neighbours don't behave like that, Stepan Stepanitch! You're not a neighbour, you're a grabber!
CHUBUKOV	What's that? What did you say?
NATALYA STEPANOVNA	Papa, send the mowers out to the Meadows at once!
CHUBUKOV	What did you say, Sir?
NATALYA STEPANOVNA	Oxen Meadows are ours, and I shan't give them up, shan't give them up, shan't give them up!
LOMOV	We'll see! I'll have the matter taken to court, and then I'll show you!
CHUBUKOV	To court? You can take it to court, and all that! You can! I know you; you're just on the lookout for a chance to go to court, and all that. . . . You pettifogger! All your people were like that! All of them!
LOMOV	Never mind about my people! The Lomovs have all been honorable people, and not one has ever been tried for embezzlement, like your grandfather!
CHUBUKOV	You Lomovs have had lunacy in your family, all of you!
NATALYA STEPANOVNA	All, all, all!
CHUBUKOV	Your grandfather was a drunkard, and your younger aunt, Nastasya Mihailovna, ran away with an architect, and so on . . .
LOMOV	And your mother was humpbacked. (*Clutches at his heart.*) Something pulling in my side. . . . My head . . . Help! Water!
CHUBUKOV	Your father was a guzzling gambler!
NATALYA STEPANOVNA	And there haven't been many backbiters to equal your aunt!
LOMOV	My left foot has gone to sleep. . . . You're an intriguer. . . . Oh, my heart! . . . And it's an open secret that before the last elections you bri . . . I can see stars. . . . Where's my hat?

NATALYA STEPANOVNA	It's low! It's dishonest! It's mean!
CHUBUKOV	And you're just a malicious, double-faced intriguer! Yes!
LOMOV	Here's my hat.... My heart!... Which way? Where's the door? Oh! ... I think I'm dying.... My foot's quite numb.... (*Goes to the door.*)
CHUBUKOV	(*Following him*) And don't set foot in my house again!
NATALYA STEPANOVNA	Take it to court! We'll see! (LOMOV *staggers out.*)
CHUBUKOV	Devil take him! (*To table for a drink. Walks about in excitement.*)
NATALYA STEPANOVNA	What a rascal! What trust can one have in one's neighbours after that!
CHUBUKOV	The villain! The scarecrow! (*Down* L.)
NATALYA STEPANOVNA	The monster! First he takes our land and then he has the impudence to abuse us.
CHUBUKOV	And that blind hen, yes, that turnip-ghost has the confounded cheek to make a proposal, and so on! (*Down* R. C. *Stuttering. Front to door* R.)
NATALYA STEPANAVNA	What proposal?
CHUBUKOV	Why, he came here so as to propose to you. (L.)
NATALYA STEPANOVNA	To propose? To me? Why didn't you tell me so before?
CHUBUKOV	So he dresses up in evening clothes. (R. C.) The stuffed sausage! The wizen-faced frump! (L.)
NATALYA STEPANOVNA	To propose to me? Ah! (*Falls into an easy-chair and wails.*) Bring him back! Back! Ah! Bring him here.
CHUBUKOV	Bring whom here?
NATALYA STEPANOVNA	Quick, quick! I'm ill! Fetch him! (*Hysterics*)
CHUBUKOV	What's that? (*To her*) What's the matter with you? (*Clutches at his head.*) Oh, unhappy man that I am! I'll shoot myself! I'll hang myself!
NATALYA STEPANOVNA	I'm dying! Fetch him!
CHUBUKOV	Tfoo! At once. Don't yell! (*Runs out. A pause.* NATALYA STEPANOVNA *wails.*)

NATALYA STEPANOVNA	What have they done to me! Fetch him back! Fetch him! (*A pause*) (CHUBUKOV *runs in. Comes down* L. C.)
CHUBUKOV	He's coming, and so on, devil take him! Ouf! Talk to him yourself; I don't want to. (*To* R.)
NATALYA STEPANOVNA	(*Wails.*) Fetch him!
CHUBUKOV	(*Yells.*) He's coming, I tell you. Oh, what a burden, Lord, to be the father of a grown-up daughter! I'll cut my throat! I will, indeed! (*To her*) We cursed him, abused him, drove him out, and it's all you . . . you!
NATALYA STEPANOVNA	No, it was you!
CHUBUKOV	I tell you it's not my fault. (LOMOV *appears at the door.*) Now you talk to him yourself. (*Exit*)

Playing the Scene

1. What motivates the actions of these characters?

2. How will a rapid pace contribute to the believability of what the characters do and say?

3. What effect will superimposed action and business have on the scene?

Other Sources for Scenes of Farce

Box and Cox by J. M. Morton

Charley's Aunt by Brandon Thomas

Farce-comedy

As the title indicates, this form is a mixture of comedy and farce. Although the primary purpose is to arouse laughter, there is nonetheless a serious, social philosophy in plays of this type.

Manner of Playing

1. Playing, generally, is not as broad as in a typical farce.

2. The characters, although exaggerated, are more believable than in true farce.

3. The underlying idea of the play should be clearly stressed.

Sources for Scenes of Farce-Comedy

Barefoot in the Park by Neil Simon

The Seven Year Itch by George Axelrod

You Can't Take It With You by Moss Hart and George Kaufman

Satiric farce

Satiric farce puts more emphasis on the idea and less on the plot action. The situations are extremely exaggerated, as in true farce. The characters show little intellectual awareness of the illogical and preposterous plot action.

Manner of Playing

1. The satiric ideas should be pointed up.
2. The actor should direct his playing to the intellectual, unemotional element of the audience.

Sources for Scenes of Satiric Farce

Boy Meets Girl by Bella and Samuel Spewack
Once in a Lifetime by Moss Hart and George S. Kaufman
Squaring the Circle by Valentine Kaytayev
The Torch-bearers by George Kelly

Satiric farce variation

A variation of the typical satiric farce is found in Oscar Wilde's *The Importance of Being Earnest*. This play might well be called a verbal farce since more emphasis is given to what the characters say than to what they do. The dominant element is the dialogue.

Manner of Playing

1. The style of playing is more in the manner of high comedy than that of a typical farce.
2. Exaggerated melody pattern and line pointing are very important.
3. Satiric ideas should be pointed.
4. There is less emphasis on business than in true farce.
5. A gay, light mood should be maintained.

Practice Selection

THE IMPORTANCE OF BEING EARNEST

by Oscar Wilde / last scene of Act II

(*In the following scene,* JACK *is highly perturbed because* ALGERNON *has come down to the country, thus exposing* JACK *before* CECILY *and* GWENDOLEN.)

JACK   This ghastly state of things is what you call Bunburying, I suppose?

ALGERNON   Yes, and a perfectly wonderful Bunbury it is. The most wonderful Bunbury I have ever had in my life.

JACK   Well, you've no right whatsoever to Bunbury here.

ALGERNON   That is absurd. One has a right to Bunbury anywhere one chooses. Every serious Bunburyist knows that.

JACK   Serious Bunburyist! Good heavens!

ALGERNON	Well, one must be serious about something, if one wants to have any amusement in life. I happen to be serious about Bunburying. What on earth you are serious about I haven't got the remotest idea. About everything, I should fancy. You have such an absolutely trivial nature.
JACK	Well, the only small satisfaction I have in the whole of this wretched business is that your friend Bunbury is quite exploded. You won't be able to run down to the country quite so often as you used to do, dear Algy. And a very good thing, too.
ALGERNON	Your brother is a little off color, isn't he, dear Jack? You won't be able to disappear to London quite so frequently as your wicked custom was. And not a bad thing, either.
JACK	As for your conduct towards Miss Cardew, I must say that your taking in a sweet, simple, innocent girl like that is quite inexcusable. To say nothing of the fact that she is my ward.
ALGERNON	I can see no possible defense at all for your deceiving a brilliant, clever, thoroughly experienced young lady like Miss Fairfax, to say nothing of the fact that she is my cousin.
JACK	I wanted to be engaged to Gwendolen, that is all. I love her.
ALGERNON	Well, I simply wanted to be engaged to Cecily. I adore her.
JACK	There is certainly no chance of your marrying Miss Cardew.
ALGERNON	I don't think there is much likelihood, Jack, of you and Miss Fairfax being united.
JACK	Well, that is no business of yours.
ALGERNON	If it was my business, I wouldn't talk about it. (*Begins to eat muffins.*) It is very vulgar to talk about one's business. Only people like stockbrokers do that, and then merely at dinner parties.
JACK	How you can sit there, calmly eating muffins, when we are in this horrible trouble, I can't make out. You seem to me to be perfectly heartless.
ALGERNON	Well, I can't eat muffins in an agitated manner. The butter would probably get on my cuffs. One should always eat muffins quite calmly. It is the only way to eat them.
JACK	I say it's perfectly heartless your eating muffins at all, under the circumstances.
ALGERNON	When I am in trouble, eating is the only thing that consoles me. Indeed, when I am in really great trouble, as anyone who knows me intimately will tell you, I refuse everything except food and drink. At the present moment I am eating muffins because I am unhappy. Besides, I am particularly fond of muffins. (*Rising*)

JACK	(*Rising*) Well, that is no reason why you should eat them in that greedy way. (*Takes muffins from* ALGERNON.)
ALGERNON	(*Offering tea-cake*) I wish you would have tea-cake instead. I don't like tea-cake.
JACK	I suppose a man may eat his own muffins in his own garden.
ALGERNON	But you have just said it was perfectly heartless to eat muffins.
JACK	I said it was perfectly heartless of you, under the circumstances. That is a very different thing.
ALGERNON	That may be. But the muffins are the same. (*He seizes the muffin dish from* JACK.)
JACK	Algy, I wish to goodness you would go.
ALGERNON	You can't possibly ask me to go without having some dinner. It's absurd. I never go without my dinner. No one ever does, except vegetarians and people like that. Besides, I have just made arrangements with Dr. Chasuble to be christened at a quarter to six under the name of Ernest.
JACK	My dear fellow, the sooner you give up that nonsense the better. I made arrangements this morning with Dr. Chasuble to be christened myself at five-thirty, and I naturally will take the name of Ernest. Gwendolen would wish it. We can't both be christened Ernest. It's absurd. Besides, I have a perfect right to be christened if I like. There is no evidence at all that I ever have been christened by anybody. I should think it extremely probable I never was, and so does Dr. Chasuble. It is entirely different in your case. You have been christened already.
ALGERNON	Yes, but I have not been christened for years.
JACK	Yes, but you have been christened. That is the important thing.
ALGERNON	Quite so. So I know my constitution can stand it. If you are not quite sure about your ever having been christened, I must say I think it rather dangerous your venturing on it now. It might make you very unwell. You can hardly have forgotten that someone very closely connected with you was very nearly carried off this week in Paris by a severe chill.
JACK	Yes, but you said yourself that a severe chill was not hereditary.
ALGERNON	It usen't to be, I know — but I daresay it is now. Science is always making wonderful improvements in things.
JACK	(*Picking up the muffin-dish*) Oh, that is nonsense; you are always talking nonsense.

ALGERNON	Jack, you are at the muffins again! I wish you wouldn't. There are only two left. (*Takes them.*) I told you I was particularly fond of muffins.
JACK	But I hate tea-cake.
ALGERNON	Why on earth then do you allow tea-cake to be served up for your guests? What ideas you have of hospitality!
JACK	Algernon! I have already told you to go. I don't want you here. Why don't you go?
ALGERNON	I haven't quite finished my tea yet and there is still one muffin left. (JACK *groans, and sinks into a chair.* ALGERNON *still continues eating.*)

Playing the Scene

1. How real are the emotions of the characters?

2. What devices may add to the comedy of the scene?

3. Should one character receive more empathy than the other or should the empathic response to each character be more or less equal?

Farce-melodrama

This type of play contains elements of both farce and melodrama as they have been previously described. There is the exaggeration and rapid pace of farce, combined with the heightened, emotional suspense of melodrama.

Manner of Playing

Follow the principles for playing farce and melodrama, as stated previously. (See *Arsenic and Old Lace*, Plate 36.)

Sources for Scenes of Farce-Melodrama

Arsenic and Old Lace by Joseph Kesselring
Seven Keys to Baldpate by George M. Cohan

Plate 36. *Arsenic and Old Lace* by Joseph Kesselring. Scene "and just a pinch of cyanide" catches the essence of farce and melodrama. Ohio State University. Director: Everett M. Schreck. Photograph: Leo Wilhelm.

FANTASY

A fantasy is based on an impossible plot action which, by various devices, the audience is induced to believe. The characters may be real in theatrical terms, but in terms of the real world, they perform impossible feats. In certain instances the characters may be wholly imaginary and otherworldly. The locale of the plot action may range from the world of reality to the "never, never land." There is an admixture of moods ranging from the delicately comic to deep pathos.

Manner of Playing

1. The principal characters should be sympathetic and appealing.

2. The actors must enter into the spirit of the play and believe, for the duration of the play at least, the premise on which the play is based.

3. The actor should be alert and sensitive to mood variations.

4. Heavy, ponderous playing should be avoided. A light, delicate touch is most appropriate for plays of this type.

5. In line delivery it is advisable to avoid an earthy, prose quality.

6. The ethereal, poetic quality of delivery is often found to be most effective.

7. For certain scenes of fantasy, background music, such as Debussy's *Prelude to the Afternoon of a Faun*, may be helpful in acquiring the appropriate mood.

Practice Selection

HIGH TOR

by Maxwell Anderson | excerpt from Act I, Scene 3*

VAN VAN DORN, *owner of High Tor, lives a carefree life on the mountain. He refuses to sell his land to a trap-rock company. High Tor is "inhabited" by the spirits of the crew and* LISE, *the Captain's wife, of the Dutch ship, Onrust, lost in the Tappan Zee some three hundred years ago.*

SCENE | *A section of the broad flat trap-rock summit of High Tor. It is night. An airplane beacon lights the scene from the right.*

(VAN *is sitting on a rock.* LISE *comes up the rocks in the rear and stands looking out to the river, shading her eyes from the beacon.*)

LISE | You who have watched this river in the past
till your hope turned bitterness, pity me now,
my hope gone, but no power to keep my eyes
from the mocking water. The hills come down like sand,
and the long barges bear them off to town,
to what strange market in what stranger town,
devouring mountains? but never, in all days,
never, though I should watch here without rest,
will any ship come downward with the tide
flying the flag we knew.

(VAN *rises.* LISE *draws back an instant, then comes down a step toward him.*)
Do you hear my voice?

VAN | Yes, lady.

LISE | Do you see me in the light,
as I see you?

VAN | Yes.

LISE | You are one of those
the earth bears now, the quick, fierce wizard men
who plow the mountains down with steel, and set
new mountains in their sky. You've come to drive
machines through the white rock's heart.

VAN   Not I. I haven't.
I hate them all like poison.

LISE   You're against them—
the great machines?

VAN   I'd like to smash the lot,
and the men that own them.

LISE   Oh, if there were a friend
among so many enemies! I wish
I knew how to make you friend. But now my voice
shrinks back in me, reluctant, a cold thing,
fearing the void between us. — I have seen you.
I know you. You are kind.

VAN   How do you know?

LISE   When I have been most lonely in the spring,
the spring rain beating with my heart, I made
a wild flower garden; none of these I knew,
for none I knew are here, flowers of the woods,
little and lovely, nameless. One there was
like a pink moccasin, another low
with blotted leaves, wolf-toothed, and many more
rooted among the fern. I saw you then
come on this garden, secret as the tears
wept for lost days, and drew my breath in dread
that you should laugh and trample it. You smiled
and then went on. But when I came again
there was a new flower growing with the rest,
one I'd not seen. You brought and placed it there
only for love of gardens, ignorant whose
the garden you enriched. What was this flower?

VAN   Wild orchid. It was your garden?

LISE   Yes. You know
the names of all the flowers?

VAN   Yes.

LISE   But then
you'd teach them to me?

VAN   Yes.

LISE
Teach me the names.
What is the tall three-petaled one that's black
almost, the red's so dark?

VAN
That's trillium.
Speaking of flowers, tell me your name.

LISE
It's Lise,
or used to be.

VAN
Not now?

LISE
I'm weary of it,
and all the things that I've been. You have a lover?
She'll be angry?

VAN
She's angry now. She's off
and gone. She won't come back.

LISE
Love me a little,
enough to save me from the dark. But if
you cannot give me love, find me a way!
The seas lie black between your harbor town
and mine, but your ships are quick. If I might see
the corner where the three streets come to an end
on sundial windows, there, a child by a fire —
no, but it's gone!

VAN
I've seen you on the hills
moving with shadows. But you're not shadow.

LISE
No.
Could one live and be shadow?

VAN
Take my hand.

LISE
I dare not.

VAN
Come, let me see your garden.

LISE
No.
I dare not. It is your race that thins our blood
and gathers round, besieging us with charms
to stay the feet of years. But I know you kind. —
Love me a little. Never put out your hand
to touch me, lest some magic in your blood
reach me, and I be nothing. What I am

I know not, under these spells, if I be cloud
or dust. Nor whether you dream of me, or I
make you of light and sound. Between this stone
and the near constellations of the stars
I go and come, doubting now whence I come
or when I go. Cling to me. Keep me still.
Be gentle. You were gentle with the orchid —
Take my hand now.

VAN   You're cold.

LISE   Yes.

VAN   Here on the Tor
the sun beats down like murder all day long
and the wind comes up like murder in the night.
I'm cold myself.

LISE   How have I slipped so far
from the things you have? I'm puzzled here and lost.

Playing the Scene

1. What is the mood of the scene?

2. What distinctions should be made in the manner of playing between the character of Van, who is of the real world, and that of Lise, who is of the spirit world?

3. What manner of vocal delivery would be most effective for this scene?

4. How much physical action, bodily contact, and intimacy seem appropriate for the scene?

Other Sources for Scenes of Fantasy

Hotel Universe by Philip Barry
On Borrowed Time by Paul Osborn
Outward Bound by Sutton Vane

Plate 37. *Mad Woman of Chaillot* by Jean Giraudoux (adapted by Maurice Valency). Scene depicting exaggeration, mixture of real and unreal, and satire and fantasy. Ohio State University. Director: Everett M. Schreck. Photograph: Leo Wilhelm.

Satiric fantasy

This type is similar to the fantasy already described except that there is more emphasis on the ideas which are satirized.

Manner of Playing

1. As in the case of true satire, the emotions of the audience should not be aroused. For example, the scene in *The Madwoman of Chaillot* in which the capitalists are sent to their death is played for its intellectual rather than emotional values.

2. The satiric ideas must be pointed.

3. A proper mixture of the real and the unreal or fanciful is essential.

(See the scene from *The Madwoman of Chaillot*, Plate 37.)

Sources for Scenes of Satiric Fantasy

The Madwoman of Chaillot by Jean Giraudoux
The Insect Comedy by Karl Čapek
Visit to a Small Planet by Gore Vidal

Farce-fantasy

As the term implies, this type of drama combines the elements of farce and fantasy: the improbable and the impossible. The plot embraces the illogical and exaggerated action of farce along with the otherworldly qualities of fantasy.

Manner of Playing

1. Before playing this comedy variation, it would be well to reexamine the principles of each of these individual types.

2. In general, the playing should be light, gay, rapid, and sportive.

Practice Selection

BLITHE SPIRIT

by Noel Coward | closing scene of Act I*

SCENE

The scene is the living-room of the Condomines' house in Kent. On the L. there are French windows opening on to the garden. Down L. there is a chair and a radiogram. Up L. a piano and a small table. At the back there are double doors leading to the hall. At R. an open fireplace. Above fireplace is a sofa. To its left a small table and an armchair.

(In order to obtain more authentic material for his novel, CHARLES *has invited* MADAME ARCATI, *a medium, to come and arrange a séance. Much to the surprise of* CHARLES, *who alone can see and hear her,* ELVIRA, *his first wife appears. Just prior to the following scene,* RUTH, CHARLES' *second wife, much upset and in high dudgeon, has left the room.)*

ELVIRA   That was one of the most enjoyable half-hours I have ever spent.

CHARLES   *(Puts down his glass on the drinks table.)* Oh, Elvira — how could you!

ELVIRA   Poor Ruth!

CHARLES   *(Staring at her)* This is obviously an hallucination, isn't it?

ELVIRA   I'm afraid I don't know the technical term for it.

CHARLES   *(Comes down* C.*)* What am I to do?

ELVIRA   What Ruth suggested — relax.

CHARLES   *(Moves below the chair to the sofa.)* Where have you come from?

ELVIRA   Do you know, it's very peculiar, but I've sort of forgotten.

CHARLES   Are you to be here indefinitely?

ELVIRA   I don't know that either.

CHARLES   Oh, my God!

ELVIRA   Why? Would you hate it so much if I was?

CHARLES   Well, you must admit it would be embarrassing?

---

* Noel Coward, *Blithe Spirit.* Copyright, 1941, by Noel Coward. Reprinted by permission of Doubleday and William Heinemann.

ELVIRA	I don't see why really. It's all a question of adjusting yourself. Anyhow, I think it's horrid of you to be so unwelcoming and disagreeable.
CHARLES	Now look here, Elvira —
ELVIRA	(*Near tears*) I do. I think you're mean.
CHARLES	Try to see my point, dear. I've been married to Ruth for five years, and you've been dead for seven . . .
ELVIRA	Not dead, Charles. "Passed over." It's considered vulgar to say "dead" where I come from.
CHARLES	Passed over, then.
ELVIRA	At any rate, now that I'm here, the least you can do is to make a pretence of being amiable about it.
CHARLES	Of course, my dear, I'm delighted in one way.
ELVIRA	I don't believe you love me any more.
CHARLES	I shall always love the memory of you.
ELVIRA	(*Crosses slowly above the sofa by the armchair to down stage* L.) You mustn't think me unreasonable, but I really am a little hurt. You called me back; at a great inconvenience I came — and you've been thoroughly churlish ever since I arrived.
CHARLES	(*Gently*) Believe me, Elvira, I most emphatically did not send for you. There's been some mistake.
ELVIRA	(*Irritably*) Well, somebody did — and that child said it was you. I remember I was playing backgammon with a very sweet old Oriental gentleman, I think his name was Genghiz Kahn, and I'd just thrown double sixes, and then the child paged me and the next thing I knew I was in this room. Perhaps it was your subconscious.
CHARLES	You must find out whether you are going to stay or not, and we can make arrangements accordingly.
ELVIRA	I don't see how I can.
CHARLES	Well, try to think. Isn't there anyone that you know, that you can get in touch with over there — on the other side, or whatever it's called — who could advise you?
ELVIRA	I can't think — it seems so far away — as though I'd dreamed it . . .
CHARLES	You must know somebody else besides Gengiz Khan.

ELVIRA	(*To the armchair*) Oh, Charles . . .
CHARLES	What is it?
ELVIRA	I want to cry, but I don't think I'm able to.
CHARLES	What do you want to cry for?
ELVIRA	It's seeing you again — and you being so irascible, like you always used to be.
CHARLES	I don't mean to be irascible, Elvira.
ELVIRA	Darling — I don't mind really — I never did.
CHARLES	Is it cold — being a ghost?
ELVIRA	No — I don't think so.
CHARLES	What happens if I touch you.
ELVIRA	I doubt if you can. Do you want to?
CHARLES	(*Sits at the* L. *end of the sofa.*) Oh, Elvira . . . . (*He buries his face in his hands.*)
ELVIRA	(*To the* L. *arm of the sofa*) What is it, darling?
CHARLES	I really do feel strange, seeing you again.
ELVIRA	(*Moves to* R. *below the sofa and round above it again to the* L. *arm.*) That's better.
CHARLES	(*Looking up*) What's better?
ELVIRA	Your voice was kinder.
CHARLES	Was I ever unkind to you when you were alive?
ELVIRA	Often.
CHARLES	Oh, how can you! I'm sure that's an exaggeration.
ELVIRA	Not at all. You were an absolute pig that time we went to Cornwall and stayed in that awful hotel. You hit me with a billiard cue.
CHARLES	Only very, very gently.
ELVIRA	I loved you very much.
CHARLES	I loved you too. . . . (*He puts out his hand to her and then draws it away.*) No, I can't touch you. Isn't that horrible?
ELVIRA	Perhaps it's as well if I'm going to stay for any length of time. (*She sits on the* L. *arm of the sofa.*)

CHARLES I suppose I shall wake up eventually . . . but I feel strangely peaceful now.

ELVIRA That's right. Put your head back.

CHARLES (*Doing so*) Like that?

ELVIRA (*Stroking his hair*) Can you feel anything?

CHARLES Only a very little breeze through my hair . . .

ELVIRA Well, that's better than nothing.

CHARLES (*Drowsily*) I suppose if I'm really out of my mind they'll put me in an asylum.

ELVIRA Don't worry about that — just relax.

CHARLES (*Very drowsily indeed*) Poor Ruth.

ELVIRA (*Gently and sweetly*) To hell with Ruth.
The Curtain Falls.

Playing the Scene

1. What degree of reality should be employed in the playing of this scene?

2. How may the fantastic situation be made believable and acceptable to an audience?

3. What devices may be used to distinguish Elvira, as a spirit character, from the real Charles?

4. Should Charles and Elvira actually touch each other in the scene?

5. How may the enjoyment of an audience be heightened by the manner in which the scene is played?

SYMBOLISM

To a degree, all art is symbolistic in that various symbols, real or imaginary, are used to convey a concept or a mood. In symbolistic dramas a greater emphasis is placed on the importance of symbols, to convey the meaning or mood, than is the case in other styles of drama. In *The Intruder* by M. Maeterlinck, the approach of death is conveyed by such symbols as the flickering lamp, the sound of a scythe being sharpened, and a disturbance among the swans in the pond. In symbolistic dramas mood is a dominant quality. The dialogue has meaning and significance beyond its literal statement.

Manner of Playing

1. The style of acting may vary from the naturalistic through the romantic to the expressionistic.

2. Acting should be low keyed and sincere.

3. Language symbols should be stressed.

Sources for Scenes of Symbolistic Dramas

Pelléas and Mélisande by M. Maeterlinck

The Failures by Henri-René Lenormand

Section Two/Representational—Presentational style of acting

As we approach the modern period of theater, it is more and more evident that many dramas do not represent one pure and distinct style. Many modern playwrights, consciously or unconsciously, have practiced eclecticism; that is, they have borrowed from one or more styles of the past as it happened to suit their purpose. Arthur Miller's *Death of a Salesman* is a mixture of realism and expressionism, as are also Eugene O'Neill's *The Emperor Jones* and *The Hairy Ape*. Ferenc Molnár's *Liliom* and Elmer Rice's *The Adding Machine* both combine realism and fantasy. Indeed, a list of mixed styles in modern dramas could be extended almost indefinitely.

Certain mixed styles of dramatic writing require an almost even distribution of the representational and presentational style of production, as exemplified in Thornton Wilder's *Our Town* which was mentioned earlier. In a production of this play the overall treatment is presentational but the individual scenes are played in the representational manner.

In such plays, the actor must decide whether his particular character falls into the representational or presentational category. He should be aware of how the mixture of styles may affect his relationship with the audience and influence the degree of actor-character versus actor-performer manner of his performance.

Manner of Playing

1. The style of playing will vary in accordance with the emphasis which the playwright has given to a particular style in the play.
2. The acting is more theatrical than is the case in most realistic productions.
3. Some characters may contact the audience directly while others play with no obvious awareness that an audience is present.

Sources for Scenes of Representational-Presentational Dramas

The Glass Menagerie by Tennessee Williams

The Lark by Jean Anouilh. Adapted by Lillian Hellman.

A Man for All Seasons by Robert Bolt

Our Town by Thornton Wilder

Section Three | Presentational style of acting

To the actor of today, whose experiences in theater have for the most part been limited to the representational, realistic style, presentational acting offers a stimulating challenge. Spanning some two thousand years of theatrical history, the presentational style, within its basic pattern, offers great variety. The actor must discover those devices which are appropriate to the particular play, its period, and its production.

CLASSICISM

GREEK TRAGEDY

The dominant characteristics of Greek tragedy are unity, simplicity, clarity, control, and orderliness. The plots are single and compact. The writing is poetic, rhythmic, and embellished. One dominant, controlled mood is sustained throughout. The characters, representing nobility of birth, mind, and spirit, are idealized and are "larger than life."

General acting principles. We know relatively little about the actual performance of a Greek tragedy in the fifth century B.C. However, there are sources from which we may build a concept of the acting style. We know that in general the theaters were large, often with a seating capacity comparable to our present day stadiums. This would of necessity require strong vocal projection, increased volume, heightened word emphasis, and precise diction. In short, the manner of delivery would approximate the declamatory or oratorical style.

If, as certain scholars believe, actors after the fifth century B.C. wore the cothurnus, or heightened boot, to give them greater stature, their movement would be inhibited or minimized. A statuesque quality would be imposed on their acting, and their long, flowing robes would further restrict movement and detailed business.

Since our modern theaters differ widely from those of the fifth century B.C., the production of a Greek tragedy today would probably not attempt to copy the ancient performance but rather strive to capture its original spirit.

Manner of Playing

1. With some variation, the overall serious mood should be maintained.
2. Vocal variety, precise diction, and inflection are essential.
3. Movement should be slow, majestic, and rhythmic.
4. Gestures are simple, large, flowing, and in the plane of the upper part of the body.
5. Sitting positions, particularly for the principal characters, are rarely used.
6. Physical contact with other characters is generally minimized.
7. The full-front, one-quarter, and profile body positions are used predominantly. (See *Oedipus Rex*, Plate 38.)

Plate 38. *Oedipus Rex* by Sophocles. Scene depicting the dignity and playing style of ancient Greek tragedy. University of Hawaii. Director: Edward Langhans. Photograph: Glenn Sears.

Practice Selection

ANTIGONE

*by Sophocles**

CHARACTERS	CREON, *King of Thebes* ANTIGONE, CREON's *niece*
SITUATION	CREON *has decreed that* ANTIGONE's *brother,* POLYNEICES, *who died in battle while leading an alien host against his native city, shall not be given burial rites. In defiance of this decree, with its penalty of death,* ANTIGONE *performs the burial rites for her brother.*
CREON	You there! You looking at the ground. Do you admit you did this, or do you deny it?
ANTIGONE	I did it; there is no need to deny it.
CREON	(*To guard*) Then you may go. Do whatever you please. You are free from blame in this treason. (*Guard exits.*) But you — tell me, and waste no words. Did you know this act was forbidden?
ANTIGONE	I knew. Why wouldn't I? Everyone knew.
CREON	And yet you had the audacity to scorn this law?
ANTIGONE	It was not God who set this law for me; nor was it Justice, who lives with the spirits that judge us. The gods frame no such laws for men. I did not think your order strong enough to overrule the gods' unwritten, steadfast laws. You're only a man. Their laws are not just for now or yesterday. They live forever, and no one knows when they were placed in us. These laws I will never break. No man of arrogance can terrorize me. Men may try me; God never will. I know I must die, that is certain — even though you never gave that order. But if my time for death comes soon, I will call it a blessing. For would not anyone be blessed with death who goes on living among as many evils as I do? So for me, at least, there is no suffering when I meet my fate. But if my poor dead brother's body had gone unburied through my fault, then the pains would torture me. For doing this, though, I will not suffer. Perhaps the things I do seem stupid to you. But then, perhaps I bear the charge of folly from a fool.
CREON	But let me tell you this: those with hardened spirits break down, all the same. Many times, the strongest iron bar, tempered and brittled in the fire, cracks and

---

* Sophocles, *Antigone.* Translated by Henry A. Strater.

shatters at a glance. I know that thrashing, bucking stallions are broken by a little bridle bit. Mere slaves are not allowed to think high thoughts. (*He turns from* ANTIGONE.) She knew her blatant sin back then, when she scorned the laws which I set forth. Sin, indeed; when she did it, and sin again to boast of it and laugh at what she did. Am I still the ruler? No — she's the ruler if she claims this power over law and stays unpunished. She is my niece, but even if her blood were closer than all others who worship at the altar in my house, she shall not avoid a fate most evil. And that sister of hers too — I blame her as much for plotting this burial. Call her in. I saw her inside a while ago, raving, and mind out of control. Like a thief, the mind which darkly plots no good is caught beforehand. I hate it deeply when someone trapped in evil deeds wants to gloss them over.

ANTIGONE   What more can you want than to kill me, since you have caught me?

CREON   I wish for no more. Having this, I have everything.

ANTIGONE   Then why do you wait? I agree with none of your logic; I never will. And in the same way, what I think can never please you. Yet how could I have an honor more worthy to remember than to give my own brother burial? All these here would say that they agree, if fear had not locked their tongues. But the sceptre brings with it many privileges. A king may say and do whate'er he wants.

CREON   You alone of all the Thebans see it this way.

ANTIGONE   They all see it too, but they bite their tongues in fear of you.

CREON   Then are you not ashamed if you think differently, apart from them?

ANTIGONE   It is nothing shameful to reverence a brother; the same womb bore us.

CREON   And was not the man who died fighting him your blood brother too?

ANTIGONE   They were of one blood, one mother, the same father.

CREON   Then how can you degrade the one by honoring the other?

ANTIGONE   His dead corpse will not accuse me.

CREON   If you honor only one, you degrade the other in proportion.

ANTIGONE   But one was not some slave that died; they both were brothers.

CREON   One destroyed this country; the other stood guard over it.

ANTIGONE   It doesn't matter. Heaven desires the burial rites for all alike.

CREON   But not that the good man shares equally with the evil one.

ANTIGONE	Who knows? This may be guiltless in the world hereafter.
CREON	Never is the enemy a friend, even when he dies.
ANTIGONE	And never can I grow to share in hate; I must share in love.
CREON	Then go to your hereafter if you must love. Love the dead there. While I live, no woman rules.

Playing the Scene

1. Is Antigone or Creon the protagonist of this play?
2. What are the dominant traits of each character?
3. In which area of the stage would the playing of this scene seem most appropriate?
4. Which body positions should be used?
5. How much and what kind of movement does the scene demand?
6. What kind of vocal delivery seems most fitting for the dialogue of the scene?
7. What is required of the nonspeaker during the long speeches?
8. How much audience empathy should each character receive?

Sources of Scenes for Ancient Greek Tragedy

The Collected Plays of Aeschylus, Sophocles, and Euripides can be used.

MODERN CLASSIC TRAGEDY

Modern classicism, although patterned on the ancient classical models, makes certain concessions to the conventions and techniques of modern theater. As a rule, the chorus is eliminated or replaced by a messenger. In T. S. Eliot's *Murder in the Cathedral*, however, the old women of Canterbury function in much the same manner as the ancient Greek chorus. Physical contact and violent action on stage, avoided in the ancient Greek tragedy, are not uncommon. The language may vary from lofty prose to poetry. The ancient classical principle of emotional restraint or the dominance of reason over emotion is not closely followed in modern classic tragedy.

Manner of Playing

1. The tragic mood, although varied, should be established and maintained.
2. Action is often more violent and impassioned than in the ancient model.
3. There is more direct and ensemble playing than was probably the case in the fifth century B.C.
4. Line interpretation should be heightened and intensified.
5. The mundane and commonplace should be avoided.
6. Pantomimic business should be highly selective and applicable.

Sources for Scenes of Modern Classic Tragedy

Daughters of Atreus by Robert Turney
Medea by Robinson Jeffers
Murder in the Cathedral by T. S. Eliot

ANCIENT GREEK COMEDY

The plays of Aristophanes are a mixture of satire, farce, and burlesque. However, behind the wit, ribaldry, and bawdy action is a serious purpose. Aristophanes, an ardent pacifist, was perhaps the first literary propagandist. He was trying, through the medium of ridicule, to correct some of the faults of his era, particularly the senseless waste of Grecian resources in continuous wars. It is helpful to remember that there is a close similarity between these plays and the light operas of Gilbert and Sullivan, except that Aristophanes' comedies are much more earthy, bawdy, and frank. (See *Lysistrata*, Plate 39.)

Manner of Playing

1. In contrast to Greek tragedy, the comedies contain a great amount of physical action and bodily contact.

2. Although a considerable amount of action and pantomimic business is indicated in the text, much more must be invented by the actor.

3. The characterizations must be exaggerated, often to the point of caricature.

4. The satiric ideas should be stressed.

5. The pace must be exceedingly rapid.

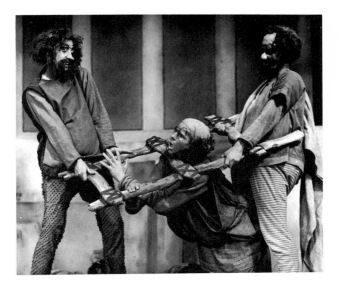

Plate 39. *Lysistrata* by Aristophanes. Scene depicting the exaggerated style of ancient Greek comedy. Southern Illinois University. Director: Christopher Moe.

Practice Selection

LYSISTRATA

by Aristophanes*

SITUATION	LYSISTRATA *has obtained an oath from the Grecian women that they will refrain from intimate relations with their husbands until the men agree to end the Peloponnesian War. The women have taken possession of the Acropolis.* CINESIAS, MYRRHINE'S *husband, has just returned from seven months in the service. There is no joy in his house without* MYRRHINE. *He comes to the Acropolis and tries to get his wife to break her oath.*
CINESIAS	As far as I can see, she's come to look a lot younger and gentler. Even when she pouts at me and acts snooty — that sort of thing itches the passions even more.
MYRRHINE	(*To her baby which a slave is carrying*) Come on, little sweetie-pie babykins. Your daddy's a bad boy. Momma's sweetie-pie is going to get a great big kiss.
CINESIAS	You heartless thing! Why'd you let those other women talk you into pulling this stunt? You're just making things tough for me, and you'll give yourself an ache, too.
MYRRHINE	Keep that busy little paw of yours away from me!
CINESIAS	But think of our home and all the stuff there that we own, you and me — a pretty poor job you've done taking care of it.
MYRRHINE	I don't give a hoot about that stuff.
CINESIAS	Don't you give a hoot about the cock poking his beak into the wool you're weaving?
MYRRHINE	Not me, by Jupiter.
CINESIAS	And the holy free-for-alls of Venus — you haven't played that game all this while. Won't you take that step back to me?
MYRRHINE	By Jupiter, not me; not unless you all make friends and stop the war.
CINESIAS	O.K., O.K., if that's what you want, we'll do it.
MYRRHINE	O.K., if that's what you'll do, I'll even forget about the rest. But not now — I'd break my promise.

---

* Aristophanes, *Lysistrata.* Translated by Henry A. Strater.

CINESIAS	But just lie down here with me a little while.
MYRRHINE	Positively not . . . though I can't say I don't like you.
CINESIAS	You like me? Then why don't you lie down with me, Myrrhine?
MYRRHINE	You silly thing! In front of the baby?
CINESIAS	Darn it! (*Calls slave.*) Here, take this kid home. O.K., now the kid's finally out of the way. Won't you lie down now?
MYRRHINE	But where around here could anybody do such a thing, poor fellow?
CINESIAS	Wherever Pan's special place is — that's fine.
MYRRHINE	Then how in the world will I get cleaned up to go back to town?
CINESIAS	You'd be gorgeous bathing in a woodland stream.
MYRRHINE	But I gave my solemn promise. Do you think I'm going to break it, silly?
CINESIAS	Blame it on me. Don't give another thought to your promise.
MYRRHINE	O.K., but let me get something for us to lie on.
CINESIAS	Forget it. The ground's good enough.
MYRRHINE	By Apollo, not me. Even though you *are* in such a state, I won't lie on the ground. (*She exits.*)
CINESIAS	The little woman still loves me; no doubt about it.
MYRRHINE	(*Enters with bedding.*) There! Lie down and get ready. I'll get undressed. But wait a minute — something else — we need to get a mat.
CINESIAS	What do you mean — mat? Not for me, anyway!
MYRRHINE	Right, by Diana. It's a tough strain on the bedpost that way.
CINESIAS	Give me a little kiss.
MYRRHINE	(*Kisses him.*) There! (*She exits.*)
CINESIAS	Wowee! Come back here in a hurry — all the way back!
MYRRHINE	(*Returning*) Here's the mat. Lie down and I'll undress. But wait a minute — something else — you don't have anything to put your head on.
CINESIAS	But not for me — I don't need a pillow.
MYRRHINE	Well, darn it, *I* do! (*She goes out.*)

CINESIAS	And here's the instrument of Hercules for her to entertain!
MYRRHINE	(*Reentering*) Get up; hop up now.
CINESIAS	All the way up already!
MYRRHINE	Really all that?
CINESIAS	Come here, Honey-precious!
MYRRHINE	I'm unhooking the girdle. Remember, now. You won't cheat on your promise about the peace treaty.
CINESIAS	By Jupiter, blast me if I do.
MYRRHINE	You don't have a bearskin rug.
CINESIAS	Damn it, I don't need it! I just want to get down to business!
MYRRHINE	Never mind; that's just what you'll do. I'll be back in a second. (*She exits.*)
CINESIAS	A guy gets itchy waiting for all this stuff to get spread out.
MYRRHINE	(*Reentering*) Raise yourself up.
CINESIAS	But it's already raised up!
MYRRHINE	Wouldn't you like me to rub some sweet oil on you?
CINESIAS	By Apollo, *no*, I tell you, not for me!
MYRRHINE	By Venus, *yes*, I tell you, like it or not!
CINESIAS	I hope that oil gets spilled, by Jupiter!
MYRRHINE	Here, put out your hand. Take some and smear it on.
CINESIAS	This oil isn't sweet at all, by the gods . . . unless its name is "Temptation" and it doesn't stink of holy matrimony.
MYRRHINE	Silly me! I brought domestic oil instead of the imported!
CINESIAS	It's fine; let it be, you divine creature!
MYRRHINE	It's foolish to use cheap stuff.
CINESIAS	The guy that first extracted oil — I hope he dies a thousand deaths.
MYRRHINE	Here, grab this marble bottle.
CINESIAS	I've got something else that's harder. Lie down, you little pest, and don't go off for anything else.
MYRRHINE	That I'll do, by Diana. Shoes off first . . . so anyway, sweetie-pie, you will vote to sign the treaty, won't you?
CINESIAS	I'll think about it. (*He leaps for her; she escapes.*) That did it. That woman's betrayed me and ruined me. Stripped for everything and she gets away.

Playing the Scene

1. What was the attitude of the ancient Greeks toward sex?

2. How does the moral code of the fifth century B.C. affect the playing of this scene?

3. Should the sex element of this scene be played straight, heightened, or played down? Which approach will be most effective in bringing out the comedy and the idea of the scene?

4. What universal comic situation and traits of character does this scene contain?

5. What is Myrrhine's motive in going after the various articles?

6. Where should this scene be played on the actor-character versus the actor-performer scale?

7. Which lines of the scene should be delivered directly to the audience?

Other Sources for Scenes of Ancient Greek Comedy

The Collected Plays of Aristophanes can be used.

ANCIENT ROMAN COMEDY AND FARCE

It is well known that the early Roman writers based their plays on the Greek models. As was true in the Greek comedies, the Roman imitators included diverse elements: farcical scenes, burlesque, comedy of manners, and a jumbling of prose dialogue with lyrical poetry. Lacking in Roman comedy is the pointed satire and literary quality to be found in the plays of Aristophanes. The Roman Plautus wrote for the masses with a dominant purpose: to make them laugh. His successor, Terence, while hewing to the line of Roman comedy, achieved a higher literary elegance and artistry. The Roman comedy characters are stock types with little depth or subtlety in characterization.

Manner of Playing

1. The acting of Roman comedy is similar to that of its Greek model.

2. Playing must be broad, lusty, coarse, and filled with inventive pantomimic business.

3. Farce playing differs from comedy in the exaggeration of situation and action.

4. The playing is predominantly toward the front of the stage.

5. Much of the playing is in the full-front body position.

Practice Selection

THE MENAECHMI

by Plautus | excerpt from Act IV, Scene 4*

(The plot of this play develops from a confusion over identical twins. MENAECHMUS SOSICLES *has arrived in Epidamnus in search of his long lost brother. Unknowingly, he has, at last, come to the very city where his brother lives. In the following scene, he meets his brother's wife, who mistakes him for her husband. He has entrusted his purse to his servant,* MESSENIO.)

MENAECHMUS   That was a pretty dumb trick I pulled a while ago when I trusted Messenio with my wallet and cash. He's probably in some bar already, soused. (MENAECHMUS' *wife looks out of the door.*)

WIFE   I guess I'll go and see if my old man's coming home yet. Why, there he is now. Well, good for me — He's bringing back my coat.

MENAECHMUS   I just wonder where that Messenio is parading around now?

WIFE   I think I'll give that bum the welcome he deserves. (*To* MENAECHMUS) Well! Aren't you ashamed to show up here before my very eyes, you poor excuse for a man? And carrying that poor excuse for a coat.

MENAECHMUS   What's all this about? What's eating you, Lady?

WIFE   Just a minute, you jerk! How dare you so much as speak to me? How dare you even mumble one word?

MENAECHMUS   What the devil did I do wrong that I can't even mumble?

WIFE   You're asking me? The stupid nerve of this guy!

MENAECHMUS   Lady, don't you know why the Greeks used to call Hecuba a bitch?

WIFE   I most certainly do not.

MENAECHMUS   Because Hecuba used to behave the very same way you're behaving now. She snarled and barked insults at everybody she saw. So now you see why they were right to start calling her a bitch.

WIFE   Oh! I simply will not stand for any more of your low-down slanders. I'd rather be a widow for the rest of my life than to take any more of those insults you cook up.

---

* Plautus, *The Menaechmi*. Translated by Henry A. Strater.

MENAECHMUS	What do I care if you can't stand your husband or not? Go ahead, leave him! Say — is this the way things are done around here? Do women just walk up to any stranger that comes along and feed him some wild story?
WIFE	What do you mean, wild story? I can't take another minute of this, I tell you I'll live as a widow. I won't tolerate any more of your weird habits.
MENAECHMUS	Well, go right ahead and be a widow, blast it! Till Hell freezes over, for all I care. Don't let me stop you!
WIFE	But just a little while ago you stood right here and claimed you didn't sneak out with this coat. Now you come and hold it right under my nose! And you're not ashamed?
MENACHEMUS	By gosh, lady, you sure have your nerve. Do you mean to stand there and tell me that this coat was stolen from you? The exact same coat some other lady gave me to get altered for her?
WIFE	Well — I — never — I'm going to get my father right now and tell him about the filth you flung at me. (*To the slave*) You there! Slave! Go get my father and see to it he gets here as fast as he can. It's an emergency! (*To* MENAECHMUS) I'm going to tell Daddy every one of your insults.
MENAECHMUS	Are you nuts? What insults?
WIFE	It was my coat and my jewelry you pilfered from this house — then you handed them over to that girl friend of yours. Or haven't I got my "wild story" straight?
MENAECHMUS	Look, lady, maybe you know some pill I can take so I can stomach this whining of yours. You've got me mistaken for somebody — I'll be darned if I know who. You're about as familiar to me as Hercules' wife's grandfather.
WIFE	Go ahead and laugh at me. Now you're going to laugh on the other side of your face. Here comes my father. Take a look, why don't you? He'll be more familiar, I'll bet.
MENAECHMUS	Why sure! I knew him with Hercules' wife's *grandmother*! I met him the same day I met you!
WIFE	Are you trying to say you don't know me? Or my father either?
MENAECHMUS	Bring on your grandfather. I don't know him either.
WIFE	Just what I'd expect. You men are all alike.

Playing the Scene

1. Which lines of dialogue should be delivered directly to the audience?

2. How may credibility, acceptance of the characters, and the situation be heightened?

3. In which area of the stage should this scene be played?

4. What devices will increase the effectiveness of the scene?

Other Sources for Scenes of Roman Comedy

The Collected Plays of Plautus

The Collected Plays of Terence

MEDIEVAL DRAMA

The dominant quality of plays of the medieval period is their naive simplicity. The writers, in their unschooled way, were learning the craft of dramatic writing. Since their primary purpose was to give religious instruction, the plays are obviously didactic. In the more secular plays, there is a lusty, earthy quality characteristic of the medieval period.

Manner of Playing

1. The acting must be sincere and dignified, particularly in plays with a strong religious message, such as *Everyman*.

2. The actor should accept the childlike, naive quality of the play and fully enter into its spirit.

3. For the secular plays, an exaggerated, farcical, bawdy action is often required. (See *A Mery Play* . . ., Plate 40.)

4. An examination of illustrated manuscripts will reveal useful suggestions on matters of posture, hand positions, and movements.

Sources for Scenes of Medieval Drama

Abraham and Isaac

Everyman

The Second Shepherd's Play

Plate 40. *A Mery Play Betwene Johan Johan, the Husbande, Tyb, his Wyfe, and Syr Johan, the Preest.* Author unknown. Scene depicting the bawdy quality of secular medieval dramas. Dartmouth College. Director Henry B. Williams.

ROMANTICISM

ELIZABETHAN TRAGEDY

In this style of drama we find a definite breaking away from the restraints of classicism. The classical unities of time and place are disregarded. Scenes of extreme violence (lacking in classicism) are presented in which emotions of the characters run the full gamut. In contrast with Greek classic tragedy, there are great variations in moods, with an intermingling of the comic and tragic. The grave-diggers' scene in *Hamlet* and the drunken porter scene in *Macbeth* are typical examples. The motivating drive of the action, whether it is an inner conflict of the character or an external force, should be determined.

Manner of Playing

1. The protagonist should be believable and sincere.

2. It is imperative that he strive to attain his goal with vigor and determination.

3. The nobility of the principal characters should be developed as the exigencies of the play may require.

4. Emotional contact with the audience should be established and maintained.

5. The lyrical and rhythmic reading of the lines should not obscure the author's meaning.

6. Pantomimic business is minimized, with only the most significant included in the action.

7. Movement and gestures are large and flowing.

Practice Selections

HAMLET

by William Shakespeare | excerpt from Act III, Scene 1

(A room in the castle. In the soliloquy, "To be, or not to be . . ." which precedes the following scene, HAMLET *has contemplated taking his own life.)*

HAMLET	Soft you now! The fair Ophelia! Nymph, in thy orisons Be all my sins remember'd.
OPHELIA	Good my lord, How does your honour for this many a day?
HAMLET	I humbly thank you: well, well, well.
OPHELIA	My lord, I have remembrances of yours, That I have longed to re-deliver; I pray you, now receive them.
HAMLET	No, not I; I never gave you aught.
OPHELIA	My honour'd lord, you know right well you did; And with them words of so sweet breath composed As made the things more rich: their perfume lost, Take these again; for the noble mind Rich gifts wax poor when givers prove unkind. There, my lord.
HAMLET	Ha, ha! are you honest?
OPHELIA	My lord?
HAMLET	Are you fair?
OPHELIA	What means your lordship?
HAMLET	That if you be honest and fair, your honesty should admit no discourse to your beauty.
OPHELIA	Could beauty, my lord, have better commerce than with honesty?
HAMLET	Ay, truly; for the power of beauty will sooner transform honesty from what it is to a bawd than the force of honesty can translate beauty into his likeness: this was sometime a paradox, but now the time gives it proof. I did love you once.
OPHELIA	Indeed, my lord, you made me believe so.

| HAMLET | You should not have believed me; for virtue cannot so inoculate our old stock but we shall relish of it: I loved you not. |

OPHELIA I was the more deceived.

HAMLET Get thee to a nunnery: why wouldst thou be a breeder of sinners? I am myself indifferent honest; but yet I could accuse me of such things that it were better my mother had not borne me: I am very proud, revengeful, ambitious; with more offences at my beck than I have thoughts to put them in, imagination to give them shape, or time to act them in. What should such fellows as I do crawling between heaven and earth? We are arrant knaves all; believe none of us. Go thy ways to a nunnery. Where's your father?

OPHELIA At home, my lord.

HAMLET Let the doors be shut upon him, that he may play the fool no where but in 's own house. Farewell.

OPHELIA Oh, help him, you sweet heavens!

HAMLET If thou dost marry, I'll give thee this plague for thy dowry; be thou as chaste as ice, as pure as snow, thou shalt not escape calumny. Get thee to a nunnery, go: farewell. Or, if thou wilt needs marry, marry a fool; for wise men know well enough what monsters you make of them. To a nunnery, go; and quickly too. Farewell.

OPHELIA O heavenly powers, restore him!

HAMLET I have heard of your paintings too, well enough; God hath given you one face, and you make yourselves another: you jig, you amble, and you lisp, and nick-name God's creatures, and make your wantonness your ignorance. Go to, I'll no more on 't; it hath made me mad. I say, we will have no more marriages: those that are married already, all but one, shall live; the rest shall keep as they are. To a nunnery, go.

(*Exits.*)

OPHELIA O, what a noble mind is here o'erthrown!
The courtier's, soldier's, scholar's, eye, tongue, sword:
The expectancy and rose of the fair state,
The glass of fashion and the mould of form,
The observed of all observers, quite, quite down!
And I, of ladies most deject and wretched,
That suck'd the honey of his music vows,
Now see that noble and most sovereign reason,
Like sweet bells jangled, out of tune and harsh;
That unmatch'd form and feature of blown youth
Blasted with ectasy: O, woe is me,
To have seen what I have seen, see what I see!

Playing the Scene

1. What is Hamlet's purpose in this scene?
2. Does Hamlet suspect that the King and Polonius are eavesdropping?
3. Is Hamlet's mind deranged, as Ophelia thinks, or is he feigning madness?
4. Is Hamlet psychopathic or a normal young man?
5. Is he in love with Ophelia?
6. Why does he tell her to go to a nunnery?
7. What is Ophelia's objective in the scene?
8. How old is she?
9. What was the nature of her background, status, and rearing, which might determine her character and her manner of playing the scene?
10. What bearing does Shakespeare's poetry have on the actor's melodic pattern, quality of voice, diction, etc.?

ROMEO AND JULIET

by William Shakespeare | Act II, Scene 5

(CAPULET's *orchard.* JULIET *has sent the* NURSE *to* ROMEO *to learn if he, in truth, plans to consummate his words of love in marriage.*)

JULIET

The clock struck nine when I did send the nurse;
In half an hour she promised to return.
Perchance she cannot meet him: that's not so.
O, she is lame! love's heralds should be thoughts,
Which ten times faster glide than the sun's beams,
Driving back shadows over louring hills:
Therefore do nimble-pinion'd doves draw love,
And therefore hath the wind-swift Cupid wings.
Now is the sun upon the highmost hill
Of this day's journey, and from nine till twelve
Is three long hours; yet she is not come.
Had she affections and warm youthful blood,
She would be as swift in motion as a ball;
My words would bandy her to my sweet love,
And his to me:
But old folks, many feign as they were dead;
Unwieldly, slow, heavy and pale as lead.

(*Enter* NURSE, *with* PETER.)

O God, she comes! O honey nurse, what news?
Hast thou met with him? Send thy man away.

NURSE	Peter, stay at the gate. (*Exit* PETER.)
JULIET	Now, good sweet nurse, — O Lord, why look'st thou sad?
	Though news be sad, yet tell them merrily;
	If good, thou shamest the music of sweet news
	By playing it to me with so sour a face.
NURSE	I am a-weary; give me leave a while.
	Fie, how my bones ache! what a jaunce have I had!
JULIET	I would thou hadst my bones and I thy news:
	Nay, come, I pray thee, speak; good, good nurse, speak.
NURSE	Jesu, what haste? can you not stay a while?
	Do you not see that I am out of breath?
JULIET	How art thou out of breath, when thou hast breath
	To say to me that thou art out of breath?
	The excuse that thou dost make in this delay
	Is longer than the tale thou dost excuse.
	Is thy news good, or bad? answer to that;
	Say either, and I'll stay the circumstance:
	Let me be satisfied, is 't good or bad?
NURSE	Well, you have made a simple choice; you know not how to choose a man: Romeo! no, not he; though his face be better than any man's, yet his leg excels all men's; and for a hand, and a foot, and a body, though they be not to be talked on, yet they are past compare: he is not the flower of courtesy, but, I'll warrant him, as gentle as a lamb. Go thy ways, wench; serve God. What, have you dined at home?
JULIET	No, no: but all this did I know before.
	What says he of our marriage? what of that?
NURSE	Lord, how my head aches! what a head have I!
	It beats as it would fall in twenty pieces.
	My back o' t' other side, — ah, my back, my back!
	Beshrew your heart for sending me about,
	To catch my death with jauncing up and down!
JULIET	I' faith, I am sorry that thou art not well.
	Sweet, sweet, sweet nurse, tell me, what says my love?
NURSE	Your love says, like an honest gentleman, and a courteous, and a kind, and a handsome, and, I warrant, a virtuous, — Where is your mother?
JULIET	Where is my mother! why, she is within;
	Where should she be? How oddly thou repliest!
	'Your love says, like an honest gentleman,
	Where is your mother?'

NURSE
           O God's lady dear!
    Are you so hot? marry, come up, I trow;
    Is this the poultice for my aching bones?
    Henceforward do your messages yourself.

JULIET
    Here's such a coil! come, what says Romeo?

NURSE
    Have you got leave to go to shrift to-day?

JULIET
    I have.

NURSE
    Then hie you hence to Friar Laurence' cell;
    There stays a husband to make you a wife:
    Now comes the wanton blood up in your cheeks,
    They'll be in scarlet straight at any news.
    Hie you to church; I must another way,
    To fetch a ladder, by the which your love
    Must climb a bird's nest soon when it is dark;
    I am the drudge, and toil in your delight;
    But you shall bear the burden soon at night.
    Go; I'll to dinner; hie you to the cell.

JULIET
    Hie to high fortune! Honest nurse, farewell.
                        (*Exeunt.*)

Playing the Scene

1. What are the dominant traits in the character of the nurse?
2. Approximately how old is the nurse?
3. How may the age of the nurse be conveyed with conviction and artistry?
4. Is the nurse telling the truth when she speaks of her aches and pains?
5. Why does the nurse withhold the news from Juliet?
6. What is the emotional relationship between the nurse and Juliet?
7. How old is Juliet? How might her age affect the playing of the scene?
8. Does Juliet believe the nurse's account of her aches and pains?
9. What does Juliet do to bring about a change in the nurse's attitude?
10. Which lines in the scene require movement for their proper interpretation?
11. What might Juliet be doing during the delivery of her opening speech?
12. Where in the scene might there be a break or pause in the movement to indicate a change in thought or feeling?
13. Is there comedy in this scene? If so, where?

OTHELLO

by William Shakespeare | excerpt from Act III, Scene 3

(*The garden of the castle. With subtle, diabolical cunning,* IAGO *has goaded the trusting* OTHELLO *until he is mad with jealousy.*)

OTHELLO   By the world,
I think, my wife be honest, and think she is not;
I think that thou art just, and think thou art not:
I'll have some proof. Her name, that was as fresh
As Dian's visage, is now begrimed and black
As mine own face. If there be cords, or knives,
Poison, or fire, or suffocating streams,
I'll not endure it. Would I were satisfied!

IAGO   I see, sir, you are eaten up with passion:
I do repent me that I put it to you.
You would be satisfied?

OTHELLO   Would! nay, I will.

IAGO   And may: but how? how satisfied, my lord?
Would you, the supervisor, grossly gape on?
Behold her topp'd?

OTHELLO   Death and damnation! O!

IAGO   It were a tedious difficulty, I think,
To bring them to that prospect: damn them then,
If ever mortal eyes do see them bolster
More than their own! What then? how then?
What shall I say? Where's satisfaction?
It is impossible you should see this,
Were they as prime as goats, as hot as monkeys,
As salt as wolves in pride, and fools as gross
As ignorance made drunk. But yet, I say,
If imputation and strong circumstances,
Which lead directly to the door of truth,
Will give you satisfaction, you may have 't.

OTHELLO   Give me a living reason she's disloyal.

IAGO	I do not like the office:
	But sith I am enter'd in this cause so far,
	Prick't to 't by foolish honesty and love,
	I will go on. I lay with Cassio lately,
	And being troubled with a raging tooth,
	I could not sleep.
	There are a kind of men so loose of soul,
	That in their sleeps will mutter their affairs:
	One of this kind is Cassio:
	In sleep I heard him say 'Sweet Desdemona,
	Let us be wary, let us hide our loves;'
	And then, sir, would he gripe and wring my hand,
	Cry 'O sweet creature!' and then kiss me hard,
	As if he pluck'd up kisses by the roots,
	That grew upon my lips: then laid his leg
	Over my thigh, and sigh'd and kiss'd, and then
	Cried 'Cursed fate that gave thee to the Moor!'

OTHELLO   O monstrous! monstrous!

IAGO   Nay, this was but his dream.

OTHELLO   But this denoted a foregone conclusion:
'Tis a shrewd doubt, though it be but a dream.

IAGO   And this may help to thicken other proofs
That do demonstrate thinly.

OTHELLO   I'll tear her all to pieces.

IAGO   Nay, but be wise: yet we see nothing done;
She may be honest yet. Tell me but this;
Have you not sometimes seen a handkerchief
Spotted with strawberries in your wife's hand?

OTHELLO   I gave her such a one; 'twas my first gift.

IAGO   I know not that: but such a handkerchief —
I am sure it was your wife's — did I to-day
See Cassio wipe his beard with.

OTHELLO   If it be that, —

IAGO   If it be that, or any that was hers,
It speaks against her with the other proofs.

OTHELLO
O, that the slave had forty thousand lives!
One is too poor, too weak for my revenge.
Now do I see 'tis true. Look here, Iago;
All my fond love thus do I blow to heaven:
'Tis gone.
Arise, black vengeance, from thy hollow cell!
Yield up, O love, thy crown and hearted throne
To tyrannous hate! Swell, bosom, with thy fraught,
For 'tis of aspics' tongues!

IAGO
Yet be content.

OTHELLO
O, blood, blood, blood!

IAGO
Patience, I say; your mind perhaps may change.

Playing the Scene

1. Why does Othello not detect Iago's dishonesty and treachery?

2. How directly or openly should Iago play to Othello?

3. How much should Othello move in this scene?

4. How much should Iago move?

5. Should the audience be aware of Iago's deception in the above scene? If so, how may this be accomplished by the actor?

6. What is the emotional key to this scene?

ELIZABETHAN COMEDY

Here we have comedies in a playful, romantic mood, a blending of the serious and comic, real and imaginary, in which we see wise fools and foolish wise men.

Manner of Playing

1. Much attention should be given to the dialogue in order to achieve the essential balance between the meaning and the lyrical quality of Shakespeare's poetry.

2. The actor is admonished to explore the depth of each character and to strive for theatrical credibility.

3. It is well to be on the alert for possibilities of comic business and superimposed action.

(See Plates 41 and 42, page 294.)

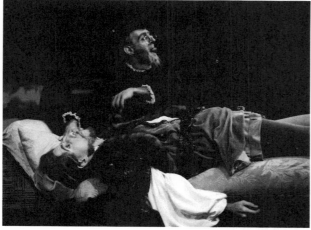

Plate 41. *Twelfth Night* by William Shakespeare. Comic devices in a dueling scene. Barter Theater '66 Season. Director: Peter Culman. Photograph: Greear Studio.

Plate 42. *Volpone* by Ben Jonson. Scene of cunning and deception. University of Miami. Director: Delmar Solem. Photograph: Ron Blakeley, University of Miami Photo Center.

Practice Selection

AS YOU LIKE IT

by William Shakespeare | excerpt from Act IV, Scene 1

SCENE	*The Forest of Arden.*
SITUATION	ROSALIND, *posing as a young man, meets* ORLANDO. *He does not recognize her as the object of his love verses.*
CHARACTERS	ROSALIND, *daughter of the banished Duke*
	JAQUES, *lord attending on the banished Duke*
	CELIA, *companion of* ROSALIND, *and daughter of* FREDERICK
	ORLANDO, *son of* SIR ROWLAND DE BOYS

(Enter ORLANDO.)

ORLANDO
Good day and happiness, dear Rosalind!

JAQUES
Nay, then, God buy you, an you talk in blank verse. (*Exit.*)

ROSALIND
Farewell, Monsieur Traveller: look you lisp and wear strange suits; disable all the benefits of your own country; be out of love with your nativity and almost chide God for making you that countenance you are; or I will scarce think you have swam in a gondola. Why, how now, Orlando! where have you been all this while? You a lover! An you serve me such another trick, never come in my sight more.

ORLANDO
My fair Rosalind, I come within an hour of my promise.

ROSALIND
Break an hour's promise in love! He that will divide a minute into a thousand parts, and break but a part of the thousandth part of a minute in the affairs of love, it may be said of him that Cupid hath clapped him o' the shoulder, but I'll warrant him heart-whole.

ORLANDO
Pardon me, dear Rosalind.

ROSALIND
Nay, an you be so tardy, come no more in my sight: I had as lief be wooed of a snail.

ORLANDO
Of a snail?

ROSALIND
Ay, of a snail; for though he comes slowly, he carries his house on his head; a better jointure, I think, than you make a woman: besides, he brings his destiny with him.

ORLANDO	What's that?
ROSALIND	Why, horns, which such as you are fain to be beholding to your wives for: but he comes armed in his fortune and prevents the slander of his wife.
ORLANDO	Virtue is no horn-maker; and my Rosalind is virtuous.
ROSALIND	And I am your Rosalind.
CELIA	It pleases him to call you so; but he hath a Rosalind of a better leer than you.
ROSALIND	Come, woo me, woo me; for now I am in a holiday humour and like enough to consent. What would you say to me now, an I were your very very Rosalind?
ORLANDO	I would kiss before I spoke.
ROSALIND	Nay, you were better speak first; and when you were gravelled for lack of matter, you might take occasion to kiss. Very good orators, when they are out, they will spit; and for lovers lacking — God warn us! — matter, the cleanliest shift is to kiss.
ORLANDO	How if the kiss be denied?
ROSALIND	Then she puts you to entreaty and there begins new matter.
ORLANDO	Who could be out, being before his beloved mistress?
ROSALIND	Marry, that should you, if I were your mistress, or I should think my honesty ranker than my wit.
ORLANDO	What, of my suit?
ROSALIND	Not out of your apparel, and yet out of your suit. Am not I your Rosalind?
ORLANDO	I take some joy to say you are, because I would be talking of her.
ROSALIND	Well, in her person, I say I will not have you.
ORLANDO	Then in mine own person I die.
ROSALIND	No, faith, die by attorney. The poor world is almost six thousand years old, and in all this time there was not any man died in his own person, videlicet, in a love-cause. Troilus had his brains dashed out with a Grecian club; yet he did what he could to die before, and he is one of the patterns of love. Leander, he would have lived many a fair year, though Hero had turned nun, if it had not been for a hot midsummer night; for, good youth, he went but forth to wash him in the Hellespont and being taken with the cramp was drowned: and the foolish chroniclers of that age found it was 'Hero of Sestos.' But these are all lies: men have died from time to time and worms have eaten them, but not for love.

ORLANDO	I would not have my right Rosalind of this mind; for, I protest, her frown might kill me.
ROSALIND	By this hand, it will not kill a fly. But come, now I will be your Rosalind in a more coming-on disposition, and ask me what you will, I will grant it.
ORLANDO	Then love me, Rosalind.
ROSALIND	Yes, faith, will I, Fridays and Saturdays and all.
ORLANDO	And wilt thou have me?
ROSALIND	Ay, and twenty such.
ORLANDO	What sayest thou?
ROSALIND	Are you not good?
ORLANDO	I hope so.
ROSALIND	Why then, can one desire too much of a good thing? Come, sister, you shall be the priest and marry us. Give me your hand, Orlando. What do you say, sister?
ORLANDO	Pray thee, marry us.
CELIA	I cannot say the words.
ROSALIND	You must begin, 'Will you, Orlando — '
CELIA	Go to. Will you, Orlando, have to wife this Rosalind?
ORLANDO	I will.
ROSALIND	Ay, but when?
ORLANDO	Why now; as fast as she can marry us.
ROSALIND	Then you must say 'I take thee, Rosalind, for wife.'
ORLANDO	I take thee, Rosalind, for wife.
ROSALIND	I might ask you for your commission; but I do take thee, Orlando, for my husband: there's a girl goes before the priest; and certainly a woman's thought runs before her actions.

Playing the Scene

1. Why does Orlando not recognize Rosalind for what she is?
2. Would Rosalind's deception be more believable in Shakespeare's day? Why?
3. What is the mood and spirit of this scene?
4. What style of delivery of Shakespeare's poetry will convey both the meaning and the lyrical quality?

ELIZABETHAN COMEDY–FANTASY

This type is similar to the comedy described in the preceding section, except that we are in a world of the fanciful and the real, intermingled with a highly romantic mood.

Manner of Playing

1. The mood must be light and vivacious.
2. The characters should have warmth and appeal.
3. The actor should strive for a distinction between the world of reality and a dream world where everything is possible.

Practice Selection

A MIDSUMMER-NIGHT'S DREAM

by William Shakespeare / excerpt from Act II, Scene 2

(PUCK *has put a love charm on the eyes of* LYSANDER, *making him despise his former love,* HERMIA, *and adore* HELENA *instead.*)

HELENA

O, I am out of breath in this fond chase!
The more my prayer, the lesser is my grace.
Happy is Hermia, wheresoe'er she lies;
For she hath blessed and attractive eyes.
How came her eyes so bright? Not with salt tears:
If so, my eyes are oftener wash'd than hers.
No, no, I am as ugly as a bear;
For beasts that meet me run away for fear:
Therefore no marvel though Demetrius
Do, as a monster, fly my presence thus.
What wicked and dissembling glass of mine
Made me compare with Hermia's sphery eyne?
But who is here? Lysander! on the ground!
Dead? or asleep? I see no blood, no wound.
Lysander, if you live, good sir, awake.

LYSANDER

(*Awaking*) And run through fire I will for thy sweet sake.
Transparent Helena! Nature shews art,

That through thy bosom makes me see thy heart.
Where is Demetrius? O, how fit a word
Is that vile name to perish on my sword!

HELENA

Do not say, so, Lysander; say not so.
What though he love your Hermia? Lord, what though?
Yet Hermia still loves you: then be content.

LYSANDER

Content with Hermia! No; I do repent
The tedious minutes I with her have spent.
Not Hermia but Helena I love:
Who will not change a raven for a dove?
The will of man is by his reason sway'd
And reason says you are the worthier maid.
Things growing are not ripe until their season:
So I, being young, till now ripe not to reason;
And touching now the point of human skill,
Reason becomes the marshall to my will,
And leads me to your eyes; where I o'erlook
Love's stories, written in love's richest book.

HELENA

Wherefore was I to this keen mockery born?
When at your hands did I deserve this scorn?
Is't not enough, is't not enough, young man,
That I did never, no, nor never can,
Deserve a sweet look from Demetrius' eye,
But you must flout my insufficiency?
Good troth, you do me wrong, good sooth, you do,
In such disdainful manner me to woo.
But fare you well: perforce I must confess
I thought you lord of more true gentleness.
O, that a lady, of one man refused,
Should of another therefore be abused!   (*Exit.*)

LYSANDER

She sees not Hermia. Hermia, sleep thou there:
And never mayst thou come Lysander near!
For as a surfeit of the sweetest things
The deepest loathing to the stomach brings,
Or as the heresies that men do leave
Are hated most of those they did deceive,
So thou, my surfeit and my heresy,
Of all be hated, but the most of me!
And, all my powers, address your love and might
To honour Helena and to be her knight!   (*Exit.*)

Playing the Scene

1. By what devices may this fantastic scene be made more believable?
2. In what area of the stage might this scene be played to best advantage.
3. Should Helena appear unattractive?
4. What emotional changes are apparent in the character of Helena?

ELIZABETHAN FARCE

This type is similar to Elizabethan comedy except for its farcical situations and the improbabilities of plot action.

Manner of Playing

1. Much inventive comic business is required.
2. A very fast pace and light mood are essential.
3. It is highly important to avoid arousing the empathy of the audience for the plight of the character.

Practice Selection

THE TAMING OF THE SHREW

by William Shakespeare | excerpt from Act II, Scene 1

(*A room in* BAPTISTA'S *house.* PETRUCHIO *of Verona has come to Padua to find a wealthy wife. In spite of what he hears about* BAPTISTA'S *daughter,* KATHARINA, *he decides that he will woo and marry her.*)

(*Enter* KATHARINA.)

PETRUCHIO   Good morrow, Kate; for that's your name, I hear.

KATHARINA   Well have you heard, but something hard of hearing:
They call me Katharine that do talk of me.

PETRUCHIO   You lie, in faith; for you are call'd plain Kate,
And bonny Kate, and sometimes Kate the curst;
But Kate, the prettiest Kate in Christendom,
Kate of Kate-Hall, my super-dainty Kate,
For dainties are all Kates, and therefore, Kate,
Take this of me, Kate of my consolation;
Hearing thy mildness praised in every town,
Thy virtues spoke of, and thy beauty sounded,
Yet not so deeply as to thee belongs,
Myself am moved to woo thee for my wife.

KATHARINA	Moved! in good time: let him that moved you hither Remove you hence: I knew you at the first You were a moveable.
PETRUCHIO	Why, what's a moveable?
KATHARINA	A join'd-stool.
PETRUCHIO	Thou hast hit it; come, sit on me.
KATHARINA	Asses are made to bear, and so are you.
PETRUCHIO	Women are made to bear, and so are you.
KATHARINA	No such jade as you, if me you mean.
PETRUCHIO	Alas, good Kate, I will not burden thee! For, knowing thee to be but young and light, —
KATHARINA	Too light for such a swain as you to catch; And yet as heavy as my weight should be.
PETRUCHIO	Should be! should — buzz!
KATHARINA	Well ta'en, and like a buzzard.
PETRUCHIO	O slow-wing'd turtle! shall a buzzard take thee?
KATHARINA	Ay, for a turtle, as he takes a buzzard.
PETRUCHIO	Come, come, you wasp; i' faith you are too angry.
KATHARINA	If I be waspish, best beware my sting.
PETRUCHIO	My remedy is then, to pluck it out.
KATHARINA	Ay, if the fool could find it where it lies.
PETRUCHIO	Who know not where a wasp does wear his sting? In his tail.
KATHARINA	In his tongue.
PETRUCHIO	Whose tongue?
KATHARINA	Yours, if you talk of tails: and so farewell.
PETRUCHIO	What, with my tongue in your tail? nay, come again, Good Kate; I am a gentleman.
KATHARINA	That I'll try. (*She strikes him.*)
PETRUCHIO	I swear I'll cuff you, if you strike again.
KATHARINA	So may you lose your arms: If you strike me, you are no gentleman; And if no gentleman, why then no arms.

PETRUCHIO	A herald, Kate? O, put me in thy books!
KATHARINA	What is your crest? a coxcomb?
PETRUCHIO	A combless cock, so Kate will be my hen.
KATHARINA	No cock of mine; you crow too like a craven.
PETRUCHIO	Nay, come, Kate, come; you must not look so sour.
KATHARINA	It is my fashion, when I see a crab.
PETRUCHIO	Why, here's no crab; and therefore look not sour.
KATHARINA	There is, there is.
PETRUCHIO	Then show it me.
KATHARINA	Had I a glass, I would.
PETRUCHIO	What, you mean my face?
KATHARINA	Well aim'd of such a young one.
PETRUCHIO	Now, by Saint George, I am too young for you.
KATHARINA	Yet you are wither'd.
PETRUCHIO	'Tis with cares.
KATHARINA	I care not.
PETRUCHIO	Nay, hear you, Kate: in sooth you scape not so.
KATHARINA	I chafe you, if I tarry: let me go.
PETRUCHIO	No, not a whit: I find you passing gentle.

PETRUCHIO

'Twas told me you were rough and coy and sullen,
And now I find report a very liar;
For thou are pleasant, gamesome, passing courteous,
But slow in speech, yet sweet as spring-time flowers:
Thou canst not frown, thou canst not look askance,
Nor bite the lip, as angry wenches will,
Nor hast thou pleasure to be cross in talk,
But thou with mildness entertain'st thy wooers,
With gentle conference, soft and affable,
Why does the world report that Kate doth limp?
O slanderous world! Kate, like the hazel-twig
Is straight and slender, and as brown in hue
As hazel-nuts and sweeter than the kernels.
O, let me see thee walk: thou dost not halt.

KATHARINA	Go, fool, and whom thou keep'st command.
PETRUCHIO	Did ever Dian so become a grove As Kate this chamber with her princely gait? O, be thou Dian, and let her be Kate; And then let Kate be chaste and Dian sportful!
KATHARINA	Where did you study all this goodly speech?
PETRUCHIO	It is extempore, from my mother-wit.
KATHARINA	A witty mother! witless else her son.
PETRUCHIO	Am I not wise?
KATHARINA	Yes, keep you warm.
PETRUCHIO	Marry, so I mean, sweet Katharine, in thy bed: And therefore, setting all this chat aside, Thus in plain terms: your father hath consented That you shall be my wife; your dowry 'greed on; And, will you, nill you, I will marry you. Now, Kate, I am a husband for your turn; For, by this light, whereby I see thy beauty, Thy beauty, that doth make me like thee well, Thou must be married to no man but me; For I am born to tame you Kate, And bring you from a wild Kate to a Kate Conformable as other household Kates. Here comes your father; never make denial; I must and will have Katherine to my wife.

Playing the Scene

1. What is the motivation for Katharina's temperament?

2. In spite of her shrewishness, should the audience hold a kindly feeling for her?

3. What are the character traits of Petruchio? Is there a danger that he may become the swaggering bully and lose audience appeal? How may this be avoided?

4. Which of Petruchio's speeches are sincere and which are facetious?

5. What action or business might Katharina execute to accompany certain of Petruchio's lines?

6. Why does Petruchio wish to marry Katharina?

NINETEENTH AND TWENTIETH CENTURY ROMANTIC DRAMA

In contrast to the classic style, romanticism presents a mixture of moods: tragic and comic. The plot is loose in structure, involved, and highly theatrical with emphasis on "big scenes" and strong climaxes. The main characters are generally idealized, larger than life, and intensely emotional. The language is predominantly poetic, rhetorical, highly emotional, and richly adorned with figures of speech and imagery.

Manner of Playing

1. Rhythmic, melodic speech in keeping with the poetic language is essential.

2. Although the action in some instances is insufficiently motivated, the actor should strive for inner truth and credibility.

3. Flowing movement and gestures are pertinent.

4. High emotional intensity is required for the big scenes.

5. Pantomimic details and business should be highly selective and significant.

6. The central areas of the stage are used predominantly, particularly for the big scenes.

7. Open, front body positions are used with great frequency.

8. Solo playing is often used.

Practice Selections

CYRANO DE BERGERAC

*by Edmond Rostand / excerpt from Act V**

SCENE   *Park of the Sisters of the Holy Cross in Paris.* ROXANE *is now in a convent, still in mourning and devoted, as ever, to the memory of her husband,* CHRISTIAN, *who was killed in the war with Spain at the siege of Arras.* CYRANO, *who has carried his undying love of* ROXANE *in his heart, comes each Saturday to visit her. Just prior to the following scene,* CYRANO *has been injured by a block of wood, thrown from an upper window. In spite of this injury, with a bandage under his white-plumed hat, he manages, although somewhat late, to keep his rendezvous with his beloved* ROXANE.

ROXANE   (*Without turning around*) What was I saying? (*She continues to embroider.* CYRANO, *very pale, his hat drawn over his eyes, appears. The Sister who has announced him goes out. He begins to descend the steps slowly, with an apparent effort to stand erect, supporting himself by leaning on his cane.*) Ah, these faded colors! How will I match them? (*To* CYRANO, *in a tone of friendly scolding*) After fourteen years, late, for the first time.

---

* Edmond Rostand, *Cyrano de Bergerac*. Translated by Robert Spanabel.

CYRANO	(*Who has managed to get to the chair, and has sat down, speaks in a gay voice contrasting with the pain in his face.*) Yes, it's stupid. Maddening! I was delayed by . . .
ROXANE	By? . . .
CYRANO	By a rather untimely visitor.
ROXANE	(*Absent-mindedly, embroidering*) Ah, yes, somewhat annoying?
CYRANO	Cousin, he was a bore.
ROXANE	Did you dismiss him?
CYRANO	Yes. I said: "Excuse me, but today is Saturday. A day when I must be at a certain place. Nothing ever makes me miss it. Call again in an hour."
ROXANE	(*Lightly*) Well, this person will want to see you, but I won't permit you to leave before this evening.
CYRANO	Perhaps I'll have to leave a little sooner. (*He closes his eyes and is silent for a moment. A light breeze causes some leaves to fall.*) The leaves!
ROXANE	(*Raising her head, gazing into the distance*) They are a soft Venetian brown. See them fall.
CYRANO	How well they fall! So brief a way from the branch to the earth, yet they know final beauty. Despite the fear of death on the ground, they wish only that their fall be a graceful flight.
ROXANE	Melancholy — you?
CYRANO	(*Collecting himself*) Why, not at all, Roxane.
ROXANE	Then let the leaves fall as they will, and tell me some of the news — My gazette?
CYRANO	Let me see —
ROXANE	Ah!
CYRANO	(*More and more pale, struggling against the pain*) Saturday, the nineteenth: the King became ill with a fever, having eaten eight helpings of grape jam. His illness was condemned for high treason, and his august pulse is now normal. Sunday, the twentieth: at a grand ball given by the Queen, seven hundred and sixty-three white wax candles were burned; Our troops, they say, have defeated the Austrians; Four sorcerers have been hung; The little dog of Madame d'Athis had to take a dose of . . .
ROXANE	Monsieur de Bergerac, hold your tongue!

CYRANO	Monday . . . nothing. Lygdamire changed lovers.
ROXANE	Oh!
CYRANO	(*Whose face is more and more changed*) Tuesday: all the court went to Fontainebleau. Wednesday: Madame de Montglat said No to the Comte de Fiesque. Thursday: Mancini was the Queen of France — or nearly so! The twenty-fifth, Montglat said Yes to de Fiesque; and Saturday, the twenty-sixth . . . (*He closes his eyes, his head bows. Silence*)
ROXANE	(*Surprised at not hearing any more, turns, looks at him and rises, frightened.*) He has fainted. (*She runs to him, crying out.*) Cyrano!
CYRANO	(*Opening his eyes, in a hazy voice*) What is it? What? (*He sees* ROXANE *leaning over him, and quickly pulls his hat down over his eyes and shrinks back, with terror, into his chair.*) It's nothing. Let me be.
ROXANE	Nevertheless . . .
CYRANO	My old wound — from Arras . . . that . . . sometimes . . . you know . . .
ROXANE	My poor friend.
CYRANO	It's nothing. It will pass. (*Smiling, with effort*) There, it's gone.
ROXANE	(*Standing close to him*) Each of us has his wound: I have mine. Always alive, it is here, this ancient wound. (*She puts her hand over her heart.*) It is here, under this faded letter, where one can still see teardrops and blood.
	(*Twilight begins to fall.*)
CYRANO	His letter! . . . Did you not say that one day, perhaps, you would let me read it?
ROXANE	His letter? You . . . you want to . . .
CYRANO	Yes . . . I do . . . now . . .
ROXANE	(*Giving him the little bag from around her neck*) There!
CYRANO	(*Taking it*) May I open it?
ROXANE	Open it . . . Read it . . . (*She goes back to her tapestry, folds it, arranges her wools.*)
CYRANO	(*Reading*) "Roxane, adieu, because I soon will die."
ROXANE	(*Pausing, surprised*) Aloud?
CYRANO	(*Reading*) "I know that it will be tonight, my darling. My heart is still heavy with love yet unrevealed. And I'm dying. Never more, never will my eyes, my glances behold . . ."

ROXANE	How you read it — his letter!
CYRANO	(*Continuing*) " . . . your exquisite beauty. My eyes will never capture your body's brightest moments. But I remember a little gesture that reminds me of you. Just to touch your forehead . . . I would cry out . . . "
ROXANE	How you read it, this letter!
	(*The darkness increases imperceptibly.*)
CYRANO	"And I cry: Adieu."
ROXANE	You read it . . .
CYRANO	"My dear, my dearest, my treasure, . . . "
ROXANE	In a voice . . .
CYRANO	"My love! . . . "
ROXANE	In a voice . . . that I have heard before. (*She comes near him, softly, without him seeing her, passes behind the chair, and leans over, silently, looking at the letter. The darkness increases.*)
CYRANO	"My heart will never leave you for a second, and I am and shall always be — even in another world — the one who loves you beyond measure, the one . . . "
ROXANE	(*Putting her hand on his shoulder*) How are you able to read now? It is dark. (*He starts, turns, sees her close to him, makes a gesture of surprise, lowers his head. A long pause.*) (*Then, in the twilight which has completely fallen, she says, very slowly, clasping her hands*) And all these fourteen years he has played this role, the old friend who came to be amusing.
CYRANO	Roxane!
ROXANE	It was you.
CYRANO	No, no Roxane, no!
ROXANE	I should have guessed when he read my name.
CYRANO	No! It was not I!
ROXANE	It was you!
CYRANO	I swear to you . . .
ROXANE	I understand all the generous deception: the letters, you were the one who . . .
CYRANO	No!

ROXANE	The dear, mad words, they were yours.
CYRANO	No!
ROXANE	The voice in the night, it was your voice!
CYRANO	I swear to you, no!
ROXANE	The soul, it was your soul!
CYRANO	I didn't love you!
ROXANE	Yes. You loved me!
CYRANO	It was he!
ROXANE	You loved me!
CYRANO	No!
ROXANE	Even now you say it with less conviction.
CYRANO	No, no, my dearest love, I didn't love you!
ROXANE	Ah, how many things have died . . . how many things have been born. Why were you silent all these fourteen years, when on this letter, which to him was nothing, these tears were yours?
CYRANO	(*Holding out the letter to her*) The blood was his.

Playing the Scene

1. Is the mood of this play basically tragic or comic?

2. Why does Cyrano conceal his love for Roxane?

3. Is Roxane a shallow character?

4. Is dialogue a dominant element in this play?

5. Is rhythm an important element?

ELIZABETH THE QUEEN

by Maxwell Anderson / excerpt from Act III*

(ELIZABETH, *queen of England, who has sentenced her ambitious young lover,* LORD ESSEX, *to be beheaded for treason against the throne, sends for him an hour before his execution. Some time earlier she had given him a ring with which he could buy his pardon. She hopes, somehow, to avoid the anguish of sending* ESSEX *to his death.*)

ESSEX
. . . I have loved you, love you now, but I know myself.
If I were to win you over and take my place
As it used to be, it would gall me. I have a weakness
For being first wherever I am. I refuse
To take pardon from you without warning you
Of this. And when you know it, pardon becomes
Impossible.

ELIZABETH
You do this for me?

ESSEX
Why, Yes,
But not altogether. Partly for England, too.
I've lost conceit of myself a little. A life
In prison's very quiet. It leads to thinking.
You govern England better than I should.
I'd lead her into wars, make a great name,
Perhaps, like Henry Fifth and leave a legacy
Of debts and bloodshed after me. You will leave
Peace, happiness, something secure. A woman governs
Better than a man, being a natural coward.
A coward rules best.

ELIZABETH
Still bitter.

ESSEX
Perhaps a little.
It's a bitter belief to swallow, but I believe it.
You were right all the time. (*The chimes ring three-quarters.*)

And now, if you'll pardon me,
I have an appointment near-by with a headsman.
He comes sharp on the hour.

ELIZABETH   You have an hour yet.
It's struck five.

ESSEX   It but struck five some time since.

ELIZABETH   It cannot go this way!

ESSEX   Aye, but it has.
It has and will. There's no way out. I've thought of it.
Every way. Speak frankly. Could you forgive me
And keep your throne?

ELIZABETH   No.

ESSEX   Are you ready to give
Your crown up to me?

ELIZABETH   No. It's all I have.   (*She rises.*)
Why, who am I
To stand here paltering with a rebel noble!
I am Elizabeth, daughter of a king.
The queen of England, and you are my subject!
What does this mean, you standing here eye to eye
With me, your liege? You whom I made, and gave
All that you have, you, an upstart, defying
Me to grant pardon, lest you should sweep me from power
And take my place from me? I tell you if Christ his blood
Ran streaming from the heavens for a sign
That I should hold my hand you'd die for this,
You pretender to a throne upon which you have
No claim, you pretender to a heart, who have been
Hollow and heartless and faithless to the end!

ESSEX   If we'd met some other how we might have been happy . . .
But there's been an empire between us! I am to die . . .
Let us say that . . . let us begin with that . . .
For then I can tell you that if there'd been no empire
We could have been great lovers. If even now
You were not queen and I were not pretender,
That god who searches heaven and earth and hell
For two who are perfect lovers, could end his search
With you and me. Remember . . . I am to die . . .
And so I can tell you truly, out of all the earth
That I'm to leave, there's nothing I'm very loath
To leave save you. Yet if I live I'll be
Your death or you'll be mine.

ELIZABETH	Give me the ring.
ESSEX	No.
ELIZABETH	Give me the ring. I'd rather you killed me Than I killed you.
ESSEX	It's better for me as it is Than that I should live and batten my fame and fortune On the woman I love. I've thought of it all. It's better To die young and unblemished than to live long and rule, And rule not well.
ELIZABETH	Aye, I should know that.
ESSEX	Is it not?
ELIZABETH	Yes.
ESSEX	Goodbye, then.
ELIZABETH	Oh, then I'm old, I'm old! I could be young with you, but now I'm old. I know now how it will be without you. The sun Will be empty and circle round an empty earth . . . And I will be queen of emptiness and death . . . Why could you not have loved me enough to give me Your love and let me keep as I was?
ESSEX	I know not. I only know I could not. I must go.
ELIZABETH	(*Frozen*) Yes. (*He goes to the door.*) Lord Essex! (*He turns.*) Take my kingdom. It is yours! (ESSEX, *as if not hearing, bows and goes on.*)

Playing the Scene

1. What is the chief obstacle which stands in the way of a love fulfillment for these characters?
2. Where are there definite changes in the emotion of each character?
3. Where is the emotional high point for each character?
4. Where are there opportunities for effective dramatic pauses?

5. In view of what is known historically about Queen Elizabeth, what voice quality might an actress use in playing the character?
6. How does the language of *Elizabeth the Queen* dictate the style of delivery?

Other Sources for Scenes of Romantic Drama

Hernani by Victor Hugo

Period Styles

The theatre's means of expression are forged by the time in which a play is written and performed, and by the contribution of the past.

Michel Saint-Denis

MOLIÈRE COMEDY

The comedies of Molière vary in type from the farcical commedia dell' arte, *Doctor in Spite of Himself*, through the artificial *The Learned Ladies* to the comparatively realistic *Tartuffe*. The plots are highly complicated and notable for their ingenious intrigue and comic situations. The richly polished language combines a mixture of satire with moral judgments of society. Yet despite the polish and superficial manners, there is a universal quality in these plays. Pomposity, hypocrisy, and deceit are universal traits of character that have appeared in all kinds and conditions of men in every age.

Since these comedies depicting the manners and customs of the seventeenth century are far removed from the experiences and situations occurring in contemporary society, most modern actors find them exceedingly difficult to comprehend and perform.

Manner of Playing

1. The actor should maintain a high degree of objectivity.
2. Elegance of posture, gesture, and movement is highly important.
3. Extensive pantomimic business should be invented.
4. An exaggerated melodic pattern and vocal inflection are essential.
5. On the proscenium stage, the downstage areas are used predominantly.
   (See Plates 43, 44, and 45.)
6. Much of the playing is full-front and in direct contact with the audience.
7. The tempo should be very fast.
8. Typical props of the period are handkerchiefs and fans (ladies), handkerchiefs and a long staff with decorations (gentlemen).

Plate 43. *The Rogueries of Scapin* by Molière. Universal types in farcical situations. Temple University. Director: Arthur O. Ketels. Photograph: R. R. Frame & Co.

Plate 44. *That Scoundrel Scapin* by Molière. Scene depicting commedia dell' arte style. Stanford Repertory Theatre, Stanford University. Director: Erik Vos. Photograph: Hank Krantzler.

Plate 45. *The Imaginary Invalid* by Molière. Comedy achieved through exaggeration of character and situation. Pennsylvania State University. Director: Frank S. Neusbaum. Photograph: Still Photo Studios, Pennsylvania State University.

Practice Selection

THE SCHOOL FOR HUSBANDS

by Molière | Act II, Scenes 5 and 6*

(SGANAREL *plans to marry his ward,* ISABELLA, *and consequently tries to prevent her from meeting young men.* ISABELLA *is in love with young* VALERE *and he with her. She must use her wits and wiles to circumvent* SGANAREL *and communicate with her lover.*)

SCENE 5

ISABELLA	(*To herself entering*) I'm afraid my lover is so full of his passion, that he does not comprehend the intention of my message; and since I'm such a prisoner, I'll run the risk of another that may speak my meaning plainer.
SGANAREL	Here I'm come back.
ISABELLA	Well.
SGANAREL	Your message has had its full effect; your man's business is done. He would have denied that his heart was sick with love, but when I assured him I came from you, he was struck immediately dumb and confounded, and I don't believe he'll come any more hither.
ISABELLA	Ha! What is it you tell me? I very much apprehend the contrary, and that he's again cutting out more work for us.
SGANAREL	What reason have you for this apprehension?
ISABELLA	You were hardly got out of doors, when, putting my head out at window to take the air, I saw a young fellow at yonder turning, who came very surprisingly, to wish me a good morning from that impertinent fellow, and flung a box directly into my chamber, in which was a letter sealed like a *billet-doux.* — I would instantly have thrown it back to him but he had gotten to the end of the street, and my heart swells with vexation at it.
SGANAREL	What knavery! The man's devoid of decency!
ISABELLA	It's my duty to send back immediately the box and letter to this cursed lover, and I shall want somebody for that purpose, for to make bold with you —

---

* Molière, *The School for Husbands.* Everyman's Library, *Poetry and the Drama*, vol. 1. Reprinted by permission of E. P. Dutton, and J. M. Dent.

SGANAREL	On the contrary, dearie, it convinces me the better of your affection and fidelity; my heart accepts the office with joy, and you oblige me by it more than I am able to express.
ISABELLA	Take it then.
SGANAREL	Well, let's see what he has dared to write.
ISABELLA	O Heavens! Do not open it.
SGANAREL	Why not?
ISABELLA	Would you give him reason to believe 'twas I! — A woman of honour ought always to avoid reading the letters a man sends her; the curiosity one then discovers, shows a secret pleasure in hearing one's self commended; and I think it proper this letter should immediately be carried to him, sealed up as it is, that he may so much the better learn how greatly my heart despises him; that his passion may lose all kind of hope henceforward, and no more attempt the like extravagance.
SGANAREL	She has certainly reason for what she says. — Well, your virtue and discretion charm me. I perceive that my instructions are rooted in your soul: and in short, you show that you deserve to be my wife.
ISABELLA	I would not, however, balk your curiosity. You have got the letter, and you may open it.
SGANAREL	Lack-a-day, I don't care; — no, your reasons are too good for that, and I am just going to discharge the trust you put in me; afterwards I shall step a little way to speak a word or two, and then come back to ease your mind.
	SCENE 6
SGANAREL	(*Alone*) How my soul overflows with joy to find her such a prudent girl! She's a treasure of honour in my family! to take the glances of love for treason, receive a *billet-doux* as a very great injury, and send it back again to her gallant by me! I'd fain know, whether upon such an occasion my brother's damsel would have acted thus. Faith, girls are just what they are taught to be. — Soho.

Sources for Additional Study of the Molière Period

Costume books of the seventeenth century

Histories of the Louis XIV period

A History of Theatrical Art, vol. 4, by Karl Mantzius*

* Karl Mantzius, *A History of Theatrical Art*, vol. 4. London: Duckworth, 1905.

Playing the Scene

1. Why is polished delivery particularly essential for these scenes?
2. What is the key to the style of this play?
3. How should the character of Sganarel be interpreted?
4. In this scene what is the relative position of the acting on the actor-character versus actor-performer scale?
5. How will mannerisms and customs of the period contribute to the effectiveness of the scene?
6. Which areas of the stage and which stage body positions should be used predominantly?

RESTORATION COMEDY

The plays of this period (1660–1700) contain a variety of elements: pure farce, the comedy of manners carried over from the continent, and the comedy of humors inherited from Ben Jonson. The theater fare reflected the manners of the Court with its boisterous spirit of an age which, with gay abandon and unrestrained levity, celebrated the end of Puritan rule. Because the life which is portrayed in the Restoration comedies is somewhat removed from the world of reality, these plays have been described as amoral. They were written to appeal to the aristocratic segment of London's society which took supreme delight in amorous adventures, intrigue, and deception. This was an age of smart conversation in which the manner of speaking and clever repartee were often more important than the content of the expression.

The dominant elements of the plays are dialogue and plot. The characters are little more than two-dimensional cardboard figures. Frequently the character's dominant trait is indicated in the dramatis personae, for example, Mrs. Frail and Mr. Vainlove.

Manner of Playing

1. Much attention should be given to the highly polished literary dialogue.
2. Because of the circumlocutory nature of the dialogue, special pitch emphasis and precise diction are needed to communicate the meaning.
3. An exaggerated melodic pattern is definitely befitting.
4. Although the characters are highly amusing, often likeable, there is generally a lack of audience empathy.

(See Plates 46, 47, 48, and 49.)

5. The actor's approach to his character should be distinctly objective. In a manner of speaking, he is standing apart from the character he is playing. In no sense does he, as in naturalism, "live the part."
6. Much emphasis and care should be given to the manners of the period: bowing, walking, standing, and sitting.
7. In this period, gentlemen walked with a definite stride, accompanied by a rotation of the hips. Fops walked with small, mincing steps.
8. The use of snuff was customary and the taking of snuff, according to Oxenford, was a studied ceremony. The snuff box was held in the left hand. The right hand tapped the lid to settle the snuff. The left thumb released the spring catch on the lid. A pinch of snuff was taken with the right thumb and second finger and deposited on the back of the left hand which was then lifted to the nostrils. In some cases, the snuff was taken directly from the thumb and second finger.*
9. The ladies made much use of the fan which "can almost be classed as a weapon; it was used for skirmishes, pitched battles, and ab-

---

* Lyn Oxenford, *Playing Period Plays*. Chicago: Coch House, 1959, pp. 218–219.

Plate 46. *The Beaux Stratagem* by George Farquhar. The rogues are engaged, man to man, in Restoration style. Carnegie Institute of Technology. Director: Bernie Engel.

solute surrender."* The overall effect of the gestures and pantomimic business should be one of high polish and affectation.

10. Graceful movement was a part of a Restoration lady's education. Movement was graceful, poised, lively, and spirited, almost to the effect of a bounce.
11. Much of the acting of the period was at center and toward the front of the stage.
12. The full-front and one-quarter body positions were used predominantly.

Sources for Additional Study of the Restoration Period

Restoration Comedy 1660–1720 by Bonamy Dobree

A History of Restoration Drama 1660–1700 by Allardyce Nicoll

Playing Period Plays by Lyn Oxenford

---

* *Ibid.*, p. 185.

Plate 47. *The Way of the World* by William Congreve. Affectation personified. University of Hawaii. Director: Edward Langhans.

Plate 48. *The Beggar's Opera* by John Gay. Note the exaggerated display of emotions as Mr. and Mrs. Peachum stare in amazement on hearing of Polly's affairs. Stanford Repertory Theater, Stanford University. Director: John Wright. Photograph: Hank Kranzler.

Plate 49. *Love for Love* by William Congreve. Note the use of the center front area, the almost full-front body positions, and the posture of individual characters. University of Iowa. Director: Peter Arnott.

Practice Selection

LOVE FOR LOVE

by William Congreve | excerpt from Act II, Scene 2

SCENE	*A room in* FORESIGHT's *house.*
CHARACTERS	MISS PRUE, *a silly awkward country girl, daughter of* FORESIGHT *by a former wife,* TATTLE, *a half-witted beau, vain of his amours, yet valuing himself for secrecy*
SITUATION	MRS. FORESIGHT *and* MRS. FRAIL *have just left the room.* TATTLE *seizes the opportunity to have an assignation with* MISS PRUE.

PRUE   What makes 'em go away, Mr. Tattle? What do they mean, do you know?

TATTLE   Yes, my dear, — I think I can guess; — but hang me if I know the reason of it.

PRUE   Come, must not we go too?

TATTLE   No, no, they don't mean that.

PRUE   No! what then? what shall you and I do together?

TATTLE   I must make love to you, pretty miss; will you let me make love to you?

PRUE   Yes, if you please.

TATTLE   (*Aside*) Frank, egad, at least. What a pox does Mrs. Foresight mean by this civility? Is it to make a fool of me? or does she leave us together out of good morality, and do as she would be done by? — Gad, I'll understand it so.

PRUE   Well; and how will you make love to me? Come, I long to have you begin. Must I make love, too? You must tell me how.

TATTLE   You must let me speak, miss, you must not speak first; I must ask you questions, and you must answer.

PRUE   What, is it like the catechism? — Come then, ask me.

TATTLE   D'ye think you can love me?

PRUE   Yes.

TATTLE   Pooh! pox! you must not say yes already; I shan't care a farthing for you then in a twinkling.

PRUE   What must I say then?

TATTLE	Why, you must say no, or you believe not, or you can't tell.
PRUE	Why, must I tell a lie then?
TATTLE	Yes, if you'd be well-bred; — all well-bred persons lie. — Besides, you are a woman, you must never speak what you think; your words must contradict your thoughts; but your actions may contradict your words. So, when I ask you, if you can love me, you must say no, but you must love me too. If I tell you you are handsome, you must deny it, and say I flatter you. But you must think yourself more charming than I speak you: and like me, for the beauty which I say you have, as much as if I had it myself. If I ask you to kiss me, you must be angry, but you must not refuse me. If I ask you for more, you must be more angry, — but more complying; and as soon as ever I make you say you'll cry out, you must be sure to hold your tongue.
PRUE	O Lord, I swear this is pure! — I like it better than our old-fashioned country way of speaking one's mind; — and must you lie too?
TATTLE	Hum! — Yes; but you must believe I speak truth.
PRUE	O Gemini! well, I always had a great mind to tell lies: but they frighted me, and said it was a sin.
TATTLE	Well, my pretty creature, will you make me happy by giving me a kiss?
PRUE	No, indeed; I'm angry at you. (*Runs and kisses him.*)
TATTLE	Hold, hold, that's pretty well; — but you should not have given it me, but have suffered me to have taken it.
PRUE	Well, we'll do't again.
TATTLE	With all my heart. — Now then, my little angel! (*Kisses her.*)
PRUE	Pish!
TATTLE	That's right — again, my charmer! (*Kisses her again.*)
PRUE	O fie! nay, now I can't abide you.
TATTLE	Admirable! that was as well as if you had been born and bred in Covent Garden. And won't you show me, pretty miss, where your bedchamber is?
PRUE	No, indeed, won't I; but I'll run there and hide myself behind the curtains.
TATTLE	I'll follow you.
PRUE	Ah, but I'll hold the door with both hands, and be angry; — and you shall push me down before you come in.

TATTLE	No, I'll come in first, and push you down afterwards.
PRUE	Will you? Then I'll be more angry, and more complying.
TATTLE	Then I'll make you cry out.
PRUE	Oh, but you shan't; for I'll hold my tongue.
TATTLE	Oh, my dear apt scholar!
PRUE	Well, now I'll run and make more haste than you.
TATTLE	You shall not fly so fast as I'll pursue. (*Exuent.*)

Playing the Scene

1. How true to real life are these characters?

2. Where would you place these characters on the actor-character versus the actor-performer scale?

3. How should the "aside" speech be delivered?

4. What style of line interpretation seems to be most effective for this scene?

5. How much movement seems inherent in the scene?

6. Should additional movement be superimposed?

Other Sources for Scenes of Restoration Comedy

The Man of Mode by Sir George Etherege
The Country Wife by William Wycherley

LATE EIGHTEENTH-CENTURY COMEDY

Comedy of Goldsmith and Sheridan

The plays of Goldsmith and Sheridan represent a breaking away from the sentimental comedy tradition of the first half of the eighteenth century as exemplified by Colley Cibber's *Careless Husband* (1704) or Sir Richard Steele's *The Conscious Lovers* (1722). Goldsmith took as his model the romantic comedies of Shakespeare, while Sheridan's plays revive the style and spirit of the Restoration. It may be said that in these plays the essence of true comedy, appealing to the intellect and not to the heart, adorned and illuminated all too briefly the eighteenth-century English stage. There are, naturally, definite similarities to the Restoration comedies: brilliant wit, barbed satire, and the vivid protrayal of the manners of the period. But there is this difference: both Goldsmith and Sheridan place more emphasis on characterization than was the case with the Restoration writers of comedy.

Goldsmith's *She Stoops to Conquer* (1773) contains obvious farcical elements and, indeed, might be played more successfully as a farce. But, as Nicoll points out, "its characterization and its delicacy of dialogue deservedly make it one of the most popular of eighteenth-century comedies."*

Plate 50. *She Stoops to Conquer* by Oliver Goldsmith. Note the exaggerated facial expressions and the profile positions, a variation from the usual full-front manner of playing. Bowling Green State University. Director: Robert R. Findlay. Photograph: Gary L. Hager Studios, Bowling Green, Ohio.

Manner of Playing

1. Emotionalism and sentimentality should be avoided.

2. It is advisable to play to the intellect of the audience.

3. The dialogue and plot elements should receive primary consideration.

4. Precise diction, exaggerated vocal variety, and satiric pointing is needed.

5. The pace is rapid; the stage movement is fluid and sweeping.

6. The characters are types, as in the Restoration comedies, but in many instances contain more depth and subtlety.

(See *She Stoops to Conquer*, Plate 50.)

---

* Allardyce Nicoll, *World Drama*. London: George G. Harrap, 1949, p. 394.

Practice Selection

SHE STOOPS TO CONQUER

by Oliver Goldsmith | excerpt from Act III

(*A chamber in* HARDCASTLE's *house.* MR. MARLOW, *a timid man, except with women of the common sort, has come seeking the hand of* MISS HARDCASTLE. *Her brother,* TONY, *in jest, has directed* MARLOW *to her house with the mistaken notion that it is an Inn.* MISS HARDCASTLE, *to attract his attentions and ease his timidity, poses as a maid.*)

MARLOW	What a bawling in every part of the house; I have scarce a moment's repose. If I go to the best room, there I find my host and his story. If I fly to the gallery, there we have my hostess with her curtsey down to the ground. I have at last got a moment to myself, and now for recollection. (*Walks and muses.*)
MISS HARDCASTLE	Did you call, sir? did your honour call?
MARLOW	(*Musing*) As for Miss Hardcastle, she's too grave and sentimental for me.
MISS HARDCASTLE	Did your honour call? (*She still places herself before him, he turning away.*)
MARLOW	No, child. (*Musing*) Besides from the glimpse I had of her, I think she squints.
MISS HARDCASTLE	I'm sure, sir, I heard the bell ring.
MARLOW	No! no! (*Musing.*) I have pleased my father, however, by coming down, and I'll to-morrow please myself by returning. (*Taking out his tablets, and perusing*)
MISS HARDCASTLE	Perhaps the other gentleman called, sir? We have such a parcel of servants.
MARLOW	No, no, I tell you. (*Looks full in her face.*) Yes, child, I think I did call. I wanted — I wanted — I vow, child, you are vastly handsome!
MISS HARDCASTLE	O la, sir, you'll make one ashamed.
MARLOW	Never saw a more sprightly malicious eye. — Yes, yes, my dear, I did call. Have you got any of your — a — what dy'e call it, in the house?
MISS HARDCASTLE	No, sir, we have been out of that these ten days.
MARLOW	One may call in this house, I find, to very little purpose. Suppose I should call for a taste, just by way of trial, of the nectar of your lips; perhaps I might be disappointed in that, too!
MISS HARDCASTLE	Nectar! nectar! that's a liquor there's no call for in these parts. French, I suppose. We keep no French wines here, sir.

MARLOW	Of true English growth, I assure you.
MISS HARDCASTLE	Then it's odd I should not know it. We brew all sorts of wines in this house, and I have lived here these eighteen years.
MARLOW	Eighteen years! Why one would think, child, you kept the bar before you were born. How old are you?
MISS HARDCASTLE	O! sir, I must not tell my age. They say women and music should never be dated.
MARLOW	To guess at this distance, you can't be much above forty. (*Approaching*) Yet nearer, I don't think so much. (*Approaching*) By coming close to some women they look younger still; but when we come very close indeed. (*Attempting to kiss her.*)
MISS HARDCASTLE	Pray, sir, keep your distance. One would think you wanted to know one's age as they do horses, by mark of mouth.
MARLOW	I protest, child, you use me extremely ill. If you keep me at this distance, how is it possible you and I can be ever acquainted?
MISS HARDCASTLE	And who wants to be acquainted with you? I want no such acquaintance, not I. I'm sure you did not treat Miss Hardcastle that was here awhile ago in this obstropalous manner. I'll warrant me, before her you looked dashed, and kept bowing to the ground, and talked, for all the world, as if you was before a justice of peace.
MARLOW	(*Aside*) Egad! She has hit it, sure enough. (*To her*) In awe of her, child? Ha! ha! ha! A mere awkward, squinting thing, no, no! I find you don't know me. I laughed, and rallied her a little; but I was unwilling to be too severe. No, I could not be too severe, curse me!
MISS HARDCASTLE	O! then, sir, you are a favourite, I find, among the ladies?
MARLOW	Yes, my dear, a great favourite. And yet, hang me, I don't see what they find in me to follow. At the Ladies' Club in town I'm called their agreeable Rattle. Rattle, child, is not my real name, but one I'm known by. My name is Jenkins. Mr. Jenkins, my dear, at your service. (*Offering to salute her*)
MISS HARDCASTLE	Hold, sir; you were introducing me to your club, not to yourself. And you're so great a favourite there you say?
MARLOW	Yes, my dear. There's Mrs. Mantrap, Lady Betty Blackleg, the Countess of Sligo, Mrs. Longhorns, old Miss Biddy Buckskin, and your humble servant, keep up the spirit of the place.
MISS HARDCASTLE	Then it's a very merry place, I suppose.

MARLOW	Yes, as merry as cards, suppers, wine, and old women can make us.
MISS HARDCASTLE	And their agreeable Rattle, ha! ha! ha!
MARLOW	(*Aside*) Egad! I don't quite like this chit. She looks knowing, me thinks. You laugh, child!
MISS HARDCASTLE	I can't but laugh, to think what time they all have for minding their work or their family.
MARLOW	(*Aside*) All's well, she don't laugh at me. (*To her*) Do *you* ever work, child?
MISS HARDCASTLE	Ay, sure. There's not a screen or a quilt in the whole house but what can bear witness to that.
MARLOW	Odso! Then you must show me your embroidery. I embroider and draw patterns myself a little. If you want a judge of your work you must apply to me. (*Seizing her hand*)
MISS HARDCASTLE	Ay, but the colours don't look well by candle light. You shall see all in the morning. (*Struggling*)
MARLOW	And why not now, my angel? Such beauty fires beyond the power of resistance. — Pshaw! the father here! My old luck! (*Exit* MARLOW.)

Playing the Scene

1. What should be the audience reaction to Marlow?

2. Is there a danger that Marlow might receive detrimental empathy from the audience? How may this be avoided?

3. Should this scene be played for comic or farcical values?

4. How may the situation be made more believable?

5. What devices and techniques may Miss Hardcastle employ in order to be convincing as a barmaid?

Plate 51. *The Marriage of Figaro* by Pierre de Beaumarchais. Intrigue, deception, and discovery. Ohio State University. Director: Everett M. Schreck.

Photograph: Department of Photography, Ohio State University.

The sentimental comedy of Beaumarchais

The most notable plays of Beaumarchais, *The Barber of Seville* and *The Marriage of Figaro* (1784), reveal a marked departure from those of Goldsmith and Sheridan. The shift is from the head toward the heart, for we see in Beaumarchais' plays definite tendencies toward romance and sentimentalism. Although his character, Figaro, is a masterpiece of comedy portrayal, Beaumarchais is primarily interested in action and intrigue. In these dramatic devices he is, indeed, a master.

Another notable characteristic of Beaumarchais' plays is the intermingling of comic action with social and political comment. Indeed, there were years of controversy before Louis XVI granted Beaumarchais permission to present *The Marriage of Figaro*. This play ridiculing the aristocracy was a most daring forerunner of the French Revolution. (See Plate 51.)

Manner of Playing

1. More emphasis should be given to characterization than is called for in the plays of Goldsmith and Sheridan.

2. A gay, rollicking, comic spirit should be maintained.

3. The social and political comments in the play should be underscored.

4. Much vocal variety is needed.

5. There is much physical action.

6. The actors should play almost entirely on their feet (really on their toes).

7. There is very little occasion to sit in the plays of this period and style.

Practice Selection

THE MARRIAGE OF FIGARO

by Beaumarchais | excerpt from Act V*

(*The* COUNT *seeks an assignation with* SUZANNE, *who is betrothed to* FIGARO. *In order to trap the* COUNT *and teach him a lesson for his perfidy, the* COUNTESS *and* SUZANNE *devise a plan. In the wedding party procession,* SUZANNE *kneels before the* COUNT *and secretly gives him a note, in which she arranges to meet him in the garden by the pavilion. The* COUNTESS *and* SUZANNE *will both go to the garden, each disguised as the other. The* COUNT *meets the* COUNTESS, *disguised as* SUZANNE, *and makes love to her.* FIGARO *observes the scene from one side and thinks that* SUZANNE *is unfaithful to him. When* SUZANNE *appears in her disguise,* FIGARO *thinks it is the* COUNTESS.)

FIGARO
(*Looking to see where the* COUNT *and the* COUNTESS, *whom he takes for* SUZANNE, *are going*) I don't hear anything any more; they've entered the pavilion. Well, that's that. (*In a changed voice*) You other clumsy husbands, who hire spies and turn for months around a suspicion without verifying it, why don't you imitate me? From the first day I follow her and listen closely; with a flick of the wrist, I get at the point. Fortunately I'm not the worrying type and her deception doesn't matter to me in the least. In a word I have everything under control!

SUZANNE
(*Coming forward softly in the dark, aside*) You'll pay for your pretty suspicions. (*In the* COUNTESS' *voice*) Who's there?

FIGARO
(*Extravagantly*) "Who's there?" He who heartily wishes that the plague had stifled him at birth . . .

SUZANNE
(*In the* COUNTESS' *voice*) Oh! Why, it's Figaro!

FIGARO
(*Looking and listening closely*) Madame!

SUZANNE
Speak softly.

FIGARO
(*Quickly*) Ah! Madame, heaven sent you here just at the right time! Where do you think your husband is?

SUZANNE
What does that ingrate matter to me? Tell me . . .

FIGARO
(*More quickly*) That Sue whom everyone thought so virtuous, who pretended to be so reserved! They're locked in there together. I'm going to call.

---

* Beaumarchais, *The Marriage of Figaro.* Translated by Charlotte F. Gerrard.

SUZANNE	(*Covering his mouth with her hand, forgetting to disguise her voice*) Don't call out.
FIGARO	(*Aside*) Oh! It's Sue! Goddam!
SUZANNE	(*In the* COUNTESS' *voice*) You seem disturbed.
FIGARO	(*Aside*) You want to fool me!
SUZANNE	We must get revenge, Figaro.
FIGARO	Is that what you desire?
SUZANNE	If I didn't, I wouldn't belong to my sex! But men have a hundred means.
FIGARO	(*Confidently*) Madame, there's no one around. Women's means are . . . the best of all.
SUZANNE	(*Aside*) How I'd like to slap him!
FIGARO	(*Aside*) It would really be gay before the wedding! . . .
SUZANNE	But what is revenge, unseasoned by a little love?
FIGARO	Even though it hides itself, be assured that deep homage is at your disposal.
SUZANNE	(*Piqued*) I don't know whether you believe that in good faith, but you don't say it with good grace.
FIGARO	(*With comic warmth, on his knees*) Ah! Madame, I adore you. Examine the time, place, circumstances, and let spite supply in you the graciousness, which my entreaty lacks.
SUZANNE	(*Aside*) My hand itches.
FIGARO	(*Aside*) My heart is pounding.
SUZANNE	But have you considered — ?
FIGARO	Yes, Madame, yes I've considered.
SUZANNE	That in anger and love . . .
FIGARO	He who hesitates is lost. Your hand, Madame?
SUZANNE	(*In her natural voice and giving him a slap*) There it is!
FIGARO	Ah! You little fiend! What a slap!
SUZANNE	(*Giving him another*) "What a slap!" What about this one?
FIGARO	And what's this? Is today the slapping day?

SUZANNE	(*Hitting him at each sentence*) Ah! "What's this?", is it? Here's one for your suspicions; and here are some more for your revenge, your deception, your expedients, your insults and your plans. Is that love? Is that the way you talked this morning?
FIGARO	(*Laughing and getting up*) Saint Barbara! Yes, that's love. Oh, lucky Figaro! Strike, my darling, till you get tired. But after I'm black and blue, look kindly, Sue, on the most fortunate man who was ever beaten by a woman.
SUZANNE	"The most fortunate!" You rogue, you weren't seducing the Countess any the less, with such a deceiving babble! Why, I, forgetting myself, was really yielding for her.
FIGARO	Could I mistake the sound of your pretty voice?
SUZANNE	(*Laughing*) Did you recognize me? Ah! Revenge will be sweet!
FIGARO	To thrash somebody soundly and still to bear a grudge — that's a woman for you! But tell me how you can be here, when I thought you were with . . .
SUZANNE	Well! It's you who are the innocent, to fall into a trap prepared for someone else! Is it our fault if, wishing to muzzle a fox, we catch two?
FIGARO	Who is catching the other?
SUZANNE	His wife.
FIGARO	His wife?
SUZANNE	His wife.
FIGARO	(*Wildly*) Ah! Figaro, go hang yourself! You didn't guess that! His wife? Oh, females, the weaker, wittier sex! So all those kisses out here?
SUZANNE	Were given to Madame.
FIGARO	And the page's?
SUZANNE	(*Laughing*) To His Excellency.
FIGARO	And earlier, behind the armchair?
SUZANNE	To no one.
FIGARO	Are you sure?
SUZANNE	(*Laughing, and shaking her fist*) Figaro!
FIGARO	(*Kissing her hand*) Your blows are jewels. But the Count's were the real thing.

SUZANNE	Now, superb fellow! Humble yourself.
FIGARO	(*Doing what he says*) That's fair; on my knees, bent well over, prostrate, my chest on the floor.
SUZANNE	(*Laughing*) Ah! the poor Count! What trouble he's gone to ...
FIGARO	(*Getting to his knees*) To achieve the conquest of his wife!

Playing the Scene

1. How may the mistaken identity be made more believable?

2. Is a high degree of reality required for this scene?

3. Should Figaro and Suzanne receive admiration and sympathy from the audience?

4. How will it affect the performance if the audience is unsympathetic?

5. What devices might Suzanne use to imitate the Countess?

6. How should the asides be delivered?

7. Wherein does the superior knowledge of the audience heighten the comedy of the scene?

8. What mood level of comedy seems most appropriate for this scene?

NINETEENTH-CENTURY MELODRAMA

Plays of this type are characterized by involved plots, two-dimensional type characters, and dialogue which is exaggerated, adorned, highly emotional, and often sentimental. In spite of this, the plays were taken seriously and were thoroughly enjoyed by the audiences of their day.

Influence of theatrical conditions. As was true of other periods, the style of acting was in part an attempt to compensate for the theatrical conditions of the period. The theaters were generally large, often with three or four balconies. As a consequence, a considerable portion of the audience was remote from the stage. The illumination, by oil or gas until late in the century, was of low intensity. Under these conditions, intimate, conversational speech and small, detailed gestures would have been ineffective. Although the overall intent of the melodramas was to achieve realism, by standards of today the acting was highly artificial. (See *Under the Gaslight*, Plate 52.)

Manner of Playing

1. Catching the flavor of the period is important.

2. Interpreting the intent of the playwright seems the best approach.

3. Making fun of the play, as is sometimes done, is a questionable procedure.

4. There is an exaggerated use of postures, gestures, and facial expressions.

5. Each character usually represents one dominant trait.

6. The "grand" style is often used in the delivery of the dialogue.

Plate 52. *Under the Gaslight* by Augustin Daly. This scene from the famous melodrama makes its own comment. University of Minnesota. Director: Frank M. Whiting.

Practice Selection

THE DRUNKARD, or THE FALLEN SAVED

*adapted by Wm. H. Smith | opening scene of Act I**

CHARACTERS   MRS. WILSON, MARY, LAWYER CRIBBS

SCENE   *Interior of a pretty rural cottage. Flowers, paintings, etc. Everything exhibits refined taste, and elegant simplicity. Table, with Bible and armchair, R. Table and chair with embroidery frame, L.* MRS. WILSON *discovered in armchair, R.* MARY *seated by table, L.*

MRS. WILSON   It was in that corner, Mary, where your poor father breathed his last — this chair is indeed dear to me for it was in this he sat the very day before he died. Oh how he loved this calm retreat, and often in his last illness he rejoiced that the companion of his youth would close his eyes in these rural shades, and be laid in yon little nook beside him; but now —

MARY   Dear mother. It is true, this sweet cottage is most dear to us. But we are not the proprietors. Old Mr. Middleton never troubled us much. But as our late worthy landlord is no more, it is generally believed that our dear cottage will be sold. We cannot censure his son for that.

MRS. WILSON   No; the young must be provided for, and willingly would I bow with resignation to that great power that loveth while it chasteneth; but when I think that you, my beloved child, will be left exposed to the thousand temptations of life, a penniless orphan. (*A knock* C. D.) Hark! who knocks? Dry your tears, my darling. Come in. (*Enter —* LAWYER CRIBBS C. D. — *comes down* C.) Good morning, sir. Mary, my child, a chair.

CRIBBS   (*Sitting,* L. C.) Good morning, Mrs. Wilson; good morning, my dear young lady. A sad calamity has befallen the neighborhood, my good Mrs. Wilson.

MRS. WILSON   Many a poor person, I fear, will have reason to think so, sir.

CRIBBS   Yes, yes. You are right. Ah, he was a good man, that Mr. Middleton. I knew him well. He placed great confidence in my advice.

MARY   Was he not very rich once, Mr. Cribbs?

CRIBBS   Yes, yes; when the times were good, but bad speculations, unlucky investments, false friends — alas! alas! we have all our ups and downs, my dear madam!

---

* *The Drunkard* was originally performed at the Museum, Boston, in 1844. It became one of the most popular of the nineteenth-century melodramas. It was presented by Theater Mart in Los Angeles from the late thirties for a period of some twenty years.

MRS. WILSON	Ah! Mr. Cribbs, I perceive you are a man, who —
CRIBBS	Has a heart to feel for the unfortunate. True, madam, it is the character I have attained, though I am not the man to boast. Have you any prospect of — that is — have you provided —
MARY	It is true then, too true, the cottage and garden will be sold?
CRIBBS	Why, what can the young man do, my dear? A gay young man like him. Fond of the world, given somewhat to excess, no doubt. But pardon me, my dear Miss Mary; I would not call up a blush on the cheek of modesty. But you know, the extravagance, that is, the folly —
MRS. WILSON	All, sir. I understand you — very much unlike his father I would say.
CRIBBS	I place great confidence in your prudence, Mrs. Wilson. I wish the young man well, with all my heart. Heaven knows I have cause to do so for his honored father's sake. (*Puts a handkerchief to his eyes.*)
MRS. WILSON	Come, come, Mr. Cribbs, he is better off. It is impiety to mourn a good man's death. His end was that of a Christian.
CRIBBS	Judge then of the interest which I take in the last remaining scion of that honored stock. But, madam, Edward Middleton. He is yet young, and —
MRS. WILSON	I think he is not more than twenty, I recollect him when a lad, a bright, blue-eyed boy, with flaxen hair, tall of his age.
CRIBBS	Twenty-three last July, madam; that is his age precisely — he is giddy, wild and reckless. As the good man says, "when I was a child, I thought as a child." (*A pause —* CRIBBS *looks around the room.*) Well, madam, business is business. I am a plain man, Mrs. Wilson, and sometimes called too blunt — and — and —
MARY	You mean to say that we must leave the cottage, sir.
CRIBBS	(*Pretending feeling*) No, not *yet*, my dear young lady — I would say it is best to be prepared, and as Edward is sudden in all his movements, and as my entreaties would never change him — why, if you could find a place before he moves in the matter, it might save you from much inconvenience, that's all.
MRS. WILSON	You impose upon us a severe task, my dear sir.
CRIBBS	Bear up, my dear madam, bear up. If I may be so officious, I would try Boston — at the Intelligence Offices there, any healthy young woman, like your daughter, can obtain a profitable situation — think of it, think of it, my good madam. I will see you again soon, and now heaven bless you. (*Exit, C. D. and off* L. — MRS. WILSON *and* MARY *look for a moment at each other, and then embrace.*)

MRS. WILSON	Well, comfort, my daughter, comfort. It is a good thing to have a friend in the hour of trouble. This Mr. Cribbs appears to be a very feeling man; but before taking his advice, we would do well to make our proposed trial of this young man, Edward Middleton. You have the money in your purse?
MARY	It is all here, mother. Thirty dollars — the sum we have saved to purchase fuel for the winter.
MRS. WISLON	That will partially pay the rent score. When this young man finds we are disposed to deal fairly with him, he may relent. You turn pale, Mary; what ails my child?
MARY	Dear mother, it is nothing: it will soon be over — it must be done. I fear this young man. He has been described so wild, so reckless. I feel a sad foreboding.
MRS. WILSON	Fear not, Mary; call him to the door. Refuse to enter the house — give him the money, and tell him your sad story. He must, from family and association at least, have the manners of a gentleman — and however wild a youth may be, when abroad among his associates, no gentleman ever insulted a friendless and unprotected woman.
MARY	You give me courage, dear mother. I should be an unnatural child, if — (*Aside*) — yet I am agitated. Oh, why do I tremble thus? (*Puts on a village bonnet, etc.*)
MRS. WILSON	(*Kisses her*) Go forth, my child — go as the dove flew from the ark of old, and if thou shouldst fail in finding the olive branch of peace, return, and seek comfort where thou shalt surely find it — in the bosom of the fond and widowed mother. (*Exit* R. D., *and* MARY, C. D.)

Playing the Scene

1. To what extent should Mr. Cribbs' villainy be apparent to the audience?
2. Why does Mr. Cribbs appear to Mrs. Wilson and Mary as a friend to be trusted?
3. For what values should this scene be played?
4. Should the actors play for laughs?
5. What was the probable audience reaction to *The Drunkard* when it was originally played in the middle of the nineteenth century?

Other Sources for Scenes of Nineteenth-Century Melodrama

Ten Nights in a Barroom by William W. Pratt
Streets of New York by Dion Boucicault

Chapter twelve
Modern Styles

For Dionysus is immortal and the theatre lives alway.
Sheldon Cheney

EXPRESSIONIST DRAMA

The expressionistic style of drama developed in Germany, or more particularly, in Berlin during the period between 1910 and 1920. Although in its pure form it did not establish a firm and lasting foothold in the theater, its influence is evident in dramas such as *Beggar on Horseback*, written in 1924 by George S. Kaufman and Marc Connelly.

In expressionistic plays idea or theme is the dominant element. All other elements of the play — plot, characterization, dialogue, spectacle, and lyrical quality — are modified, exaggerated, or distorted for the sake of expressing the prevailing theme more forcibly. All the devices known to the theater — narrator, chorus, aside, soliloquy, projections, flashbacks, sounds, music, and dance — are utilized. Rhythm is often used for its emotional and theatrical effect. As a rule, the plot structure is loose, consisting often of episodic scenes or pictures which present various facets of the dominant idea. The scenes often have little logical or sequential relationship. The dialogue may be fragmentary or telescopic, or it may consist of long, emotional speeches. The characters may be realistic, fantastic, symbolic, grotesque, mechanized, or puppet-like. In some expressionistic plays the audience sees the play through the distorted vision of the central character.

Manner of Playing

1. A sufficient degree of reality to achieve audience acceptance, credibility, and understanding should be maintained.
2. Primarily, the meaning of the play must be communicated.
3. A great range of all the vocal elements is required.
4. Pantomimic business is highly selective and significant.
5. Movement, often unmotivated, sometimes machine-like, is used for its theatrical effectiveness as well as to underscore the theme.

Practice Selection

THE ADDING MACHINE

by Elmer Rice | Scene 2*

SCENE
An office in a department store. Wood and glass partitions. In the middle of the room, two tall desks back to back. At one desk on a high stool is ZERO. *Opposite him at the other desk, also on a high stool, is* DAISY DIANA DOROTHEA DEVORE, *a plain middle-aged woman. Both wear green eye shades and paper sleeve protectors. A pendent electric lamp throws light upon both desks.* DAISY *reads aloud figures from a pile of slips which lies before her. As she reads the figures,* ZERO *enters them upon a large square sheet of ruled paper which lies before him.*

DAISY
(*Reading aloud*) Three ninety-eight. Forty-two cents. A dollar fifty. A dollar fifty. A dollar twenty-five. Two dollars. Thirty-nine cents. Twenty-seven fifty.

ZERO
(*Petulantly*) Speed it up a little, cancha?

DAISY
What's the rush? To-morrer's another day.

ZERO
Aw, you make me sick.

DAISY
An' you make me sicker.

ZERO
Go on. Go on. We're losin' time.

DAISY
Then quit bein' so bossy. (*She reads.*) Three dollars. Two sixty-nine. Eighty-one fifty. Forty dollars. Eight seventy-five. Who do you think you are, anyhow?

ZERO
Never mind who I think I am. You tend to your work.

DAISY
Aw, don't be givin' me so many orders. Sixty cents. Twenty-four cents. Seventy-five cents. A dollar fifty. Two fifty. One fifty. Two fifty. I don't have to take it from you and what's more I won't.

ZERO
Aw, quit talkin'.

DAISY   I'll talk all I want. Three dollars. Fifty cents. Fifty cents. Seven dollars. Fifty cents. Two fifty. Three fifty. Fifty cents. One fifty. Fifty cents. (*She goes on bending over the slips and transferring them from one pile to another.* ZERO *bends over his desk, busily entering the figures.*)

ZERO   (*Without looking up*) You make me sick. Always shootin' off your face about somethin'. Talk, talk, talk. Just like all the other women. Women make me sick.

DAISY   (*Busily fingering the slips*) Who do you think you are, anyhow? Bossin' me around. I don't have to take it from you, and what's more I won't. (*They both attend closely to their work, neither looking up.*)

ZERO   Women make me sick. They're all alike. The judge gave her six months. I wonder what they do in the work-house. Peel potatoes, I'll bet she's sore at me. Maybe she'll try to kill me when she gets out. I better be careful.

Playing the Scene

1. What is the attitude of each character toward the other?

2. Are the comments of each character a true expression of his feelings?

3. May the content of the lines in this scene be taken literally?

4. Which lines of dialogue are not supposed to be heard by the other character?

5. How may the actor differentiate, in his delivery, between the dialogue which consists of the character's inner thoughts and the lines which the other character is supposed to hear?

Other Sources for Scenes of Expressionist Drama

Beggar on Horseback by Marc Connelly and George S. Kaufman

From Morn to Midnight by Georg Kaiser

The Dream Play by August Strindberg

The Emperor Jones by Eugene O'Neill

The Theatre of the Soul by Nikolai Evreinov

EPIC DRAMA

Epic drama deals with themes of larger scope than is usually the case in tragedy. Typical of epic drama is Brecht's *Mother Courage* which is a chronicle of the Thirty Years' War. The epic plot is usually loose, fragmentary, and episodic. Idea, the dominant element, is often given a direct, didactic, and propagandistic treatment. The language may vary from journalistic prose to poetry, with frequent interpolations of songs. The characters are generally realistic but may, as is the case with expressionism, vary in the degree of lifelike representation.

Brecht, the chief exponent of epic drama, advocates minimizing the emotions of the characters while stressing the idea of the play. This is not to say that scenes in epic drama are not emotional or that the emotion is not conveyed to the audience. Brecht seeks an alienation of the audience. By this production device the audience is induced to think rather than feel.

Manner of Playing

1. In certain respects, the epic style of acting stands at the opposite pole from naturalism.

2. Instead of living the part, the epic actor seems to stand apart and comment on the character.

3. The dominant purpose is to de-emotionalize the scene while stressing the idea. (See Plate 53.)

Plate 53. *The Skin of Our Teeth* by Thornton Wilder. Note the exaggeration of characterization which emphasizes the idea. Eastern Illinois University. Director: E. G. Gabbard. Photograph: Bertram Studio, Charleston, Illinois.

Practice Selection

THE PRIVATE LIFE OF THE MASTER RACE

by Bertolt Brecht | Section 9*

(*It is evening. A woman is packing. She is picking out the things she wants to take with her. Sometimes she takes an article out of the bag again and puts it back in its place so that she can pack something else. She hesitates a long time over a large picture of her husband which is on the dressing table. In the end she leaves it where it is. Getting tired of packing, she sits for a few moments on a suitcase, her head propped on her hand. Then she goes to the telephone. . . . She hangs up and calls no more numbers. She has been smoking. She now burns the little book in which she has looked up the telephone numbers. She walks up and down a couple of times. Then she begins to speak. She is trying out the little speech which she wishes to make to her husband. One sees that he is supposedly sitting in a certain chair.*)

THE WIFE

Yes, I'm packing. You mustn't act as if you hadn't noticed in the last few days . . . Fritz, everything is tolerable except one thing; that we're not looking each other in the eyes during the last hour that remains to us. That they shall not achieve — the liars who set everyone lying. Ten years ago when somebody thought no one could tell I was Jewish you quickly said; "Oh, yes, they can tell." And I liked that. It was clear-headed. Why evade the issue now? I'm packing because otherwise they'll take away your position as chief surgeon at the clinic. And because they already cut you there to your face and because already you can't sleep at night. I don't want you to tell me not to go. I'm going in a hurry because I don't want to have you tell me I *should* go. It's a question of time. Character is a question of time. It lasts for a certain length of time, just like a glove. There are good ones that last a long time. But they don't last forever. Incidentally, I'm not angry. And yet; I am. Why should I always be so understanding? What's wrong with the shape of my nose and the color of my hair? They want me to quit the town where I was born lest they should need to give me butter. What kind of men are you all? What kind of a man are you? You people discover the Quantum theory and let yourselves be bossed by half-savages; you have to conquer the world, but are not allowed to have the wife you want. Artificial respiration and every shot a hit! You're monsters or the bootlickers of monsters. Yes, this is unreasonable of me, but what use is reason in such a world? There you sit watching your wife pack and say nothing. The walls have ears, don't they? And you all say nothing! One lot listen and the other lot hold their tongues. Christ! I should hold my tongue too. If I loved you, I'd hold my tongue. I love you really. Give me that underwear. Those have sex appeal, I'll need them. I'm thirty-six, that's not too old, but I can't do much more experimenting. It mustn't be this way in the next country I come to. The next man I get must be allowed to keep me. And don't say you'll send money, you know you can't. And you shouldn't act as if it were for four weeks. You know it and I know it too. So don't say, "Well, it's only for a couple of weeks," as you hand me the fur coat I won't need till winter. And let's not talk about shame. Oh, Fritz! (*She stops. A door is heard opening. She hastily puts herself to rights. Her husband comes in.*)

THE HUSBAND	What are you doing, tidying up?
THE WIFE	No.
THE HUSBAND	Why are you packing?
THE WIFE	I want to get away.
THE HUSBAND	What do you mean?
THE WIFE	We've talked sometimes about my going away for a time. Things are not too good here these days.
THE HUSBAND	That's a lot of nonsense.
THE WIFE	Shall I stay then?
THE HUSBAND	Where do you intend to go?
THE WIFE	To Amsterdam. Away from here.
THE HUSBAND	But you have no one there.
THE WIFE	No.
THE HUSBAND	Why don't you stay here then? You certainly mustn't go on my account.
THE WIFE	No.
THE HUSBAND	You know I've not changed, don't you, Judith?
THE WIFE	Yes. (*He embraces her. They stand, silent, between the bags.*)
THE HUSBAND	And there's nothing else to make you go?
THE WIFE	You know the answer to that.

THE HUSBAND	Perhaps it isn't so stupid. You need a breather. It's stifling here. I'll bring you back. Two days on the other side of the frontier, and I'd feel much better.
THE WIFE	Yes, by all means.
THE HUSBAND	This business here can't last too long. A complete change will come — from somewhere. All this will calm down again like an inflammation. It's really a misfortune.
THE WIFE	It certainly is. Did you meet Shoeck?
THE HUSBAND	Yes, that is, only on the stairs. I believe he's sorry again they cut us. He was quite embarrassed. In the long run they can't hold us intellectuals down like this, however much they hate us. Nor can they make war with completely spineless wrecks. These people are not so unresponsive if one confronts them boldly. When do you want to leave?
THE WIFE	Quarter past nine.
THE HUSBAND	And where shall I send the money?
THE WIFE	General delivery, Amsterdam, perhaps.
THE HUSBAND	I'll get myself a special permit. My God, I can't send my wife away with ten marks a month! What a mess everything is in. I feel awful about it.
THE WIFE	When you come for me, it'll do you good.
THE HUSBAND	To read a paper for once that has something in it!
THE WIFE	I called up Gertrude. She'll look after you.
THE HUSBAND	Quite unnecessary — for a couple of weeks.
THE WIFE	(*She has begun to pack.*) Hand me the fur coat now will you?
THE HUSBAND	(*He gives it to her.*) After all, it's only for a couple of weeks. (*Dim out. The Panzer is heard.*)

Playing the Scene

1. Do you find the emotion of the scene under-developed for the sake of the dominant idea?

2. Does this scene contain inherent possibilities for a highly emotional and dramatic effect?

3. What devices are used to underplay the emotion of the scene?

4. What is Brecht's purpose in this scene?

5. Try different styles of playing this scene: (1) with emphasis on the emotional content, (2) with emphasis on the idea. Which treatment seems most appropriate and effective?

Other Sources for Scenes of Epic Drama

Mother Courage by Bertolt Brecht

The Skin of Our Teeth by Thornton Wilder

AVANT-GARDE: "THE THEATRE OF THE ABSURD"

Avant-garde refers to a group of dramatists (other artists as well) who wish to break with the conventional, established forms and conventions of the theater and launch out into new modes of expression. As Ionesco, a prominent member of this coterie, expresses it, "The avant-garde man is the opponent of an existing system."* Although the plays of this group differ widely in subject matter and style, there are a number of characteristics which permeate their writings: varying degrees of formlessness, a philosophy of hopelessness and negation of life, and a lack of definite goals or objectives. This radical, bizarre character of the avant-garde plays has earned for them the title "Theatre of the Absurd."

---

* Eugene Ionesco, "The Avant-Garde Theatre," *The Tulane Drama Review*, 5 (December 1960): 45.

In reality, the break with traditional theater by the avant-garde writers is so great that one can no longer discuss their plays in such Aristotelian terms as unity of plot structure, character motivation, and significant, sequential dialogue.

The avant-garde writer has so little concern for plot that it is futile to expect a beginning, middle, and end of the action. Indeed, the suspense of the drama centers not so much on how the play will end, but rather on what surprising or illogical event will happen next. Certainly, not the least appeal of an avant-garde play for the audience is the game of trying to figure out what it all means.

The characters lack personality, in the usual sense, and often are without real names. They may be symbolical, allegorical, or mere mouthpieces for the playwright's ideas. Because of the puzzling actions of the characters, combined with their complete lack of individuality, a certain alienation effect comparable to that of Brecht's epic theater is produced in the audience. As a result, the spectator is not likely to empathize emotionally with a vague, puzzling character or one far removed from the norms of life.

Perhaps one of the most characteristic features of the Theatre of the Absurd is the playwright's use of language. The exponents of this theater group feel that in our society the ability to communicate has broken down. Even if the sharing of thoughts and feelings were possible, there is nothing to communicate. This concept accounts in large measure for the generally meaningless, nonsequential, irrelevant quality of the dialogue. Although one may not be able to find a rationale for an individual line or speech, often in toto the playwright's meaning may be evident. Traditionally, language is the chief medium of thoughts and emotions. But it is not unusual in the Theatre of the Absurd to receive more meaning from the action than from the dialogue.

Yet despite their absurd, bizarre characteristics, these plays possess a certain, somewhat indefinable audience appeal. As Esslin points out, "They prove that exits and entrances, light and shadow, contrasts in costume, voice, gait and behavior, pratfalls and embraces, all the manifold mechanical interactions of human puppets in groupings that suggest tensions, conflict, or the relaxation of tensions, can arouse laughter or gloom and conjure up an atmosphere of poetry even if devoid of logical motivation and unrelated to recognizable human characters, emotions, and objectives."*

Manner of Playing

1. Very few general principles may be stated which will apply to all the plays of this genre.

2. Each play will require a special approach.

3. The actor should determine, if possible, the author's purpose.

4. If the author's purpose seems to convey the concept that human beings are illogical puppets or automatons, this characteristic may be portrayed in mechanical movements and arbitrary speech patterns.

5. The author's viewpoint in terms of the overall mood should be fully ascertained.

6. Does the play seek to provoke laughter, gloom, or despair?

7. Although the characters have little individuality in the play script, each character must, of necessity, acquire some personality in actual performance.

Plate 54. *Oh Dad, Poor Dad, Mama's Hung You in the Closet and I'm Feelin' So Sad* by Arthur L. Kopit. The absurd situation here is readily apparent. Eastern Illinois University. Director: E. G. Gabbard. Photograph: Bertram Studio, Charleston, Illinois.

---

* Martin Esslin, "The Theatre of the Absurd," *The Tulane Drama Review*, 4 (May 1960): 4.

Practice Selection

OH DAD, POOR DAD, MAMMA'S HUNG YOU IN THE CLOSET AND I'M FEELIN' SO SAD

by Arthur L. Kopit | excerpt from Scene 3*

SCENE

The scene is a lavish hotel room in Havana, Cuba. At stage left is the entrance to the suite. On the rear wall is hung a glass case with a red axe inside it and a sign over it that reads, "In Case of Emergency, Break." Upstage right is a balcony with Venus's-flytraps. Stage right is a door to the master bedroom.

(*The door opens.* ROSALIE *enters.*)

(*She is dressed in an absurdly childish pink dress with crinolines and frills — the picture of innocence, the picture of a girl ten years old. Her shoes are black leather pumps and she wears short girlish-pink socks. Her cheeks have round circles of rouge on them — such as a young girl might have who had never put on makeup before.*)

ROSALIE

There's something bothering you, isn't there? (*Pause — coyly*) What's-a matter, Jonathan? (JONATHAN *does not answer at first but stares off into space — frightened, bewildered.*)

JONATHAN

(*Weakly*) I never thought I'd see you again. I never thought I'd talk to you again. I never thought you'd come.

ROSALIE

Did you really think that?

JONATHAN

She told me she'd never let you visit me again. She said no one would *ever* visit me again. She told me I had seen enough.

ROSALIE

But I had a key made.

JONATHAN

She . . . she hates me.

ROSALIE

What?

JONATHAN

She doesn't let me do anything. She doesn't let me listen to the radio. She took the tube out of the television set. She doesn't let me use her phone. She makes me show her all my letters before I seal them. She doesn't —

ROSALIE	Letters? What letters are you talking about?
JONATHAN	Just . . . letters I write.
ROSALIE	To *whom*?
JONATHAN	To people.
ROSALIE	*What* people?
JONATHAN	Oh . . . various people.
ROSALIE	Other girls? Could they be to other girls, by any chance?
JONATHAN	No. They're just to people. No people in particular. Just people in the phone book. Just names. I do it alphabetically. That way, someday, I'll be able to cover everyone. So far I've covered all the "A's" and "B's" up to Barrera.
ROSALIE	What is it you say to them? Can you tell me what you say to them . . . or is it private? Jonathan, just what do you say to them!?
JONATHAN	Mostly I just ask them what they look like. (*Pause. Suddenly he starts to sob in a curious combination of laughter and tears.*) But I don't think she ever mails them. She reads them, then takes them out to mail. But I don't think she ever does. I'll bet she just throws them away. Well if she's not going to mail them, why does she say she will? I . . . I could save the stamps. Why must she lie to me? Why doesn't she just say she's not going to mail them? Then I wouldn't have to wait for letters every day.
ROSALIE	Guess why I had this key made.
JONATHAN	I'll bet she's never even mailed one. From Abandono to Barrera, not one.
ROSALIE	Do you know why I had this key made? Do you know why I'm wearing this new dress?
JONATHAN	She doesn't let me stand in the window at noon because the sun is too strong. She doesn't let me stand in the window at night when the wind is blowing because the air is too cold. And today she told me she's going to nail shutters over the windows so I'll never have to worry about being bothered by the sun or the wind again.
ROSALIE	Try and guess why I'm all dressed up.
JONATHAN	She tells me I'm brilliant. She makes me read and re-read books no one's ever read. She smothers me with blankets at night in case of a storm. She tucks me in so tight I can't even get out till she comes and takes my blankets off.

ROSALIE   Stop talking about that and pay attention to me!

JONATHAN   She says she loves me. Every morning, before I even have a chance to open my eyes, there she is, leaning over my bed, breathing in my face and saying, "I love you, I love you."

ROSALIE   Jonathan, isn't my dress pretty?

JONATHAN   But I heard everything tonight. I heard it all when she didn't know I was here. (*He stares off into space, bewildered.*)

ROSALIE   What's the matter? (*He does not answer.*) Jonathan, what's the matter?

JONATHAN   But she must have known I was here. She *must* have known! I mean . . . where could I have gone? (*Pause*) But . . . if that's the case . . . *why did she let me hear?*

ROSALIE   Jonathan, I do wish you'd pay more attention to me. Here, look at my dress. You can even touch it if you like. Guess how many crinolines I have on. Guess why I'm wearing such a pretty, new dress. *Jonathan!*

JONATHAN   (*Distantly*) Maybe . . . it didn't make any difference to her . . . whether I heard or not. (*He turns suddenly to her and hugs her closely. She lets him hold her, then she steps back and away from him. Her face looks strangely old and determined under her girlish powder and pinkness.*)

ROSALIE   Come with me.

JONATHAN   What?

ROSALIE   Leave and come with me.

JONATHAN   (*Fearfully*) Where?

ROSALIE   Anywhere.

JONATHAN   What . . . wha . . . what do you mean?

ROSALIE   I mean, let's leave. Let's run away. Far away. Tonight. Both of us, together. Let's run and run. Far, far away.

JONATHAN   You . . . mean, leave?

ROSALIE   Yes. *Leave.*

JONATHAN   Just like that?

ROSALIE   *Just like that.*

JONATHAN   But . . . but . . . but . . .

ROSALIE   You want to leave, don't you?

JONATHAN	I . . . I don't . . . don't know. I . . . I . . .
ROSALIE	What about the time you told me how much you'd like to go outside, how you'd love to walk by yourself, anywhere you wanted?
JONATHAN	I . . . I don't . . . know.
ROSALIE	Yes you do. Give me your hand. Stop trembling so. Everything will be all right. Give me your hand and come with me. Just through the door. Then we're safe. Then we can run far away, somewhere she'll never find us. Come, Jonathan. It's time to go. I've put on a new dress just for the occasion. I even had a key made so I could come and get you.
JONATHAN	There are others you could take.
ROSALIE	But I don't love them. (*Pause*)
JONATHAN	You . . . you *love* me?
ROSALIE	Yes, Jonathan. I love you.
JONATHAN	Wha-wha-why?
ROSALIE	(*Softly*) Because you watch me every night.
JONATHAN	Well . . . can't we stay here.
ROSALIE	*No.*
JONATHAN	Wha-wha-whhhhy?
ROSALIE	Because I want you *alone.* (JONATHAN *turns from her and begins to walk about the room in confusion.*) I want you, Jonathan. Do you understand what I said? *I want you for my husband.*
JONATHAN	I . . . I . . . can't, I mean, I . . . I want to . . . go with you very much but I . . . I don't think . . . I can. I'm . . . sorry. (*He sits down and holds his head in his hands, sobbing quietly.*)
ROSALIE	What time will your mother be back?
JONATHAN	Na — not for a while.
ROSALIE	Are you sure?
JONATHAN	Ya-yes.
ROSALIE	Where is she?
JONATHAN	The usual place.
ROSALIE	What do you mean, "The usual place"?

JONATHAN	(*With a sad laugh*) The beach. (ROSALIE *looks at* JONATHAN *quizzically.*) She likes to look for people making love. Every night at midnight she walks down to the beach searching for people lying on blankets and making love. When she finds them she kicks sand in their faces and walks on. Sometimes it takes her as much as three hours to chase everyone away. (ROSALIE *smiles slightly and walks toward the master bedroom.* JONATHAN *freezes in fear. She puts her hand on the doorknob.*)
JONATHAN	WHAT ARE YOU DOING!? (*She smiles at him over her shoulder. She opens the door.*) STOP! You can't go in there! STOP! (*She opens the door completely and beckons to him.*)
ROSALIE	Come.
JONATHAN	Close it. Quickly!
ROSALIE	Come, Jonathan. Let's go inside.

Playing the Scene

1. What seems to be the author's purpose in this play?

2. What does the character Jonathan represent?

3. What does the character Rosalie represent?

4. What devices does Rosalie use to seduce Jonathan?

5. How would the different devices which Rosalie uses be reflected in her vocal delivery?

Other Sources for Scenes of Avant-Garde Drama

The Bald Soprano by Eugene Ionesco

The Caretaker by Harold Pinter

The Sandbox by Edward Albee

CONCLUSION

In Part Two it has not been our purpose to present an exhaustive study of all the styles of plays, but rather a selection of the most representative types which should be most useful to the actor. Any attempt to include a complete list of styles would be futile, if not impossible. No doubt new styles will emerge in the future as the playwright seeks new modes of expression.

Index

ABCDE79876543210